To Philip –
Best Wishes for
Christmas 1996

FROM: Mother and Dad

THE BEST YEARS
OF OUR LIVES

THE BEST YEARS OF OUR LIVES

Paul Wilson

**WIGAN'S RISE FROM SECOND DIVISION
TO SUPER LEAGUE**

Foreword by Maurice Lindsay

MAINSTREAM
PUBLISHING

EDINBURGH AND LONDON

First published in Great Britain in 1996 by
MAINSTREAM PUBLISHING COMPANY
(EDINBURGH) LTD
7 Albany Street
Edinburgh EH1 3UG

ISBN 1 85158 775 6

A catalogue record for this book is available
from the British Library

Typeset in Book Antiqua
Printed and bound in Great Britain at The
Bath Press Ltd, Bath

To my family; to everyone in the rugby league family; and to anyone else who has ever thought that rugby league might be a teeny bit more interesting than rugby union.

'I try and steer all my boys towards playing rugby league; I think it's the best game in the world. But I understand why a lot of them prefer soccer. You don't have to be brave to play that.'

Derek Birchall
Rugby master, Deanery High School, Wigan

Contents

Foreword

Wigan Rugby League Club, its history and its people have played such an immense part in my life that being asked to write a foreword for a book associated with the club's recent past is nothing less than a privilege.

I have discovered that, all over the world, when the name of Wigan is mentioned everyone starts to talk excitedly about the rugby club. I am not surprised! Wigan stands for pride, passion and commitment to the glorious world of rugby league. Players, directors and supporters alike know that to be involved with the Wigan club is something special. Throughout its long and illustrious history the club has remained dominant in rugby league and universally respected throughout the world of sport. The most recent years, however, have undoubtedly been quite exceptional.

As I write this foreword, so many memories come flooding back and so many remarkable and talented people spring to mind. None of us will ever forget the irrepressible smile of Henderson Gill, who was one of the first to bring back a sense of joy to the Wigan terraces. Or the significance of Shaun Edwards, whose signing signalled a revival in the flow of local talent. There are wonderful memories of the sensational John Ferguson and the mercurial Brett Kenny, culminating in the excitement of Wigan winning the Challenge Cup in 1985 for the first time in 20 years. We will also remember the many subsequent open-topped bus journeys from the outskirts of Wigan when the Challenge Cup was being brought home to Central Park and paraded in front of upwards of 40,000 people.

The club's success simply went onwards and upwards. Each season seemed to bring with it new stars, more trophies, and a growing number of wonderful fans. Just after the Challenge Cup victory in 1985 was the most important event of them all: the arrival of the incomparable Ellery Hanley, surely the greatest single figure in Wigan's recent history and certainly the most influential player I ever signed. The club also captured the best coaches in the world in Graham Lowe, John Monie and Mr Rocksolid himself, Graeme West. Heady days never seemed to end. The town of Wigan was rising to new eminence and its townsfolk were enjoying life like never before.

I once said to a journalist that being the chairman of the Wigan club was like riding a roller-coaster of success when there were only ups and no downs. The club was at a low ebb in 1979, and suffered the indignity of being relegated to the second division and having no players considered worthy of international selection. In the subsequent years all that changed, resulting in an incredible record in 1992 of 14 Wigan players being selected to tour Australasia with the British Lions. I was Tour Manager that particular year, and one of my proudest moments was when we beat Australia in front of a packed house in Melbourne with nine Wigan players in the side. The British forwards dominated their Australian counterparts, not something anyone was used to seeing. The whole of the British pack that night was made up of Wigan players.

Along the way, the club had victories as far apart as Milwaukee in the United States and a famous triumph, against all odds, in Australia when Wigan lifted the 1992 Sydney Sevens Trophy. I will never forget that particular competition. When Wigan ran out onto the field a local commentator described the great Andy Gregory as looking like a milk bottle on legs. He was silent as Andy later collected the trophy, after Wigan had swept all before them to stun a massive Australian audience who had become used to their all-conquering heroes defeating all-comers.

My own departure, later in 1992, to become the chief executive of the Rugby Football League in no way reduced the tempo. A dynasty had been created and it was impossible to stop the momentum. The show was on the road and what a fabulous show it was. There were so many stars and so many gala nights that even this book would need extra chapters to describe them all.

That incredible night in 1987 when Wigan beat Manly will live long in everyone's memory. There were almost 40,000 in the stadium and I think everyone stayed to celebrate until the early hours of the morning. The cellars of the clubhouse were empty the next day following the greatest party I can ever remember. Another great milestone was Wigan's revenge over St Helens at Wembley in 1989. The scoreline of 27–0 in Wigan's favour brought great comfort to all the old-timers who had suffered at the hands of the Saints at Wembley in 1961 and 1966. The defeat of another old enemy, Widnes, at Wembley in 1993 was one more sweet occasion, as it was Widnes who had last beaten Wigan at Wembley in 1984 with the aid of Joe Lydon and Andy Gregory, two of Wigan's favourite sons. All that had changed, and Wigan had gone from hardly ever playing at Wembley to never losing at Wembley.

The Wigan club became such a part of my life that leaving in 1992 was a great wrench. Memories never leave you, however, and I can still see the grin of Wigan's famous old scout, Billy Cunliffe, as we sat in the Royal Oak, next to Central Park, following the Challenge Cup final win in 1985. B[...] Wigan man first and last, and althoug[...] no longer with us, I am sure he will be u[...] heaven scanning the pages of this book an[...] having arguments as to whether Martin Offiah is better than his beloved Billy Boston. It matters not, because great names such as these wonderful players are just two among the legion who have proudly worn the cherry and white and done full justice to the club's traditions.

There have been many other heroes too including people who never actually took the field, like the faithful staff who joined the club with me in 1979 and are still there today, a testimony to their love of the club.

This book covers all those wonderful years, and Paul Wilson tells the tale in an enthralling and almost mystical way. Paul, of course, was part of the story himself, having worked for local newspapers at a time when the Wigan phenomenon was actually unfolding. That still-continuing story has resulted in the players becoming household names throughout the country and, indeed, the world. The Wigan club had been almost totally responsible for the rugby league revival and the national spotlight the game now finds itself under. The cherry and whites are synonymous with style and class, and that is the way it should be.

So many of us were fortunate enough to be a part of the Wigan story. We were all privileged – those who displayed their skill and courage on the pitch and those who stood back and applauded – and I doubt that anything in my sporting life will ever come as close to comparing with the thrill of those special days. Tears were few and joy was abundant – they really were the best years of our lives.

M.P. Lindsay
Chief Executive, Rugby Football League, and Wigan Director, 1979–92
June 1996

ly was a
h he is
o in

duction and Acknowledgements

If it is true that an era has ended at Wigan, or for rugby league in general, then that era – the best years of our lives – will be encapsulated in this book. I should say at the outset, however, that this was not the original intention. When this account of 15 years in the life of Wigan Football Club was first conceived, there seemed no end in sight to the Central Park club's dominance, no Super League storm clouds were visible in Australia, and the idea of Gary Connolly playing for Harlequins seemed as improbable as hearing Will Carling describe him as the best centre in Britain. As improbable as it still seems, in other words.

But clearly rugby's landscape is altering quickly, and altering beyond all recognition. In as much as the Super League in this country was formed with the stated intention of attracting blue chip sponsors and millionaire businessmen into the game, rugby league is already fighting a losing battle, since all those people have rushed instead into the new, professional rugby union. It may be that rugby league as it has been known and loved, either as an exciting and skilful spectator sport or in its other role as a useful and surprisingly accurate metaphor for life in the north of England, will not survive intact. Its passing will be an occasion for mourning, since, in a very real way which is not always appreciated outside Lancashire, Cumbria and Yorkshire, this is a game which touches people's lives.

Perhaps this is too gloomy a forecast, since rugby league has been examined and pronounced dead on innumerable occasions in the past, only to cling to life and eventually regenerate itself in a more vivid capacity than ever. This is precisely the story this book has to tell. When Maurice Lindsay, the present chief executive of the Rugby Football League, invested some of his own money in the Wigan club at the beginning of the '80s, he was warned off in no uncertain terms by former directors who had had their own fingers burned. 'Don't throw good money after bad. The game has gone.' Lindsay thought otherwise, and nine Challenge Cups, eight league titles, eight Regal trophies, five Premierships, five County Cups, three World Club Challenge triumphs and a Sydney and a Middlesex Sevens later, you would have to concede he had a point. Wigan won more in the space of 12 years than virtually anyone else could dream of winning in a lifetime. But the sub-plot of this book, unintentional at first but unavoidable by the end, is the consequences of Wigan's dominance for the rest of the game. The club credited with revitalising rugby league was eventually charged with strangling it.

A personal view is simply that the last 15 years were a hell of a good time to be in or around Wigan, and that whatever is going to happen will eventually happen. It is certainly not up to individual clubs to worry about the effect their own success might be having on the wider game, and a game that is too weak to do anything about one club winning all the prizes and monopolising all the fun is almost certainly going to be too weak to resist either the friendly advances of Rupert Murdoch or the hostile ones of professional rugby union.

The former threat is relatively new; the latter one has been around for as long as the game of rugby league. In future seasons, perhaps not too many years away, when we are all playing one code, the fact that rugby league managed to survive, loud and proud, for over 100 years will come to be seen as a miracle. The odds were always stacked against it, but the pleasure it gave, even on wintry afternoons at Widnes or Whitehaven, was immense. Outsiders have never been able to understand quite why that should be. I hope this book can shed a little light on the subject.

I must apologise. I was writing in the past tense there. I am sure rugby league will continue to give pleasure at places like Widnes and Whitehaven, even if not on wintry days any more. At least I wish I was sure. As it is, I am sure of only two things. One is that the game of rugby will continue to be played in Wigan, under whatever banner, and that the area will continue to produce outstanding players for whatever handling code requires them. If this is not to be rugby league, I would prefer it to be rugby union, or some sensible hybrid between the two established codes, than some ersatz, made-for-television insult to the memory of real rugby league. Rugby union now appears to know what spectators want to see. It has merely been pretending to be clueless for the past 100 years. I would rather watch a real game of rugby at Central Park, even if it involves 15 players a side and the odd lineout, than anything involving crash-helmets, time-outs and Wigan Red Sox. You can only go so far in chasing a new audience before you alienate your old one.

The second thing of which I am sure is that the last 15 years at Wigan have been special, remarkable, unrepeatable. No one else is going to match those achievements: few clubs in any sport will ever regularly turn out teams of such staggering quality. Maurice Lindsay, Jack Robinson and all the others, I salute you. The last 15 years have been a privilege and a pleasure. Worth writing a book about.

Finally, I would like to acknowledge gratefully the time and co-operation both the above gentlemen generously gave to assist me in the writing of this book. I would like particularly to thank Maurice for kindly supplying a foreword, and Jack for finding time to speak to me when several other more pressing matters were claiming his attention. I am especially indebted to Shaun Edwards for his help with chapter eleven; Andy Goodway, Andy Gregory, John Pendlebury, David Stephenson, Phil Clarke and Joe Lydon for happily reminiscing over old times; and Maurice Bamford, Doug Laughton, Alex Murphy, Colin Clarke, John Monie, John Dorahy and Graeme West for their insights into coaching. I would like to take this opportunity to wish Phil Clarke and Nicky Kiss good luck and good health for the future as they recover from serious medical conditions.

Although I was around in Wigan for the whole of the 15 years in question, I don't necessarily remember all of it without prompting, and I am happy to acknowledge the assistance of fellow journalists Dave Hadfield, Paul Fitzpatrick, Martin Richards, Peter Aspinall, John Benn and Neil Barker, in providing accurate information upon request. I never did get to grips with the statistical side of the game, and my thanks are due to Anne Dempsey and Paul Ogden for their reliability in that department, while for the excellent pictures in this volume I am indebted to photographer Frank Orrell and *The Wigan Observer* for granting permission to use his work. I am grateful to my own employer, *The Observer*, for permitting this project, to Mainstream for their help in realising it, and to Trevor Smith for his early spadework.

The title of this book, incidentally, was provided inadvertently by a comment from Dot Houghton, a friend and one of Wigan's keenest followers. I am also sworn to mention Winston Higham, Chris Leyland and Chris Docherty, without whose impromptu coaching sessions in the bar of the Swan or the Bowling Green this book would probably have been finished more quickly, but less enjoyably. But the biggest thanks in the production department go to my wife, Janet, for the initial encouragement and the food and drink passed up to my lonely work station in the attic. Without her, this book might never have been completed at all.

Paul Wilson
Wigan, September 1996

CHAPTER ONE

Ancient History

'The directors have turned the best club in the league into a complete and utter joke.'

Friday, 11 April 1980: Castleford 21, Wigan 13 . . . Relegation happens in sport, it doesn't have to be the end of the world. Every team hits a rough patch from time to time, but the good ones can bounce back. Sometimes, as in the case of Manchester United in football or Hull FC in rugby league, the experience can even be an opportunity to take stock and come back fitter and stronger.

None of these things were being said about Wigan in 1980. Most people in rugby league knew that second division teams like Huddersfield and Batley had once been great, but it was almost impossible to reconcile their glorious pasts with the impoverished present. Neither of these two teams were ever going to be famous again: they had accepted a humbler station in life with the Doncasters, the Huytons and the Keighleys of rugby league's division two, inhabited for the most part by clubs who never had any designs on fame in the first place. Batley's Gallant Youths and Huddersfield's Team of all the Talents only lived on in old men's memories, and Wigan appeared destined for this unhappy fate.

The only difference was that you didn't have to be of pensionable age to remember Wigan's glory years. Prominent throughout rugby league's 85 years of existence, the club's last golden era had been as recent as the '60s. Few could now remember precisely what had happened to Huddersfield or Batley, at what point they gave up hope of the lush green pastures of success and settled for the stony soil of sporting subsistence, but Wigan were undeniably going the same way, here, in the present, and the spectacle was morbidly fascinating. The outbreak of melancholia which accompanied Wigan into division two had less to do with the actual demotion than the fear that greatness might have left the club. Wigan had been edging towards relegation for several seasons and, though the players could usually be relied upon to show some fight on the pitch, the club's supine directors appeared to accept defeat all too readily. The '70s generally had been a thin time for rugby league, and now one of the game's legends was losing the will to live. If

. . . The way we were . . . George Fairbairn and the Wigan squad which gained promotion from the second division in 1981. Back row (l to r): Regan, Nanyn, O'Neill, Vigo, Breheny, Hollingsworth. Centre: Ramsdale, Clough, Boyd, Greenall, Ratcliffe, Butler. Front: Wilf Smith (assistant coach), Braithwaite, Fairbairn, Coyle, Williams. Kneeling: Bolton, Kiss.

Jimmy Hornby makes a break against Leeds.

Wigan could lose their greatness, so could the game. Underlying the concern at the club's sickness was a deeper, unspoken worry about the health of the game as a whole.

Cliff Webb, *The Wigan Observer*'s rugby writer of the time who also doubled up as church correspondent, described the defeat at Castleford as 'the saddest day of my life'. He was choked, he said, as he watched the Wigan lads giving everything they had in a last, desperate bid to keep their hopes alive: 'to think that a club which has represented the very best in rugby league for most of the century has come to this'. Sophisticated Wigan followers, an editorial in the paper chipped in, do not want to watch a team of triers. They want to watch a team of winners.

'The board must take the blame', a page one story thundered. Editor Jack Winstanley spoke of a creeping paralysis that had seen the club stagger from crisis to crisis. 'Like many who knew Wigan intimately when it was *the* rugby league club the world over, I have seen this coming for close on ten years.'

As if to confirm that the lack of foresight and fighting spirit stemmed from the boardroom, director Martin Ryan unwisely appealed for a return to a single division. 'Clubs like Huddersfield, Barrow and Swin-ton will never come back under the present system, and I think Wigan will soon be in the same boat. Only Humberside clubs can exist on their gate money these days, for all the crowds the rest of us get we might as well switch back to playing on Saturday afternoons.'

One of the most fondly remembered of Wigan players, Ryan never quite managed to cut the same adventurous dash as a director, but though hindsight makes it tempting to scoff, he was only actually wrong about his own team. Clubs like Barrow and Swinton are possibly worse off now than ever, and it is a long time since either Humberside club was able to exist on its gate money. The point is that while no one could have predicted the spectacular heights to which Wigan would rise in the 15 years following relegation to the second division, problems with the game's structure and financial viability were considerably easier to identify. This will be worth remembering later, at around the point in this story when Wigan stop earning universal congratulation for pulling them-selves up by their bootstraps and setting an example for others to follow, and begin to attract criticism for actively damaging the game. It was Wigan's good luck to discover

Danny Campbell in typically rampaging form against Widnes, with Billy Melling in the background. Note that Wigan's shirts, not to mention hairstyles, are more old-fashioned that those of their opponents.

their salvation: their misfortune to be saddled with the responsibility for everyone else's. Some say they have killed the British game, others argue it would have died long ago without them. What is beyond dispute is that Wigan are a sporting phenomenon, possibly without parallel anywhere in the world, and yet 15 years ago people would not have been able to comprehend such a thing.

Returning to our story and that April night in 1980, several hundred Wigan fans had gone along to Central Park for the Friday evening 'A' team match; partly out of habit, partly because they wanted to follow events from Castleford and be close to the club if the news was as bad as they feared. They were doubly disappointed. The news from Castleford was every bit as bad as they had feared, but the club simply never bothered to announce either the running score or the final result from Yorkshire. The 'A' team game ended and the players left the field. Many fans lingered behind, feeling sure an announcement of some sort would be made (it was less easy then to follow rugby league matches on local radio) but after a few minutes of complete silence the floodlights were switched off, plunging the ground into symbolic darkness. Within seven years, Wigan would become club champions of the world on an unforgettable night when fireworks lit up the sky and 37,000 fans were shoehorned into Central Park, but in April 1980 the club had a lot to learn.

Sunday, 14 September 1980: Fulham 25, Wigan 5 . . . Anyone who expected Wigan to romp gaily through their second division fixtures had been cruelly disabused in the opening league game at York, where the visitors not only lost 22–17 but had a fourth player dismissed in a season barely a fortnight old.

14

Just when *The Wigan Observer* thought it was safe to lay off the 'Day of Disaster' type headlines for a while, they were wheeled out once again. In retrospect, however, the calamity which overtook Wigan on that sunny afternoon in west London looms larger in the memory, a very public humiliation all the greater for being wholly unexpected.

Fulham were new, so freshly formed that the league had allowed them an extra fortnight to get organised, and this was their inaugural fixture at Craven Cottage, where they would henceforth be helping pay the rent. Wigan, the most illustrious name handy

Extremely rare picture of Maurice Bamford and a successful Wigan signing. Mike Scott, from Halifax, was the only one of Bamford's trio of Yorkshire imports to make the grade at Central Park.

in the second division, had been selected to add a touch of history and pageant to the occasion. Everyone could see a pratfall coming, except the hapless victims. Fulham may have been new to Craven Cottage and the game new to the capital, but few of their players were new to the game. Only a team of Wigan's monumental complacency could mistake Widnes in disguise for a harmless bunch of southern *ingénues*, but that is exactly what the visitors did. 'The coach going down was like a party, coming back it was like a funeral,' said Wigan scrum-half Ness Flowers. 'I don't think any of us thought for a minute about losing, to be honest.'

There was very little reason for this misplaced confidence. Fulham had been put together shrewdly by Reg Bowden, himself a more than able scrum-half with plenty of shelf-life left, using proven, northern-based players with first division experience. It showed. If the scoreline does not quite suggest the extent of Fulham's superiority it is because Wigan managed to squeeze on to the scoresheet in the last minute, and because these were still the days of the three-point try. A parade of former Wigan greats had taken place on the pitch prior to kick-off, but long before the end Billy Boston and Co. were peeping through their fingers at a grotesque mismatch. Just looking at the teamsheet brings a shudder, even after all these years. Fulham's team that day was: Risman; Cambriani, Aspey, Noonan, McCorquodale; Eckersley, Bowden; Van Bellen, Karalius, Lester, Gourley, Allen, Hull. Wigan were: Fairbairn; Ramsdale, Willicombe, Davies, Hornby; Coyle, Flowers; Townend, Pendlebury, Smith, Clough, Hollingsworth, Boyd.

Afterwards it was open house for the nation's media in the Fulham dressing-room, as Bowden trilled like a canary about the bright future for his team and for rugby league in London. Across the corridor the difference was marked. The visitors' dressing-room door remained locked for over an hour, and no one got a peep out of Wigan player-coach George Fairbairn.

But what really made the situation grotesque was the irony. Wigan could have transformed their fortunes by signing a captain and number seven half as handy as Bowden. It was painfully evident that players of his calibre were either not being approached, or, scarcely a more comforting reflection, preferred to travel the length of the country to play for a fledgling side with an uncertain future rather than risk involvement with a gutless, witless, beached whale of a club like Wigan. On the way back north from London, an argument with directors over whether non-playing reserves were entitled to egg, sausage and chips at the motorway services led to South African winger Green Vigo walking out on the club. More worrying for the increasingly restless supporters were the players who had never walked in. Bowden only joined Fulham because his first-team place at Widnes had gone to a teenager called Andy Gregory, an obvious, natural talent for whom a succession of schoolteachers and coaches had been predicting an international future. Those schoolteachers and coaches, like Gregory himself, came from Wigan. The young scrum-half had been born, raised, educated and taught rugby in the town, but had decided to look elsewhere for a professional career.

Saturday, 9 May 1981: Manchester City 1, Tottenham Hotspur 1 . . . Most people remember the 1981 FA Cup final between Tottenham Hotspur and Manchester City for its replay, and the virtuoso goal by Ricky Villa which sealed the London side's success. Maurice Bamford has a more vivid recollection of watching the original draw at his home in Leeds, because during the half-time interval the telephone rang and changed his life.

Bamford achieved a degree of fame in the '80s as coach at Wigan, Leeds and Great Britain. As he is fond of remarking, only one other person has completed that triangle, and Eric Ashton was awarded the MBE. But in May 1981, Bamford was merely the unsung coach of Huddersfield, a side which, unlike Wigan, had just failed to climb out of division two. Huddersfield, in fact, had finished fifth, the highest position attainable without the attendant unpleasantness of being promoted, coming down again next year, and losing a lot of heart, money and support in the process. With four teams going up each season from a division of only 15 clubs, decent sides had to try quite hard not to get promoted, especially if, like Huddersfield, they had managed to beat three of the quartet above them. The exception, oddly, was Whitehaven, the fourth-placed team who struggled badly in the top flight and who won only two games all season, but nevertheless returned to haunt Bamford when he needed it least.

So while Huddersfield's failure to secure promotion did not necessarily reflect poorly on Bamford's coaching, it scarcely had first division clubs beating a path to his door. A previous spell at Halifax had demonstrated a motivational flair and an ability to make the best of limited resources, but small miracles at struggling Yorkshire clubs do not constitute a reputation. If Bamford was recognised at all outside the West Riding it was for bearing more than a passing resemblance to Polish trade union leader Lech Walesa, or for a brief moment of local television notoriety after no fewer than six players had been sent off in a Huddersfield–Wigan match the previous season, some of them for biting. He had no inkling his coaching credentials were being scrutinised beyond the Pennines, and Wigan would have been among the last clubs he would have suspected of harbouring an interest. Which is why he got a shock when destiny came calling, at half-time in the FA Cup final, in the form of an invitation from Jack Robinson, a Wigan director, to discuss the coaching vacancy at Central Park.

'It was,' Bamford says, with the slightly misty-eyed overstatement for which he is famous, 'like being asked to join Manchester United. Any coach who thinks anything about himself, if he gets the chance, has got to say yes to a club like that. Just to be associated with Wigan is an honour.'

These sentiments may seem unremarkable now, but the parallel between Wigan and Manchester United was far less evident in 1981. True, both clubs had recently experienced a season in the second division, but rugby league's then second division was not remotely comparable to the football version. Rugby league only had two divisions, and the second served as the basement, as well as the level just under the first. It is fair to say a majority of its clubs were only there because there was no third or fourth division to fall into. There would always be a place for Wigan in any history of rugby league – founder members of the Northern Union, first winners at Wembley, home of all-time legends like Jim Sullivan, Joe Egan, Billy Boston and Brian McTigue – though history

Colin Whitfield represented one of Wigan's best bits of transfer business in the 1981–82 season, arriving from Salford in a swap for Trevor Stockley and Roy Heaney. Roy who? Precisely.

was precisely what the club appeared to be heading for. What Robinson omitted to tell Bamford, at their introductory meeting anyway, was that another season in the second division would finish Wigan for good. 'Even with a toe-hold in the first division it was the hardest thing in the world to turn the club round,' Robinson said. 'If we had slipped

back into the second division again we would have sunk without trace. Debts alone would have crippled us. That's how bad things had become. The club had been trading on the past for far too long, dealing in empty promises and ignoring the empty coffers. The attitude seemed to be that whatever happened, *Wigan* would be all right, but the reality was that we were nearly taken over by the soccer club at the start of the '80s. Had we been relegated a second time, there is no question but that we would have been forced to move in with Wigan Athletic.'

The infamous Craven Cottage débâcle was a good example of Wigan's irrational belief in their own infallibility. 'We all thought we were going to win,' said scrum-half Flowers. 'It never occurred to us that Fulham had put quite a handy side together, we just thought we were going to teach a load of southern upstarts how to play rugby league.'

That Wigan were hardly in a position to teach anyone how to play should really have occurred to Flowers earlier, since he had turned his back on rugby union in South Wales to try his hand as a professional. It was not a rewarding experience. Wigan's 'professionalism' did not even extend to finding Flowers his promised job in the area, and after a few seasons, spent mostly in the reserves, he returned home. Surprisingly, he is not bitter. 'I don't have any regrets, except maybe that I went to Wigan about five years too soon,' he said. 'But I don't fool myself I would have got anywhere near the first team once the success started happening, I couldn't even hold down a place when they were terrible.'

If Wigan were slightly less terrible by the time Bamford arrived, it was mostly down to the purchase, midway through the second division season, of Castleford scrum-half Gary Stephens for £35,000. Ending the argument between Flowers and Bernard Coyle over the number seven shirt, and providing some much needed leadership and experience at half-back, Stephens was instrumental in helping Wigan secure promotion. Bamford was delighted to have such a reliable lieutenant on the pitch, so much so he made Stephens his captain almost straightaway, but he soon discovered his scrum-half did not share Flowers's happy-go-lucky personality. Stephens struck even fellow Yorkshiremen as being something of a moaner, and spent much of the 1981–82 season at loggerheads with his coach. 'He was

constantly complaining the team wasn't good enough,' Bamford explained. 'Well it wasn't. You didn't need to be a genius to see that, but no one particularly wanted reminding all the time. Gary was good when we were winning, but you need a leader when the chips are down as well, and when things went badly he was a little bit too fond of sulking and pointing the finger at others.'

The question of leadership had been uppermost in Bamford's mind since meeting Robinson at Birch services on the M62 and agreeing to come and meet the Wigan board. He knew then he was almost certain to lose George Fairbairn, the club's one player of undisputed international class and the man who had led Wigan out of the second division in his first season as player-coach. Optimistic, but not blindly so, Bamford knew life would be hard in the first division for a team which had only managed to finish its previous campaign as runners-up to York in the second division. And he was well aware that he was inheriting substantially the same team which had been relegated the year before, only without its leading light. Fairbairn was not of a mind to stick around once he had been relieved of coaching responsibilities. Bamford made keeping the Great Britain full-back his priority on joining the club, but Fairbairn said he was sickened by the way the directors had handled the matter – 'I was the last to know' – and never played for Wigan again. He was sold for a then record £72,500 to Hull Kingston Rovers in June 1981, the directors at least receiving a fair price for their last major asset, but scarcely inspiring confidence for the coming season.

'Plenty of people asked me at the time why I was going to Wigan, but to be honest it only took me a second or two to make up my mind,' Bamford said. 'It was just one of those things, like being asked to coach Leeds and then Great Britain a few years later, that I had dreamed about. Wigan has always had a magic for me. My family was a rugby league family, people like Boston and McTigue were gods in our house, and though I sensed that Wigan had never really replaced those two, and had been suffering slowly since the mid-'60s, I was overwhelmed at being asked to try to bring some of the glory back.'

Very few coaches would have described the challenge ahead in those terms, and it may have been an early example of Robinson's shrewd character judgement that he zeroed in on someone willing to link the past and the future without dwelling too long on the uncomfortable present. Or it could just have been luck. Certainly Robinson, a new boy on the Wigan board who felt the club needed a coach capable of dragging it into the modern era and had taken on himself the responsibility of finding one, believes luck played a big part in the Wigan story. But then again, he was not faced with a wide choice of candidates.

'There was a dearth of good British coaches,' he said. 'Or at least there was a dearth of good ones willing to come to Wigan. The club had a graveyard reputation. It had already crossed my mind that we might need to look outside the country and bring someone from overseas to shake the club up a bit, if only because a complete newcomer might be unaware of the sense of hopelessness surrounding the club, and come without any preconceptions. But there was no money to wave around in those days, and my co-directors raised enough objections to employing a Yorkshireman, let alone an Australian. Plus, we were hardly in a position, in terms of playing staff or level of support, to try anything so ambitious and see it fail through lack of resources. We needed a bit of stability first of all, a few good results. I thought Maurice was a man who could put us back on our feet.'

Bamford duly arrived, with plans for three-day camps at Lancaster University and the revolutionary idea of stepping up training from two to three nights a week which were quite grandiose for the time. They wouldn't have impressed any visiting Australians, but the whole point of British rugby league in the early '80s, in the comfortable cocoon of insularity which existed before the 1982 Kangaroos and the lifting of the international transfer ban, was that Australia was too far away to worry about. Just how insular and parochial the game could be was forcibly impressed on Bamford at his first visit to Central Park, when he discovered the talk of his household, the club he had placed on a pedestal, was being run by small-minded men capable of cold-shouldering an enthusiastic new recruit simply on account of his birthplace.

A director called Arthur Stone thought Wigan should not be talking to Yorkshire coaches, and told Bamford so, and Martin Ryan threatened to resign if such a foreigner were appointed. 'I was ashamed at what Maurice had to put up with on his first visit,' Robinson recalled. 'Some of the directors were unforgivably rude to his face.' Bamford gave as good as he got, however, which impressed Robinson, and in turn the new coach was pleased to hear some plain speaking from his champion. 'Jack told me not to worry about the other directors,' Bamford explained. 'He said they were all talk, and that Ryan wouldn't have the chance to resign because he would be sacked first.'

Here was Bamford's first introduction to something strange about the Wigan board. Junior directors do not normally overrule their senior colleagues, but Robinson appeared to pull rank on Ryan. It was also noticeable how another young and energetic newcomer, a sometime accountant, plant-hire contractor and bookmaker called Maurice Lindsay, usually spoke for the club, despite having been on the board even less time than Robinson. These two gave every impression of running the whole show, and in a few years they were, but in 1981 they did not get their own way without a fight. 'We only just got Maurice Bamford installed as coach,' Robinson recalled. 'Basically the board wanted a Wigan man, failing that, a Lancastrian. Maurice got in on the third count, that at least he was English, but the whole episode was typical of the way the club was being run. Eleven out of every 12 items up for discussion at board meetings would get deferred. There were too many directors, and the only thing they ever agreed about was that junior members should pour the tea. We simply could not get any business done, it's impossible in a situation like that. Maurice [Lindsay] and I began plotting how to get rid of the others right from the start.'

Wigan's gang of four. Left to right are club directors Jack Hilton, Tom Rathbone, Maurice Lindsay and Jack Robinson. Just pretend the Challenge Cup is not in the picture. It certainly wasn't in 1982.

The change from a cumbersome, 12-man board to a streamlined, quick-thinking and quick-operating panel of four was the biggest single factor in Wigan's transformation from the laughing stock of the early '80s to the slick machine which was dominating the game by the end of the decade. Officially the revolution happened after Bamford had left – that is, it was formally announced midway through the following season – but in reality the power balance had begun to shift before his arrival. The sub-plot to the Yorkshireman's difficult season in charge was one of boardroom upheaval. The club Bamford left was being run quite differently from the one he originally joined, even if the change may not have been immediately evident from the outside. But Bamford was on the inside, and

had he picked up earlier on the new mood he might have lasted longer than a season, though one fears a flexible attitude and the ability to adapt to rapidly changing circumstances were never among his strong points. Sometimes, listening to the immodest blend of nostalgia and I-know-it-all-ism he peddles as a local radio pundit, one wonders if the penny has dropped yet. In the end what did for him at Wigan was what had initially recommended him to the club – he was rooted in the past.

Nevertheless, the difficulties Bamford faced that season should not be underestimated. Coping manfully with a thoroughly disenchanted playing staff – in the wake of Fairbairn's departure senior professionals like Steve O'Neill, Denis Boyd, John Butler and Billy Melling had all indicated a desire to continue their careers elsewhere – the new manager supervised a satisfactory start to the 1981–82 campaign. Interest in the Lancashire Cup was predictably ended by Widnes, but only after a brilliant solo try by Stephens had brought Wigan through a tricky first-round tie at Carlisle. Like Fulham the previous season, the newly formed Cumbrians were playing their first-ever game of rugby league, at home against Wigan. They were not quite such unknown quantities, since three of their players – Boyd, Hollingsworth and Davies – had moved from Central Park in the close season. Wigan, meanwhile, boasted three newcomers of their own at Brunton Park. Mick Scott, Steve Nicholson and Jimmy Birts, all from Yorkshire, were the summer signings Bamford had made with the proceeds from the Fairbairn sale. Wigan's team for the first game of the season on 16 August 1981 was: Birts; Ramsdale, Stockley, Nicholson, Hornby; Foy, Stephens; Hodkinson, Kiss, O'Neill, Melling, Nanyn (Scott), Smith.

Jimmy Hornby, a winger of comically lugubrious appearance who nevertheless enjoyed a place in the affections of the Central Park crowd, might have had a hat-trick of tries at Carlisle, but dropped three passes. Cliff Webb, of *The Wigan Observer*, was inclined to be sympathetic, pointing out that the passes, from Foy and Nicholson, were decidedly poor. This was all too typical. This was Wigan at the start of the '80s. A team of triers, not spectacularly inept, but not particularly good at rugby league either, if the object of the game was to win matches and draw crowds. Hornby at that time could often be caught gesturing theatrically to the crowd, arms spread wide in despair or fists beating the ground in frustration, indicating that if only the ball had come at the right time or at a catchable height he would have beaten the cover and scored in the corner. Wigan fans back then had little else to smile about, and enjoyed this joke. A story about Hornby that Bamford used to enjoy, possibly apocryphal but still illustrative of how much has changed at Central Park, concerns the season under Vince Karalius. Disgruntled at the paucity of a win bonus, one player had unwisely complained that Karalius was 'a typically tight Widnes bastard' behind the coach's back, but well within earshot. The fearless and famously combative Karalius promptly challenged whoever had made the remark to step outside the dressing-room and repeat it. After several minutes waiting alone in the corridor, Karalius informed the now silent gathering that as a Wiganer could not possibly be expected to take on a Widnesian on his own, he would fight any four of them. Another nervous interlude followed, before the dressing-room door opened and to Karalius's surprise, Hornby emerged on his own. 'Can I go home, please?' he asked. 'You see I'm not from Wigan, I'm from Billinge.'

In the circumstances it was perhaps not all that surprising that Wigan's return to first division action, a 25–8 home victory over Whitehaven, drew a 'crowd' of just 3,478. The average age of those spectators would have made an interesting comparison with the present as well. Mostly male, middle-aged and older, Wigan's audience was literally dying off. The same was only slightly less true of the game as a whole. Barely a thousand more people were at Leeds the following Saturday to see Wigan pick up a surprising 36–23 away victory, after trailing

18–5 in the first half. Two league games, four points. 'That will take some of the pressure off us on Wednesday,' a beaming Lindsay remarked after the Headingley match. Wednesday was the shareholders' annual meeting and, sure enough, expected criticism of the way the club was being run failed to surface. There had been plenty of stinging rebukes in the local press – 'The directors have turned the best team in the league into a complete and utter joke,' wrote Paul Ogden, of Ashton in Makerfield – but on the night, shareholders contented themselves with a pot-boiling debate on whether or not a ban on unruly Warrington supporters was feasible. Only one interchange was noteworthy. Chairman Jack Hilton was pleading poverty, as usual, to charges of not investing sufficiently in first-team players of quality, when he was asked whether the club had explored the possibility of shirt sponsorship, as several other teams had now begun to sprout logos. 'As a matter of fact we have,' said Hilton, revealingly. 'We have asked around town, but we can't find anyone who wants to be on our shirts.'

It was not difficult to see why. Eight matches after the shareholders' meeting, Wigan were still on four league points, and supporters were much less happy about setting a new postwar record for consecutive defeats. The story was a familiar one. Wigan had simply not been good enough against first division heavyweights like Widnes, Warrington, Leigh and Bradford in the league, and had been unable to repeat their Headingley success when drawn at Leeds in the John Player Trophy. But that was not all. The crowd was on Bamford's back over the performances of the Yorkshire players he had brought in, Birts in particular. Scott was considered a useful acquisition, Nicholson less so, but poor Birts, for whom Bamford had paid Halifax £22,000, was an unmitigated disaster.

Damned with faint praise from the outset, when even Bamford conceded his new purchase was a sound defender and reliable goalkicker but 'not the best runner of the ball in the world', the full-back lost his confidence to such a degree when Wigan began losing that he could no longer be trusted with the goalkicks. Once it emerged Wigan were interested in Colin Whitfield, available at £65,000, Birts was visibly broken. The board had to act quickly, Robinson explained, because Bamford appeared blind to the player's shortcomings. 'Just one look at Birts was enough to make us question our coach's judgement,' Robinson recalled. 'I remember seeing him run out for the first time and thinking, "Crikey! What have we done here?" He was spindly looking, slow and nowhere near strong enough. And that was before he lost his confidence. It taught us a lot, that signing. In the beginning Maurice and I simply assumed that Maurice Bamford knew something we didn't. He was a coach, after all. A couple of games later we were forced to the conclusion that our coach didn't know as much as we did. It wasn't quite that simple, but certainly we never worried about backing our own instincts, after that.'

Birts had to go. He had become an acute embarrassment. He was probably not the worst player Wigan have ever had – he was simply an average performer promoted beyond his ability – but now enjoys, if that is the word, local notoriety as a by-word for public failure and an example of Bamford's dead hand in the transfer market. The real problem was that Bamford's unbending loyalty to a protégé would not allow him to admit a mistake. Birts was just having a rough patch, he would come through in the end. The board had no wish to make Birts feel more at home by returning to the second division, however, and could not risk a public spat with their coach so early in the season, so the club accepted a £10,000 loss on the deal and packed the full-back off to Carlisle. Birts had played just 12 games in Wigan colours.

It was an expensive lesson, but one well learned. Wigan eventually secured Whitfield without a penny changing hands, let alone Salford's anticipated £65,000. In what still looks like one of the deals of the decade, Salford were persuaded to part with their speedy and stylish utility back in exchange for Trevor Stockley and Roy Heaney. The former was a useful centre destined never to fulfil his potential at a succession of clubs and who had already asked for a move. The latter was a sometime Bolton Wanderers footballer who only ever played a handful of games of professional rugby. Wigan, under Robinson and Lindsay, were growing up quickly. Classy, competent and above all confident, Whitfield had everything Birts lacked. He would have represented the first shining example of the board's new policy of bypassing Bamford and buying their own players, had he not been preceded a few weeks earlier by the unconventional and unignorable Henderson Gill.

CHAPTER TWO

A Spark of Life

'Professionalism, true professionalism that is, was still just a pipedream.'

Maurice Lindsay and Jack Robinson went with Billy Cunliffe, the club's chief scout, to watch Rochdale's transfer-listed winger in a second division game at the Athletics Grounds, then a dilapidated stadium visibly coming to the end of its usefulness. Lindsay takes up the story: 'It was the old greyhound track stadium, and there were only a couple of thousand spectators, if that. At that time neither Jack nor myself had any experience in assessing players, we weren't quite sure what to do or what to expect. Billy could make certain observations about a player's strengths and weaknesses, but he couldn't make the decision about buying him. That was up to us. When we had mentioned Henderson Gill to Maurice Bamford he told us not to touch him with a bargepole.

'So we were sneaking out of school, really, we were going behind the coach's back being at Rochdale at all. But although the game was a bit drab, we knew we were on to something as soon as Henderson got the ball. The whole crowd rose to its feet. Suddenly there was atmosphere and excitement, where previously there had been silence. Henderson only got the ball about half a dozen times in the whole match, but every time it was the same. He would go charging forward, giving it every-thing he'd got, and the place would come alive. The only entertainment on offer was when he had the ball, and we knew imme-diately that he would respond to a bigger stage. We were looking for someone with a bit of flair, a character to set the town talking. Bamford wanted grafters all the time, laikers he called them, but we wanted a crowd pleaser in the Billy Boston tradition.'

Wigan picked up Gill for £23,000, but agreed to put out a figure of £30,000 at the request of Rochdale chairman Jack Grindrod, who was in a hurry to sell the player but did not want supporters to realise how desperate was the club's need. Even at the lower price, Lindsay and Robinson had to put their hands into their own pockets to pay Rochdale. The Fairbairn money had been spent, and although cash in small amounts was coming into the club from the sale of players like John Butler and Steve O'Neill, there was no float to fund team-strengthening.

'We had to spend a bit of our money to show some of the other directors we meant business,' Lindsay explained. 'One of our long-running criticisms of them was that they lacked the guts to compete in the transfer market. Before we bought Gary Stephens – and we bought him on the drip because we didn't have anything like £35,000 lying around at the time – the club's transfer record was £16,000 for John Butler. This was at a time when Hull and Hull KR were spending tens of thousands on players like Steve Norton and Trevor Skerrett. They were miles ahead in the bravery stakes. Wigan directors didn't want to spend any money, yet they expected any player they brought to the club to be capable of winning the Challenge Cup. It was an unrealistic and ultra-conservative policy which was getting us nowhere. We had been arguing for ages that you only get what you pay for, and stressing the need to be a bit more adventurous, so this was our moment to put up or shut up.'

Lindsay and Robinson put up for Gill, and immediately felt more adventurous. Big,

Glynn Shaw was just the sort of rough, tough forward Maurice Bamford had been asking the board to buy. At the wrong end of his career when he joined Wigan, but fondly remembered for two great seasons.

woolly rasta hats were not in common use as items of training-night headgear in 1981, and Lindsay was less confident he was signing the new Billy Boston when he travelled over to Rochdale to meet Gill and complete the deal. 'His appearance would have raised a few eyebrows in the Central Park boardroom,' Lindsay said. 'But he was lovely to talk to, and very keen to come to Wigan. I thought: "This lad's got the right attitude, at least." I confess I wasn't thinking that later in the season when he went to a nightclub in London and didn't bother turning up for our match at Wakefield the next day, but incidents like that were few

and far between. You never knew quite where you were with Henderson, that was part of his charm, but he gave us terrific value over the years. Definitely not bad for a first signing.'

It was a pity the coach did not see things quite the same way. Sometimes, as with Whitfield and later with David Stephenson, Bamford could claim to have had the idea first before standing back to let the directors get on with the transaction, but it was all too clear which party was making the decisions when Wigan bought Gill. Bamford was furious. He had spent the last few weeks insisting the club needed 'a big, hairy-arsed forward' – at one point he even enquired after Whitehaven's 31-year-old captain Gordon Cottier – and a quality stand-off. He was distinctly unimpressed to be handed a winger of any description, but especially one of erratic manner and uncertain temperament, and one whose price-tag dictated he would have to be accommodated in the first team.

Bamford denies ever having said he didn't want Gill, which would be an impolitic admission after the winger's glorious decade at the club, but he made it abundantly clear at

Henderson Gill . . . unorthodox, occasionally unreliable, frequently unstoppable. Maurice Bamford didn't want him, Maurice Lindsay and Jack Robinson 'sneaked out of school' to buy him from Rochdale. A landmark signing who could easily have ended up at St Helens. But then again, so could Martin Offiah.

the time that he wished the directors would listen to what he did want. 'Wingers weren't costing us games,' he said. 'We were short of strength in the pack and experience in the backs. As a team we lacked savvy. And I didn't see what good a youngster like Gill was going to do us, however promising he was supposed to be.'

It looked as if Bamford had been overruled, which he more or less had been, though that

was not quite the whole story. 'We had been disappointed with Bamford's initial signings,' Robinson said. 'Scott was a sound player, in fairness, but Nicholson and Birts were just not good enough. We decided pretty quickly that in future our policy would be for directors to undertake major signings.'

Robinson and Lindsay, that is. The pair would no more have trusted their co-directors to deal in the transfer market than they would have sent Bamford on a talent-spotting trip to Yorkshire. But the popular impression that Gill was signed just to spite Bamford, to show him what a real rugby player looked like, is incorrect. 'The timing was a little unfortunate in that respect,' Robinson admitted. 'Gill had been available most of the season, even St Helens had been considering signing him, and think how differently things might have turned out had he gone to Knowsley Road. I wanted him all along, but as usual, I couldn't get the other directors to agree. His signing cropped up at every board meeting for six or seven weeks, but every time we decided to wait. God knows what for. Finally, and we were incredibly lucky that no one else had signed him in the meantime, I got the go-ahead and we bought him the very next day. We knew the coach wasn't looking for a winger, but this was the start of our new signing policy. We were only going to sign quality players from now on, and we were going to sign them when they became available, rather than when we needed them.'

Anchored on the exceptional judgement Robinson and Lindsay showed in assessing a player's worth to the club and value on the market, this policy was to stand Wigan in excellent stead for years to come, but Gill's presence in the side did not bring about an immediate upturn in fortune. He made a losing début away at Barrow, where newly transferred Billy Melling had a predictably big say against his old club. This was the same Billy Melling who, four matches earlier, had responded to Bamford's pre-match instruction not to throw out any silly passes in the home game against Widnes by giving

Gary Stephens was not Maurice Bamford's favourite captain or travelling companion, though when he wanted to play he could lift Wigan above second-division mediocrity.

Mick George an interception try in the opening minute. Barrow were otherwise ordinary, it was Wigan's uninspiring team selection, featuring the decidedly ponderous half-back partnership of Walsh and Flowers, which virtually guaranteed the fifth defeat in a row. But Gill's performance almost made the trip worthwhile. He took a try well, and cancelled a certain Barrow score by racing back 50 yards to surprise Hadley as he strolled under the Wigan posts. It was barely perceptible as a turning point, too trifling even to consider as an omen, but Gill appeared to be made of the right stuff. Wigan followers had almost forgotten what initiative, eagerness and athleticism looked like.

Gill scored another try in the JPS defeat at

Leeds, when Bamford was criticised for playing a less than fully fit Stephens, but before a home match against Hull brought up Wigan's seventh defeat in a row, the club was involved in a flurry of transfer activity. The Whitfield deal went through, Salford preferring Stockley and Heaney to Martin Foy plus cash, but Widnes turned down a double approach for Glynn Shaw and Eric Hughes – the fearsome forward/clever back combination Bamford had long been seeking.

Whitfield made his début in the next game, away at York, the sort of fixture any team looking to avoid relegation had to have down as a banker. York won 24–20. The script was all too familiar. Jeff Townend, a prop who had once played for Wigan, scored the winning try, John Pendlebury dropped the ball over the line in the final minute. To complete the sense of *déjà vu* from the previous season, Wigan had Alan Hodkinson dismissed by referee John Holdsworth, whose fussiness over scrum technicalities had irked the prop all afternoon. Bamford looked haunted afterwards, a man who had wanted to take Wigan into the history books and had managed it with a postwar record losing run. He gave Pendlebury an unnecessarily hard time over the missed chance, and later apologised, blaming the strain he was working under. Which was real enough. Not only were Wigan at the wrong end of the table and falling, Bamford now had a shrewd idea his services might not be required next season whether relegation was avoided or not.

The losing run came to an end with a 16–5 home defeat of Wakefield, in which Gill performed so brilliantly Harold Box was obliged to flatten him with one of his choicest late tackles. By the time Wigan travelled to Fulham in late November they had finally acquired Shaw from Widnes, and Bamford's boast that in Hodkinson, Kiss and Shaw he had the best front row in either division was not far off the mark. Age was against both props, but no one was going to take liberties with that threesome. Wigan's team at Craven Cottage was: Whitfield; Hornby, Nicholson,

Wigan took a risk on David Stephenson in 1982, not because the Salford centre was not big, strong or skilful enough, but because he had A levels and a rugby union background. Nevertheless, he lasted seven glorious seasons, and with Gill provided a solid platform for future team building.

Wood, Gill; Foy, Stephens; Hodkinson, Kiss, Shaw, Trundle, Scott, Pendlebury. Only Hornby and Pendlebury survived from the débâcle of the previous season, and the latter in a different position. The result was different too, Wigan winning an exciting game with the help of a couple of tries from Gill and a drop goal from Whitfield. In December 1981 the great Brian McTigue died at the early age of 51. It would be pleasant to imagine he did not have to go to his grave without witnessing the first flowerings of the club's revival. Victory at Fulham was followed by two straight wins against Leeds and Featherstone, vital points in the bag, and Gill's

irrepressible form earned him a Great Britain call-up. 'A credit to the board's foresight,' commented a sheepish Bamford. While Wigan were making it four in a row against Featherstone, Gill scored a hat-trick on his international début in France.

It couldn't last, of course, and although Wigan could cope with a New Year's Day defeat at fogbound Warrington, where Shaw was sent off for punching Dave Chisnall in one of the few parts of the pitch the referee could see clearly, losing at home to lowly Barrow brought everyone back down to earth. It was an unprofessional performance, Wigan scoring three tries to Barrow's two but

27

giving away a stream of penalties which Ian Ball gratefully accepted.

Off the pitch, Stephens was unhappy, which was nothing new. He complained that the distance between Castleford and Wigan was too far to travel, something which never seemed to have occurred to him before, and said he had lost his appetite for the game. This was odd, since Bamford gave him a lift to training nights anyway, along with Scott and Nicholson. With the last two it was a matter of convenience, but Bamford had the impression that if he didn't drive Stephens over the Pennines he would stop playing. 'He had a bad attitude for a captain and it was starting to be a problem,' Bamford said. 'Those car journeys were a pain, because Gary would talk about money all the time. He always wanted more, he permanently felt he was not getting what he deserved, although sometimes he would vary it by claiming to have been paid more than he really had, just to wind the others up. He never talked about playing, or gave any indication of enjoying the game, just about money. He was utterly mercenary. I didn't really want to hear all this, I felt like I had a foot in both camps, but when I finally offered to ask the board for a bit of extra cash he said not to bother because he was looking for a move anyway. He didn't reckon Wigan were capable of winning anything. He was annoying like that. I remember once even Mick Scott told him to sort himself out or shut up, and Mick was one of his mates. I could have done with changing my travelling arrangements really. I can't imagine John Monie or any of the modern coaches putting up with nonsense like that, but that was how the game was then. True professionalism, the sort you see at Wigan today, was just a pipedream.'

Stephens did not get his move but managed to talk himself out of the captaincy, Bamford handing the job to £10,000 new boy Mal Aspey, a pre-Challenge Cup deadline signing from Fulham. In point of fact, very little about Aspey was new or boyish, he was an old hand with rather less left in the tank than Wigan possibly imagined, but he had the necessary experience and in 17 games he 'did a job' for Bamford. That things were looking up was evident from a 13–10 home win over Hull KR, Fairbairn and all, and although two successive defeats followed at Widnes and Hull, Wigan continued to climb away from relegation danger when Stephens scored two tries against his old club as Castleford were beaten 17–8. A young Shaun Wane appeared at loose forward in the Castleford match, and had a fine game until he was injured. He did not realise then that this would be the story of his career. One of a trio of promising forwards who emerged together from the Wigan St Patrick's amateur club, Wane came to Wigan at the same time as Mike Gregory went to Warrington and Andy Platt went to St Helens. For a while there was lively debate over which club had picked up the best player, until injuries began to blight the careers of Wane and Gregory. Platt went on to have the longest and most illustrious career, and gave most of his best years to Wigan, who paid St Helens £140,000 for the privilege in 1989. In 1982, the significant point about Wane was that he was one of the first local players of genuine promise to sign for his local club. Wigan St Patrick's at that time were more famous for producing players like Andy Gregory and Joe Lydon and packing them off to Widnes.

Wigan delighted their fans on the eve of their attractive Challenge Cup first-round tie at St Helens by paying Salford £55,000 for David Stephenson. This was quite a capture. Salford had already turned down £40,000 of Hull KR's money plus £40,000-rated forward Phil Hogan for their Under-24 international centre. Wigan clinched the deal by offering cash, albeit in staged payments, gambling that increased attendance would pay the steadily mounting bills. Even in rugby-mad Wigan this was a long way from a foregone conclusion, although small things like breaking the club transfer record on the eve of the Challenge Cup deadline were bound to help. Supporters appreciate that sort of gesture, it makes them feel the club is at least trying.

Stephenson was the sort of strong, skilful centre any coach would like in his side, though he had the sort of background – rugby union and the odd A-level – which does not always translate into a successful career in rugby league. It was an expensive signing which could have gone wrong, but fortune again favoured the brave, and instead it went immediately and spectacularly right. Stephenson could not have wished for a better début than the one he made in a rousing 20–12 Cup victory at Knowsley Road. Shaw, Scott and the rest of the pack were magnificent, the tireless tackling of the whole team was an embodiment of the defensive virtues Bamford always preached, but no one made more impact than Stephenson, who weighed in with two tries and a cheeky drop goal.

Short of beating Saints at Wembley, nothing makes a Wigan fan happier than beating Saints away from home in the Challenge Cup. There were some very happy Wigan fans on that Saturday night in February, but happiest of all were the club's directors after the next round. Wigan's reward for their unexpectedly dashing performance at St Helens was a home tie against Widnes, the holders of the Cup. This, unfortunately, meant the end of Wigan's participation. Widnes, under Doug Laughton, were on their way to Wembley again and in no mood to be trifled with, but the home side emerged with honour intact after a narrow and exciting 7–9 defeat had kept the crowd on its feet throughout. And what a crowd. The attendance of 17,467 for the Widnes game was Wigan's best for five years, the atmosphere at a packed and expectant Central Park something few of the team were old enough to remember. Wigan scored first through Aspey, and spent the rest of the match looking for more, but found the Widnes defence just too well organised. Although lacking the injured Hodkinson and suspended Shaw, Wigan themselves defended ferociously, but could not quite keep it up for 80 minutes and were undone when a moment of Gregory magic conjured the decisive try for Cunningham.

Wigan were disappointed, naturally, but at the same time encouraged. A large chunk of Stephenson's transfer fee was paid off already, but for perhaps the first time the club could see beyond the immediate necessity of paying the bills. The directors had been proved right. The Wigan public had not lost interest in rugby league, they just knew the difference between a second-rate team and one worth watching. Given a level of commitment from the boardroom, and a measure of success on the pitch, Wigan could rely on big gates. The only question now was how far the club wanted to go.

'I think it was probably around that time the directors realised they were sitting on a goldmine,' Bamford said. 'The smart ones, I mean, the ones who eventually took over. I think initially they had been trying to turn the club round, just aiming to get it back up to first division standards, when suddenly they saw a potential that was sky high. Widnes, for instance, could win every trophy in sight and not attract 17,000 spectators. Most clubs were the same way. The Hull clubs were getting the biggest attendances then, but they had had several seasons of success and only rarely drew gates of that size. Wigan were still finding their feet. That crowd against Widnes certainly opened my eyes. It was quite a shock to find 17,000 waiting to see us when we had been playing to gates of four or five thousand all season. I always knew that Wigan were big, or at least capable of being big, but that was the first occasion I really appreciated what it meant.'

Unfortunately the Cup was not the whole story for Wigan or for Bamford. League defeats at Leigh and Hull KR had put the club back in the relegation zone, and although a first away win at Castleford for ten years appeared to have clinched survival, Wigan slipped again by losing at home to Bradford by a single point. With six matches to play they only needed two wins to ensure safety, one if the teams below them kept losing, but it was hard to see where that victory might come from after a dispirited Wigan went all the way to Whitehaven to play a rearranged league

Martin Foy was an enigma, a classy stand-off whose lack of commitment frustrated Maurice Bamford. The coach once arranged to send him to Huyton on loan, just to provoke a reaction. Foy won the Man of the Match award in the 1983 John Player Special Trophy final, but drifted out of the game after a few more seasons.

game on a Wednesday afternoon, and ended up becoming the struggling Cumbrians' first scalp of the season. Prior to Wigan's arrival, Whitehaven's league record read: played 24, lost 21, drawn 3. Bamford admitted that giving the relegation certainties their first win had been his nightmare all season, and his worst fears were borne out in a dismal 8–5 defeat. 'That was the worst day of my time at Wigan,' Bamford admitted. 'It was a cold winter's day, there was hardly a crowd on because it was such a strange time to play a match, and we should have had a try in the last minute but Peter Stoddart got away with a blatant elbow.' Wigan's team had a strange look

about it too. Some players were unavailable through work commitments, and as Stephens was having another of his stand-offs with the coach, John Pendlebury was pressed into service as emergency scrum-half. 'I was young at the time so I just did what I was asked,' Pendlebury said. 'I was usually happy to be in the team at all, because I wasn't Maurice Bamford's cup of tea that season. He didn't know where to play me, and he was still accusing me of costing Wigan the game against Widnes by holding on to the ball too long with a two-man overlap. I was guilty, I had to admit, and playing that game at Whitehaven was like a punishment. Gary

Stephens had fallen out with Bamford again, and the spirit in the squad was very low. I think we were beaten at Whitehaven before we even ran out for the game.'

It was hard to imagine anything worse than that, but the sight that greeted supporters travelling to Wakefield the following Sunday probably qualified. A bevy of Wigan directors was standing in the club car park, in turn peering anxiously at their watches and then down the road. They continued to do this until approximately five minutes before kick-off, at which point they resigned themselves to the conclusion that Henderson Gill was not going to turn up. Nor did he, being 200 miles away. Wigan had little choice but to forgive their player and concoct some elaborate excuse about injury for the local press, which was a bit of a waste of time since every fan who had been to Wakefield knew they were lying. Wakefield, another team about to be relegated, should have represented two points for the taking, but Gill-less Wigan went down 17–14. Relegation was now frighteningly possible. Bamford, who had been talking of a top eight place a few weeks earlier, pronounced himself angry, heartsick and frustrated at his side's ability to win games against bigger clubs but lose momentum when faced with weaker opponents. The euphoria of only a month earlier seemed as much of a pipedream as true professionalism.

Wigan lost at St Helens on Good Friday too, although at least the five teams below them kept losing. This was eventually Wigan's salvation. A very welcome two points arrived from the home fixture against Fulham on Easter Monday, and a 23–5 win over listless St Helens in the final game of the season, rearranged from Christmas, provided a highly flattering final safety margin of five points. In between, there was a humiliating defeat at Featherstone to keep things in perspective. A pedestrian Featherstone side secured its own survival with a 26–14 win, despite the Wigan directors putting up the biggest bonus of the season in an effort to end the uncertainty before the final day of the season. Wigan had

to hope Wakefield, Fulham, Whitehaven and York would keep losing, and in the end they obliged. Castleford finished fifth from bottom, with Wigan a place above them. But if Bamford had secretly been hoping for a reprieve on the back of his Cup success, he knew he had blown it by the time Wigan blew up at Post Office Road. 'I came away absolutely sick,' he said. 'A coach doesn't send out a team to play badly, but rightly or wrongly the coach carries the can.'

Rightly or wrongly, Bamford was dismissed within days of the end of the season. As Wigan had lost six of their last eight matches, and could have been relegated had any of the bottom four clubs mounted even a modest revival, he could not seriously expect anything else. The only thing more predictable than Bamford's sacking was the ensuing outbreak of sentimentality. 'I don't want to leave, and I feel very hurt,' the coach told Wigan fans. 'I have been haunted all season by the feeling that names of other coaches like Laughton, Benyon and Grainey are being bandied about. I gave Wigan my best and now I fear my rugby career could be over.'

Bamford need not have worried on the last account, in fact he may have been disingenuous in pretending he had nowhere else to go. He had already made a verbal agreement to take over at Bramley, and in the event had a choice between the second division club and Featherstone, whose members were so impressed by his gruff geniality they voted to offer him their coaching position, despite a long tradition of only appointing from within the club or the village. From first Yorkshireman at Wigan to first stranger in Featherstone, Bamford had come a long way in a year, and within a few more years had gone all the way to Leeds and Great Britain.

'Wigan put me on the map, but I'd like to think I did the same for them,' Bamford said. 'They could so easily have gone straight back down again. Wigan's achievements that season might not look much compared to what has happened since, but compared to what went before it was a significant improvement. They were crying out for new faces, virtually the whole team had to be changed in just one season. And we avoided relegation, which was the main goal. But perhaps that bit of success in mid-season did for me, perhaps that's when the directors began to want something better. I think I could have made Wigan a lot better in another season, but the directors wanted a big-name coach like Alex Murphy by that time and I was made a scapegoat. Which saddened me, but when I left I received 148 letters and cards from Wigan fans who appreciated what I had done for the club. I don't think many Wigan coaches have been as well liked. I can't argue now that the directors did not do the right thing, the record speaks for itself. The time was right for one of the big clubs to do something dramatic, but never in my wildest dreams did I ever imagine any club would do what Wigan have done. If you had told me ten or 12 years ago a club would win at Wembley six, seven, eight years on the trot, I would have laughed. It wouldn't have been thought possible. Wigan have more than bridged the gap back to their old glory years, and fair play to them, but no one, not even Robinson and Lindsay, are entitled to take all the credit. They didn't know it all, not then anyway. One snowy night I remember those same directors wouldn't let Billy Boston into the club. Robinson and Lindsay were still new at the game then. Like I say, it was a learning process for everyone. A joint effort.'

Neither director disputes this observation, but Bamford still had to go. Not just because the last few weeks of the season had shredded everyone's nerves, but because Bamford had signed Birts and opposed the purchase of Gill. Characteristically, Bamford has no regrets. 'I would have put my house on Birts,' he said. 'He played his bollocks off for me at Halifax. He was arguably the best all round full-back in the second division, but Central Park was just too big for him. You can't foresee that, and when it happens, there's very little you can do about it.' On the subject of Gill, Bamford insists his opposition was not to the player, but to Wigan's back-to-front manner

of team-building. 'Gill turned out to be a marvellous winger, if I'm honest I will admit I underrated him at first, but the best winger in the world is not what you need when you are constantly being beaten up front and outplayed at half-back,' he said. 'Something very similar happened to me later in my career at Leeds. I was told that the club had put together a package worth £350,000 over five years to bring Jonathan Davies from Welsh rugby union. I asked where they intended playing him and was told stand-off, to which my reply was "stand-off to what?" Leeds had a pack then which was even weaker than Wigan's had been. The whole team was weak. Davies would have been murdered if I had thrown him into that side in that position. He got a much better deal at Widnes, being brought gradually into an already strong team, but if Leeds had bought him first people would have been expecting miracles, the results would have been disappointing, and there would have been no money left to do anything about it. I managed to persuade Leeds to spend their money on Garry Schofield and Lee Crooks instead, and I was much happier with that transaction. You've got to get the basics in place before you go shopping for luxuries, and that's what I tried to tell Wigan over Gill.'

Wigan's whole approach in the past 15 years could be said to amount to a rebuttal of this sensible but rather uninspiring theory. 'Bring on the entertainers' has been the club's unofficial motto. Get the crowds in, give the punters what they want, and use the profits to strengthen the team when necessary. Leeds actually won very little with Crooks and Schofield, whereas with Davies in their side they might have increased attendances sufficiently to bankroll a later bid for the pair and had the Welshman's matchwinning talent into the bargain. No one will ever know now, but one could at least understand Bamford's reasoning. Considering Wigan had hired him to put the club back on its feet, rather than win prizes for artistic impression, he was entitled to feel the rules had been changed midway through his term.

Possibly the directors recognised this, certainly when the sad day of parting arrived Robinson felt sorry for the coach he had brought to the club only a year earlier. 'Maurice looked very down, he seemed to be taking it hard, so I went over to commiserate with him, as I had been the one to bring him,' Robinson said. 'I wished him all the best for the future, hoped we could still remain friends, all the usual things. Then he said something which amazed me. He said he had tried his best, which was fair enough, no one could have worked harder for the club than he had. That was one of the reasons we all felt so uncomfortable. But then he said he couldn't see where he had gone wrong, and if he had his time again he would do everything exactly the same. "Even Jimmy Birts?" I asked him. "Especially Jimmy Birts," he replied. I knew then we had made the right decision. Maurice is correct in saying we were all making mistakes that season, but some of us were learning from them. I would be the first to admit that Maurice [Lindsay] and myself made lots of little errors, but we tried our best not to make the same mistake twice, which might be why we never went disastrously wrong. We felt we were learning fast, but Maurice Bamford was either unwilling or incapable of learning anything new. That final conversation took quite a weight off my shoulders.'

Bamford had one last appointment in Wigan, honouring a commitment to award the prizes at Wigan Schools end-of-season presentation evening. He received a tremendous ovation, and was so overcome by the warmth of his reception he was unable to speak for several minutes. Earlier the same day, elsewhere in town, the scenes were rather less emotional as Wigan's new coach Alex Murphy breezed into Central Park.

CHAPTER THREE

A Giant Awakes

'Open up, Mrs Brown. We've won the cup!'

At Murphy's earliest introduction to Wigan supporters, he made a promise which was music to their ears. 'This club has been under-achieving. We are going to get Wigan winning trophies again, and we are going to get back all those supporters who have been on loan to Wigan Athletic.'

On both counts, Murphy was as good as his word. No one can take that away from him, and it might even be true to say the coach was instrumental in putting Wigan on the path to success. Certainly Wigan perked up immediately Murphy arrived, challenging for the championship instead of flirting with relegation, and the combination of the game's most colourful personality and most famous club was popular with everyone from sports editors to spectators. Record books do not tell the whole story, they give no indication of how chaotic it all was at the time, but they give the distinct impression that Murphy and Wigan were good for each other. And they were. It is only the notion that this was in any way deliberate or preplanned which is inaccurate.

Wigan wanted a big-name coach. 'We were still buying ordinary players,' Lindsay explained. 'We decided the only way to improve the overall quality of the squad was to get a coach who had vision.' This more or less ruled Murphy out straightaway. The man Lindsay and Robinson had in mind was Widnes's Doug Laughton. The theory that Wigan employed Murphy because they swallowed his myth and believed they were getting the best coach in the country is a non-starter. Lindsay the bookmaker was a big friend of Murphy the inveterate gambler, and

knew exactly what reality lay behind the legend. There is another theory, which suggests Wigan were quite hard-headed about the whole business and simply took what they wanted from Murphy before discarding him when he was no longer useful. Apart from making both parties out to be cleverer than they really were, this is far too neat to be true. Nothing in the two years Murphy was at Wigan was ever neat, nothing was that straightforward, very little was even as it appeared. It was the best fun Wigan fans had had in ages.

Fun, of course, was not what the Wigan directors were looking for as they deliberated over a successor to Bamford. Robinson had again floated his idea of bringing a coach from Australia, but the general opinion was that it made sense to first try the best Britain had to offer. In Robinson and Lindsay's opinion, that meant Laughton, who had produced a succession of dynamic Widnes sides on a tight budget. In the opinion of the rest of the board, it meant Murphy who, in addition to being a genuine, card-carrying legend, had just guided humble Leigh to an improbable championship. The senior Wigan directors would not be the first or last old men to be seduced by the sheer privilege of rubbing shoulders with one of the game's all-time greats, but at an early stage in the debate Robinson stood up to be counted. 'I was against getting Murphy, and I said so,' he recalled. 'It wasn't anything personal, just that I thought the club needed someone with his career in front of him. To me Murphy represented the past, his best days were behind him. You couldn't knock his achieve-

Brian Case was one of Alex Murphy's best signings for Wigan, a workaholic prop forward who was still giving excellent service at Central Park long after the coach had departed.

ments, but I sensed he was coming to a time in his life when he had done enough in the game, and probably had had enough of it as well. I thought we should be looking forward. I was possibly the only director who thought this, and certainly the only one to come out and say it. A couple of years later Murphy threw it back at me, saying he had never had the support of all the directors, which wasn't strictly true. I had argued against his appointment, but once he joined us I backed him, even when the others were calling for his head. I couldn't see the point of falling out with him then. It was too late. We knew what we were getting, we still went out and got him, so we had to put up with him. If I've learned one thing in life it's that you don't change people.'

There was another lesson Robinson was still to learn, however. Which is that logic and common sense can only take you so far, and then luck takes a hand. 'It's very strange,' he said, 'but Alex turned out to be a lucky signing for us. Laughton was the best choice, the most sensible option, I am convinced of that. But if we had got him instead of Alex we might never have gone on to be so successful

so quickly. There are dozens of instances like that, where we went one way instead of another, and I often wonder what would have happened if we had gone down a different path. We seemed to always have luck on our side, though of course we didn't realise it at the time.'

Murphy, like the departing Bamford, was perfectly well aware Laughton was the Wigan board's first choice. Or at least Robinson and Lindsay's first choice. Lindsay went to see the Widnes coach one night at his home, where he explained his ambitious plans for Central Park and asked the former Wigan captain to return and spearhead the club's revival. 'Doug listened politely, but turned me down,' Lindsay said. 'Or at least I thought he did. Over the next couple of days I became unsure. I remember walking down his garden path and saying goodbye at the gate, thinking what a lovely man Doug was and what a pity it was he wanted to stay at Widnes. Then I was asleep in bed the following morning and the phone rang at 5 a.m. It was Doug. He said he had changed his mind, and asked me if I had pen and paper handy. He seemed surprised when I said I hadn't, and told me I would have to be a lot sharper if he was coming as coach. Eventually I found a pencil, and wrote down the names of five players he wanted to buy, then went back to bed. The phone rang again at 7 a.m. It was Doug, asking whether I'd seen the papers. I hadn't. He tutted at that too, then said some player or other had become available and would I add him to the list? I was beginning to wonder what Widnes had been putting up with all this time, but I planned another meeting with Doug to make sure he had a deal. Suddenly he rang again to tell me he'd changed his mind again. He couldn't quite see Wigan taking off and had decided to stay where he was, but would I consider becoming vice-chairman of Widnes?'

Laughton denies the last charge. 'I used to joke that Maurice Lindsay would be the best signing Widnes could make, but that was all,' he said. But the rest is substantially true. Laughton turned down Wigan and spent the rest of his career wondering why. 'I still can't really explain it. I was on 50 quid a week at Widnes when Maurice came calling, and he offered me £35,000 a season. He said they wanted the best and were prepared to pay for it. I said I'd think about it, but as soon as he'd gone my wife told me to take it, because it was the kind of offer I might never be made again. I had to agree. I didn't want to leave Widnes, and I had my own business so money wasn't exactly a pressing concern, but no one in his right mind would refuse that kind of pay rise. And it wasn't just the money, either. I liked the way Maurice sold the club and the job. The Wigan directors, when I had been at the club, were very old-fashioned – I only left because I didn't think they did enough to keep Eric Ashton as coach – but Maurice was completely different. My wife and I both thought the same thing – he was going places, whether I joined Wigan or not.

'So I called him and told him I would come, then I went to tell Widnes, who were broken-hearted. I wasn't on a contract, there was absolutely no reason why I should not just walk out and join Wigan, but call it loyalty or principle, I felt I would be letting friends down. So I told Wigan I still wanted to come, but only in another season. They contacted me and told me Alex Murphy was ready to come straightaway, probably trying to force my hand. I said I wasn't ready to leave, and that was that. They got Murphy, which was absolutely the right thing to do. I stayed at Widnes, which was unquestionably the wrong thing. Most of my friends at the club began to leave, and within a year I'd gone myself. I've always been a man for quick decisions, I'm like Maurice in that respect, and I often wonder why I didn't stick with my original plan. It's not even as if I'm a great believer in loyalty. I certainly didn't owe Widnes anything, and like any coach at any club, I knew I wouldn't get much loyalty in return if things began to go wrong. A few bad results in this job and you're out the door, whoever you are. In hindsight I regret not joining Wigan, but there are a lot of things in my rugby career I regret. I don't lose sleep over it. In time I went back to Widnes and was very happy, then I had four good years at Leeds. I'm not complaining.'

Laughton contacted Murphy to wish him well at his new club. The two are not great friends, but Laughton genuinely wanted Wigan and Murphy to succeed. 'Like everyone else, I believed the game needed a strong Wigan,' Laughton said. 'People used to say that all the time back then, you don't hear it so much now. I don't think anyone realised how strong Wigan were going to get.'

When the club ended several weeks of summer speculation by appointing Murphy in June 1982, there were signs that Wigan were at least thinking big. The former Leigh, Salford and Warrington boss was to head up a four-man coaching team at Central Park. Coming in to assist Murphy would be Bill Ashurst, a former Wigan favourite who had been helping out at Wakefield Trinity after a spell playing in Australia, and Alan McInnes, a schoolteacher and ex-Salford player whose brief reign as caretaker coach at the Willows ended when Mal Aspey jumped ship from Central Park to coach the Red Devils. Wigan were surprised, having imagined they had the services of Aspey the player, but in no position to complain after spiriting Murphy out of the championship celebrations in Leigh. Murphy, by a nice irony, was a pioneer of the coaching route out of a playing contract, having used just such a ruse to leave St Helens in the '60s. The fourth member of the coaching quartet, with special responsibility for youth development, was another former Wigan player, Geoff Lyon.

In spite of this surprising degree of delegation, Murphy remained the main man. 'We now have the top coach in the game, and in Phil Worthington the top administrator too,' said Jack Hilton in welcoming Murphy. 'This pursuit of excellence has always been our aim.' Ever the diplomat, Hilton must have conveniently forgotten the Laughton business, just as he deemed it wisest not to mention that club secretary Worthington, who considered he had exceeded the normal adult dose of Murphy during his years at Warrington, had started to look for another job as soon as he realised his past was coming back to haunt him. Worthington was gone by September, quoting 'personal reasons' for returning to a job in local industry. Something else Hilton failed to mention was the parting shot from Brian Bowman, the Leigh chairman who was unhappy at the manner of Murphy's departure from Hilton Park but not exactly sorry to see him go.

'Alex wasn't on a contract at Leigh, there was nothing improper about our approach, but after the deal had been announced I rang Brian to check we were still friends,' Lindsay explained. 'He said no, he hated the lot of us and would never approve of the whole business, but then he suddenly seemed to cheer up. "Listen," he said. "I've got just the thing to go with Alex, and you can have it as a present. There's a great big box of headache tablets on my sideboard and I've just realised I won't be needing them any more."'

By 1982 Murphy was well on his way to becoming a caricature of himself – one frivolous publication circulated in Leigh suggested Wigan had got their man by passing him a drugged betting slip – but the

laughing soon stopped when his new team opened the season with four straight wins. Wigan again began the season at Carlisle, this time with a league match against the newly promoted Cumbrians, and were made to struggle by a side whose summer captures from New Zealand included a youthful Dean Bell. But Wigan had not been inactive in the transfer market either. Brian Juliff, a £25,000

Henderson Gill's strength and determination takes him through four Leeds challenges for the crucial score in the 1983 John Player Special Trophy final. The winger injured a shoulder in the act of scoring and played no further part in the game.

signing from Wakefield, made his début on the wing at Carlisle, and the winning try in the 10–7 victory was scored by Jimmy Fairhurst, Murphy's first recruit, a Burton-wood-based scrum-half for whom Blackpool Borough had been persuaded to accept a couple of Wigan reserve players.

Jinking Jimmy, as he quickly became known, was an instant hit with Wigan supporters, and a good example of Murphy's instinctive, rather than logical, approach to team-building. The coach's first decision on joining Wigan had been to reappoint Gary Stephens as captain. Nothing wrong with that, although somewhere in Yorkshire Bamford probably allowed himself a chuckle. Then Murphy decided team spirit was non-existent, so he signed Fairhurst, knowing him to be the sort of confident, wise-cracking character who could help lift morale in the dressing-room and on the pitch. 'I needed someone who could do a specific job for me,' Murphy explained. 'Jimmy probably wasn't the greatest player in the world, but he was popular and positive and he lifted everyone's spirits.' Nothing wrong with this reasoning either, except that Fairhurst played in Stephens's position. So Murphy's new captain almost immediately found himself out of the team. His new £25,000 winger,

with a solo try from 60 yards out. This looked suspiciously like the start of something big. The league champions and now the Challenge Cup and John Player Special Trophy holders had just been despatched within a couple of days, and when Salford turned up for a first-round Lancashire Cup tie they became Wigan's fourth victims of the season.

Winners at last. Alex Murphy's team in celebratory mood at Elland Road. A bit ragged, perhaps, by the standards of later years, but Wigan were out of practice in 1983. Note the semi-detached and serious-looking Graeme West on the extreme right.

Juliff, must have been similarly confused. Within three games of his arrival he was playing in the pack, as Murphy dropped a heavy hint to the board that he considered a new second-row forward a priority signing.

The strange thing was that, initially anyway, Murphy's improvisation worked a treat. In the first home league match of the season Wigan actually beat Leigh. Then, in front of a second consecutive crowd of over 10,000, mighty Hull were overwhelmed 23–8. Once-timid Wigan took the fight straight to their illustrious opponents, with Shaw, Kiss, Scott and Campbell excelling in the pack, and Fairhurst setting the seal on a resounding win

There was no doubt about it, the giant was stirring. Fairhurst implored the Wigan players to shout and chat to each other during games, saying he had never known such a quiet team, but confidence, even flamboyance, did not take long to spread. Nicky Kiss, criticised by some supporters for over-lavish celebrations after scoring against Hull, defended himself articulately. 'I care about Wigan doing well, I want to celebrate when we score, especially if I'm the scorer,' he said. 'I've seen too many lukewarm Wigan players in the past. A lot of the players I've known here could hardly be bothered to put their hands together in support of their team-mates.'

Kiss, a casual dresser at the best of times, chafed somewhat when Murphy decreed that Wigan players would henceforth turn up for games in regulation blazers and slacks, but conformed in the spirit of solidarity sweeping through Central Park. This spirit spread to the terraces. Prior to the start of the season Lindsay had appealed for a cherry and white army of support, a band of followers in favours to rival the black and white hordes who travelled everywhere with Hull, and made replica shirts available to the public. Sales of these never took off until a kit redesign the following season persuaded a dubious public that Wigan shirts really could double up as fashion items, but a prediction by Murphy that Wigan could one day exceed Hull's attendances began to look less fanciful once Central Park had savoured the experience of out-shouting their Humberside counterparts.

If ever there was a time to launch a boardroom coup this was it. Immediately after the Hull game four Wigan directors – Jack Hilton, Maurice Lindsay, Tom Rathbone and Jack Robinson – announced they would be willing to inject up to £112,000 into the club, in the form of a debenture loan re-payable in 1995, in exchange for total control. The four were the directors principally responsible for the upturn at the club in the previous 12 months, and by this time most supporters and shareholders realised it. Lindsay, a former plant-hire contractor and occasional bookmaker who joined the board in 1979, was the public face of the venture; Robinson, who ran a successful business exporting English bric-à-brac to America, was the long-term Wigan supporter who provided most of the rugby knowledge. Driving back disconsolately from a heavy defeat at Leeds a couple of years earlier, Robinson had deter-mined to join the Wigan board to see if he could run the club any better, reasoning simply that he could not possibly run it any worse. Now he was trying to take it over.

Robinson and Lindsay were the prime movers behind the regeneration of Wigan and the boardroom cull they quickly deemed

necessary, but they were not rash enough to attempt it on their own. Although pros-perous, neither had sufficient funds to simply buy-in and take over, and both knew only too well how quickly a rugby club could drain the wealth of anyone unwary enough to attempt to run it as a plaything. The whole point of Robinson and Lindsay was that they were not unwary, and neither had they any intention of running Wigan as a plaything. They simply felt running Wigan as a business would be a step in the right direction. When the board, or a portion of it, had been cop-pering up to buy Henderson Gill the previous season, Robinson and Lindsay's money had been topped up by a donation from Rath-bone, proprietor of a long-established bakery firm and one of the few wealthy men at the club. Though hardly as dynamic as the other two, Rathbone had proved himself both useful and forward-thinking, and although his big car, big coat and big cigar image sat a little uneasily with his partners' earnestly hands-on approach, his solid, dependable presence was welcomed. As was that of Hilton, owner of a modest chain of sports shops and far from a major financial player or visionary leader, but possessed of what Lindsay described as 'a quiet wisdom'. Unusually for a former player, Hilton was a progressive voice on the board, at least in touch with the modern game. He quickly assessed what was happening to the club and signed up with the new regime, amid accusations of disloyalty from other directors. 'Jack Hilton was a latecomer to the scene,' Lindsay explained. 'In the beginning there were just three of us – Jack Robinson, Tom Rathbone and myself – but he came to us and said that although he hadn't got much money to spare, he would raise what he could if we would have him along. He was very supportive of our ideas, was obviously genuine in his concern for the club and, being well known and respected in town, was able to provide a friendly face for the revolution.'

So Hilton came on board for the knock-down price of £10,000, favourable terms which further incensed those directors who were soon to discover they were not wanted at any price. Even today, Lindsay regards Hilton as one of the few old-timers who will hold his hands up and admit that standards have improved since his playing days. 'Most former players live in the past,' Lindsay said. 'They don't always say it, but they usually hate to give credit to their modern counterparts, because they think the game's gone soft, or got too easy, or some other such nonsense. Jack has never been like that. There must have been times during his early years on the Wigan board when he was appalled at what he saw on the pitch, but when we got the team right he was the first to admit the players were training harder, running faster and performing more consistently than anyone had in his day.'

However flexible his outlook, Hilton's immediate advantage to the breakaway group was a link with the past. Not only had he played with distinction for Wigan and Great Britain in the '50s, he was chairman of the old board and he continued to be chairman of the new board, lending an irreproachable continuity to the venture which his co-plotters would have found impossible to buy. Cynics at the time suggested this was the only reason for Hilton's inclusion, that he was retained as a mere figurehead for Robinson and Lindsay's designs on the club. A lot was said at the time which was a good deal less complimentary, but not much of it was repeated when the debenture loan finally came up for repayment, and Central Park shareholders queued to have their photograph taken with the world's foremost collection of rugby league silverware. Robinson, Hilton and Rathbone looked on indulgently. Apart from the departure of Lindsay, who left in 1992 to run the game, no less, the Wigan board reached 1995 intact, a fair achievement for any group of directors, something of a miracle for anyone involved in running a rugby league club. Rathbone clearly knew what he was talking about in 1982, when he explained why this particular group of four directors should be given the chance to run the club. 'We work very well together and have the utmost confidence in each other. We also think a

smaller board is more appropriate in this day and age, as the four of us can reach decisions easily and quickly.'

In 1982, however, this was pretty radical thinking, and the six directors who would have to willingly stand down to enable the scheme to succeed did not like it one bit. Not that the rump of the board was united on the issue. The old board was incapable of uniting on an issue, that was the point of the takeover. The six – Alf Close, Harry Gostelow, Peter Higginbottom, Tim Moran, Martin Ryan and Arthur Stone – all had different points of view, as was their habit. Some, like former chairman Gostelow, made dissenting noises but were basically tired of the responsibility and secretly pleased to be handed an honourable discharge. Others, particularly the relatively young Higginbottom, could see what the gang of four was trying to do, agreed with it, and just felt sad to be excluded. But most felt resentful, mistrusting both the motives and the abilities of the Central Park four, especially after the club announced a record £80,000 loss on the previous season. A letter printed in *The Wigan Observer* from 'Interested shareholders', almost certainly supplied by, or on behalf of, one of the threatened directors, asked: 'Are these four people not partially responsible for the plight in which the club finds itself? What evidence is there that these four can suddenly produce dynamic leadership?'

A good question, but when a shareholders' meeting eventually debated the issue on 2 November, the four were seen to have judged their audience accurately, or at least done enough already to suggest they could keep up the improvement. The debenture scheme – basically a conditional loan, which all shareholders were invited to subscribe to for the right to a greater say in the running of the club, but over £100,000 of which was found, as planned, by the four directors – gained a 90 per cent vote of confidence. Ryan spoke out against the plan, claiming the new directors simply wanted him off the board. This was a mistake, since the shareholders were evidently in agreement. 'They don't want *my* money,'

Ryan complained, adding that his cash offer to join the breakaway board had been refused. Robinson took the stage and informed the gathering that Mr Ryan's money would have been welcome a year earlier, when loans were needed from directors to buy players, but at that time there had been none forthcoming.

Jimmy Firhurst, Nicky Kiss and Barry Williams help chair captain Colin Whitfield around Elland Road.

Higginbottom was more supportive, even though he was talking himself out of a job. 'We don't want to have to start selling players like Gill and Stephenson, they are our future,' he said. 'I think anyone willing to put £35,000 into this club ought to have a say in how it is spent.' But the mood of the meeting was best caught by a couple of shareholders, speaking from the floor. First Dave Whelan, a millionaire local businessman who would quickly become pally with the new regime and feature prominently in the Wigan story for the next decade, weighed in with a few powerful words which virtually carried the vote on their own. 'For the last 20 years this club has been a horror story,' he boomed. 'The most famous club in the world has been the most diabolically run. I think we should support these four brave men.' The meeting duly did, though not before Harold Heyes, a popular and outspoken voice from the terraces at shareholders' meetings over the

years, had injected a note of comedy. 'It's fear of the unknown that worries people,' he said. 'We don't mind walking the plank with you on this, we just want to make sure there are no sharks swimming about down below.'

Somewhere between these two speeches was the defining moment that set Wigan on the path to greatness. It can all be traced back to a Tuesday evening three days before Bonfire night in 1982, or at least from a '90s perspective it can. Back then, no one was quite sure for a while, least of all Murphy and his increasingly erratic performers on the pitch. We left them, if you recall, with team spirit sky high after opening the season with four successive victories. The run came to an end with the next match, away at Warrington, but the Wigan revival was dealt a much more severe blow when Fulham came to Central Park in the second round of the Lancashire Cup (this is not the place to go into rugby league's geographical complexities, but Fulham played in the Lancashire Cup because they began life as Widnes in disguise. Widnes, of course, is in Cheshire; Central Park itself is in Greater Manchester) and produced a scintillating performance to win 15–4, the home side being unable to manage a single try. Wigan at this time never really expected to win the Lancashire Cup – for years the only purpose they served in the competition had been to provide a neutral ground for the final – but Fulham were in the second division, for heaven's sake. Presented with an opportunity to stroll into the semi-finals Wigan just managed the strolling part, watching bemused as Crossley and Bowden put on an exhibition of fast, incisive rugby.

Murphy reshuffled his pack and managed to save face with a notable victory at Hull KR, but when that was followed by a draw at Oldham it was back into the transfer market. Or to be more precise, the transfer trade. 'Wigan promised there would be money to spend on players, and in a way there was,' Murphy said. 'But what they didn't make clear was that there would only be money for players the board wanted. I went to them asking for reinforcements and they told me there were no funds available at the moment, because they were signing a Kiwi forward Cec Mountford had put them on to. According to Cec, he was the best in the Southern Hemisphere. I thought at the time it sounded too good to be true, but I said nothing. He wasn't due for a few weeks so I just got on with trying to find my own reinforcements.'

Murphy came up with Lee Bamber, a 23-year-old prop who was on Blackpool Borough's list at £12,000. If there was a reason why an enormous, powerfully built and aggressive player from the Widnes area was languishing on Blackpool's list at such a knockdown price, Murphy didn't bother to find out. Neither did he find much of the money. He simply selected a reserve player, Dave Regan, whom Blackpool were more than happy to take in exchange, and did the deal. No matter that Regan had been at Central Park nine years and was coming up for a testimonial. No matter even that Regan had stepped into the breach at Hull KR the previous week and performed heroically. It was this last factor which upset Regan, a patient player who knew he had to make the most of his first-team chances. 'After the Hull KR game Murphy told me that if I continued to play that way the number 10 shirt was mine,' he said. 'Next thing I know, he's sending me to Blackpool, so I blew my top.' Regan refused to go, and ended up being banned from Central Park by Murphy, but Bamber duly arrived, went straight into the team, and won the Man of the Match award in a victory over Bradford.

Bamber won the Man of the Match award in his next game too, and as the opponents on this occasion were Australia, and not just any old Australia but the fabulous 1982 tourists, it began to look as if Murphy had unearthed a real find. This was only the second game of the Kangaroo tour, and Australia had their midweek side out, except that players like Miles, Lewis and Mortimer did not yet realise they would spend the next couple of months playing second fiddle to the likes of Meninga, Kenny and Sterling. Neither did anyone have

an inkling that these tourists would be the first in history to go through Britain and France undefeated. Consequently, no one immediately realised how impressive a feat it was for Wigan to hold them to a 13–9 scoreline. As the tour progressed it became painfully obvious that British rugby league was suddenly in the business of being thankful for small mercies, but Wigan could at least hold their head up and say they gave Australia a game, their four-point margin of defeat proving to be the nearest anyone came to matching the Invincibles. Henderson Gill's try, scored with characteristic aplomb from an initial break by Danny Campbell, was one of only seven the Kangaroos conceded in 15 games in Britain, and Wigan's effort looked all the more creditable when the Test series began and Great Britain were rolled over to the tune of 40–4. Wigan might have edged closer too, or possibly even managed a draw, but for gamely going for a winning try in the closing minutes and eschewing a number of kickable penalties. In the end they paid heavily for the inexperience of their full-back, Barry Williams, who faltered early in the game under a succession of steepling kicks from Australia, but no one was complaining. A crowd of over 12,000 saw a proper contest between a British side and Australia, something about to become a very rare commodity indeed.

Williams, a local player who had been given his chance by Murphy and seized it willingly enough, stayed in the side for most of the season, taking advantage of Whitfield's successful conversion to centre, until he was eventually undone by a change in rules which obliged full-backs to field a lot more high kicks. But at least he lasted the season. Bamber, despite his dream start, played just eight games for Wigan. By Christmas he was staying away from the club amid lurid rumours of his fondness for petty crime, at which he seemed singularly inept, judging by the number of times he got caught. He would have been far better sticking with the rugby, at which he at least showed promise. 'I'm very disappointed with that lad,' Murphy confessed. He wasn't the only one. Lee Bamber was shot dead six years later in a Widnes pub, a victim of the chaotic and violent lifestyle he had chosen for himself and his own apparent determination to be one of life's losers. He was 28.

Back in 1982, Wigan shot up the table with convincing wins over Halifax, Barrow and Workington, the increasingly reliable Gill helping himself to five tries in the three games and cementing his position as crowd favourite. It would have been around this time that TV commentator Ray French informed the nation that Gill was the sort of player who bobbed up and down like a corkscrew, an unintentional slip which nevertheless described the winger's eccentric action pretty accurately. Gill was fast and elusive but unusually strong for a winger of the time, with sufficient upper-body power to literally throw off unsuspecting tacklers, occasionally over his shoulder. It was hard to know when a Gill run had come to an end, and he was always capable of making his own space in which to operate, whether he received the ball on the wing or in the middle of the field. 'If you think Hendy is elusive on the field,' Murphy once quipped memorably of an unconventional player and famously erratic trainer, 'you want to try catching him on the telephone.' In the early years, Gill's popularity with the crowd and his usefulness to the team were chiefly centred around his ability to create something out of nothing, which he was asked to do rather too often. It would be another few years before anyone had the bright idea of seeing what he could do with an overlap.

With Stephenson, Gill was drafted into the Great Britain side for the second Test, as the selectors belatedly realised the size of their task against Australia, but neither could do anything to prevent a defeat only slightly less comprehensive than the first. The one item of good news on the international front was that Cec Mountford's man had arrived. All 6 ft 5 in Kiwi second-row Graeme West (27) had to do was live up to his billing. Wigan had certainly acted decisively on the advice of

Mountford, a New Zealander who captivated Central Park in the '50s – West had signed a five-year contract and brought over his young family.

'As soon as we saw Graeme, both the player and the man, we knew this was the sort of figure we could build a team around,' Lindsay said, in his new capacity as Wigan vice-chairman. Murphy's initial, typically flip response – 'Would any local basketball teams please get in touch' – betrayed his reservations. After watching West make his début, admittedly in difficult conditions, in a rain-lashed defeat at Leeds, Murphy knew he had a problem. It wasn't that West was a bad player, he obviously had his strong points as he demonstrated with two tries and no fewer than four assists to rout Featherstone on his home début. But he was not the player Murphy wanted. 'I was after someone to lead from the front, the type of forward who would break down a door rather than climb over it,' Murphy said. 'When West came I thought fair enough, we'll have him, but we still need someone else. So I had this slight difficulty. I had to let the directors know that the best player in the Southern Hemisphere was not quite what I was looking for.'

This difference of opinion over the new regime's most adventurous signing threatened to drive a wedge between coach and directors, and the fact that Murphy and West never managed to hit it off with each other would have long-term repercussions for the club and both individuals. But in the short term, things began to look rosy at Central Park very soon after West's arrival. At Christmas 1982, Wigan rediscovered that infallible cure for dressing-room disharmony, a cup run.

Apart from an unhappy Stephens going on the transfer list at £35,000 prior to Wigan's visit to his old club in the first round of the John Player Special Trophy, there seemed nothing particularly fateful about a trip to Castleford in a competition in which the club had always fared poorly. Devised in 1971, the JPS Trophy had begun to be taken seriously midway through the '70s, and though never remotely rivalling the Challenge Cup in the affections of supporters and players, had demonstrated its potential when over 25,000 turned up at Leeds for an all-Humberside final the previous year. Even allowing for Wigan's decline in the '70s, their record in the competition was dismal. Minnows like Barrow and Blackpool had reached JPS Trophy finals in their time, yet in 11 attempts Wigan had never even reached a semi, and had gone out at the first- or second-round stage on no fewer than nine occasions.

So expectations were not exactly high at Wheldon Road, but interest soon rose after West scored one of four tries in a 16–10 victory, and Wigan were drawn at home to St Helens in the next round. A crowd of 12,172, the best of the season to date, turned up to watch Wigan give a convincing impression of a team destined for cup success. Which is to say, they played quite badly but still won. Beaten in the scrums and struggling for possession most of the game, Wigan were also handicapped when Whitfield's goal-kicking touch suddenly deserted him. The centre missed all his shots at goal, but in the brief periods when they had the ball Wigan used it to advantage and outscored Saints by three tries to one, Ramsdale (2) and Stephenson getting the touchdowns in a 9–5 victory.

The reward was what looked like a very fair chance of breaking the semi-final duck, a third-round tie at second division Salford. The reality was the hardest game of the campaign, with Murphy being lectured in the dugout by referee Fred Lindop as Wigan sweated out a gritty 5–4 win. Possibly Lindop's tolerance of Salford's spoiling tactics made the margin of victory closer than it might otherwise have been, but apart from the break by Williams which allowed Stephenson to set up the only try of the game for Pendlebury, Wigan could congratulate themselves on another sterling defensive effort. They had conceded only one try in the last two rounds, and it wasn't just the forwards doing the work. With three-quarters like Ramsdale and Stephenson displaying hitherto unsuspected relish for moving up quickly to

nail opposition runners before they hit full stride, Wigan were acquiring a genuine reputation as a difficult team to break down.

New Year's Day 1983 brought its traditional encounter with Warrington, only this time it was a JPS Trophy semi-final, at the neutral venue of Knowsley Road, St Helens.

Not the prettiest of trophies, but a good line in the lap of honour. John Pendlebury, Martin Foy, Glyn Shaw and Barry Williams show off the John Player Special Trophy, with Henderson Gill tagging on behind.

With the nation watching live on BBC, Wigan raced to a 15–6 half-time lead through tries from Gill, Stephenson and Jeff Clare. The last was a 17-year-old amateur, a junior discus and shot putt champion who played centre or second row for St Patrick's in his spare time and had found himself rapidly propelled through the Central Park ranks by Murphy. The coach's habit of shoving youngsters straight into the first team regardless of age or experience was another point on which Murphy was at odds with his directors, who inclined to the modern, enlightened view that too much too soon could damage immature and unformed players and ultimately prove wasteful. To this day Murphy remains unrepentant: 'As a young player at St Helens I was coached by the greatest coach of them all. You can keep your Graham Lowes and your John Monies, Jim Sullivan was in a different galaxy. I always remember what he told me, and I've stuck by it wherever I've been. His advice to me was that if you are good enough you are old enough, and if you are quick enough you'll make it. That's all there is to it, really. It's that simple.'

Whatever the Wigan directors thought privately about pitching a 17-year-old rookie into a major semi-final, they had to admit Clare handled it well. Coming on as a substitute for the injured Williams, Clare sent Gill over for a try in the corner, then added one himself before the interval. In the second half, Wigan carried on playing with the same attacking bravado, and almost came unstuck. Had they been more experienced cup campaigners they would doubtless have battened down the hatches and tried to protect their lead, but lacking that professional edge which only comes with experience they were either unable or unwilling to change their game plan on the hoof. In the circumstances the only sensible policy was to carry on as they had been doing, but their incautious approach allowed Warrington back in, and Wigan had to hang on grimly for a 15–14 win, their second successive one-point margin. Warrington, in fact, scored four tries to Wigan's three, and ironically the winners were indebted to Whitfield's goalkicking for their passage to the final. Despite being petitioned by supporters to find a new goalkicker as Whitfield went into the semi-final with only two goals to his name from his last 11 attempts, Murphy kept faith with his centre, and was rewarded by three crucial goals from four attempts at Knowsley Road, including one from the touch-line. In contrast, Warrington's ultra-reliable Steve Hesford, a goal machine whose accuracy had been Wigan's downfall on innumerable occasions in the past, had an uncharacteristic off-day, missing four out of five shots. Wigan might have scraped into the 1983 JPS final, but call it Murphy's luck or Murphy's magic, something seemed to suggest their name might be on the trophy this year.

Wigan already knew their final opponents would be Leeds, who defeated Widnes in a tryless first semi-final at Huddersfield, but there were three weeks to wait until the big event. There was plenty to be getting on with in the meantime. Almost as soon as they reached the final, Wigan audaciously declared they would be happy to play Leeds at Elland Road. Although a neutral venue in the strictest sense, the home of Leeds United was hardly equidistant between Central Park and Headingley, the latter being a mere three miles along the ring road. Lindsay patiently explained that undersoil heating was a consideration for a televised final in January, and that Elland Road could offer the seating and corporate entertainment facilities which geographical half-way houses such as Swinton and Huddersfield all too obviously lacked, but essentially this was an early expression of the club's burgeoning confidence. Wigan simply weren't bothered where the final was to be played. Considerations such as which side of the Pennines hosted the game, or minute calculations about which team had to travel the furthest, belonged to the parochial past. For their first major final in 13 years, Wigan were not going to baulk at an hour and a bit on the motorway. 'We'll play it on the moon if need be,' Lindsay said. 'We'll take 10,000 supporters wherever we go. Wigan fans like a day out.'

Prior to the final, it was announced that £12,000 worth of debenture stock had been taken up by shareholders, leaving £100,000 to be found jointly by the four directors. On the field, Wigan kept up their unbeaten home record in the league with a 20–8 defeat at Castleford, the half-back partnership of Fairhurst and Martin Foy showing up well, but the game was marred by an injury to Clare, who departed in the first half with a broken leg, and dreams of appearing in a final shattered. Off the field, Stephens, for whom no offers had been received, indicated he was willing to come off the transfer list and fight for his place, and Wigan strengthened their pack considerably by picking up Brian Case from Warrington. A solid, if unspectacular, prop of deceptive strength and mobility, Case had been out of the game for ten months as a result of a dispute at Wilderspool, during which his transfer fee had been reduced from £80,000 to £45,000. Wigan secured him for significantly less than that, but Warrington still showed a tidy profit on a player Murphy had originally signed for £300 as a 17-year-old in 1975. 'I went along to a summer school at Wilderspool,' the St Helens-born Case explained. 'Alex told me if I played as well as I trained he would take me on.'

Case made his Wigan début in a comfortable 31–12 win at Workington, the last league game before the JPS final, an occasion which saw Ramsdale become the first Wigan player to fall foul of the newly introduced sin bin. Chiefly famous for rarely saying boo to a goose in an otherwise blameless career, the saintly Ramsdale must have wondered how he came to be first in the queue of sinners in a side which featured quick-tempered individuals like Kiss, Pendlebury and Shaw.

On Saturday, 22 January 1983, motorway police reported what could only be described as a caravan of cherry and white coaches safely crossing the Pennines on the M62. Lindsay had predicted 10,000 supporters, and asked for them all to be sporting the club colours, and he was not disappointed in either respect. Of the 19,553 present at Elland Road that afternoon, well over half were shouting for Wigan, and shout they certainly did. Despite the fact that Leeds were virtually playing at home, the atmosphere arrived courtesy of Central Park. It was another triumph in the increasingly confident relationship between the club's new management and its traditional support. Lindsay had said the Wigan public would back a successful team, here was evidence. Lindsay had gone as far as to predict that Wigan would cross the Pennines and still out-shout Leeds, and the travelling fans took extra pleasure in making this prophecy come true. No one was guessing then where this heady game of trust and obedience would end up, the almost forgotten excitement of taking part in a cup final was enough for anyone involved with Wigan over the past few years;

but there was an unmistakable sense of adventure in the enterprise, a hope that this might be the way things would be in the future.

Leeds, like their outnumbered fans, turned up for an ordinary cup final, little realising they would be facing men on a mission. Experience was on their side – Leeds had twice been successful at Wembley in the late '70s and since then had collected Premiership and Yorkshire Cup winners medals – age was not. Key players such as Dyl, Holmes, Dick and Ward were approaching the veteran stage, and although that crucial central quartet possessed all the craft and class of the great Headingley team of the previous decade, they no longer possessed the pace, and having both Rayne twins sidelined by injury scarcely improved the outlook.

Nevertheless, it appeared experience would prevail in a tense, rather featureless first half. Wigan went ahead through a Whitfield drop goal in the seventh minute, but appeared nervous and inhibited as if over-awed by the occasion, and spent most of the first period trapped in their own half defending their line. Fortunately, they now had the best defensive record in the league, and Leeds were restricted to a couple of Dick penalties, answered by one from Whitfield, which saw the Yorkshire side turn round 4–3 up. It might have been 7–3, or worse, had not Dyl been held on his back over the line when a try seemed certain. The Dyl of old might have scored, but on this occasion the Wigan line just held, and Leeds never came as close again.

Leeds tired in the second half, Wigan didn't, and some of their confidence returned as the game began to swing in their favour. Leeds were still seeing most of the ball, however, and it took an inspired substitution by Murphy to make things start happening for Wigan. In the 50th minute the coach brought off West and sent on Case. The new arrival was a favourite of Murphy's, West was not, but personal feelings aside, the substitution was justified by results. West had been having a quiet game, toiling away but not doing much damage, not responding at all to the big match atmosphere. Case, somewhat blasé about JPS finals having won three already with Warrington, immediately made Wigan look more menacing and helped win six of the last eight scrums, whereas five of the previous six had gone to Leeds.

Seven minutes after Case's arrival, Wigan scored the game's first try. Stephenson found Gill on the left wing and, though presented with only a glimpse of the line and little room in which to operate, the winger dipped his shoulder and bravely put his speed and strength to good use in battering through Mark Campbell, Heron and Hague. Impact with Hague at the moment of scoring in the left corner forced Gill to retire with a shoulder injury, but the damage was done. When Whitfield, who had been playing with a broken nose since the first half, kicked long and true from the touch-line, Wigan went 10-4 in front and Leeds heads started to drop. The rest of the game, in contrast to its first period, was almost exclusively fought out in the Leeds half of the field. Leeds resisted Wigan's somewhat predictable attacking moves until five minutes from the end, when they were caught out by a set play following a penalty, substitute Juliff accepting Scott's short pass to beat the surprised Hague and Sykes on a run to the posts. Whitfield's goal was a formality, and Wigan had their first trophy since the reorganisation of rugby league into two divisions in 1973. In terms of major trophies, if the JPS Trophy is ranked with the Challenge Cup, the Championship and the Premiership, ahead of lesser competitions such as the county cups or BBC2 Floodlit Trophy, Wigan's 15-4 Elland Road success was the first occasion for rejoicing since the Wembley victory against Hunslet in 1965.

Now, 18 years is a long time to wait, and Wigan had a lot of rejoicing to do. What the rest of the country made of the 1983 JPS Trophy final is unclear, it was hardly the most entertaining or distinguished of games, but the atmosphere alone made it memorable. Wigan made unusual underdogs. They had supporters who expected success and who knew how to celebrate, and could normally be relied upon to bring more of these to any particular game than the side who were actually expected to win. The 1983 JPS Trophy final marked the opening of an entertaining era in which Wigan gatecrashed all the best parties but were still regarded as *arrivistes*. For maybe four or five more years Wigan could go into major finals without being expected to win. All too soon this would change, and some of the fun went out of it once Wigan never expected to lose, but that's racing ahead a little. In January 1983, Wigan and fun were just getting reacquainted.

Martin Foy, a quiet, reserved stand-off whose uncertain attitude the previous season had so frustrated Maurice Bamford that the coach had telephoned Geoff Fletcher and fixed up a loan period at Huyton just to frighten him, was nominated Man of the Match. He had played well, but in a game without an outstanding contribution from any individual, Foy only shaded the decision ahead of Campbell and Pendlebury. Leading the celebrations on the pitch, predictably, was Kiss, demonstrating to a horrified TV audience how to drink a bottle of champagne but still spray your mates with the foam. The photographs of the team with the trophy tell many a story. An incredibly young looking Stephenson appears to be celebrating for the first time. Ramsdale, on the front row, is not looking at the camera, he's still peering down at his medal in its box. Shaw, on the back row, is waving a scarf and undoubtedly looking forward to a few pints afterwards, while Fairhurst and Kiss are singing at the top of their voices. Whitfield, the captain, nurses a sore nose and the trophy, Scott gives a clenched-fist salute while Gill, in a tracksuit, joins the group at the edge. At the opposite end, a clean-shirted West looks preoccupied and solemn, a peripheral figure hardly joining in.

If West needed cheering up when he came off the field, Murphy failed to provide the necessary words of reassurance. The coach's only comment on the substitution was a terse and less than diplomatic: 'No one is guaranteed a first-team place now.' But West already knew better than to expect sympathy from Murphy, he was wising up to the coach's brusque manner with every passing day. 'When he pulled me in that final, I couldn't really complain,' West said. 'But I remember sitting in the dugout sort of half-watching the game, feeling a bit fed up and sorry for myself, when we got a kick at goal. I didn't think anything of it, but suddenly I heard this voice boom out: "Come on then, what are you waiting for? Get on with the sand bucket!" I thought no, he can't possibly mean me, he wouldn't be petty enough to ask that. But of course he did, and he was. So I pulled myself up, and trotted on with the sand for Colin Whitfield. I was blazing when I went out, but Colin said something that made me laugh, and I calmed down a bit and saw the funny side. As I got back to the dugout I made like I was going to throw the sand in Murphy's face. I only dummied the action, but he thought it was for real. He ducked, and Bill Ashurst ducked as well. That made me laugh. I thought that was very funny.'

If West thought he had a problem, the sight of Gary Stephens hovering around the dressing-room in a suit put his plight into perspective. The player who had once moaned that Wigan were never going to win anything had managed to miss their moment of glory. 'I'm pleased for the lads, naturally,' Stephens said. 'But this has been one of the worst experiences of my life.' The sheer novelty of Wigan turning out to be a winning side was not lost on Ramsdale, either. The winger was still sitting in the tunnel, gazing at his medal, after everyone else had got changed and gone upstairs for a drink. 'I can't believe it,' he said weakly. 'I've actually won something.'

Back in Wigan, there were plenty of people echoing the same sentiment, all looking for a drink. Trouble was, in those Saturdays of yore, the pubs did not open until 7 p.m., and the return of the cherry and white caravan had begun to disgorge groups of thirsty pilgrims on to the cobbled market square about an hour too soon. The group containing your correspondent made straight for the Park Hotel, a rugby pub still in its prime in 1983, a couple of years before it was scandalously sacrificed to make way for the ramp of a multi-storey car park. The door was firmly barred, as we all knew it would be. One of the more intrepid of our number, now a Wigan publican in his own right, addressed the redoubtable landlady through her letterbox. 'Open up, Mrs Brown. We've won the cup!' Predictably, Mrs Zetta Brown, upright pillar of Wigan society and widow of Tom Brown, a man who had travelled to Australia in 1932 and brought back a couple of Kangaroos to Central Park and who served as chairman of the Rugby League Council in the '40s, was not having any of it. Or us. 'The doors of this establishment will open at the appointed time, and not a moment sooner,' an austere voice replied from within. 'And Wigan haven't won the cup yet. If it's not Wembley it's not the real thing.'

Fortunately, the rest of town was not so sceptical. During the next few weeks, every school, club and workplace in Wigan must have been treated to a close-up of the none-too-lovely John Player Special Trophy, as, encouraged by their coach, the players made the most of their achievement. But even as Murphy was milking the applause, he managed to sour the situation remarkably quickly. West's difficult introduction to English rugby continued when a dubious Paul Woods tackle in a Challenge Cup preliminary round game against Cardiff left him nursing a broken jaw and facing a six-week lay-off, but a rare win at Bradford was evidence Wigan's confidence was still high, and the capture of Oldham St Anne's scrum-half, Mike Ford, a young player several clubs had been watching, was also encouraging. But when the first round proper of the Challenge Cup arrived, Castleford came to Central Park and put Wigan's Wembley dreams firmly in perspective. A 17–7 home defeat was just as emphatic and unanswerable as the one Fulham had inflicted in the Lancashire Cup earlier in the season. After the JPS success, which had seen Castleford beaten on their own ground, the Wigan players had been speculating that this could be their year for Wembley. They were wrong. Wigan met Castleford four times in the 1982–83 season, and won every game except the one that mattered most.

Cup disappointment was bad enough, but nothing new. What followed was worse for being unexpected. The first home league match after the JPS final brought high-flying Hull KR to Central Park, a meeting Granada Television were keen to broadcast on their new rugby league action programme. Wigan were beaten at home for the second week in succession, a try and a goal from Whitfield being the only high points in a 21–5 defeat, but if Granada had contented themselves with filming just the action the occasion might have passed unremarked. Instead, the cameras followed the disconsolate Wigan players up the tunnel and into the dressing-room, and thousands of late-night viewers had the privilege, if that is the word, of witnessing an Alex Murphy bollocking first hand. It was not a pretty sight. This was ten years before England football manager Graham Taylor unwisely allowed a camera crew to follow him around, and many viewers were shocked by the amount of swearing. Less sensitive souls, and those capable of accepting industrial language as part of an industrial game, were still shocked by the unimaginative nature of Murphy's profanities. Here was a man with a reputation for motivation, magic even, standing in a cramped room full of beer bottles and abusing his players in a manner which was indistinguishable from that of the most boorish terrace drunk.

It was clever television but appalling PR, and what made viewing all the more grimly fascinating was the differing reactions of the players. Some looked ready to hit Murphy, some looked downcast and contrite, some looked as if they weren't even listening. Stephenson, who had not had a good game, came in for some particular stick, Murphy publicly ridiculing him for not working hard enough and making excuses to avoid training. He looked uncomfortable at the

time, and the passing years have scarcely softened the indignity. 'It was horrendous, a real low point in my life, not just my career,' he said. 'Having to sit there taking that crap was bad enough, but to have it broadcast on

Three coaches, a cheesed-off Kiwi and a sand bucket. They say every picture tells a story, but Graeme West is better at telling this one. From left on the Wigan bench at full time at Elland Road are Henderson Gill, Alan McInnes, Bill Ashurst, Alex Murphy, West and Jeff Clare.

television was intolerable. Once the programme had gone out, and all the criticism started rolling in, Alex apologised to the players. He said he didn't know the camera was there, which was a bit rich, considering it was virtually sitting on his head.'

What Murphy now says is that he was led to believe the camera had been switched off. 'I was conned, tricked very badly,' he explained. 'The only reason we let them film in the dressing-room in the first place was because we had just put up some motivational slogans, and Granada said they would like to show them. After the game, the first thing I asked was what the camera was doing there. I was told it was not running. I got the shock of my life when I went home and watched the match. The next morning I had to go round to my mother's to apologise for the language. Then I went to see Paul Docherty, Granada's head of sport. He asked me what I was moaning about, and said the viewing figures were excellent. I said I hadn't come to moan. I'd come to kill him.'

The best this damage limitation exercise

can do for Murphy is depict him as gullible, but whether duped by the camera crew or not, no one put the words into his mouth. His shortcomings as a coach and a communicator were the talk of the game for a few weeks, and try as he might, Murphy could not find anyone but himself to blame. 'It was a mistake, one of my biggest ever,' Murphy admits now. 'I still say I was sold down the river, there is no way I would have knowingly let Granada broadcast that dialogue, but there's no doubt I overreacted. I was too wound up, if the truth be known. We had gone out of the cup the week before, now we had let the supporters down with a really poor display at home and on television. I was annoyed with the players, and I let my disappointment get the better of me. I should have taken a few deep breaths or gone for a walk for ten minutes. But I didn't, I gave the players a blast when they walked off the field, and the television people were clever enough to catch it. I'll never live it down, but that is not how I normally behave in a dressing-room. People think I'm like that all the time, and it's just not true. I don't normally shout, swear or bully players. I was just exasperated that day with David Stephenson. Great player – I signed him for Salford, don't forget – but a bit of a mammy's boy. He was always crying off training because of his job. I tried to be as flexible as I could, and told him if he did the business on the field I would allow him some leeway, but I didn't like his attitude in that particular game and something snapped.'

Stephenson smiles at the suggestion that the performance the TV cameras caught was out of character for Murphy, a one-off produced by special circumstances. 'I wouldn't go as far as to say Alex was like that every week,' he said diplomatically. 'But we were all familiar with that side of his character. He's a decent enough bloke with a good sense of humour, and some weeks we all got on well together, particularly if we were doing well. But he could be a bit of a ranter, his management techniques were from the dark ages.'

This evaluation offers a clue to why Murphy was so distrustful of Stephenson. He was hardly a troublemaker or a likely focus for dressing-room unrest, but he was and is articulate. Murphy had come across the odd educated player before, but Stephenson, along with Pendlebury, West and Kiss in the Wigan team of the early '80s, was one of a new breed of career professionals, not in the game for a few extra quid at the weekend, but to see how much they could learn and how far they could go. If they disagreed with the coach on some aspect of playing or training they were likely to say so. If they had an idea of their own which they thought might improve performance, they were likely to volunteer it. Murphy could never really cope with this sort of input from his players, try as he might to be modern. In any rugby team there will always be players who will run through a brick wall for the coach, and players who would rather think of a way to climb over it. Murphy was better with the former, but could accommodate the latter at a push. Now he was confronted by players who were asking whether the brick wall was really necessary in the first place. This was a coach who had once sent on a substitute to give a message to a labouring forward. 'What do you want me to tell him, boss?' the sub shouted from the touch-line prior to taking the field. 'Tell him, tell him . . .' Murphy's voice trailed off as the forward made another expensive mistake. 'Tell him he's a toe-rag.'

It was not unusual for Murphy to have to deal with players more articulate than himself, but having to cope with players who were not afraid to question his rugby intelligence was something new. He could not adapt, not in time anyway, and tried to mask his insecurity by becoming increasingly authoritarian. It didn't work. Even the loyalists in the side became fed up eventually, and Murphy came to regard the quartet of West, Pendlebury, Stephenson and Kiss as a disruptive and unhealthy influence within the club.

The late-night television horror-show was merely a revealing insight, however. It did not destroy morale overnight. After drawing the next match with Widnes, Wigan went on to win four league matches in succession, a run of form which took them into the top four and put them firmly in the title running. West came back after his injury with a try against Carlisle; the dynamic front row of Shaw, Kiss and Case was simply terrorising opponents; and with Foy and Fairhurst sparkling at half-back (Stephens was back on the list and staying away after failing to regain his place), Wigan were suddenly championship contenders to be taken seriously. The moment of truth came at The Boulevard, Hull, on a Tuesday night in March. Hull were title rivals, after proving one of the most consistent sides of the season, but Wigan had beaten them at Central Park back in August and were probably playing better now. One mighty performance on Humberside could simultaneously damage Hull and set Wigan up for the half dozen easier matches which remained.

A large cherry and white contingent made the trip to the end of the M62, but the night ended in anticlimax. Shaw, Wigan's tower of strength, their talisman of invulnerability, broke his leg after a couple of minutes. The game was up, and Wigan knew it. Hull were brilliant in a 23–6 victory which also left Ramsdale and Fairhurst nursing injuries, even with Shaw on the field for 80 minutes Wigan would have struggled to live with them. Without him the season was over, even though Wigan won their next four games and briefly touched the top of the table for the first time in memory. Their last, theoretical chance of the title disappeared with a 9–9 draw at Featherstone, and the league campaign petered out with a last-day defeat at Widnes,

Hull pipping their neighbours Hull KR to the title on the same afternoon. The Premiership was even more disappointing, Wigan going out in the first round at home to Leeds, but all things considered, it had been an encouraging and enjoyable season. A trophy on the sideboard and third place in the league would have been beyond the dreams of Wigan fans only a couple of seasons ago. More encouraging even than results was a new spirit about the place. After the Good Friday success against St Helens, a letter in *The Wigan Observer* told a charming story of two small boys on the perimeter fence, one telling the other to look out for Henderson Gill. 'But which one is he?'

'Oh, you'll know him when you see him. He always has his socks rolled down.'

Whether it was Murphy, or the new board, the exciting players and improved results, or a combination of all four, some special chemistry seemed at work. Perhaps it was because the rugby team had spent so long in the doldrums, but Wigan Athletic, the football team across town, barely got a look-in again. It seemed everyone in Wigan, with the possible exception of West and Stephenson, was enjoying their rugby again. The next season was eagerly anticipated. And as the supporters' club announced Shaw their player of the year, followed by Scott and Campbell, history was being made at the other end of the country in Bristol, where a 16-year-old Wigan schoolboy named Shaun Edwards, already captain of the English Schools rugby league side, achieved a remarkable double by leading out England Schoolboys against Wales at rugby union.

CHAPTER FOUR

Frightened to Death by Bramley

'I always knew having Alex as coach would change our relationship. I thought I might fall out with other directors because of it, but I never imagined we would end up falling out with each other.'

The summer of 1983 was the last before the long-overdue lifting of the international transfer ban. A year later, every self-respecting club in the league would have a representative out on tour with Great Britain, prowling Australia with an open cheque-book. The unopposed excellence of the 1982 Kangaroos had ended most of the flimsy arguments for keeping the ban, and those same Kangaroos were the quarry for English clubs once free movement was re-established, but Australia was still forbidden territory in 1983. Graeme West was there, captaining New Zealand in the second trans-Tasman Test and scoring a try to help Graeme Lowe's Kiwis achieve a stirring 19–12 victory over the Aussies at Lang Park, Brisbane, but the only thing stirring back home in Britain was the usual summer silly season.

Putting two and two together and making five, a couple of papers ran stories suggesting the disenchanted West would not be returning to Wigan, but the club responded quickly to scotch such gossip, which, in due course, was seen to be groundless when the player reported back in good time for the new season. Next local sensation was the 44-strong Great Britain training squad drawn up by Frank Myler to prepare for the 1984 tour Down Under, which included several second division players but not a single Wigan man. Murphy was predictably furious, for the media's benefit, advancing the claims of Gill and Stephenson but appearing to forget Case, who in the event was the only player from the club to make the trip.

In the real world, Wigan's St John Fisher High School beat Featherstone High to become English RL school champions for the second time in three years, with Shaun Edwards outstanding. This was not a fabricated silly season story, but the real thing. Wigan had already received several letters from supporters and well-wishers urging them not to miss out on the teenage prodigy, mindful of the club's recent history of allowing notable home-grown talents like Joe Lydon and Andy Gregory to slip through their fingers and flourish at rival clubs. Keith Holden, like Edwards the son of a former professional, was another highly promising schoolboy talent maturing at approximately the same time, and Lindsay confirmed Wigan were watching the pair closely with a view to signing both. This was encouraging, in that Lindsay at least appeared to be on the ball, and unlikely to repeat his predecessors' mistakes in dismissing either player as too small or too greedy, but the club's record was still a millstone around the directors' necks. Players of Edwards and Holden's age were simply too young to remember anyone who was any good joining Wigan from school. The Wigan board needed to re-educate the town's talent that the route to Wembley did not necessarily begin at Widnes.

Edwards, in particular, came to be regarded as a touchstone. The 16-year-old was famous throughout rugby circles, and it was clear from a number of leading professional clubs who had already expressed interest he was sure to have a big future. Wigan could not afford to miss him. Lydon and Gregory could scarcely be blamed for choosing Widnes, such was the laughably unattractive alternative their home-town club presented at the time they became available, but if Wigan were claiming to be a serious force again, if they wanted to be taken seriously by the rest of the game, they had to get Edwards. Fail, and the last two years might as well not have happened. Cliff Webb, covering the inter-schools final for *The Wigan Observer*, expressed the predicament succinctly: 'If Wigan allow

Keith Holden (with ball) and Steve Hampson. Two of the brightest young talents at Central Park in 1984.

Edwards to move anywhere except Central Park when he is 17 they will have egg on their faces for years to come.'

This touched a nerve at the club. So jumpy were Wigan about the situation that Lindsay responded in the local newspaper the following week. 'We have made him the biggest offer we have ever made to a junior, but we can't let Edwards write his own cheque,' the Wigan vice-chairman said. 'We will match what anyone else offers, within reason, but we have to count on a bit of local loyalty too.' The identity of the Edwards to

whom Lindsay was referring is debatable. Ostensibly, Wigan were asking Shaun to be reasonable, though anyone capable of reading between the lines was aware that the appeal for loyalty and moderation was directed at Edwards senior, the player's father, Jackie. A former Warrington scrum-half and contemporary of Murphy's whose highly promising rugby career had been cut short by injury, Jackie Edwards had taken an extremely close interest in every stage of his son's development, and was the last person to let Shaun sell himself cheaply or unwisely. Lindsay, a long-term friend, probably knew all along he had Jackie's trust, and felt the Edwards family shared his confidence in the future at Central Park, all that worried him was Jackie's ability to drive a hard bargain. The bookmaker knew he was facing another gambler here, but a canny and successful one, someone shrewd at assessing long odds and capable of turning knowledge into profit. Not that Jackie needed much nous in this instance, just nerve. He was, after all, holding the ace, and Lindsay knew it. Hull KR had promised to top any offer, Jackie casually revealed, and he still had to see Widnes, Oldham and Leeds. Lindsay began to show signs of exasperation. 'It would help us considerably if Jackie would state a figure,' he said, more in hope than expectation. 'Instead of constantly telling us our offers fall short of what is wanted.'

Keith Holden junior, four months older than Edwards, signed for Wigan with little ceremony on his 17th birthday in June, his arrival all but upstaged by the number of people leaving Central Park. Wigan's annual summer clearout of players deemed surplus to requirements included eight free transfers, including one extremely disgruntled Jimmy Hornby. 'He has no realistic chance of playing in the first or the "A" team, and no one is automatically entitled to a testimonial,' was Murphy's somewhat curt explanation. That Hornby was unlikely to figure in Murphy's plans for the coming season was undeniable. He was approaching the end of his career, and after a season spent mostly on the sidelines found few clubs were interested in taking him (Oldham eventually signed him) even as a gift. But the point was that Hornby was not looking for a transfer. The denial of a tenth season at Wigan also meant he was denied a testimonial. As Hornby had unquestionably been a first-team performer for most of his time at the club, most supporters shared his sense of grievance. A testimonial would not have cost the club a great deal; in all probability it would not have realised a great deal for Hornby either. However, it was the principle which was significant. Hornby was not to be allowed to bow out gracefully, and his admirers among the Wigan supporters were not going to get the chance to show their appreciation for his years of histrionic gestures and the odd sparkling try. Hornby had lost his first-team place, he was not wanted any more, he was out. There was no room for sentiment at the new Wigan.

There was suddenly no room for Bill Ashurst either. Murphy's coaching assistant was not part of the summer clearout, but he was summarily dismissed after just one season. The reason was never made clear at the time, and has been a matter for conjecture since. Needless to say, each man's account of the parting differs wildly from the other's, but as Murphy and Ashurst have both been known to tell the odd whopper in their time, both are unreliable witnesses when it comes to a disagreement between them. Both offer extremely amusing critiques of the other's character – Ashurst maintaining Murphy sacked him because he was doing his job too well and was frightened of the competition; Murphy claiming Ashurst's later conversion to Christianity only came about because he had so many sins to repent – but reading between the lines, the problem seems to have stemmed from the split dressing-room. Delegation had been Murphy's big idea when he arrived at Central Park, but if Lindsay's quote at the time can be believed (it probably wouldn't pass a lie detector test, either) the coach had had enough of it after one season. 'Bill did a great job for us, but Alex has told us he intends to take a bigger share of the actual

coaching next year, and there is no point having two people doing the same job,' Lindsay said.

Diplomatic and delicately phrased as this statement was, it nevertheless contained confirmation of something fans had long suspected. That Murphy had not been doing much of the coaching. It had been said that Colin Clarke, his assistant at Leigh, deserved

Kerry Hemsley in full flow. The big Australian was a success as Wigan's first big name import, but was less impressive in the 1984 Challenge Cup final.

a far bigger share of the credit for that club's 1982 championship than Murphy had been prepared to concede, and now it was being suggested that Ashurst had been doing a lot of the work at Wigan. It appears Ashurst's mistake had been to get too close to the players, not something Murphy was ever likely to do. By sanctioning Ashurst's removal, in fact, Wigan may have been trying to persuade Murphy to spend more time with his charges. As Murphy saw it, his job was to sign players, pick the side, and gee them up on Sunday afternoons. Anything else – from tactics to training routines to assessing the performance of the junior sides at the club – could safely be left to an assistant. Except when the assistant began to join with the players in questioning the coach's role, in which event the assistant had to go. It was significant that one of the few players to speak up for Ashurst was Nicky Kiss, one of the dressing-room militants, whose personal dislike of Murphy intensified from this time on. Supporters were not privy to these behind-the-scenes machinations, although the ones who attended 'A' team matches on a regular basis were aware that the club had a coach who did not.

Set against this was the success Murphy had undoubtedly brought the previous season. Wigan's average gate had leapt by 2,000 to 7,426, the best for ten years, and only Hull, some 4,000 per game in front, were better supported. As the new season approached, Murphy defended the club's apparent lack of interest in the transfer market, claiming the club had no money to spend and that all the players available were too expensive. This was not the can-do, season ticket-shifting tone Lindsay wanted to hear, and Murphy received another ticking-off for being too downbeat. 'If top quality players become available, we will always do our best to sign them,' Lindsay said, effectively correcting his coach. 'As a matter of fact we hope to be able to announce the capture of a big-name overseas Test forward when the season starts.'

This had to be another New Zealander, as that country was not governed by the international transfer ban, and turned out to be Mark Broadhurst, a fearsome prop currently starring with West for the Kiwis. Ironically, he was exactly the sort of player Murphy had said he wanted when Wigan signed West, proving the board did listen to the coach's opinions. Broadhurst was tough, uncompromising and capable of leading from the front, but he also led Wigan up the garden path. At the last minute he opted to join Hull KR, leaving Lindsay, in his own words, 'absolutely shattered'. The Wigan vice-chairman was still inexperienced in the tricky business of signing players from the other side of the world, but still guileless enough to talk openly of his disappointment. 'We must have spent over £300 on telephone calls and cables, and I really thought we had him,' Lindsay said. 'What a let down!' Lindsay would miss his man on the odd occasion in the future, but rarely let his own guard drop to such an extent. Another signing fiasco once the season started, when Wigan announced the capture of Kiwi scrum-half Shane Varley, only to see him join Leigh instead, taught Lindsay never to even discuss names until the ink was dry on the contract. Leigh's coach, Tommy Bishop, had once had Varley at Workington, and after reading of his intention to join Wigan, used his prior acquaintance to divert him to Hilton Park. Wigan were doubly annoyed. Not only had they inadvertently alerted rivals to a player, they felt the New Zealand authorities should have kept to a gentlemen's agreement and not let Leigh jump the queue. 'We played by the rules and lost,' Lindsay said. 'Leigh behaved in a most underhand manner, and got the player.' From now on, Wigan would deal in secret, and only announce successful signings as *faits accomplis*. And if Lindsay was ever crossed, or disappointed in a deal, he would suffer in silence. Failing that, he could always be relied upon to come up with a few hundred words on why Wigan never wanted so-and-so in the first place.

Thought to be keen on signing a ball-playing forward, Wigan had also botched the signing of Harry Pinner of St Helens for £40,000 during the close season, and had been forced to scrap an exchange deal for York's Brendan White when Gary Stephens, who was supposed to travel in the opposite direction, announced his retirement. But with West back from New Zealand and Glyn Shaw back after injury (sadly, never quite the same player again), Wigan opened the season with away wins at Salford and Wakefield, the latter including a sad but resigned Bill Ashurst.

The much-vaunted shirt redesign was unveiled in the first home match of the season, against Leigh. A thinly disguised copy of Hull's best-selling garment, with irregular hoops in cherry and white as opposed to black and white, it was the closest Wigan got to resembling champions as they subsided to a resounding 26–12 defeat before a crowd of 9,000. Lancashire Cup hopes, not that Wigan entertained any, failed to survive a first-round trip to Widnes, and after three defeats in the next three league games, away at Hull and at home to Bradford and Widnes, Murphy was suddenly looking at a losing run which threatened to match Maurice Bamford's. Almost from the off, he had been playing Holden, the 17-year-old signed in summer, at scrum-half in place of the injured Fairhurst. 'I don't want to, but there's no one else,' the coach explained. The plucky Holden gave a good account of himself, and scored a try in the defeat at Hull, but other problems were beginning to mount up for Murphy. Martin Foy picked up an injury, and the performance against Bradford was so poor that Wigan were booed off Central Park. John Pendlebury asked for a transfer and was made available at £35,000, after getting the distinct impression Murphy did not want him around. 'Murphy keeps on about needing a new loose forward, and the club have made it quite clear they don't think I am the answer to their problems,' he said. Mick Scott was dropped for the Widnes league game, and Colin Whitfield picked up another broken nose, causing him to contemplate quitting. No sooner had Wigan fixed up a loan deal for Hull centre Tim Wilby, itself a sign of increasing desperation, than Kiss demanded a transfer on learning that Wigan had signed the New Zealand hooker Howie Tamati.

Worst of all, a promising youngster called David Lyon signed for Widnes. Nothing particularly unusual about this, except that his father, Geoff, happened to be on the coaching staff at Central Park. An embarrassed Lyon senior promptly resigned, a second member of Murphy's four-man coaching team to leave the club after barely a season, but this was hardly the consideration uppermost in the directors' minds. With the ongoing Edwards negotiations still at a delicate stage, the idea that even people within the club thought Widnes a better bet for the future was highly damaging to Wigan, who had to endure several days of extremely unflattering publicity.

Just when a diversion was needed, the international transfer ban was lifted, and Wigan were able to announce the capture of one Kerry Hemsley, a powerhouse prop in the Broadhurst mode, from Australian club Balmain. Frank Stanton, the coach of the 1982 Kangaroos, rated Hemsley the best prop in Australia, but even without the big sell from Down Under, Lindsay and the Wigan directors thought they were on to a good thing. Extremely large, with a pre-punk hairstyle and a passion for powerful motor-cycles, Hemsley was every inch the wild colonial boy. If the Wigan directors thought he would capture the public imagination and put more bums on seats they slightly over-estimated his capabilities, but Hemsley did at least inject a splash of colour into a season beginning to look gloomy.

Before Hemsley arrived Wigan ended their losing sequence with victory at Whitehaven, but Kiss was sent off in a bad-tempered game and Murphy had to endure some criticism from travelling supporters. The following week almost 8,000 people packed the cramped Hilton Park ground to see Hemsley and Tamati make their débuts at Leigh, the latter replacing Kiss at hooker. On an absolutely filthy day, two well-matched sides provided classic derby entertainment in pouring rain, though some of the play also bordered on the filthy, with Varley allegedly spitting at his opposite number Holden, and Tamati lasting 11 minutes before visiting the sin bin for flattening Leigh danger-man Woods. On the debit side, Whitfield missed four shots at goal from seven attempts, Woods kicked four penalties while Tamati was off the field, and Wigan lost 24–18, giving Leigh yet another double over their supposedly more illustrious neighbours. On the other hand, Wigan had looked very good at times and contributed fully to a thoroughly enjoyable game, Hemsley had managed to look fearsome despite only climbing off a flight from Sydney the previous night, and Tamati at least showed spirit and had picked on the right opponent. But star of the show was Holden, who played one of the games of

Bringing the fun back to Central Park. Steve Hampson and members of the crowd enjoy Henderson Gill's showmanship after scoring. Gill, of course, is the one with his socks rolled down.

his young life, and left no one on the return journey to Wigan regretting that Varley had chosen not to come to Central Park.

The big news in October 1983 was that Shaun Edwards finally did decide to come to Central Park. Quite whose idea it was to have BBC *Breakfast Time* cameras cover the momentous signing, on the stroke of midnight on his 17th birthday, is unclear, it has variously been ascribed to Jackie, who liked the romance; Murphy, who wanted the kudos; and Lindsay, who valued the publicity. A similar dispute subsequently evolved, as Edwards quickly began to fulfil his potential and establish himself as one of Wigan's greatest-ever players, over who was responsible for

actually signing him. Murphy still likes to bill himself as the man who signed Shaun Edwards, as if he had had to convince the club of the player's worth, while Lindsay and Robinson take the view that, thanks to their own efforts, Wigan were finally in a position to offer a promising career to a talented local youngster, and the deal just happened to go through on Murphy's watch.

But the truth is that Shaun Edwards was never a conventional prospect or a conventional signing. Jackie signed him up for a rugby career at an age when his contemporaries were signing up for sweet-shop treats and Sunday school outings. To an extent both lives had been lived for the day Shaun turned professional. There was an element of Jackie's own career, cruelly terminated at the age of 23, being lived through his son, and a suggestion that Shaun might have given up too much of his childhood to please his father. To say Jackie brought his own experience to bear on his son's career would be to qualify for the understatement of the century, and the parental guidance did not stop when Shaun began to make his own way as a professional. Six years later, when Shaun himself was 23 and already owner of more caps and medals than his father could have dreamed of, Jackie sounded off in public when his son was left out of Great Britain's first Test against New Zealand. When Shaun's pivotal role in ensuring victory in the second Test was not sufficiently stressed in some newspapers, their rugby league correspondents received letters bearing a Wigan stamp. Not of complaint, exactly, more of instruction. 'That's Jack all over,' Lindsay said. 'Over-protective, perhaps, but with his son's interests at heart. Shaun was never going to be anything else than a professional rugby player, you see. His whole future was mapped out from an early age.'

Lindsay remembers Shaun as a child of 11 or 12, coming round to the house to borrow rugby magazines. 'Jackie had a library of Australian rugby league videos before most people had videos. He had never been to Australia, but he was thoroughly immersed in the latest coaching theories. Jackie took his son's rugby education in hand from day one, and as a result, when Shaun arrived on the schools rugby scene, he was almost the finished article. Not only did he have the full range of skills, he had an Australian attitude. He was miles ahead.' Wigan were not miles ahead in 1983, but Jackie, who keeps a cool head for business calculations under his trademark trilby, did not make a bad choice of club for his boy. The record contract for a

He hardly ever knocks-on, never gives a bad ball, always backs up and reads a game quicker than anyone else. He's perfect. It's just a good job he didn't want to be anything else.'

These attributes had to be taken on trust when, bright and early on 17 October 1983, a nation and its cornflakes witnessed what at first appeared to be an attempt on the record for the number of people able to squeeze into the front room of a terraced house, but eventually transpired to be the occasion of a

The teams take the field for the 1984 Challenge Cup final, Alex Murphy and Vince Karalius leading out Wigan and Widnes respectively. Second in line Shaun Edwards appears eager to get on with it; much further back in the Widnes line are Joe Lydon and Andy Gregory.

schoolboy was renegotiated within a couple of years as success began to roll in. Wigan and Edwards were delighted with each other. It took Shaun most of his career to give the impression he actually enjoyed playing rugby – he was never one for unnecessary exuberance on the pitch, and was well into his 20s by the time he managed to convince anyone he was even aware of life away from it – but there was no doubt he was very good at what he did best. 'Intensity is the word that sums Shaun up,' Lindsay said. 'He is the most driven character I have ever met. He is also probably the most naturally talented, even more so than Andy Gregory or Ellery Hanley.

cheque for £35,000 passing into the possession of Edwards senior. Young Shaun, saddled with the difficult role of looking worth every penny of the record contract while sitting on the family sofa, smiled a lot but said little. Murphy said more, without managing to match his remark of a week previously, when asked if the protracted Edwards saga was nearing a conclusion. 'Yes, I think a decision has been reached,' he said. 'I've seen white smoke coming out of Jackie Edwards's hat.'

Within days of joining Wigan, Edwards had the opportunity to see some Australian excellence first hand, coupled with some of the reasons why British coaching methods were lagging behind Southern Hemisphere standards. The Queensland state side was on tour, and presented with the prospect of facing the likes of Gene Miles, Wally Lewis and Greg Dowling in a team that was virtually Test strength, Wigan decided to call an extra training session. Recent form had not been inspiring, and Wigan had an injury crisis on their hands, but the real problem was that Murphy normally went greyhound racing on the night in question. 'I personally watched Alex take training that night, because I knew he wanted to go to the dogs,' Lindsay said. 'I watched him change into a tracksuit, board the coach, and set off. An hour later, still uneasy, I drove down to the training ground. No Alex. Kerry Hemsley told me he had changed out of his tracksuit on the coach, had a car waiting for him at the training ground, and that we would lose by 40 points on Sunday. He wasn't far wrong. Queensland beat us 40–2.'

Edwards watched the game, in which Queensland's dynamic full-back, Joe Kilroy, was outstanding, and was observed making notes. At least someone at the club was taking things seriously, though Murphy maintains his fondness for greyhound meetings over training sessions has been overstated. 'It is completely false to suggest I was never seen at training,' he said. 'I might have missed the odd session for legitimate reasons, but I don't recall ever going to the dogs when I should have been taking training.' There is room for debate on this point, given that Murphy's idea of leading a training session often amounted to little more than setting the players off on a run or an exercise before disappearing. One wag once forwarded the coach's name in response to the standard programme question-naire prompt 'Who would you most like to meet . . .', but behind all the jokes and accusations lay a simple and obvious reality. Murphy's concept of coaching was based on the two-nights-a-week model he had been familiar with since his playing days. Modern coaches, of the type Murphy described dismissively as 'clipboard and video men', went into the job a lot more deeply than that.

Monday might be spent watching the video of the previous day's game and devising training routines for the rest of the week; Tuesday might be spent watching tapes of the next opponents, and as well as the two or three sessions with the first-team players during the week there would be 'A' team and youth team progress to check up on. One man did not have to do everything, but the chief coach certainly needed to keep involving himself in all these matters and more. It was basically a full-time job, and the ironic thing was that Wigan not only realised this but were prepared to pay on such a basis, only to find themselves dealing with a coach whose attitudes, as Robinson had perceptively remarked at the outset, belonged to the past.

The importance of watching 'A' team games was amply demonstrated when a former Warrington player called Ian Mather fixed up a couple of trial games for his friend, a young rugby union full-back called Steve Hampson. A player with the Vulcan club in Newton-le-Willows, Hampson had become disenchanted with his team-mates' unambi-tious attitude to training, and the policy of selectors at a Lancashire RU trial who seemed to rate educational background and accent higher than ability to perform on the pitch. 'I just grew out of union,' Hampson said. 'I didn't know an awful lot about league, Newton not being a particularly strong area for the game, but I knew I wanted to train harder, get fitter, see how far I could go.' Mather initially took the 21-year-old Hampson to Swinton, where he created such an impression in a couple of 'A' team trials that Wigan had to move faster than they had expected. 'Alex Murphy called me up in person and invited me for a trial,' Hampson recalled. 'I couldn't believe what was happening.' Murphy did not turn up in person to watch Hampson play against Leigh's 'A' team, however, leaving it up to chief scout Billy Cunliffe and the board to make the decision. Fortunately, Hampson made the decision very easy, playing with such confidence and flair that Tommy Bishop, a coach who did attend 'A' team matches, almost snapped him up for Leigh right under Wigan's noses. There were two astonishing things about Hampson. First was his strength, built up in his day job as a drayman, which belied his less than imposing stature. Second was his nerve. Whether jumping to catch a high ball cleanly, a skill at which he had few equals, or running to clear from his own line through the heavy midfield traffic, Hampson always managed to look almost cheekily nonchalant, as if he had been performing this sort of simple task every day of his life. His composure in what were only his third and fourth games of rugby league certainly impressed Cunliffe. 'He'll be frightening when he gets a bit of experience,' the scout said after Hampson's second trial. 'He's got great hands and bags of confidence, it was hard to spot a weakness. I think he might be slightly suspect when it comes to tackling players head on, but we can work on that.'

Hampson was duly signed, and quickly found himself upstaging Shaun Edwards when the pair of them made their first-team début in a home tie against York in the John Player Special Trophy. It was typical of Murphy to blood both so quickly, but Edwards needed to be paraded after his high-profile signing, and a 30–13 stroll against second division opposition was as good an opportunity as any. Nor was there a case for letting Hampson moulder in the stiffs. He was four years older than his fellow débutant at stand-off, and had already demonstrated in the 'A' team that he was unlikely to be intimidated by senior professionals. Nor was he. Edwards was steady on his début, Hampson sensational. It was the beginning of an unlikely love affair between Central Park and a late starter from Newton-le-Willows. The sight of Hampson positioning himself under a towering kick, catching cleanly then clearing his line in one seamless sequence became such a commonplace that fans began to take it for granted. He only knocked-on once in the entire 1986–87 season, for instance, and when he did, the silence was deafening. 'The crowd usually wait for me to make the catch before making a noise,'

Hampson said. 'It goes quiet when the ball is kicked in the air, then if I catch it I can hear the roar. It's a great feeling and it gives me a buzz every time. I wouldn't swap places with anyone.'

With young Holden still holding his place in the team, Fairhurst was pushed to the sidelines, and soon found himself on the transfer list after an argument with the board. Fairhurst claimed he had no quarrel with Holden – 'the lad is playing well and it's up to me to win my place back' – and denied he had asked for a move, but the board, who seemed to dislike either his attitude or his friendship with Murphy, made him available at £15,000. There were no takers.

Hampson, Edwards and Holden all played together in a narrow defeat at Oldham, but Edwards was rested for Salford in the JPS second round, and Fairhurst came back as a stand-off and received a fractured jaw for his pains. A brilliant hat-trick of tries by Gill and one from promising young forward Brian Dunn helped Wigan to a 24–15 victory and a trip to Widnes in the next round. With Stephens staying away, Fairhurst out and Foy nursing a hamstring injury, Murphy had little option but to play his two 17-year-old half-backs. If he had been able to play Hampson as well Wigan might have survived the trip to Naughton Park, where Vince Karalius was now in charge following Doug Laughton's summer departure, but Hampson had picked up a leg injury. Pendlebury, of all people, was pitched in at full-back, which could scarcely have improved his less than cordial relations with Murphy, and Wigan were beaten 20–15, although the youngsters gave a good account of themselves in a generally encouraging performance.

With only the league to concentrate on during December, Wigan put together an impressive run of four victories over Whitehaven, Hull, St Helens and Castleford, with Edwards recording his first try for the club in the last game, taking a pass from the newly rehabilitated Stephens. Hull had arrived with Peter Sterling at scrum-half, having secured one of the stars of the 1982

Kangaroo tour on a short contract, but Stephens, returning from self-imposed exile just when his club needed him most, kept the livewire Australian safely under wraps. Hampson fielded all the kicks Hull could throw at him, which was plenty, and Whitfield scored a late penalty to secure a 14–12 win. A Wigan substitute in that game was chunky loose forward Wayne Elvin, another Australian, but only an international in the sense that he had brought himself half-way round the world to try his luck in England. He found a receptive coach in Murphy who, whatever his limitations, could never be accused of not giving newcomers a chance. Players on the first-team periphery were often frustrated by the coach's apparent indifference to their ability, not to mention all those toiling away unseen in the 'A' team, but complete strangers knocking on the door with their kit in an airport duty-free bag were welcome anytime. Another of this new breed, freed by the relaxing of the international transfer ban, was Mark Cannon, a stand-off who had played a few games for St George in the Sydney Premiership. Except that on the way over he heard Wigan had just signed Edwards, and concluding that the club's stand-off requirements would be filled for the foreseeable future, introduced himself as a second row. No problem. After a couple of games in the 'A' team, now being looked after by Colin Clarke, Murphy's former assistant at Leigh, Cannon was in.

More importantly, perhaps, Hemsley was out, returning to Australia in the New Year as agreed to prepare for the new season with Balmain. Wigan's winning run came to an end entirely predictably at Post Office Road, where an unhappy Murphy became involved in an unseemly scuffle with gloating Feather-stone supporters, and bad quickly turned to worse when further defeats followed at Hull KR and at home to Warrington. Stephenson went on the list at £45,000 following the 24–10 defeat at Craven Park, after Murphy blamed him for losing form and speed, and, more bizarrely, for not protecting Edwards. The teenager's youthful good looks had been

permanently altered when Rovers' Aussie import John Dorahy left him needing five stitches and looking for one of his front teeth. Edwards was entitled to some protection, and the disagreeable Dorahy richly deserved a taste of his own medicine, but it was news to Stephenson that these duties rested with him, as opposed to one or more of the forwards. Murphy dropped Stephenson and Whitfield for the Warrington game, and brought back

The lonely walk back. Losing captain Graeme West leaves Wembley in a pensive mood after the 1984 Challenge Cup final defeat by Widnes.

Kiss when Tamati reported sick, but so dire was the Wigan performance the coach was forced to admit his regular three-quarters had been missed. They were reinstated for the next game, a Challenge Cup first-round tie at lowly Bramley. Kiss, to his disgust, was not.

Murphy also dropped Stephens for the Cup match, so as to have Holden and Edwards in tandem at half-back. This was a logical and adventurous selection, but disenchantment had spread like a contagious disease through the whole side, and not even the most promising half-back partnership in the country could make Wigan look like a

Shattered dreams. Dennis Ramsdale and Steve Hampson after the 1984 Challenge Cup final.

team that Saturday in February, let alone potential Cup winners. Bramley were destined to finish eighth in the second division that season, level on points with the preposterous Kent Invicta, yet Wigan could only scrape a 10–10 draw at McLaren Field. It was a scrape, too. Wigan tries came from West and Gill, but only Hampson's courageous tackling earned a replay. 'Wigan were frightened to death by Bramley,' wrote Cliff Webb in *The Wigan Observer*, reporting the embarrassment in tones suggesting he had barely got over the shock himself.

If dressing-room morale was low before the Cup tie, it plumbed new depths in the immediate aftermath. For several weeks it had been apparent that all was not well between the Wigan players and their coach, indeed between the Wigan players and each other. West, now captain and writing a

column for *The Lancashire Evening Post*, had been openly critical of Murphy. The coach had responded by criticising his captain back until, enraged at what he regarded as unhelpful coverage of the obvious splits in the camp – between coach and directors, coach and players, and increasingly between club and supporters – he suspended all communication with the local newspaper. So, as Wigan prepared for their Wednesday night replay against Bramley on 15 February 1984, local reporters were unable to provide either confirmation or denial of the intriguing and persistent rumour that a blade had been produced by one of the players in a dressing-room argument, or gain an official comment on the widespread understanding that Murphy's association with the club would be terminated as soon as the team went out of the Challenge Cup.

No one imagined that particular disappointment would be very long in arriving, certainly not anyone who witnessed the shambles at Bramley. Yet sport is never predictable, and something wholly unexpected happened in the replay. Wigan won it at a canter. There was nothing especially remarkable about a 34–4 home win over second division opposition, but the way Wigan put their recent troubles behind them was impressive. Partly this had to do with Cannon coming clean about his real position. Murphy dropped Edwards and Holden for the replay and paired Cannon with Stephens at half-back. This smacked of desperation, he could not have known how effective the Australian would be, but the result was spectacular. Cannon was transformed, the best player on the pitch, scorer of two confident tries in a victory which, early stage of the competition and lowly opposition notwithstanding, left supporters looking forward to the next round and talking of a possible cup run. Relegation briefly reared its head when Wigan lost their next match at Fulham, but when Cannon scored another couple of tries in the Challenge Cup second-round victory over Oldham at Central Park, Gill also chipping in with a pair in a 30–6 victory, Murphy's reprieve was complete. The whole town was talking about Wembley, rifts between club and local press were quickly healed in the interests of selling more tickets (over 9,000 had watched the Oldham game), and buoyed by the new mood of optimism at the club Wigan put themselves out of harm's way in the league table by winning their next four championship games in a row.

Cannon, meanwhile, positively revelling in his new role as local hero, cancelled his scheduled return to Australia and postponed his university studies in Queensland to stay with Wigan until the end of the season. The squad was further strengthened by the acquisition of hard-working back-row forward Ian Potter from Leigh and old-fashioned prop forward Neil Courtney from Warrington. Both had played under Murphy before and were well known to the coach, neither was signed in time to be eligible to play in the Challenge Cup this time round.

Edwards, now playing on the wing as Murphy tried to juggle his successful half-back partnership with the necessity of having his teenage prodigy actively involved some-where, scored a hat-trick in the home league match against Wakefield before Wigan went to St Helens for their Challenge Cup quarter-final. It was not an easy draw, though Saints were not enjoying the best of seasons, and there was an unmistakable confidence among the travelling supporters in the 20,000 who packed into Knowsley Road. The pitch was so muddy that Wigan appeared in Saints' second strip at half-time, the players having become almost indistinguishable after only a few minutes, but there was no doubt which side was enjoying the Cup luck. Wigan were losing 7–4 with ten minutes remaining, when Pendlebury, a player Murphy had been frantically trying to substitute for several minutes, finished a four-man passing move to put Wigan in front. They never looked back, with Stephens, Elvin and Case keeping St Helens on the rack, Whitfield adding a couple more goals and Cannon adding a second try before the end to keep his record of scoring in every round.

Wigan's Cup luck continued to work like a charm after the quarter-final was over. Second division York had managed the shock of the round by beating Castleford 14–12 and, to a mixture of disbelief and euphoria, Wigan were drawn against the Minstermen in the semi-finals, thus managing to avoid a potentially ruinous pairing with Widnes or Leeds. The hard part was already behind, after an absence of 14 years Wigan were as good as at Wembley.

Suddenly the shirt sponsorship deal which had proved so elusive arrived in time for the Elland Road semi-final, Wigan businessman and rugby supporter Dave Whelan seizing an opportunity to get his JJB Sports chain of shops some national exposure.

In the Wigan match programme for the league game against Fulham, the last fixture before the semi-final, the 'View from the Terraces' column, penned by an obscure local journalist under the pseudonym Doug Stand, had this to say about the remarkable events of recent weeks:

> Once upon a time, in a dark part of the wild northern lands, a gracious king held court in a fair and splendid castle. The king's name was Alex, and his court was known for miles around, for the chivalry of his knights and the distinctive oval table around which they sat.
>
> At the time our tale begins, King Alex was going through a bad patch. Although his dashing exploits were held in awe throughout the land, the old magic no longer seemed to be working. Not enough dragons were being slain, it was said, and the knights were arguing amongst themselves. All this time King Alex sat in a high tower and sulked, and the people of the land grew weary.
>
> One day, incensed by a series of vitriolic messages chipped into the castle walls by irate stonemasons, King Alex decided to consult the court sorcerer.
>
> 'Merlindsay,' quoth the king. 'What can I do to get the people of this fair land off my back?'

'Wise king,' quoth back Merlindsay, 'you must go and see the Black Knight at the place they call The Griffin. He will give you sound counsel.'

So King Alex journeyed forth to the lair of the mythical beast, where the Black Knight drew him into a dark corner. 'Verily, good king,' he counselled, 'many miles from here is a great castle with twin towers, where deeds of passing great glory are performed. Go there, and bring back the Holy Grail.'

'Hang on a minute,' quoth King Alex. 'I've heard of this Holy Grail. Isn't this the one you have to be spotless, honest and pure just to look at?'

'Thou hast hit the nail on the head,' quoth the Black Knight. 'Thou art a good king, wise and strong in the hunt, but spotless, honest and pure is stretching it a bit. Go and find thyself a champion.'

'A fair knight from a distant land?' quizzed King Alex.

'Correct,' quoth the Black Knight.

So the king sallied forth, sorely troubled as to where he could lay his hands on such a champion before the Holy Grail deadline. But the wizard Merlindsay had been at work in the king's absence, and when Alex returned to his castle he found the place full of fair knights from distant lands, all talking in strange tongues and playing with Excalibur in the robing-room.

'Right you lot,' quoth Alex. 'We're up for t'Holy Grail. I need a knight in shining armour, pure in thought and fair in deed.'

An embarrassed silence followed, as the knights of the oval table variously cleared their throats, fidgeted with spurs, and sheepishly polished bits of their armour.

'I've only been to Pemps twice,' ventured Sir Galahad, at long last. 'And I'm a stand-off really, not a second rower.'

'Verily thou sayest sooth,' quoth King Alex, getting into the lingo in his excitement.

So began the quest for the Holy Grail, which next week takes our intrepid adventurers over the mountains to the east to do battle for admission to the fabulous castle in the south. The people of the land are no longer weary and disgruntled, and King Alex and his court are almost restored to their former glory.

Which is just as well. For as a peasant scanning the Central Park honours board observed this week, Wigan appearances at Wembley are getting rarer than unicorn droppings.

No one seriously imagined York, in their first semi-final since 1931, would upset Wigan's plans, even after the close shave against Bramley three rounds earlier, and nor did they. In the event, neither Wigan nor York played particularly well on a waterlogged and slippery Elland Road surface, though mainly due to Stephens's organisation, the first division side always remained in control. Tries by Whitfield and Scott, the latter an opportunist effort which owed something to luck and something to the conditions, pushed Wigan out to 14–2 in front before Chris Harrison scored the try of the afternoon for York to help make the final scoreline more respectable at 14–8.

Stephens, who had almost joined York earlier in the season, was delighted to be at Wembley for the first time, even if he did have to sweat on a possible ban after being dismissed at Castleford in the league match which followed the semi-final win. Not for the first time in his Wigan career, he asked to come off the transfer list. 'I didn't want to go to York, that's all. I'd rather retire than play second division football at 30. I did take my ball home for a while, I admit that, but Alex Murphy gave me another chance. I was upset about being dropped for the first-round game at Bramley, but fortunately I was recalled for the replay, and now I'm at Wembley.'

Wigan managed to sell £20,000 worth of Wembley tickets in the first two hours of trading, despite the fact that Widnes, those seasoned cup campaigners and most hard-nosed of professionals, were waiting in the final. The portents were not good. Widnes had knocked Wigan out of the JPS Trophy earlier in the season, won at Central Park and would complete a league double at Naughton Park four games before the Cup final. On the other hand, Wigan's confidence and sense of purpose was visibly growing. A night match at Warrington in the month prior to the final attracted only a few diehard supporters. It seemed just the sort of fixture a team with one eye on Wembley did not need and would probably lose. Instead, Wigan put on one of the shows of the season, trouncing Warrington 34–6 on their own ground with Hampson, in particular, having one of the games of his life. Widnes were the favourites for Wembley, there was no doubt about that, but Wigan could claim to be a match for anyone on their day.

The visit of Hull KR to Central Park a month before the final was not one of their days. Far worse than the 30–14 mauling by the eventual champions was the sight of Hampson departing on a stretcher, his leg badly broken, his Wembley dream in ruins. Anyone with an interest in fairy tales, which meant just about everyone in the 10,000 crowd, had a lump in their throat. 'The break was my own fault,' Hampson admitted. 'Instead of just tackling George Fairbairn I tried to pull him over. Keith Mills [club physio] came onto the field and started looking at my knee. I lifted my leg up and showed him my ankle – it was swinging about in the breeze. Funnily enough, the pain only came later, I suppose I was in shock at first. And although everyone commiserated with me about missing Wembley, I didn't feel all that sorry for myself. I was blasé about the whole thing, because we had got there in my first season. It was too easy, in a way. It only struck me later how hard it is to get there, and that some of the game's greatest players have never been. I didn't even realise at that time what a big occasion it was, until I went to the final on crutches and lived the experience with the rest of the team.'

Defeat at St Helens in the last league match of the season cost Wigan a top eight place, but

the same week Kerry Hemsley arrived back in town, having returned specially for the final. Wigan were putting all their eggs into the Wembley basket, but no one seriously expected them to do anything else. The last couple of months had proved a financial godsend to the club, a lifeline to its beleaguered coach and a fillip to the whole town. Wigan teemed with cherry and white as thousands of supporters left for the final on Friday and Saturday mornings. Wembley

Should he stay or should he go? Maurice Lindsay, caught looking over his coach's shoulder, appears to be in two minds over Alex Murphy's popularity with fans at the 1984 Wembley homecoming. The coach was sacked before the start of the following season.

Way was a sea of cherry and white as Wigan fans effortlessly outnumbered and out-celebrated their Widnes counterparts before the game, and after the final thousands turned up to welcome the team back to Central Park.

It was the perfect weekend, apart from the 80 minutes of action it was built around. After all the anticipation and excitement, the 1984 Challenge Cup final made harrowing viewing for anyone with a cherry and white perspective. Defeat Wigan supporters could take, in their heart of hearts most of them realised Widnes might have an edge in class and an awful lot more Wembley experience. But the manner of the 19–6 defeat was hard to bear. Only the Wigan supporters put in anything like a Wembley performance that day, on the pitch the team failed miserably to raise its game, or even to play as well as it had been doing in the weeks leading up to the final. The result was the most one-sided and uninteresting Wembley occasion for years, never in doubt from the moment Keiron O'Loughlin juggled and finally caught John

It's over. Alex Murphy after losing to Widnes at Wembley in 1984.

Basnett's pass to score the opening try for Widnes. Hemsley scored a try for Wigan four minutes from the end, but although this made the final scoreline marginally more respectable, it hardly justified the big Aussie's airfare and neither could it conceal the fact that all five overseas players in cherry and white – West, Cannon, Tamati and Elvin were the others – flopped badly on the day. 'We just froze,' Murphy admitted. 'Wembley gets to some players like that, and there's not much you can do about it.'

Wembley didn't seem to affect any of the Widnes players like that, however, even first-time Challenge Cup finalists like Joe Lydon.

Widnes only had one overseas player in their side, the splendidly reliable Kevin Tamati, and he didn't freeze either. But the very worst thing for Wigan supporters to stomach, not that anyone begrudged Lydon his Lance Todd trophy for Man of the Match after two majestic long-range tries which provided the only highlights of a mediocre afternoon, was the damage inflicted by the Widnes trio who were playing against their home team. 'Wembley dream shattered by three Wiganers' cried *The Wigan Observer*, encapsulating events with its usual succinctness. It was true. Apart from O'Loughlin, the former Wigan player who had opened the scoring, and Lydon, the St Patrick's starlet who came of age in the 1984 final, the most influential player on the field had been Andy Gregory, picking up the second Wembley winners medal of a glittering career at the expense of the club who had let him slip through their fingers. When Lydon ran the length of the field for his second try, in fact, Gregory was accused by Wigan supporters in the crowd of making an abusive, two-fingered gesture, an allegation the scrum-half has always hotly denied.

Just about the only Wigan player to impress was Gill, who tried his utmost all afternoon without ever getting a chance to show his true value, although Scott, Pendlebury and Edwards did not do too much wrong. Edwards, playing at full-back, became the youngest player ever to appear in a Wembley final at just 17 years, six months and 19 days, but this distinction was little consolation at the time. 'He was in tears afterwards, he felt he'd let the side down,' Murphy said. 'He hadn't, of course, if anything it was the other way round. I put my arm round him and told him he had nothing to cry about. I told him he was a great player and he would learn and grow stronger from this experience. I know that to be true, because I got thrown in the deep end once or twice in my time. You either sink or you swim, but you cope, and the experience never harms you. I did exactly the same thing with Gary Connolly at St Helens in 1989. Some people said I was rushing him, but I don't think you need to protect great players. Gary didn't particularly enjoy that afternoon, just as Shaun didn't in 1984, but they didn't let anyone down. When I made my Test début at the age of 18 in Australia we suffered a thrashing and my inexperience was exposed. My captain, Alan Prescott, wasn't very pleased and told me so, but he said if I got picked again I was to play my natural game. It felt like I grew up overnight, and I never forgot that. Shaun Edwards didn't even let himself down in the 1984 final, never mind anyone else. And look at the player he has become since. In my book he is the greatest Wigan player ever. Possibly not the best player Wigan have ever had, but the greatest player the town has produced. That's quite a compliment, when you think of Joe Egan, Brian McTigue, Ken Gee, Andy Gregory and all the rest, but however you stack it up Shaun has to be out there in front. And he grew up that day at Wembley in 1984.'

After the final, in the cavernous players' tearoom at Wembley, the contrast in demeanour between the two teams told its own story. Widnes players chatted volubly in large groups, leaning back in chairs, sitting on tables, planning their evening's entertainment with wives, girlfriends and club officials. This was their fourth visit in six years, and they were familiar with the surroundings and the routine, as easy and relaxed as a group of friends meeting in a favourite hotel. Members of the Wigan party were doing the exact opposite. Standing alone, or in small groups of two or three, talking nervously, not really knowing what to say, from time to time gawping at their surroundings like tourists trying to take it all in. Lindsay and Robinson stood together. They had a hundred matters to think about, from the homecoming the following day to the future of their coach, but Lindsay was already collecting his impressions of the big day out with a view to doing a few things differently next time. The following year, in fact. 'We'll be back,' Lindsay said. 'We'll show them next year.' Frankly, your correspondent did not believe him, but he made with the understanding

nod, as sympathetic listeners are apt to do in moments of private grief and high emotion. The idea that Wigan, who had just made their first appearance at Wembley for 14 years and played like over-awed schoolboys, would even want to be back next season was preposterous. Supposing they met Widnes in the first round? Or Bramley on a good day? What most Wigan supporters wanted was to slip off quietly for a few stiff drinks of the amnesia-inducing variety, but though Lindsay was visibly shattered by the crushing disappointments of the day, his quick brain was at work already. 'Look at this lot,' he said, indicating the Widnes party with a wave of his hand. 'They are the professionals. They have done their work, now they are having a good time. We've been enjoying ourselves since we got to Wembley, and that's the difference. Just getting here was enough for us, we weren't focused enough on winning the match itself. Did you see the teams as they took the field? Our players were all waving to the crowd and looking for their girlfriends in the stand. Widnes didn't do any of that. They kept their heads down, concentrating on the task ahead. Now they are having a good time, and we look like we've been to a funeral. We've been taught a lesson today, we've still got an awful lot to learn, but we can do it. This will only increase our determination to come back next year and get it right.'

What neither Lindsay nor Robinson did at this juncture, directly at any rate, was criticise the coach or his players, though Murphy's position must have been uppermost in their minds. There is no doubt the directors were ready to sack Murphy half-way through the season. The Cup run saved his skin, but unexpectedly, the Cup run had taken Wigan all the way to Wembley. The town had been delighted to renew its acquaintance with the Challenge Cup final after a 14-year absence, as would be amply demonstrated the Sunday after Wembley when Murphy and his players arrived home to a reception which put Widnes's in the shade, and Wigan didn't even have the Cup to wave from the open-topped bus. Did this count as failure? Could a coach be dismissed in these circumstances? Wigan thought not, and let the situation ride over summer. It had been better to go to Wembley and lose rather than not go at all, and at least it ought to be possible to build on the experience.

The summer of 1984 was a busy one, with Great Britain on tour in Australasia (sole Wigan representative: Brian Case) and just about every first division club following the international party around trying to sign up the best of their opponents. Lindsay went Down Under with the capture of Australian Test centre Gene Miles uppermost in his mind, Murphy went for his usual holiday in France. By the time the pair were reunited at Central Park for the start of the 1984–85 season, word was out that Miles was not coming, but Wigan had secured the services of brilliant Kangaroo stand-off Brett Kenny instead. There would also be a winger, an uncapped Eastern Suburbs player called John Ferguson. 'John who?' Murphy asked.

Kenny could only come in December, but would stay to the end of the season. Ferguson would be here for the start of the season, but would have to fly back in February.

International transfers between hemispheres, British clubs were beginning to find out, were fraught with complexities due to the overlapping seasons. Murphy was not happy about not having Miles, possibly because rivals St Helens had just announced the capture of Mal Meninga, the Australians' other powerhouse centre, and told Lindsay so. By the time of the Wigan Summer Sevens on 19 August, with Wembley just a receding memory, the two men had already had several frank exchanges of views. Their friendship, as Lindsay had always suspected it might, had been sorely tested. Lindsay's friends now were Robinson, Rathbone and Hilton, men he regarded as partners in a challenging but worthwhile endeavour. The sense of partnership with Murphy was missing. Rather than providing an extra shoulder to the wheel, a new insight into solving a problem, all too often the coach was the problem. It was something of a vicious

circle. The more Murphy felt excluded the more petulantly he reacted. The more quarrelsome he became, the less the directors trusted him. Robinson said I told you so, but could not see any grounds for severance. Lindsay felt Murphy was holding the club back, and was beginning to regret keeping him on over summer. By August, Murphy was perfectly well aware of the precariousness of his position, but this only hastened, rather than delayed, the inevitable collision.

The argument, when it came, was petty and trivial, though at a less superficial level it reflected all the above tensions. The Summer Sevens are a traditional curtain-raiser to the new season at Central Park. Unlike the Locker Cup, the annual charity event against Warrington on the final weekend of the close season which regularly sees old scores settled, the Sevens, played the previous weekend, are an undemanding run in the sun, the gentlest of re-introductions to competitive rugby for eight teams of players and a few thousand spectators. Wigan won the competition in 1984, as they had occasionally managed to do in previous seasons, and the players duly began to spend their afternoon's pay, topped up by a modest winning bonus, at the bar. Murphy did not receive any bonus, and when he came to the office to ask for one Lindsay at first thought he was joking. The coach was not joking, however, and ignoring Lindsay's sarcasm, rephrased his request into a demand. If something snapped in Lindsay at this point, presumably because his employee and erstwhile friend stood revealed as a mercenary and a greedy one to boot, something also snapped in Murphy at around the same time, presumably because Lindsay was sitting there preaching while counting the afternoon's takings. Peeling off a few notes from the stack, Lindsay hurled them contemptuously across the desk with one or two choice remarks in Anglo-Saxon. Murphy flew at him, and for a few brief seconds the pair wrestled. A horrified Billy Cunliffe, the chief scout who was the only witness to the flare-up, tried to separate them, realised he couldn't, and ran for help. Tom

Rathbone arrived just as the scuffle was ending. Neither combatant being in peak condition, the bout would not have won many points for technical merit, but Murphy, who had been athletic once, must have landed at least one good punch, because Lindsay sported a black eye for most of the following week. A telephone had been dislodged from the desk in the excitement. That telephone, an authentic but peripheral detail of the quarrel, became the talk of the whole game the following day when Wigan sensationally announced that Murphy had been sacked.

The official reason was gross misconduct, but within hours Wigan was buzzing with the rumour that Murphy had thrown a telephone at Lindsay and caught him squarely in the eye. Within a day or so, this already salacious tale had been highly embroidered. British Telecom's catchphrase of the time – 'It's for yoo-hoo' – became the punchline of thousands of jokes. The reality was quite straight-forward, Murphy and Lindsay had grown tired of each other and the former had voluntarily given the latter a pretext for his dismissal. The legend, however, had a life of its own. 'I felt like the man who shot Jesse James,' Murphy said. 'Every time I went out the tale was getting more and more fanciful. I was supposed to have knocked Maurice across a table, then he fell backwards across a chair and it splintered, and the variations on the telephone theme were just unbelievable. There were half a dozen new ones every day. I didn't enjoy any of this, either, because it was just beginning to occur to me that I might have made the biggest mistake of my life. I have had plenty of time to think about it since, and now I am certain that falling out with Maurice was the biggest mistake of my career, certainly the most expensive. I might have been at Wigan for another ten years. I might have still been there now. Looking back, that day and the television incident in the dressing-room the previous season are the two biggest regrets of my career. Those were two very big mistakes. I am still counting the cost of making an enemy of Maurice. I'll probably regret it for the rest of my life, but I swear I never threw a telephone at him.'

Murphy is possibly deluding himself about the length of time he could have stayed at Wigan had he been able to keep his nose clean. Lindsay laughs at the suggestion of Murphy sticking around for another decade, and says he is definitely deluding himself. Murphy claims they have patched up their friendship, Lindsay denies it. 'I don't say Alex and I are still at each other's throats, over the years we have had business with each other and we have a professional relationship now, but things can never be the same as they once were. That was always the danger in bringing a personal friend like Alex to the club. I always knew that having Alex as coach would change our relationship. I thought I might fall out with other directors because of it, but I never imagined for a moment we would end up falling out with each other.'

It would have been even more difficult for Lindsay to foresee the day when he was glad of a bust-up with Murphy, because it gave him the opportunity to get rid of him, but that is how it happened. What Wigan could not bring themselves to do in the aftermath of Wembley, they did three months later, and it was all Murphy's fault. 'It was an unpleasant incident, but it had its positive side,' Lindsay said. 'It cleared the air wonderfully. Alex can say what he likes, but the fact is we went backwards in his second season. Getting to Wembley had more to do with being drawn against York in the semi-final than anything we were doing on the pitch. We were incredibly lucky to get to the final that season, we didn't even qualify for the Premiership play-off in the league. Alex would have been sacked long before the end of the season but for the Cup run, and he knew it.'

The Wigan of later years would have parted company with an unsatisfactory coach immediately after the final, or at least at the end of the season. Exactly ten years after Murphy's departure the club did just that, to a coach who had brought in the Champion-ship and Challenge Cup in first season at

Central Park. Waiting until the eve of the following season made no sense, but it is important to remember, Lindsay says, that the Wigan directors were still inexperienced in these matters in 1984. 'We bottled out, I suppose,' Lindsay said. 'We took the easy option, until the situation became untenable. Wigan would not do that now, but there hasn't always been such confidence in the boardroom. Murphy was still a popular coach in 1984, not everyone knew what we knew, and although we could have terminated his contract after Wembley, we just weren't bold enough to do it.'

Murphy does not see it quite like this. 'It's quite simple,' he said. 'Maurice sacked me because he wanted all the attention for himself. He always wanted to be number one, Mr Wigan, and while I was around I was deflecting some of his glory. Reporters would congratulate me and ask me questions, and Maurice didn't like that. So I had to go, and I was fool enough to give him the opportunity. It's all in the past now, and my departure didn't exactly make the wheels fall off at Central Park, but I don't think I get the credit I deserve for my part in the club's success. In fact, I know I don't, because I don't get any credit whatsoever. When I first went to Wigan I drew up a plan for the future, which they have followed in every detail. Everything I recommended they have done, from taking on fitness specialists, to lighten the load of the coach, to signing world-class players, including overseas ones on three-year contracts. I told them to do all that and they did, after I had gone. The world-class players came pouring in after I had gone, but

I had to put up with Mark Cannon and Kerry Hemsley. The board brought Hemsley back for Wembley, not me, because he had put a condition into his contract without me knowing. That's the way it was all the time. I didn't know anything about West or Tamati until they arrived, and all I knew then was that they were not what I wanted. And I wasn't on anything like £35,000 a year either, if that's what Doug Laughton was really offered. I wasn't even on half that. I'm used to clubs with no money, I've spent my entire coaching career at hard-up clubs, and Wigan were no exception. But Wigan were the only club to tell me there was no money in the kitty then go out and buy players behind my back.'

Murphy's affronted tone and injured pride have survived the intervening years almost intact, but they were even better at the time. One morning in 1984 *The Lancashire Evening Post* received a telephone call from an irate Murphy demanding to know how much West was receiving for his weekly captain's column, where his robust views had quickly gained him a readership. The sum was a modest fifteen pounds. Murphy was quite pleased. 'I'm thinking of paying him fifteen quid a week not to write it.' Even Lindsay, like Robinson, agrees that the Murphy rollercoaster was an enjoyable ride, a special time for the club. 'The best thing about Alex, apart from his outstanding record as a player, is that he is undoubtedly a charismatic figure capable of great fun and wit,' Lindsay said. 'He swept into Central Park like a wind and freshened everyone up. The worst thing was the knowledge, the absolute certainty, that that wind would die, and it did. It blew itself out.'

CHAPTER FIVE

Wembley Glory

'Some of our tries were sheer magic.'

The title of this chapter is a cliché, and not only that but one of the most obvious and casually over-used of the sports writer's set of stock phrases. Wembley is synonymous with glory. To play there at all is an achievement, to feature in a cup final is an undeniably glorious thing to do. Finish on the winning side and you are automatically entitled to trail clouds of the stuff.

Wembley these days likes to call itself the Venue of Legends, trading on the myth we are only too willing to swallow, even though we know the reality does not always match up. For there are dull cup finals as well as exciting ones, humdrum internationals as well as World Cup finals, and any number of occasions, in football and in rugby, where the magnitude of the event manifests itself negatively in a pragmatic approach to winning or a constraining fear of losing. We all have a loose approximation of the ingredients our ideal Wembley final should contain – two good teams, for a start, a close game and a plot with several twists and turns; liberal helpings of bravado and panache; the deserving winners just shading the plucky losers by virtue of producing spectacular scores at crucial moments; these scores to be audacious in their inception or breathtaking in their execution, preferably both, so we can mentally re-live them for years afterwards – but this is an agenda owing more to schoolyard fiction than to real life. Part of the attraction of watching sport is the excuse it allows for childlike optimism, but most grown-ups realise that cup finals will rarely live up to such impossible expectations.

The 1985 Silk Cut Challenge Cup final

between Wigan and Hull did. It was sensational from start to finish, probably the best of all time, certainly the most memorable of the television era. The 1996 final contained three more tries, and has a strong claim to be the most exciting in memory, but it also contained a high count of basic errors and by that time anyway, rules had been none-too-subtly altered to encourage high scoring. Back in 1985, *The Guardian*'s Frank Keating called the final the most voluptuous exhibition of rugby it had ever been his privilege to witness. Had it been a rugby union match, a national holiday would probably have been announced in its honour and the BBC could have given the tape of Barbarians v. All Blacks in 1973 a much-needed rest and shown something else for a change. It was only rugby league though, so the nation as a whole did not go off the rails with excitement, and the media continued to be unaccountably fascinated by scoreless football matches and dreary rugby union encounters dominated by drop goals, penalties and pushover tries.

For once, however, rugby league supporters were not up in arms about the shameful neglect of their sport. It was a source of some annoyance that praise in most quarters for the 1985 final was only grudging, but the match itself had been such a thrilling confirmation of everything rugby league stood for – skill, strength, speed and vibrant spectacle – that the game stood back and savoured a rare opportunity for self-congratulation. The 1985 final was not quite a watershed, nothing that happened during the '80s was as monumentally significant as the

Kangaroo tour of three years earlier, but it was a welcome indication that the game was travelling in the right direction. The '70s had been a difficult period for British rugby league, with declining gates, dilapidated grounds and little money or new support coming in. The game had become deeply unfashionable, even in the North, and dangerously introspective. Wigan and Hull were two of the clubs helping reverse these trends in the '80s, a decade when optimism reigned, ambition knew no bounds, and what

John Ferguson in action against Castleford. A superbly balanced runner, with deceptive strength and uncanny ability to ride the heaviest challenges.

would later became known as the feelgood factor was high among those sections of the community not having their collars felt on picket line or poll tax protest. From a '90s perspective it is tempting to wonder which was the most illusory, the revival in rugby league's fortunes in the mid-'80s or the corresponding boom in the nation's economy. But both felt real enough at the time, and the 1985 final appeared to offer evidence that, in rugby league's case at least, the return to rude health had not been stage-managed or

cynically manipulated. After the grey years of the '70s and the trouncing by Australia in 1982, it was a pleasure to see spring sunlight at the old stadium illuminate such a colourful and compelling spectacle. True, there were a record ten overseas players involved in the 1985 final, but that still left 20 home-grown players, including some of Britain's most exciting young talents, to share the record ten tries and 52 aggregate points. Those totals, a professional coach or a purist would argue, imply a measure of defensive naïvety, and indeed both Wigan and Hull could be faulted for throwing everything into attack and attempting to win by outscoring rather than containing the opposition. But not by spectators. Purists and professional coaches have their own ideas about what constitutes an ideal final, everyone else was perfectly content with this one. Even the losing players and supporters consoled themselves with the heartening thought that any sport capable of producing such a showpiece could not be doing too much wrong.

And Wigan won. More or less everything Maurice Lindsay had said at Wembley the previous year came to pass. Wigan returned at the first opportunity and succeeded in style. Considering the club's recent history, and the fact they had begun the season without a coach, there was something of a fairy-tale aspect to it all. Except that is another cliché, and this chapter is already in danger of becoming overloaded. But as we return to August 1984, and a Central Park still shell-shocked by Alex Murphy's departure, there are no apologies for the original one. If ever a team went to Wembley and covered themselves in glory it was Wigan in 1985, and as with all the best schoolyard fiction, the most stirring of all triumphs was all the more exciting for being accomplished against the odds.

As Murphy walked out of Central Park, he almost passed John Ferguson on the way in. Ferguson, you will recall, was Wigan's side bet in the great Australian sweepstake. Not Brett Kenny, who would only arrive just before Christmas, and not Gene Miles, who would not be arriving at all, Ferguson was an uncapped, Aboriginal winger from the Eastern Suburbs club who looked suspiciously older than his stated age of 29. Ferguson's exact age will probably never be known, it has been a subject for debate in both England and Australia, but his 'playing age' alone was enough to incense Murphy. 'Alex thought I was out of my mind signing a 29-year-old, and privately said so,' Lindsay explained. 'When I called from Australia to tell him the news I had to calm him down. First he was disappointed about not getting Miles, then he was up in the air about signing another unknown, and a geriatric one at that. He wanted to know why I wasn't signing any famous players. I already had Kenny, as a matter of fact, but I could not announce it just yet. Alex knew St Helens had got Meninga, that was what was putting the pressure on. He knew this season was going to be different to the last, and that backpackers and B-list celebrities would not be good enough.'

Murphy was correct, but by the time the season came around, he no longer had Wigan's worries on his shoulders. The men supporting that heavy burden were Colin Clarke and Alan McInnes, the assistant coaches who had been hurriedly promoted to take charge of the first team following Murphy's sudden exit. They didn't know anything about Ferguson either, beyond the fact that he was due to arrive the weekend before the season started, in time to be introduced to the Wigan crowd prior to the annual Locker Cup charity match against Warrington. A smallish chap (5 ft 9 in) in a large overcoat, Ferguson made more of an impression on the Wigan players than the supporters, chiefly for getting through more cigarettes than even David Stephenson or Nicky Kiss thought wise. The Australian's rugby ability was yet to be ascertained, but if ever Wigan needed a chain-smoking champion, they would know where to look.

The odd thing about Ferguson was that he had remained an unknown quantity in an age when video recorders and satellite transmissions were making the Sydney Premiership increasingly accessible to rugby league followers in Britain. It was not as if only the members of Kangaroo tour parties were familiar to fans in Wigan and elsewhere, thanks to the enterprise of various pubs and clubs around town, and in most rugby league

John Ferguson sets off for the line in his 'farewell' appearance in England, the Challenge Cup quarter-final at Warrington in 1985. Graeme West and Shaun Wane look on admiringly.

strongholds, it was now possible to keep tabs on most Winfield Cup games on video, albeit a week or two after the event. But Ferguson, who had only turned professional late in his career, and then with the unfashionable and soon-to-fold Newtown club, was an underrated talent even in Australia. On Newtown's closure he joined Easts, a more high-profile Sydney club, but despite consistent form and several tries, never attracted the attention of the Australian selectors. It was while playing for Easts, however, that Ferguson was spotted by Jim Hartley, Jack Robinson's brother-in-law, who was in Sydney on a business trip. Lindsay followed up the tip, went to watch Ferguson in action in 1984, and the rest is history – Wigan history, at any rate.

One person in Lancashire to whom the name of Wigan's new signing did mean something was freelance journalist Dave Hadfield, who had spent a year in the Southern Hemisphere at the start of the '80s and had regularly watched Ferguson playing for Newtown. 'He was an extremely exciting

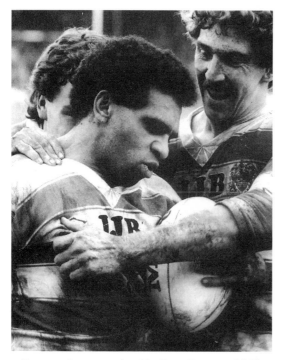

Ferguson is congratulated by Brett Kenny and Mike Ford after his wonderful try against Warrington.

player and a great crowd pleaser,' Hadfield said. 'As soon as I heard Wigan had signed him I was full of admiration. Someone at Central Park had clearly done their homework. Ferguson was a sure-fire winner who was certain to go down well in England. I knew Wigan were always on the lookout for the type of player to light up the crowd like Billy Boston used to do, and I thought Ferguson could do exactly that. The only possible doubt about him was how well he would adapt to English conditions, but he did fine. I don't think he ever enjoyed the cold weather here, I don't imagine he seriously considered coming back for another season, but while he was here he was just as good as I thought he would be. No, in fact he was probably even better.'

The statistics show that Ferguson scored 24 tries in 25 appearances for Wigan in 1984–85, but the statistics do not tell the whole story. Some of Ferguson's tries had to be seen to be believed. Not endowed with remarkable physique or blessed with exceptional pace, Ferguson simply had a precious gift of going

past defenders. Deceptively strong, he appeared to possess some sort of spring-loaded, self-righting suspension which enabled him to ride the heaviest challenges, and you could never tell, no matter how many tacklers ganged up on him, whether Fergie would beat half of them or all of them. He also had an uncanny ability to pre-empt a tackle by sleight of foot. Even when almost at a standstill he could produce footwork nifty enough to leave quality opponents floundering, an ability never better demonstrated than when scoring Wigan's opening try in the 1985 Challenge Cup final. Dane O'Hara probably still wakes up in the middle of the night with visions of Ferguson oscillating in front of him. But we are getting beyond ourselves. Returning to the start of the season, where Ferguson scored a début try in an away win at Castleford in the opening league game, Wigan supporters quickly became aware they were in for a treat. Watching Ferguson was a true privilege, especially for those younger members of the Central Park crowd who had been brought up on the lean years and only had second-hand accounts of former glory. Kenny, when he arrived, would doubtless be brilliant, but would never belong to Wigan. He was doing us a favour coming at all. With Ferguson it was the other way around. Here was someone the crowd could take to their hearts and get proprietorial about – few seemed to want, or even rate, him in Australia, after all – and Ferguson behaved throughout as if it was Wigan who were doing him a favour.

And in a sense they did. Ferguson's stock in Australia shot up after his successful season in England, to the extent that he finally wore the green and gold at the grand old age of 30. Coming at a time when Australian rugby league players were contemplating retirement at that age, this international début was still the more surprising, particularly as in all likelihood Ferguson was even older. But as Lindsay said after first checking Ferguson out at Easts: 'As soon as I saw him in action I knew we had to have him. Caps, age, reputation did not matter. He was simply breathtaking. I knew he would be a sensation in England.' Lindsay's hunch was proved correct by Ferguson's style and try-scoring prowess. Not all of his tries were spectacular, though a lot were, and so were many of the runs with which he created tries for teammates. Neither did Ferguson specialise in feats of unstoppable strength or incredible speed. He just scored tries that were improbable, in that it was difficult to imagine anyone else scoring them; and made opportunities by beating the first man so regularly you could put money on it. The 'buzz' factor Lindsay had been looking for was back. When Ferguson got the ball, Central Park positively tingled. 'The lad is fabulous,' said Billy Boston, showing typical generosity to Ferguson's age as well as his exploits on the wing. Midway through the season, Jack Hilton went even further. 'Ferguson must be one of Wigan's best-ever signings,' the chairman said. 'How he missed out on international selection I'll never know. Surely the Aussies can't have *four* wingers better than him!'

Hilton was right, Ferguson was one of the best wingers in Australia. No Eric Grothe perhaps, but certainly worth a place in any touring party, if not the Test side itself. According to Hadfield, his late arrival on the professional scene and his Aboriginal background both counted against him. 'When you look back to pre-1985, the Australian neglect of Ferguson does seem pretty scandalous,' he said. 'He had always been a very useful player for Newtown, even though he had to live off scraps all the time. He was never going to score hat-tricks there, with the limited opportunities that came his way, but he was obviously talented and his partnership with the other Newtown winger, Ray Blacklock, was quite interesting. They used to support each other, run off each other, and sometimes even swap wings with each other, all adventurous stuff well ahead of its time and not greatly appreciated in the rigid Australian game. But even when Ferguson joined Easts he was ignored until Wigan spotted him. At that time it was difficult to

get out of the Australian team, once you had been selected you had to bomb fairly drastically to lose your place, and Ferguson had a reputation, wholly undeserved in my opinion, for going walkabout. He was not held to be reliable, in other words it was thought he might miss matches or training

Fergie's farewell. Wigan's favourite winger is chaired off by Neil Courtney and Danny Campbell (hidden behind Shaun Edwards) at Wilderspool. No one knew then that Ferguson would be back for Wembley, though a lot of people were hoping.

sessions without explanation. Of course this could simply have been anti-Aboriginal prejudice, but coupled with his late start and the uncertainty about his exact age, it was enough to keep him off centre stage until Wigan arrived.'

Wigan were not wholly altruistic in this enterprise, one of the consequences of Ferguson's low profile in Australia was that his expectations were similarly modest, and the English club took advantage of the situation to pick up a bargain. All Ferguson cost Wigan was £4,000, a trifling amount even for the time. Wally Lewis asked nearly that much per game at Wakefield Trinity. Ferguson was one of the few players worth £4,000 per game, but these were days of

Henderson Gill leaves Gary Kemble for dead en route to the Wembley try line . . .

innocence and moderation, and £4,000 was all he got for six months work, plus winning bonuses, of which, thanks to him, there were plenty. Becoming a local hero might be glamorous, but no one ever said it was well paid.

Colin Clarke was deputised to pick Ferguson up from Heathrow airport on the morning of the Locker Cup meeting with Warrington, the newly installed joint coach and his new player driving straight back to Wigan to catch the game. 'I was in a hurry, this was my first game in charge, and though it was only a friendly I naturally wanted to be back at Central Park as quickly as possible,' Clarke said. 'So we were shooting up the motorway in the outside lane, and about half-way home John suddenly asked me if I would mind stopping for a minute. So I pulled into the next services, expecting him to want to use the toilet, but he didn't. He stepped out of the car, pulled out a packet of fags and lit up. I didn't realise he was such a heavy smoker. I told him he could have had a cigarette in the car, but he realised I didn't smoke and said he preferred not to. So my first impressions were a bit confused. On the one hand I had just taken charge of a professional athlete who

could not go three hours without a cigarette, but on the other hand John was a very courteous and considerate person. When we got back to Wigan I asked him if he felt like playing against Warrington. He said no, but very politely.'

This was the second eventful Sunday in a row for Clarke, a former Wigan hooker who had won a winners medal in the 1965 Challenge Cup final, but had famously had to sit out the 1966 Wembley débâcle against St Helens through suspension. The previous weekend he had found himself in the middle of the Murphy–Lindsay row, unaware that within 24 hours it would lead to his elevation from 'A' team to first-team coach, in partnership with Alan McInnes, the club's erstwhile fitness trainer. 'I was up in the bar after the Sevens when Murph walked in,' Clarke said. 'I could see straightaway he was uptight about something. I bought him a drink, but he seemed distracted. He said he'd just had an almighty bust-up with Lindsay, but left it at that. He finished his drink and went home. I didn't think that much of it, he was always having bust-ups with Lindsay, but the next minute Maurice himself arrived at the bar, looking decidedly flustered and a little worse for wear. He wasn't battered or bleeding or anything, but his face was beginning to swell, and it was obvious he had been shook up. I still remember what he said. He bought a couple of drinks, trying to remain calm, then he just turned and said: "Well, he's gone and done it now."'

Clarke would only learn the full implications of the row the following morning, when Lindsay informed him of Murphy's dismissal and invited him to take over the coaching with McInnes. Both men agreed. Despite the precipitate circumstances, there was no question of taking over as caretakers until someone more famous could be found. It was as if the club had been prepared for such an eventuality. Certainly Clarke was aware that Murphy had come close to the sack before, notably after the Queensland game, and assumed Lindsay and the board had a plan of action to hand. Both

. . . and celebrates his touchdown with one of the most radiant grins ever to illuminate the stadium. Mike Ford (7), Steve Donlan (4) and Shaun Edwards (1) are the first to arrive with congratulations.

Clarke and McInnes were respected names in rugby league with solid coaching credentials, and although neither had ever succeeded by themselves at a big club, the pairing was as promising as any of the alternatives the English game had to offer. 'I think Maurice wanted the best of me and the best of Alan,' Clarke said. 'We each had our strengths, our own areas of expertise, and we complemented each other. I had no worries about taking over Wigan or working with Alan. We both knew each other quite well by then and had developed a mutual respect and an appreciation of what needed doing at the club.'

All the same, with due respect to Clarke and McInnes, it was a low-profile appointment after Wigan's chase of Laughton and connection with Murphy, and their stated desire only to be associated with the very best. The policy of only recruiting 'big-name' coaches seemed to have been put on the back boiler, although having tried a few, Wigan's reluctance to court any more was understandable. Bamford had been a disappointment, and an expensive one in terms of his outlay on players of inferior quality. Although not a big name when Wigan first hired him, Bamford certainly was now,

having joined Leeds after leaving Central Park *en route* to his eventual installation as coach of Great Britain. Yet, the Wigan board still believed they knew more about rugby players than he did. Murphy had been a far bigger disappointment, because the expectation had been greater, and even Laughton, the coach Wigan had originally targeted, was out of the game and looking unlikely to return. Never a predictable man at the best of times, Laughton left Widnes at the end of the 1983 season for a reason never satisfactorily explained, though to judge from the frequency with which he was encountered on licensed premises the following year he had more than a few sorrows to drown.

By this time also, Lindsay and Robinson were convinced they could spot and sign players, in both Britain and Australia, and put a team on the pitch capable of winning most of its matches, and so only needed a coach to supervise the training sessions and work on dressing-room morale. If a coach, however famous, was going to be more of a hindrance than a help in that direction, as Murphy had been, he could be dispensed with. Having put so many of the pieces of the jigsaw together

Another Wembley try from the very top drawer. Brett Kenny opens his legs, so to speak, and shows his class.

themselves, the Wigan directors were wary of inviting anyone in to undo the good work. The club was not so much anti-coach as anti-personality. The directors had come to believe that professional players do not necessarily have to be coerced into performing by the force of a coach's aura, and were looking for someone to work harmoniously with themselves and the playing staff, instead of making fresh waves. Clarke and McInnes did not come with big reputations, that was part of their attraction. Their great advantage was that their method of working was already familiar and acceptable to directors and players. They were unlikely to spring any unpleasant surprises.

Nor did they, although stand-off Mark Cannon sprang one of his own when he asked for considerably more money to play another season. Within days of his appointment Clarke was summoned by Lindsay to deal with a player who claimed he would return to Australia if his contract was not substantially improved. 'He was trying me out,' Clarke said. 'He was asking for a huge amount of money, which would have caused us problems all along the line if we had agreed. I

think he had me down as an inexperienced coach who might give in to his demands rather than take a stand. Maurice just asked me what I wanted to do, I think he was watching for my reaction too. I said Cannon could go home if he wanted to, but he couldn't have the money. He backed down and continued to play for us, though not as well as he had played the previous season. I was doubly relieved. Not only had I faced down my first challenge, I had avoided paying over the odds for a player who was not as good as we all thought he was.'

The opening-day win at Castleford was followed by a home defeat at the hands of Bradford, for whom Ellery Hanley excelled, and an away defeat (what else?) at Leigh, but Wigan supporters in 1984 could accept these inconsistencies cheerfully enough. At the end of September, Wigan hammered Leeds 30–14 at Central Park, with Cannon claiming a couple of tries, then a week later managed their usual collapse at Featherstone. There were no calls for the heads of Clarke and McInnes, however, for in the next game Wigan won through to the Lancashire Cup final with an away defeat of Salford. This was almost uncharted territory. Wigan's last appearance in the county cup final had been in 1980, during their season in the second division, when no one had expected them to beat first division Warrington but no one had anticipated them losing quite so embarrassingly either. The club's last winning appearance in the county final had been in 1973. This may not seem such a distant memory, but it should be remembered that only 16 teams took part in the Lancashire Cup, including the likes of Blackpool, Runcorn, Rochdale and several other second

Aussie pride. Brett Kenny and John Ferguson show off the 1985 Silk Cut Challenge Cup in the tunnel at Wembley.

division sides. With only three wins necessary to reach the final, there was little excuse for decent teams not making the semi-final stage on a more or less regular basis, and expecting to win the thing every few years. Wigan's limp record of one win and two losing appearances in the previous ten years was overshadowed by the likes of Widnes (five wins in the same period), Warrington (two wins) and even Workington Town (four consecutive appearances from 1976 to 1979 and one win, against Wigan in 1977).

A feeling that this might be Wigan's year began when Widnes were overwhelmed 28–8

before a crowd of 10,000 in the first round at Central Park, and persisted when Swinton were outclassed 32–6 in the next round on a balmy evening at Station Road. Ferguson scored a couple of tries that night, and Ian Potter, the muscular forward signed too late to play at Wembley the previous season, chipped in with another. Spotted in the crowd was Nicky Kiss, the hooker who had hardly been seen at Wigan in the final months of Murphy's reign. Howie Tamati having returned to New Zealand, Wigan's number nine shirt was being filled by Paul O'Neill, an Under-21 international signed from Salford, but Kiss announced his intentions of making a comeback. 'Now that Murphy has gone, the coast is clear,' he said. This was bad news for O'Neill, a talented but lightweight player destined to discover, after a couple of seasons on the periphery, that coaches were always likely to prefer the extra experience and strength Kiss had to offer.

After the Willows semi-final, which saw Wigan haul back an 8–2 deficit to run out 19–8 winners, there was good and bad news. The good news was that St Helens's easy victory over Leigh in the other semi-final had set up the first Saints–Wigan final in the Lancashire Cup's 80-year history, surprising in view of the strength of the deadly rivals and the essentially parochial nature of the competition. The bad news was that St Helens were running into hot form, thanks in no small part to their Australian mighty man, Mal Meninga, who had set Saints on a winning streak from the day he arrived with two typically muscular tries against Castleford. Proud as Wigan fans were of Ferguson, they had every respect for Meninga. There was nothing deceptive about the burly Queenslander, what you saw was precisely what you got. Meninga was tall, powerfully built, with exceptional pace for a big man, a shrewd rugby brain and a deft pair of hands. Oh, and he was a useful kicker as well. More or less perfect, in other words, the type of player a computer would design if you asked it to come up with an individual capable of winning matches on his own. At this stage of his career, stealth, guile and subtlety played little part in Meninga's game. They didn't need to. Defences, especially English ones, normally caved in to his strength and speed. He scored 28 tries in 31 games for St Helens in 1984–85, mostly by running in straight lines, and created many more for his supporting cast.

By the time the Lancashire Cup final came round Meninga had managed only five games for St Helens, but they had all been victories. Wigan supporters, familiar with

Two coaches, one prize. Alan McInnes and Colin Clarke in the Wembley dressing-room with their crowning achievement. That's the back of the author's head, behind the Challenge Cup.

Meninga's awesome performances for Australia against Great Britain, knew only too well what havoc he was capable of creating. Two things happened prior to the final to put Wigan fans in good heart, however. The first was winning home advantage. County cup finals were normally played on neutral grounds, but as the attendance for Saints v. Wigan would clearly be greater than anything Warrington or Salford could accommodate, and there was insufficient time to take the game to a football stadium, it was decided to stage the game at either Knowsley Road or Central Park. A coin was tossed, and Wigan won. Over 26,000 people eventually packed into Central Park for the final, the first true

capacity crowd at Wigan for years and 10,000 more than Wilderspool could have held.

The other reason Wigan had to be cheerful was their performance in the league match prior to the final: a 30–10 away win at Hull KR, the defending champions, who were on their way to retaining their title. Ferguson was brilliant. Those Wigan fans who did not already realise a special talent was in their midst had their eyes opened. So did the rest of the game. The following description comes from 'Don't Expect Miracles', a chapter on Wigan's 1984–85 season I contributed to Dave Hadfield's *XIII Winters*. It is not laziness which prompts me to recycle the odd extract, simply the knowledge that having relived the events of this particular season at least four times for different publications, I am unlikely to improve upon my earlier efforts at this late stage.

Rovers had so far not lost a match all season. Fortress Craven Park was pretty well impregnable, and few Robins supporters would have been expecting Wigan to ruffle any feathers. The first defeat of the season had to come some time, of course, but 10–30 at home to Wigan was not on anyone's agenda. Especially as Rovers barely got a look-in, spending most of the afternoon chasing the shadows of the visiting wingers.

Henderson Gill scored a hat-trick, while Ferguson contented himself with a single touchdown – but it was Fergie's match. Rovers just couldn't get near him, and his part in the final try was simply sensational. Running from his own line, he drifted around Prohm, accelerated past Laws, and dummied the by-now exasperated Fairbairn. Just short of the Rovers try line he was stopped by Clark, who had crossed from the opposite wing – but so too had Gill, and when Edwards continued the move, there was literally nothing left of the home defence to keep the winger out. 'We have been telling people all the time that Fergie is a world-beater,' Colin Clarke said. 'Perhaps now they will start to believe us.'

They did, but when Wigan ran up against St Helens's world-beater in their very next match, the contest was not even close. Mighty Mal scored two tries, made two tries and strode off with the Man of the Match award, and that was before half-time. A fairly creditable second-half fightback from Wigan, when tries from Gill, West and Kiss reduced a 24–2 interval deficit to a more respectable-looking scoreline of 26–18, could not disguise the fact that the home defence had melted away when Meninga had done little more than breathe on it. Wigan had been slaughtered by their arch enemies in a cup final on their own ground. To add insult to injury, Saints' Australian had done as he pleased, while Wigan's had scarcely figured in the game. It was difficult to see how life could be lived again after such an embarrassment. What use was Brett Kenny arriving in December now? The damage had been done. Saints–Wigan cup finals, as any supporter of either side would confirm, are few and far between, and to the indignity of the two Wigan defeats in the '60s on the only occasions the sides had met at Wembley had now been added this virtual walkover in the Lancashire Cup.

Having had their illusions crushed almost as comprehensively as at Wembley the previous May, Wigan set about ringing the changes. Mike Ford, a promising teenage half-back, was given a run in place of Fairhurst at Halifax, Keith Holden got a chance a week later at Workington. Nick Du Toit, an enormous South African rugby union player who had made his own way to Wigan and asked for a trial, made his début on the right wing in the easy John Player Special Trophy first-round win over Huddersfield.

Kenny flew in just too late to prevent Wigan sliding out of the JPS Trophy, a notable Ferguson try against Leeds providing the only highlight in a 10–4 defeat at Headingley, but made a winning début at Warrington a week later. And after that game Wigan simply kept winning, with Kenny coming more and more to the fore, and the wingers in particular enjoying a succession of

field days. Kenny's long pass to the wing was something to behold. From almost anywhere on the field, often without warning, the stand-off would suddenly hurl towards either touch-line a pass which appeared destined only for the crowd until Ferguson or Gill – especially Gill – arrived on cue at the last

Superman and chain smoker. John Ferguson has a crafty fag out on the Wembley pitch after the Cup success against Hull.

moment, and some unsuspecting defence would realise there was little point even starting the chase.

All through December Wigan kept winning, and the sequence was not even interrupted by the Boxing Day visit to Knowsley Road, where Kenny and Holden and a superb pack performance helped atone for the Lancashire Cup final defeat with a welcome 30–22 victory. Meninga, closely watched by Stephenson, was less of a menace this time. 'I think in the Lancashire Cup final we made a mistake by trying to gang up on him,' Colin Clarke said. 'Everyone was looking to someone else to stop him. Before Boxing Day, I just had a quiet word with David Stephenson, to remind him it was down to him to tackle Meninga.' And how, exactly, did Clarke motivate his centre for this daunting task? 'I told him if he let him through again he would find himself in deep fertiliser.'

Wigan won all their matches in January, too, though because of the freezing weather there were only two of them. Ferguson was due back in Australia on 24 February, and as he neared the end of his stay, every week without a game was considered wasted by Wigan supporters as unimpressed as he was by the appalling British weather. When the conditions did relent though, Fergie gave double value to make up for what fans had been missing. Two tries against Widnes at the end of January were followed by four against Castleford at the beginning of February, the latter game arguably his most famous individual performance. From *XIII Winters*:

> Central Park was blissfully stunned. I have several photographs and indeed, a specially commissioned painting of the various trails of destruction Fergie left that day. But the overriding mental impression is of a cartoon strip in the *Beano* style, with our hero scooting effortlessly all over the pitch, little puffs of air at his heels illustrating every acceleration, while in the background a series of hapless opponents crash into each other, give futile chase, or lie helplessly prostrate.

After the Castleford victory, Wigan's seventh in a row since Kenny's arrival, came the first two rounds of the Challenge Cup, concertinaed into successive weekends because of the time lost to the weather. Ferguson would be able to play in both before flying home. Prior to the Challenge Cup deadline Wigan had failed with a £75,000 bid for Widnes scrum-half Andy Gregory, on the Naughton Park list at £150,000. Though thrilled with the success of this season's foreign imports, Wigan were mindful of their promise to field home-grown sides in the long term, and were anxious to recapture the most famous of the local products to leave town in the bad old days. Widnes, however, were not at all keen on this repatriation programme for Wiganers. Gregory had not played for them since the opening day of the season as he nursed some convenient grievance. Although Widnes were resigned to losing a player who was clearly angling for a move to a wealthier club, they had no intention of letting him go to Wigan, whom they suspected of unsettling him in the first place. So in the end, as the deadline approached, Widnes told Wigan that Gregory was not for sale for less than the full amount, then set up a hurried exchange deal with Warrington which saw the scrum-half move to Wilderspool with £75,000-rated forward John Fieldhouse travelling in the opposite direction. As Fieldhouse never really settled at Naughton Park, and Gregory remained unhappy at Warrington, Widnes had effectively cut off their nose to spite their face. Obviously they resented having to sell the player at all, but as a selling club, even a reluctant one, they failed in their duty to squeeze the best possible price out of the buyer. Gregory ended up at Wigan two years later, but Warrington, not Widnes, were the recipients of the record £130,000 transfer fee. By the time Gregory arrived at Central Park, his fellow Wiganer and erstwhile Widnes team-mate Joe Lydon was already there. Widnes had not wanted to sell him either, but by 1986 were so desperate for funds they felt they had no choice but to accept Wigan's £100,000. Widnes did eventually learn their lesson, stinging Wigan for an eye-watering £440,000 for Martin Offiah in 1992, though it did not come as a complete surprise to learn that almost every penny of that fee was needed to cover debts.

So, with Gregory bound for Wilderspool, Wigan bit their lip and signed Steve Donlan, Leigh's classy stand-off or centre, for £25,000, 24 hours before the deadline. Most of this money was raised by the sale of John Pendlebury to Salford, a deal which disappointed some fans and surprised a few more. Pendlebury was a very useful player. 'Our players' panel is now so big, we are getting lots of enquiries from other clubs,' chairman Jack Hilton explained. 'But we are not prepared to part with top-class players, just those on the fringe.' The fact that Pendlebury was on the fringe was a measure of Wigan's progress in recent seasons, his transfer was the first example for years of a quality player being unable to hold down a first-team place at Central Park, which is why it made everyone a little nervous. Before leaving, Pendlebury had only one question. 'What's Kevin Ashcroft like as a coach? I've heard he's a clone of Alex Murphy.'

Wigan's first-round Challenge Cup tie against Batley was played at Burnden Park, where Bolton Wanderers had undersoil heating, and was more memorable for the strength of support in the Sweet Green Tavern and other local hostelries than the one-sided 48–6 win. Cherry and white replica shirts were now *de rigueur*, Bruce Springsteen's *Dancin' in the Dark* was on every jukebox, and with the welcome warmth of the sun hinting that spring was around the corner, Wigan's thoughts automatically turned to Wembley. By the time Kenny, Ferguson et al had negotiated the next obstacle – a tricky away tie at Warrington – it was clear that Wigan not only had a side capable of making a quick return to the capital, but one capable of putting up a decent performance when it got there. The 24–14 win at muddy Wilderspool was Fergie's farewell match, and a more memorable send-off could not have been scripted. Warrington, whose ranks now included a peeved-looking Andy Gregory, could only stand and watch as tries

by Kenny, Gill and, most unforgettably, Ferguson, plus six goals from new kicker Stephenson, swept Wigan into the quarter-finals.

From *XIII Winters*:

Fergie's farewell try is indelibly imprinted on the mind. When Kenny received the ball in his own half and looked up, most of the Wigan contingent knew what was about to happen. The ball was duly swung out to the right to Stephenson, then on to Ferguson, and the winger's gallop to the line from beyond half-way out, with

Shaun Edwards once looked young shock. An impossibly youthful teenage full-back shows off the Challenge Cup at the 1985 homecoming.

Kenny in perfect step, pointing and shouting encouragement, was captured brilliantly by television and stills photographers alike.

But this was not just a leaving party. Warrington were a good side who had been confidently beaten. Amid the disappointment of the previous year's Wembley let-down, the Wigan directors, notably Maurice Lindsay, had promised that the club would be back. It had not seemed a likely prospect, but their wishful thinking now appeared to be taking shape, and this time it was due less to luck than good judgement.

After the game Wigan completed the signing of Phil Ford, the Warrington winger, for a steepish £40,000. Signed too late to be eligible for Challenge Cup games, Ford simply had to deputise for the departed Ferguson in the remaining 14 league games, a tall order which he actually accomplished quite well, beginning with two tries on his début in the home defeat of Hull KR. A former rugby union player from Wales, Ford had plenty of pace and a more than useful sidestep, and at this stage of his career, after learning the game at Warrington, was hungry for honours and pleased that his professional career seemed to be taking off. Wigan seemed to have done another sharp piece of business in the transfer market, even if they were still faced with the prospect of getting to Wembley without Ferguson or Ford.

Without doubt the toughest tie in the 1985 cup run was the quarter-final at Bradford. Odsal was in the throes of redevelopment and 15,000 people turned up to watch the game at what was basically a building site, making the atmosphere at the north of England's foremost hole in the ground even more surreal than usual. The game would simply not have taken place under present-day safety regulations, but danger and discomfort were a long way from most spectators' minds as one of the closest and most nerve-wracking cup ties imaginable got under way. The action was almost unbearably exciting. Every time Hanley got the ball, Wigan were in danger of conceding yards if not points; therefore Bradford's understandable plan was to give him the ball at every possible opportunity. This was the season in which Hanley became the first player for 23 years to score 50 tries in a season, and it was easy to see how. He was not a natural stand-off, but in that position he saw a great deal of the ball, and he certainly knew how to run with it. Even with half the Wigan side hanging off him Hanley still seemed capable of scoring or setting up a try, and in a torrid, physical encounter fought out at close quarters like a boxing match, the Bradford man was more of a threat than Kenny. The contest bore no

resemblance to the open, running games Wigan had recently been dominating, and only an extraordinary degree of collective determination allowed the visitors to defend a one-point lead during a second half when Bradford threw everything at their line bar the bulldozers.

Wigan held on for a 7–6 win, a drop goal from Mike Ford providing the slender margin of victory, though there might have been a little more daylight between the teams had Gill been able to run to the posts after crossing in the corner for his try. Instead, he was mobbed by his own fans as soon as he crossed the whitewash, resulting in a kick at goal from a wider angle than it need have been, resulting in no extra points. This sounds ludicrous, and indeed it was, but so was the situation which had several rows of Wigan supporters watching the game from portable seats just behind the Bradford in-goal area. It was that kind of day. But Wigan were through to the semi-final.

The winning run finally came to an end after 11 consecutive victories when Wigan were held to a draw in their league match at Halifax. Coming only three days after the monumental effort at Odsal, avoiding defeat at the hands of the enterprising Halifax team stuffed full of Australians was quite an achievement. But Wigan knew they would soon have to make a choice. The run of eight league wins Kenny had inspired had taken them briefly to the top of the table following their second victory of the season over Hull KR, but if they continued to pursue success on two fronts there was a good chance of falling between both stools. The double of Challenge Cup and first division championship had never been achieved in the modern era, and was not considered a serious proposition. Rugby league seasons almost always ended with a backlog of fixtures to play off in a hurry – this one, because of the severe winter, certainly would – and teams who only had their final league position to play for usually had to raid their reserves to make up the numbers around the end of March and the beginning of April. Anyone still in the Cup, with a realistic chance at Wembley, would do so as a matter of prudence. No team was far enough ahead of the first division pack, in terms of quality or quantity of players, to jeopardise success in one competition by going flat out in another. Back in those innocent, amateur days of 1985, clubs were content to share the trophies around. One major was enough. Anyone parading the championship trophy or the Challenge Cup from an open-topped bus in April or May was universally considered to have had a successful team.

So when Wigan met Hull KR in the Challenge Cup semi-final at Elland Road on 23 March, more was resolved than the identity of the Wembley finalists. Rovers, like Wigan, were still in with a theoretical chance of a double. Once knocked out of the Cup, beaten by 18 points to 11 and by Wigan's overpowering determination to return to Wembley, they knuckled down to the league and secured a second successive champion-ship. Had the Elland Road result been reversed, Wigan might well have managed the same feat, though it is perhaps more likely they would have suffered a damaging hangover. Rovers were not the first team to discover that Wigan had set their heart on Wembley this season, although the sight of West striding massively out of defence in the second half to beat Fairbairn on a 50-yard run and send Stephenson cantering to the posts for a try that signalled their quick return, was perhaps the most remarkable evidence yet that the previous year's losers were out to make amends.

As in the quarter-final, Ferguson was absent and Kenny unusually subdued, conspicuous mostly for his defensive work, but Wigan no longer looked for individual inspiration, they seemed to have become a team of winners. Juliff, a surprise choice on the right wing, opened Wigan's account with a try in the right corner, brilliantly engineered by Wane at the expense of a knee injury which ruled the unlucky young prop out of the final. Wane could only watch as Miller and Clark scored tries which kept Rovers in with a

shout at 12–11, before Man of the Match West made his second telling intervention. The Wigan captain's earlier barnstorming run had produced a try at a crucial time, regaining the lead for Wigan just when Rovers seemed poised to forge ahead; now West used his height to advantage, popping a basketball pass out of a tackle for Gill to score. There were other heroes, too. Mike Ford played well enough to secure a Wembley shirt at the end of the first season. Courtney clung on to Broadhurst for a solid 80 minutes. Perhaps more important still, Scott clung on to the waistband of Clark's shorts for a couple of seconds, long enough to prevent a certain score which could have dramatically affected the outcome.

Wigan were at Wembley again, and the club lost no time in confirming that Ferguson would be flown back for the final. Video compilations of his 22 tries in 24 games were already being eagerly devoured by fans with withdrawal symptoms, and now there was to be one last appearance in the flesh. At Wembley. With Brett Kenny. It was like a dream.

Suddenly, so was the league. A bad one. Wigan managed to beat Oldham at home in the first match after qualifying for the Cup final, only to be confronted by a suicidal programme of three away matches in Yorkshire in the space of five days. They lost to Hull, Leeds and Bradford in rapid succession, the margins of defeat increasing as the team became progressively weaker and visions of the title receded from view. Wigan lost at home to St Helens, too, and although the Wembley-bound contingent in a huge Good Friday crowd of 19,768 were able to smile indulgently about that, there was no denying that the next Central Park defeat, at the hands of already-relegated Hunslet, was worrying. But that was the only slip in Wigan's last half dozen league games. The remaining five were all won, helping Wigan finish third, five points behind Hull KR and two behind St Helens.

All that remained, prior to setting off for Wembley, was an awkward and unwanted

Premiership first-round play-off against Hull at Central Park. By virtue of victory in an epic semi-final against Castleford which went to a replay, Hull were the team awaiting Wigan at Wembley a week later. Wigan won the dress rehearsal 46–12, with Phil Ford, who would not be playing at Wembley, weighing in with four tries. The victory meant little. Very few of the team Hull turned up with would be playing at Wembley either.

The final, on 4 May, turned out to be rugby league's 50th at Wembley, an occasion marked by a parade of representatives from each previous showpiece. Henry Coates represented Dewsbury, beaten by Wigan in the first-ever Wembley final in 1929, while from 1984, Joe Lydon, as the previous year's Lance Todd Trophy winner, represented Widnes. Jack Hilton nipped down from his seat in the directors' box (Lindsay, the Wigan vice-chairman, led out the players that year under an agreement between the four directors to rotate the honour between them) to appear as Wigan's representative from the 1951 final, and Joe Egan and Eric Ashton (1948 and 1959) were also in the procession, but predictably the biggest cheer was reserved for Billy Boston (1966). Equally predictably, the loudest boos, in fact pretty much the only boos, were for Alex Murphy (1971). Murphy had at least seen this coming. 'I'm really looking forward to going out there,' he said with heavy sarcasm in the media suite before the game. 'There will be 50,000 Wiganers booing me, 40,000 Hull speccies booing me, and the other 10,000 will probably feel like joining in as well.'

The reason Murphy was in the media suite was because, although back as coach at Leigh for an improbable third spell, he was deriving most of his income at the time from his secondary stock in trade, the gift of the gab. An outspoken columnist in several news-papers, Murphy was on duty at Wembley as match summariser alongside Ray French in the BBC's television commentary box. The deficiencies of the BBC's rugby league coverage have been well documented over the years, and this is not the appropriate place

to enter the boring debate about comedy northerners which began with Eddie Waring, so suffice to say that the French–Murphy partnership, a double dose of dreary St Helens accents and abysmal syntax, is never going to be remembered as a high spot of the corporation's sporting output. Those Wigan supporters who had left the video recorders running, however, returned home to find they had an extra treat in store. French had been his usual excitable self in a final which offered plenty to get excited about, but Murphy, a mixture of envy, resentment and palpable prejudice against Wigan in general and West in particular, had unintentionally provided a minor cult classic. In much the same way as schoolboys in the '70s could recite whole chunks of Monty Python dialogue parrot-fashion, so to speak, now Wiganers appreciated the irony of Murphy's idiotic non-sequiturs. The ripest lines, such as Ferguson having a bad leg, delivered with impeccable comic timing seconds before the winger scooted 50 yards for his second try, and West being so knackered he was taking five minutes to get up off the floor, were still enlivening social gatherings in the '90s.

A feature of the final not immediately obvious to the 97,801 present at Wembley, but picked up by the television cameras and commentary team, was the extraordinarily relaxed demeanour of Kenny prior to kick-off. Hands stuffed deep into the pockets of his tracksuit top, his right one offered in only the most perfunctory way as the teams were introduced to duty dignitary the Earl of Derby, Kenny appeared positively casual about the Wembley experience. Seemingly in a private trance, as if listening to some invisible Walkman, Kenny was either deeply unaffected by the pre-match tension and the ritual preliminaries, or determinedly switched-off. The television commentators made a half-hearted attempt to build his apparent indifference to shaking the Earl of Derby's hand into a diplomatic incident, but once the match was under way, it was obvious Kenny was very switched on indeed. He was up against his Parramatta and

Kangaroo half-back Peter Sterling in the 50th final. The fact that Hull had reached Wembley under the brilliant scrum-half's guidance was no accident. Australian Test stars like Meninga at St Helens and, to a lesser extent, Grothe at Leeds, had been value for money signings and box office successes, but the two clubs at Wembley were the ones who had recognised that to galvanise the whole team, rather than just add glamour at centre or wing, the pivotal roles of stand-off and scrum-half are the most important. At scrum-half, Sterling was able to spread his influence and add confidence to the whole Hull operation, a service similar to the one Kenny had provided for Wigan. There was no doubt where the contest within the contest would take place. Team-mates in Australia and friends off the pitch in England, both Sterling and Kenny had come for a Challenge Cup winner's medal, the final being correctly perceived Down Under as the biggest occasion the British game has to offer. Only one could take it home. Something had to give, and it was Sterling who was in tears at the end of the game, after a performance which would have won him the Lance Todd Trophy in any other year. Sterling was tireless, courageous, inspirational and ingenious, but his friend Kenny was simply transcendent. People have argued for years that even though Hull lost the game, Sterling should have been the Man of the Match, and the prosaic truth is that Kenny probably only shaded him because the votes were counted before the end of the game, with Wigan still in a strong position. But this does not mean the members of the Rugby League Writers' Association necessarily made the wrong decision. Take out the sympathy for Sterling and the admiration for the late Hull fightback he orchestrated, and you still have a flawless performance from Kenny. No one has ever come closer to perfection in a Wembley final. Ferguson's blessed opportunism may have been just as vital to Wigan's cause, but Kenny never put a foot wrong all afternoon, playing the game of his life to inspire a famous victory. And if that's not worth the Lance Todd Trophy, what is?

For the record, the teams that day were as follows. Hull: Kemble; James, Evans, Leuluai, O'Hara (Schofield 58); Ah Kuoi, Sterling; Crooks (capt.), Patrick, Puckering (Divorty 58), Muggleton, Rose, Norton. Wigan: Edwards; Ferguson, Stephenson, Donlan, Gill; Kenny, Ford; Courtney, Kiss, Case (Campbell 55), West, Dunn, Potter. Sub: (not used) Du Toit. Hull coach Arthur Bunting left promising youngsters Schofield and Divorty on the bench, only introducing them after Wigan had taken a 28–12 lead. Were he to have his time again he might consider having Schofield on from the start, if only for his goalkicking. Both teams scored five tries, but whereas Gill and Stephenson kicked four goals between them, in the continued absence of Whitfield, Crooks only managed two for Hull, hence the four-point margin which gave Wigan a 28–24 victory. Clarke and McInnes had opted for two forwards on the bench, preferring Du Toit's versatility and short burst explosiveness to the claims of the unlucky Juliff and Scott, though in the event the big South African was himself unlucky. Had Wigan continued to cruise to victory, Du Toit would undoubtedly have been given a run at the end, but Hull's incredible fightback (they scored 12 points in the last 16 minutes and would have been likely winners had the game lasted five minutes longer) left no room for risk-taking.

Enough of these preliminaries. Here is the final, as reported by this correspondent for *The Wigan Evening Post* in 1985. Readers who do not want such minute detail, more than a decade after the event, may skip it if they wish. I do not propose to relive all Wigan's finals in this book, indeed the very frequency of them in the '80s and '90s means concision will be necessary to avoid repetition, but this was the launchpad for all the club's later success, and is still regarded as the best ever Wembley. You might detect a slight Wigan bias in what follows, for which I make no apologies. There is nothing in the rules about local journalists having to be impartial.

If there was any such thing as a neutral spectator in the record crowd at Wembley, he probably knew straightaway he was witnessing the greatest Challenge Cup final of all time.

For the rest of us, the realisation took a little longer. You would think that when he has just seen ten of the most exciting tries ever scored at Wembley compressed into a throbbing 80 minutes, plus a dazzling display of half-back artistry which lived up to all its pre-match billing, the average rugby fan would go home happy. But the average fan at Wembley was wearing either black and white or cherry and white like the players, and was put through an identical gamut of emotions.

For Wigan there was initial worry, then exhilaration, followed by tension and finally relief. Hull went through optimism, extreme pessimism, then hope and ultimately frustration. Wigan's victory would have been the greater had they managed a final flourish, but to deny Hull their magnificent fightback would have detracted from the greatness of the final. The losers may be rueing their missed goal chances, but Wigan should not be denied credit for forcing their opponents out wide. Hull's conversion attempts were invariably from more difficult positions from Wigan's, and Wigan never once opened up down the middle the way Hull did when Edwards raced to the posts.

Despite the final quarter, few could seriously argue that Wigan were not worth their win, just as few could object to Kenny receiving the Lance Todd Trophy ahead of his great rival Sterling. The brave little terrier snapping defiance and single-handedly organising the Hull fightback might have won over the emotional voters, but Kenny made a coolly clinical appeal to the intellect. The Wigan stand-off scored one superb try and was crucially involved in three others. The only Wigan try which could not be traced back to Kenny's hand was the last, when Ferguson seized on a grounded pass, ironically from Sterling.

Kenny also got through a prodigious tackling stint, popped up under his own posts to collect the occasional Sterling bomb, and never wasted an ounce of effort in steering Wigan to success. But it was Sterling who struck first, as Wigan spent the first quarter struggling to break out of their half. After Crooks's early penalty goal, it was Sterling who ran purposefully across the field, stood up in a tackle that Donlan will probably prefer to forget, and squeezed the ball out to his brother-in-law, Muggleton. A quick pass sent Kemble racing for the right corner, and the full-back cleverly committed Edwards and Gill before a reverse ball left James an easy opportunity.

Crooks missed the goal, but Wigan did not look confident at this stage. Stephenson had unwittingly started the Hull attack by failing to find touch with a penalty, and memories of last year's final began to stir. They needn't have. Ferguson touched the ball for the first time in the 15th minute, but accomplished enough with it to suggest more and better things lay in store. Ferguson breezed past two defenders before Kemble felled him with a textbook tackle, an exercise the Hull full-back shortly had to repeat to stop Gill on the opposite wing. If the match had ended there and then, Kemble and his compatriot O'Hara would have emerged with reputations intact, but the next 40 minutes or so were unkind to the Kiwi duo, from the moment Kenny surprised the Hull defence by working the ball out of a tackle near the line. Potter, the equally surprised recipient, threw a high, wide pass out to Ferguson's wing where, despite having to rock back on his heels to pull the ball from the air, the Australian managed to beat O'Hara from a standing start. In a good position near the touch-line the Hull man appeared to have all the angles covered, but Ferguson first caught him flat-footed with one of his bewildering shimmies, and then went round him as though he had half the pitch in which to work, even managing to bring the ball in towards the posts through Muggleton's desperate challenge over the line. Gill kicked a still tricky conversion with his customary nonchalance, and Wigan were back level. Psychologically, perhaps, they were in front, having coped with Hull's initial thrust and proved capable of scoring from far more limited opportunities.

Ferguson's score acted like a shot of adrenalin on Wigan, both relaxing the side and reminding them of the heights they could reach. Stephenson missed a penalty and the chance to put Wigan in front for the first time, but Kenny kept up the pace with a devastating try just before the half hour. Sweeping onto a neat ball from the tireless Ford, completing a runaround move with West, Kenny surged through a gap, looked for support and at the same time saw a route open up to the line. Accelerating almost imperceptibly with little apparent effort, Kenny took on Kemble on the outside and won hands down, completing a curving 50-yard run with a try in the left corner.

Stephenson converted this time, though a Crooks penalty pulled two points back for Hull, but leading 12–8, Wigan were not content to play out the rest of the half. Their third try, in the 39th minute, was the boldest of the lot, a direct result of their confident cross-field style. West, on the right, was in at the start of a passing move deep in Wigan territory which saw the ball riskily transferred across the face of goal to the opposite wing, where Kenny picked out Stephenson with a stunning 30-yard pass. Stephenson did his centre's work well, aided by a somewhat over-eager challenge from James, giving Gill a clear run up the left touch-line with Sterling flapping ineffectively at his ankles. Once more it was down to Kemble to halt a Wigan player in full stride, and the Hull man underestimated Gill's pace over 70 yards. Already out of position,

Kemble could not make up enough ground to mount an effective check, and a lot more than a flailing pair of arms was required to stop Gill at his most determined. The most thrilling of touchdowns having been concluded with one of the most radiant grins ever likely to grace Wembley, Wigan turned round 16–8 ahead, Stephenson having missed the goal.

No matter, three minutes into the second half the Wigan fans were sent into rapture by what looked like a game-clinching try from Edwards. James misfielded a kick, Ford and Kenny worked a classic dummy from the set piece and the stand-off set off for the posts. This time Kemble was in position, but Edwards had raced alongside in support, Kenny's pass was timed to perfection, and the youngster savoured a moment he will enjoy for the rest of his life. Gill added the goal, but if Wigan were thinking of a landslide, Sterling had other ideas. Breaking for the right-hand corner leaving Kenny in his wake, Sterling was covered by Edwards on the line, but just before the tackle the scrum-half offloaded cleverly for Evans to ground the ball. Crooks missed the kick, but Hull had made their point. They were not about to take anything lying down. The Hull comeback can be traced to that moment of defiance which dented Wigan's air of invincibility, but the crucial moment in the game arrived in the 51st minute, with Wigan leading 22–12. Hull were on the attack when the hapless O'Hara dropped the ball on the left wing, though had Sterling's pass been up to his usual standards of precision the winger might not have made such a complete mess of accepting it. As it was, O'Hara and Muggleton scrambled in vain for the loose ball on the touch-line, right under the noses of the coaches on the bench. They scrambled in vain because the ball wasn't there any more. Ferguson, swooping from nowhere like some hungry bird of prey, had snatched it as soon as it bounced. Most ordinary wingers would have settled for just grabbing possession, but of course the whole point about Ferguson is that he is no ordinary winger. Gathering the ball without breaking his stride, Ferguson was speeding down the touch-line before O'Hara and Muggleton fully appreciated the danger as, too late, Kemble wearily realised that here was another two-horse race in which he was destined to finish second.

Ferguson beat the full-back so comprehensively that he was able to leave Gill another straightforward conversion from by the posts, a point missed by those claiming the final was lost for want of a goalkicker. Campbell took over from Case at this stage, though a more effective substitution was Hull's introduction of Divorty and Schofield for Puckering and O'Hara. Instantly Norton figured more prominently in the game. The wily loose-forward had been contained with difficulty for an hour, but now began to run the show. A fine tackle from Gill was needed to halt James in the 62nd minute, but three minutes later Wigan buckled under the pressure. Norton and Rose were involved in the move which put Leuluai in for a walkover try, though there was some justification for Wigan's claim that Divorty had 'crossed' and effectively shielded his colleague. Crooks missed the conversion, and Hull's success ratio failed to improve in the 74th minute when Schofield had a go, after Sterling's precision pass had enabled Divorty to crash through Stephenson on the line. Hull had now come back to 28–20 down, and Wigan, desperate for a chance to slow the game down, were unable to gain possession in the closing stages. Restarting the game after Divorty's try, Wigan rather inadvisedly kicked off with a short hop to the wing, and Leuluai took a short ball from Ah Kuoi to burst through Potter and Dunn at an alarming speed. Edwards had no chance once the famous

sidestep came into operation, and Leuluai scored without a Wigan hand being laid upon him, though Ford, capping a notable performance which was not as far behind Sterling's as the disproportionate head-lines suggested, chased the Hull centre out towards the touch-line to prevent an easy goal from under the posts. Schofield should still have kicked the goal, but didn't, and Wigan made the most of this small reprieve to regain the ball, their composure, and eventually the Silk Cut Challenge Cup. Those final few minutes, Kenny later admitted, were the longest of his life. Everyone in cherry and white knew exactly what he meant.

In the Wembley tearoom afterwards, where a year earlier Wigan players had slumped disconsolate and weary, all was now animated chatter. 'A brilliant advert for the club and the game,' Alan McInnes thought. 'All credit to Hull for coming back, but I thought we deserved to win. Some of our tries were sheer magic.' His chairman agreed. 'You couldn't ask for a better day,' Jack Hilton said. 'None of the players from the previous Wembleys could remember a more exciting final.' Neither could his vice-chairman. 'Everything was fabulous, it's been a marvellous day for Wigan rugby,' said a beaming Lindsay, adding, 'John Ferguson was out of this world. I wouldn't begrudge flying him over if it had cost ten times as much.'

Ferguson himself was all modesty. 'I still can't believe my luck,' the winger said after the game. 'Playing out there was a great privilege, winning was even better. To score two tries was just the icing on the cake. I'm seriously thinking of retiring now, I couldn't go out on a higher note.' Needless to say Fergie didn't retire, but in the Wembley dressing-room in 1985 he had no way of knowing a couple of Grand Finals in Canberra colours and long overdue inter-national recognition lay in store on his return to Australia. One player who did retire shortly after the 1985 final, not through choice but through an unfortunate arm injury, was prop Neil Courtney. 'I have to thank Wigan for giving me the chance to do what every rugby player dreams of doing. I thought my chance had gone.'

Kenny, as might be expected, was cool and almost calculating in victory. 'I thoroughly enjoyed the game, it must have been a terrific spectacle. I've got what I came for now, and it

quite what the future had in store, was wide-eyed in teenage wonder. 'Scoring that try was something I'll never forget – I felt on top of the world.' So did Gill. 'Brilliant, man, especially scoring my try. I just flicked a switch and went into overdrive, and Gary Kemble was nowhere . . .'

Wigan's atonement for 1984, and for all the barren years since 1965 for that matter, was

Homecoming 1985. Wigan's first Challenge Cup for 20 years, and it's safe to say the fans are pleased.

feels great. I was a bit worried in the last ten minutes though, they were the longest of my life.' Sterling was generous in defeat. 'I was bitterly disappointed when the final hooter went, but I suppose we made mistakes early on. You have to hand it to Brett Kenny though – he's the best stand-off in the world.' Brian Dunn, transferred to Rochdale shortly after his brief moment of glory, struck a traditional note. 'Everything happened so fast, it was just a blur. Even walking up the steps was all over before it sank in.' Everyone says that about Wembley finals, but this one really had been fast. 'It was incredible, both teams were playing 100 mph rugby all the time,' David Stephenson said. 'I remember thinking, after about 20 minutes, that this pace could not possibly continue, but it did. And I don't even want to think about those last ten minutes.' Edwards, who like Ferguson did not realise

complete. Having kept their promise and returned to Wembley, they had graced the stadium with a wonderful performance and surpassed even their own expectations. We should really leave them there, in the rosy glow of a job well done, with Ferguson flying back to Sydney and forgetting to pick up his winning pay packet in all the excitement, and Ford and Gill securing short-term contracts in Australia on the strength of their cup final performances, but unfortunately this was not a Hollywood production but a rugby league one, and the season did not end at Wembley. The Premiership final at Elland Road was due the following Saturday, and Wigan had the small matter of a semi-final at St Helens to fit in first.

Preposterously, the league originally scheduled the game for Monday, just two days after Wembley. On appeal they relented, and granted an extension until Tuesday evening, a massive three days after Wembley. Wigan had got what they wanted out of the season and were in no mood for Premiership trifles – only teams who have failed to win anything else all season could get worked up about a spurious competition expressly designed to keep the turnstiles clicking and the cash coming in as long as possible – but if the opponents were St Helens there was pride at stake and an obligation to perform. It was a genuine dilemma. In the event Wigan sort of half-played at Knowsley Road. Which is to say, they made a good start, competed for about an hour, then fell away in the final quarter to leave Saints with a 37–14 scoreline which flattered them. In the circumstances this was understandable, acceptable even, but what was problematic was that some players appeared more 'tired' than others. Around half the side seemed keen to get into another final, while the other half was looking no further than the full-time bath. Supporters were left with the nagging feeling that had Wigan agreed on a common policy they could have trounced Saints and prevented Meninga having another field day against Hull KR in the final. Phil Ford, who had not been involved at Wembley, was desperately trying to make up for the disappointment by finishing the season on a high, and one could sense his frustration when colleagues failed to respond to his exhortations. Kenny, in particular, appeared to have his thoughts fixed on the first flight home, and it was no great surprise when

he subsequently admitted, in an interview in Australia, to not trying terribly hard. Allegations that Kenny actually 'threw' his final match to hasten his return home came to cloud the stand-off's splendid season in England, though there is no evidence to suggest that anything so dishonourable took place. Yet in a way, Kenny was dishonest. Wigan supporters knew what he was capable of, even when tired, and because the whole team now revolved around him, his non-participation was bound to have a telling effect. It might have been better to skip the game and give someone more enthusiastic a chance, though such a course would hardly have made Kenny any more popular. It was a no-win situation, and Clarke, for one, sympathised with his player. 'A lot of the things said about Brett's performance in that game were unfounded, and many were unfair,' Clarke said. 'I think it was obvious to everyone that his heart wasn't in it, but to look at the situation from his perspective, he had just won at Wembley, an occasion he compared with the Australian Grand Final. And in Australia, the season ends with the Grand Final. The two best teams fight out the finale, then everyone has a good drink and breaks up for the summer. There aren't even any midweek games in Australia, let alone Tuesday night fixtures in lesser competitions coming just three days after the major showpiece, so I think the whole situation was foreign to him. He couldn't understand the point of it and, to be honest, neither could I.'

CHAPTER SIX

Getting Ahead

'I was amazed when the club said they weren't satisfied. It had seemed like a
marvellous season to me.'

The difficulty for Wigan now was following such a brilliant season. Almost anything would be an anticlimax, but immediately after the excitement of Wembley had died down, the club did something unusual in rugby league at the time, something which would have a far-reaching effect on the game as a whole.

What Wigan did, in a nutshell, was decide they wanted more. This may not seem such a revolutionary policy statement, but the prevailing attitude at the time was one of resting on laurels and savouring success. Winning the Challenge Cup, especially in such style, would have kept most clubs going for a couple of seasons. After such a long time in the wilderness, Wigan had every right to accept all the congratulations and sit back. It had taken five years, but Wigan's team was now the envy of the league, and even if Kenny and Ferguson had to be replaced there was still unmistakable quality running right through the side. West had proved himself an admirable pack leader and superb captain. Edwards, still in his teens, was already picking up international honours and looking worth every penny of Wigan's investment. In Gill and Phil Ford, Wigan had a pair of wingers as good as any in the domestic game, and exciting young half-backs in Mike Ford and Holden. Hampson, that most instinctively talented of full-backs, was back for another full season after missing virtually the whole of the last one, and Case and Potter had stiffened the pack performance immeasurably. What the last two prodigious workers lacked in explosiveness and panache, Du Toit seemed set to provide. The South African had found a berth in the second row, and for a short while anyway looked capable of rampaging through any English defence. Wigan might have needed one or two new signings, just to keep the supporters happy and provide healthy competition for first-team places, but they already had a side which appeared capable of putting more trophies on the Central Park sideboard.

That is not how the directors saw it. As soon as he could, Lindsay flew out to spend the close season in Australia, to find a couple of replacements for Kenny and Ferguson of similar, if not quite equal, calibre. 'It was important to keep the momentum going,' he said. 'Brett and John hadn't just been successful on the playing front, they had been immensely popular with supporters. Wigan fans liked the idea of having the best Australia could offer playing in cherry and white, and so did we. It was perhaps a short-term approach to team-building, but it was the right thing to do at the time. Our game had been starved of excitement, and these guys could provide it. We knew if we found players worth watching, Wigan supporters would come and watch them, so that's what we did. We went for the best.'

During the time Lindsay was away, Clarke took to referring to him as 'Moses'. 'Because,' the coach explained, 'he's gone to the promised land.' After the previous season there was no reason to doubt Lindsay's eye for a player or his ability to persuade them to come to Wigan, so Clarke and McInnes at Central Park were quite happy to wait and see what Moses provided. Lindsay's mission was made easier by the resplendent Wembley success which was still fresh in the memory. Not a great deal of English rugby league is watched in Australia, but Wembley is an annual ritual. It had been Wigan's good fortune to win the Challenge Cup final in the first full season after the lifting of the international transfer ban, and the presence of a high-profile Australian like Kenny in the

Ellery Hanley, new for 1986.

team, and the impression made by several of his team-mates in cherry and white, had boosted the club's stock Down Under. Most Aussies were keen to do what Kenny had done, and spend a season in the dreary old place in return for a winner's medal at Wembley, and Wigan were seen as a good bet for a ticket to the twin towers.

Lindsay went to talk to Gene Miles (again) and Wally Lewis, but returned home with Greg Dowling, a Test prop forward from Queensland who had gained brief notoriety (and no little admiration) during summer by

having a toe-to-toe fight with New Zealand hard man Kevin Tamati; and Steve Ella, a delightfully nimble half-back who could play almost anywhere in the back line and whose international appearances for Australia had been limited only by the excellence of Kenny, Lewis and the rest ahead of him. Hull and Oldham were also in the chase for Ella, Roger Millward had gone to Australia to sign Dowling for Hull KR, but Lindsay was able to swing both deals for Wigan. There were more Australians coming over to England than ever before for the 1985–86 season, but Wigan were content in the knowledge they had two of the best. The value of quality, rather than quantity, would soon be underlined by the inevitable quota restrictions on overseas players, imposed when it became clear that some clubs would happily fill their team with Australians if it meant short-term success.

But Dowling and Ella were not the only players Lindsay signed in Australia. While in Sydney the Wigan vice-chairman sought out Oldham's Andy Goodway, then playing a summer stint for Manly, and booked him for a switch to Central Park on his return. Goodway, playing at prop forward or second row and eventually earning the captaincy, had been one of the very few successes on Great Britain's ill-fated 1984 tour, hence the offer from Bobby Fulton to return the following summer. Goodway had a success-ful season at Manly too, he was clearly a player destined for the top, but potential buyers found two things off-putting. One was the price. Oldham valued him at £100,000 and were not even considering anything under £50,000. The second was Goodway's bad-boy reputation. A headstrong personality, rather than a conventionally suspect temperament, had marked out Goodway as difficult to handle. Apparently happy to exasperate coaches and colleagues alike, Goodway rejoiced in the nickname BA (for Bad Attitude) and was generally thought to be trouble. The combination was enough to put off most clubs, but not Wigan. Lindsay liked what he saw, was pleased to report back from Australia that Goodway was not in fact a child-eating monster with two heads, and recommended that Wigan pay Oldham £65,000, a then record fee for a forward, for his services. It turned out to be one of the best investments Wigan ever made, especially as they recouped money from Leeds in 1992 after seven years of peerless service, and it was one of the easiest. With rival clubs not exactly beating a path to Oldham's door, Lindsay found the player himself positively anxious to sign.

'I remember Maurice pulling me at the Sydney Cricket Ground,' Goodway said. 'He introduced himself and asked me if I was enjoying myself in Australia, then asked me if I wanted to play for Wigan and whether this amount of money would be all right. It was certainly all right by me. I just said yes three times in quick succession, and that was it. I went back to playing for Manly, I never heard anything else about the deal until I got home. I imagined there were still things to sort out, or that Wigan had changed their mind, but Oldham told me I had been sold, and that was it. The move came just at the right time for me. I was 24, and looking for something bigger. I had enjoyed playing for Oldham, I wouldn't have had a problem staying there longer, but I was ready for something to take me further on. It wasn't a question of money, though obviously that came into it. I almost decided to stay at Manly because I was so impressed with what they had to offer. When I went out I didn't know whether I would be good enough for them, but it went well and naturally I got to enjoy playing at that level. When you see what a big, ambitious club can do for you it really opens your eyes. There's no going back after that.'

Lindsay persuaded Goodway that Wigan was the big, ambitious club he was looking for, and on arrival at Central Park he was not disappointed. 'The scale of everything was impressive after Oldham. The size of the ground, the support for the club, the position the club enjoyed in the town. I was looking for something a bit more professional, and that's what I found. The whole approach was different, there was a relaxed but serious attitude to training and playing. Wigan appeared to have thought everything through. It was just more professional, in a word.'

Professional in comparison to Oldham perhaps, though Wigan of the mid-'80s would strike today's highly paid Central Park professionals as pleasantly amateurish. This was the season, nevertheless, when Wigan

Andy Goodway, another of Wigan's 1986 acquisitions, takes up the ball.

put most distance between themselves and the rest of the league, and professionalism had a lot to do with it. A brief digression here about professionalism and amateurism, two words which both rugby codes have wrestled with for over a century without ever appearing to fully understand. A professional, in sport as in any walk of life, is not just someone who receives payment for an activity, but someone who receives sufficient payment to make that activity his primary source of income. A professional footballer, for instance, pays his mortgage and feeds his family from the wages his club pays him. Football is his core activity. A non-league player, on the other hand, might play to a high standard every Saturday afternoon and even receive payment for his endeavours on the pitch, but if he holds down a job as a fireman or estate agent to meet his household expenses, that is his true profession and he is only an amateur footballer. Amateur is derived from the Latin verb *amare* – to love – and literally means to do something for love, not money. The fact that money may occasionally be involved is neither here nor there. Semi-professionalism is a contradiction

Greg Dowling in action during his single season at Central Park.

in terms. It is possible to be paid for more than one thing, but you can only have one main income. In this sense, for almost the last 100 years, rugby league and rugby union have both been amateur pastimes. Attitudes to money have defined the codes down the years, but the amount of money in either, until very recently, was not enough to make giving up the day job advisable.

Wigan, taking their lead from Australia as usual, decided to change all that. In point of fact the world's first rugby professionals were probably in the union code, either in France or New Zealand, Italy or South Africa, all countries with a high regard for the 15-a-side game and a suspiciously high proportion of

prosperous individuals with no other visible means of support. But the first true professionals, in terms of both paying tax and of spending the whole week in structured preparation for the game at the weekend, were in Australian rugby league in the early '80s. And the first one in England was Andy Goodway.

Wigan had quickly worked out that Australians were not from another planet, as Alex Murphy had rather feebly suggested when confronted with the excellence of the 1982 Kangaroos, and derived their superior physiques and fitness levels from long hours in the gym. There was actually a little more to it than that. There was skills work at training, diet, rest, self-assessment and programmes for putting in extra conditioning work at home, but the essential point was that the Australians were self-made athletes. Given the time and the right training regime, you could improve on what God had given you. The more time you put in, the bigger and the better you could get. It followed that clubs could get ahead by paying their players enough to go full time. It also followed that if the Australians could make it work, so could Wigan.

The full implications of Wigan going full time were not immediately apparent, least of all to Goodway. 'Maurice told me how much money I was going to get, and I just said yes, that will do nicely,' Goodway said. 'It was much more than I had been on at Oldham, and it struck me straightaway that I could now afford not to do anything else, but I wasn't quite ready to be a full-time rugby player. That seemed too big a leap, I couldn't imagine what I would do with all the spare time, so I got the club to fix me up with a little job as a greenkeeper at a local golf course. I didn't really do much work there, of course, I spent most of my time lazing about and playing golf, but it meant I could do as much training as I wanted and be available whenever the club wanted to put on a special session. There was no need to be full time when I first went to Wigan, we still basically trained two nights a week like everyone else, but I started to do more on my own, then the club began calling meetings during the daytime, and almost without realising it I became a full-time player.'

Most of Goodway's contemporaries at Central Park could tell similar stories. Because they mostly tended to be young, like Edwards, who was still living with his parents, or unemployed, or engaged in casual work of the type that could easily be fitted around rugby commitments, few players even noticed the shift of emphasis from part time to full time. One who did was Stephenson, who happened to be pursuing a career in computer accounts for an insurance company which he had no intention of sacrificing, but initially there was no urgency. Wigan were prepared to be flexible. Stephenson continued to work shifts, Case carried on with his bricklaying and Hampson still made his rounds as a drayman. Wigan's generous wage levels drew the odd comment from outside the club, but no more than that. The general feeling in the game was that if Wigan wanted to pay over the odds it was their own business. So it was, but Wigan hadn't finished yet. Before the season was a month old Wigan added something even more astounding than the Challenge Cup, two Australian Test players, the captain of Great Britain and the country's first professional pay scale to their portfolio. In September 1985 Wigan bought Ellery Hanley.

Even by that stage of the season it was clear Bradford's 55-try hero from the season before had set his face against playing any more rugby at Odsal. A dispute over money was apparently responsible for his non-appearance against Warrington on the opening day of the season, and as Bradford's league campaign continued without him, it became obvious that Hanley was hoping to be transfer-listed, in the safe knowledge that someone was keen to come along and buy him. It looked very much like Hanley had been tapped by another club, and Wigan were prime suspects. It wasn't just that they were out to sign Great Britain internationals and had been throwing their money around

of late, it was because they were the only club making bold signings. If Goodway had been considered risky by the rest of the league, Hanley was doubly so. Goodway's 'crimes' amounted to little more than making off with a Christmas turkey which Oldham were intending to raffle, and expressing discontent at Australian players coming to the club for a short holiday and earning more money than

Ellery Hanley leaves Brian Johnson floundering to score in the 1985 Lancashire Cup final against Warrington, to Nick Du Toit's evident amusement.

he did. The 24-year-old Hanley had done rather more than that, and had found himself on the wrong side of the law during his years as a teenage tearaway in Bradford.

Rugby league is at heart a conservative game, and Northern were not inundated with inquiries for a player with a police record, even if he had shot to prominence in 1984–85 by scoring 12 tries on the Great Britain tour and more tries in the league than in his three previous seasons put together. This was just as well, since Bradford had no intention of selling him. Hanley's first transfer request was turned down. The impasse between club and non-playing player only increased when in an attempt to explain to supporters how unreasonable Hanley was being, Bradford disclosed that he was asking for wages of

£1,000 a week to stay. This revealed the extent of Bradford's desperation. They did not see themselves as a small club or a selling club, but someone was offering Hanley wages they could not afford (not that Wigan, in 1985, were paying anyone £1,000 a week, nor did they intend to) and there was very little they could do about it. Contracts were brought in later in the decade as a direct result of Andy Gregory, in similar circumstances, threatening a restraint of trade action which would have blown the league's whole transfer system to pieces, but even freedom of contract, as has been seen in football as well as rugby, does not contain all the answers. Clubs are still liable to lose players who fancy going elsewhere for higher wages, unless they are prepared to lose money and the player's services just to prove a point. Once a player informs his club he no longer wishes to play for them and would be happier somewhere else, a fundamental contract has been broken which it is beyond legal paperwork to rescue.

So Bradford suffered and sulked, their fans felt betrayed and wrote agonised articles in *Open Rugby*, but in the end Hanley left Odsal and turned up at Central Park. Phil Ford and Steve Donlan, two players who had only arrived at Wigan the previous season, crossed the Pennines in the opposite direction as make-weights in a record £150,000 deal. Ford, who had missed out on the 1985 Cup final and was aware Wigan were on the verge of continued success, was disconsolate. Donlan, in his thirties and grateful that his brief sojourn at Wigan had enabled him to appear in a winning side at Wembley, was more philosophical. 'We professionals aren't in it for the romance,' he said. 'You sign yourself away when you take a club's money and from then on you can be bought and sold like a piece of meat. As a pro I'll try and do my best for Bradford, though I did not expect to be playing there. I can't really blame Wigan, they are doing what they think is best, and although I'm sorry to leave I'm still glad I came.'

Donlan was as good as his word, and gave Bradford reasonable service, as did Ford prior

to moving on again to Leeds. Both players were competent, journeymen professionals, although Donlan's age was against him and the £65,000 joint valuation of the pair was a shade optimistic. It was hard to conclude Bradford had got the best possible price for Hanley, particularly when they went out and splashed the £85,000 cash element of the transfer on Terry Holmes, an elderly and injury-prone Welsh scrum-half whose best days in rugby union were already behind him and who all too predictably broke down in

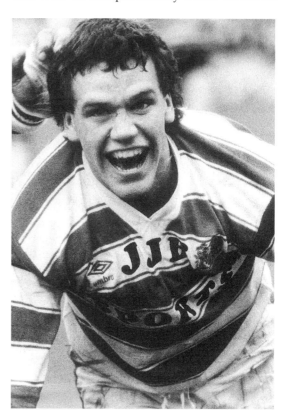

Mike Ford after scoring in the 1985 Lancashire Cup final.

rugby league. Bradford without Hanley soon subsided into a very ordinary side indeed. Wigan were about to become extraordinary, having just signed the most remarkable player of his era for a relative song. 'It was probably the best deal we ever struck,' Lindsay explained. '£150,000 was a lot of money for the time, it didn't exactly feel like picking up a bargain, but that is how it turned out. Ellery would have been good value at four times the price, I don't think Wigan would have been anywhere near as successful without him, and there is no doubt we got him cheaply.'

Lindsay denies making an illegal approach to the player or offering him financial inducements to leave Bradford, claiming Hanley had worked out his future for himself. 'The first time I ever met him was during the summer of 1985, on the Central Park car park,' he said. 'He was a great pal of Henderson's at the time and he had come over to meet him, or something. He was in Manchester quite a lot, it wasn't that unusual to see him in Lancashire. I knew he was in dispute with Bradford over money, that much had been in the papers, and I think he had just threatened not to start the season for them if they failed to improve their offer. I asked him how it was going, very politely, and he replied in the same calm tone that things were not going very well. He said he thought he would soon be looking for another club.

'That was it really, that was the only contact between us, but I thought it was safe to assume that Wigan would have as good a chance as anyone if it came to an auction. Ellery obviously wasn't the sort of player who would be looking for a move to another Yorkshire club just because it was close to home. So I immediately rang Bradford to register an interest, if and when he became available. I was put onto a chap called Barry Stamper, who was actually the head of SGS Glazing, the club sponsors. He told me Jack Bates, the chairman, was very keen to keep him, but the rest of the board were concerned that agreeing to the wages Ellery was asking would wreck the club's pay structure. I was quite hopeful after that, and two weeks later, as Barry Stamper had suggested they might be, Bradford were ready to talk. Barry Seabourne [Bradford's coach] told me he would want some of our players. I immediately suggested Phil Ford, because Colin Clarke had told me just a couple of days earlier that he wasn't happy with his attitude

and would be looking to replace him. To my surprise Seabourne accepted my suggestion, and then asked if he could have Donlan as well. I couldn't believe my luck. With all respect to Donlan, he was at an age where we would have been looking to trade him anyway. What we would have done if Bradford had asked for one of our best young players, like Shaun Edwards or Mike Ford, I honestly don't know. We were expecting some really hard bargaining, but in the end it was quite easy. They took two of our least indispensable players, and even agreed to take the £85,000 in instalments. The best thing about that was that when Bradford asked for the final one early, they knocked £2,500 off because we were able to help them out. So we actually got Ellery for £82,500, on the drip. It was a terrific piece of business.'

Andy Goodway, Nicky Kiss and Nick Du Toit celebrate the Lancashire Cup victory at Knowsley Road in 1985.

Wigan were helped by the fact that rival clubs were not queuing up for Hanley's services – 'A few clubs made noises,' Lindsay said, 'but when it came down to it most of them were as scared of his demands as Bradford had been' – and by the player's own inclination to move onwards and upwards. 'Ellery is not just a rugby league genius, he's a pretty smart thinker as well,' Lindsay said. 'He had worked out that to maximise his playing potential and earning capacity he would need to be with a more successful club, perhaps *the* most successful club, and he had looked around and recognised that Wigan were going to be the next shooting star. We were just at that immensely satisfying stage when leading players were beginning to want to join us. We didn't have to do a lot of persuading any more, and coming from where we had been, that was a really good feeling.'

Even in instalments, £82,500 was still a cash record in 1985, and a large outlay for a club which had already been spreading its money around. But Lindsay reckoned Hanley would pay for himself within a season. 'We had been quite successful, but I felt we were still quite a long way from saturation point,' he said. 'Our crowds only averaged about 8,000 or 9,000 a week, and I calculated Ellery in the team would put on at least 3,000 at the gate. We were charging people £3.50 to get in then, so I worked out we might take another £10,000 per game. With 13 league matches in a season Ellery would easily pay his own way, and any increased attendances in cup games would be pure profit.' So the deal was done, and Lindsay met with Hanley for the formality of thrashing out personal terms, only to discover that nothing involving this player was ever going to be a formality. 'Getting Bradford to sell him was a doddle compared to signing Ellery himself,' Lindsay explained. 'He turned up with his adviser, John Fitzpatrick, and over the course of several meetings gave me the most gruelling time I have ever experienced. Until I began negotiating with Ellery Hanley I knew nothing about life. I thought I was a tough cookie, and I had quite a bit of experience in signing players by this time, but I had never encountered anyone so resolutely aware of where he was going and what he wanted, and so absolutely determined not to back down. There were times when it actually got quite unpleasant, but when it was over and we had reached agreement, Ellery just shook hands

and we forgot all about it. That was how he was in everything. Even more so than his playing ability, which of course was immense, I would say what set Ellery apart was his fantastic commitment. He was incredibly focused on his rugby, never late for training, a dream to coach, the ultimate professional. He came to represent the spirit, the whole attitude of the club, and players and spectators responded to his presence. He could be difficult off the field, but on it he was without equal. We didn't realise all this at the time we bought him, of course, we just knew he was a good player and wanted him in our team, but we got a hell of a lot for our £82,500.'

By the time Hanley arrived, Wigan looked in need of such a superman. After opening the season with an easy win over Hull KR in the inaugural Charity Shield game on the Isle of Man, Wigan lost their first three league games in a row – the last defeat of the sequence, by an irony which did not escape Bradford supporters, coming at Odsal. Questions were asked in the Central Park boardroom. 'I'm not worried,' Clarke told his directors. 'I think someone should be,' Robinson told his coach. New boy Gary Henley-Smith and soon-to-depart Phil Ford both scored tries in the first victory of the season, over Fulham in the Lancashire Cup, on the eve of the Hanley signing. Henley-Smith was an unknown New Zealand sprinter who turned up at Wigan at just the right time for a game on the wing. Not only had the club just agreed to trade Phil Ford, they lost Gill with a broken leg in the opening league game against Castleford. The unlikely Henley-Smith never really made it, moving to Fulham before the end of the season and then disappearing back to obscurity, but like Phil Stott, another unknown winger who arrived at Central Park from the Vale of Lune RU club and ended up at Barrow, his handful of games helped Wigan out of a tight spot.

A crowd of 15,000 turned up for Hanley's début in the next league game, at home to Widnes, allowing Lindsay and his fellow-directors a self-satisfied smile. Spectators were for the most part enthralled by a terrific 32–10 victory, though Hanley's part in the proceedings was overshadowed by other events. Two Widnes players were unlucky enough to suffer broken legs in separate incidents. Steve O'Neill recovered from his and was back the following season. Less

bizarre Andy Kelly drop goal had consigned Wigan to a fourth league defeat at Hull KR, brought St Helens to Central Park. It also brought an 18,000 crowd to witness Ella's début, the Australian almost literally stepping off the plane and onto the substitutes' bench, and taking the field after

Elland Road revisited. Wigan win the 1986 John Player Special Trophy.

fortunate was Steve Rogers, the Kangaroo centre making his début for Widnes, whose illustrious career ended on 22 September in Wigan. Even when due allowance was made for these cruel blows to the visitors' strength and morale, all were agreed Wigan's new-look side looked exciting, but it was the pace and power of Goodway and Du Toit in the back row which caught the eye. Hanley made a quiet début at centre in a team which still featured Whitfield and Fairhurst.

Hanley's first try arrived in his next game, a not altogether convincing 22–20 defeat of Salford in the Lancashire Cup. New captain Goodway also scored as Wigan built an 18–2 interval lead, but Australian import Neil Baker inspired a Salford recovery which only just ran out of time. The semi-final, after a

an hour to score a try in a 30–2 victory. His compatriot, Dowling, scored another, but both Australians were upstaged by two brilliant scores from Edwards in the most convincing Wigan performance to date. Victory over Graham Lowe's New Zealand tourists four days later confirmed that Wigan were on the mend, and even the most hardened sceptic had to admit that a 34–8 thrashing of Warrington in the Lancashire Cup final was a satisfying achievement.

A match which kept a Knowsley Road crowd of almost 20,000 entertained offered a good opportunity to measure Wigan's progress over the past five years. The 1980 final, between the same clubs at the same ground, had attracted only 6,000 spectators and presented extremely poor fare, Warrington hardly needing to stir themselves to brush aside clueless, second division Wigan. Now here were Warrington with Andy Gregory in their side, and not only that but Les Boyd and Phil

winner's medal only in a contest for petulant behaviour, got himself dismissed before the end for stamping on Du Toit under his own posts. Since the more regularly offending

Début try for Joe Lydon, playing in the unusual position of stand-off, against Hull in 1986.

Blake, two of the most astute Australian signings any British club had ever made. They ended up on the wrong end of a record 34–8 scoreline, despite leading 8–2 at one stage, and the margin of victory would have been more emphatic still had not Stephenson missed five goals and Goodway and Hanley scorned inviting try opportunities. As it was, Wigan scored five tries to Warrington's one, having set the tone for what was to follow from the kick-off, when Boyd caught the ball and was promptly knocked flat on his backside by Du Toit. Ella scored two individual tries and demonstrated how he gained the nickname Zip Zip; Edwards, Hanley and Kiss also claimed tries. Dowling, Du Toit, Mike Ford and Whitfield all ran Ella close for the Man of the Match award – Warrington simply did not know where the next moment of danger would come from. Andy Gregory, who would have won a

Rathbone was already off the field for a late tackle on Potter, this criminal breach of discipline left Warrington with 11 men for the final few minutes, reduced to a series of blatant obstructions to prevent more Wigan tries. Warrington did not help themselves by self-destructing, but their frustration in the face of overwhelming Wigan superiority was understandable. If the 'total football' concept can translate from soccer to rugby, the idea that any player can perform any function and that attacks can spring from anywhere on the pitch, the 1982 Kangaroos pioneered it. Wigan were merely the first club side to copy it, and the 1985 Lancashire Cup final was an early indication that they were on the right track. Warrington were not the only club side destined to experience utter frustration.

With the county trophy on the sideboard for the first time in 12 years, and Ella, Dowling, Goodway and Hanley all bedding down nicely in the side, Wigan went on a 13-match winning spree, shooting up the first division table in the process and securing a place in the John Player Special Trophy final for the second time in four years. Along the way there was a terrific 28–6 league victory at Leeds, a 62–0 home thrashing of Featherstone after which Rovers coach Allan Agar resigned, and an entertaining 34–12 win at York during which Stephenson, struggling to line up a goalkick in the November gloom, was assisted by a spectator who ran on with a cigarette lighter. 'It was very funny,' said Stephenson. 'Of course, I would have preferred a cigarette as well, but you can't have everything.' A day earlier, in the second Test against the touring New Zealand, a Great Britain side featuring Hanley, Goodway, Potter and Edwards triumphed 25–8 at Central Park, the first glimmer of hope on the international horizon for years. West, recalled to international duty by the Kiwis, could not make an impression on his adopted home ground, although the series was eventually squared with a draw in the final Test at Elland Road.

Wigan reached a JPS final against Hull KR by beating Mansfield, Wakefield and Warrington in the earlier rounds and accounting for second division Leigh 36–8 in the semi-final at St Helens, with Hanley claiming four tries *en route* and a fit again Gill chipping in with three. The last, rather disappointingly one-sided game was more notable for an unusual hat-trick by prop forward Dowling, and for what happened immediately afterwards. The BBC *Grandstand* cameras, at Knowsley Road to cover the semi-final live, were hijacked after the final whistle by a Lindsay positively bursting with pride and self-importance. They were led to the St Helens boardroom, where South African rugby union internationals Ray Mordt and Rob Louw were waiting to sign Wigan contracts with a suitably telegenic flourish. Hanley might have been Lindsay's best-ever signing, but this was surely the Wigan vice-chairman's finest hour. Mordt and Louw had in fact been touting for professional deals for a couple of months, and Hull and St Helens

had expressed an interest in Mordt, a strong-running winger who Wigan had been tracking for several years. Like those clubs, Wigan quickly realised the pair wanted to stay together, but unlike their rivals, Wigan agreed to accommodate them both in a double signing worth around £75,000. But that wasn't the point. The point was that almost as if anticipating a less than thrilling match, Lindsay had a trick up his sleeve for the television audience. And although the twin signing was perhaps not as audacious a coup as club and television commentators made out, it was the very height of audacity to commandeer not only live television but the St Helens boardroom for five minutes of blatant Wigan self-promotion.

The winning run came to an end three days before Christmas with a pulsating 12–12 draw at Halifax, who were shaping up under Chris Anderson as one of the surprise packets of the season. Chiefly famous the season before for signing so many Australians the league felt compelled to restrict the number of overseas players a club could field, Halifax had been more discriminating this season and much more successful. The irony was that Anderson himself had only arrived at Thrum Hall because Hull KR needed to shed an overseas player quickly to comply with the new limit of five. Unwittingly, Rovers lost one of the country's shrewdest coaches. Any team containing Anderson was likely to be superbly well organised, and although Hanley scored twice at Thrum Hall, a combination of a cramped ground, a tight defence, and a brilliant display at full-back by the explosive Queenslander, Joe Kilroy, was enough to hold Wigan for the first time in 14 matches.

Wigan got back to winning ways at home to St Helens on Boxing Day, but more significant than the 38–14 scoreline was the crowd, a new first division record of 21,813. Hanley was all but paid for already, and as the winning run continued at Warrington and at home to lowly Swinton, Lindsay's 'back-of-a-matchbox' calculations were further vindicated by an attendance of over 12,600 for the latter.

Wigan's 11–8 victory over Hull KR in the JPS Trophy final at Elland Road was a much lower-key occasion than the one which had taken place at the same venue three years earlier. The game was dourly defensive and fairly forgettable (not that the 1983 final had been a classic), won by Wane's early try from close range and a Mike Ford touchdown which climaxed a rare handling move. Euphoria in the 17,573 crowd was conspicuous by its absence. Wigan's horizons had widened considerably in three short years. Whereas in 1983 the JPS Trophy had been received as a rival to the Holy Grail, in 1986 it was more realistically perceived as a minor prize in the grander scheme of things. A return to Wembley was uppermost in every Wiganer's mind, and the present team actually looked capable of winning the championship. Three overseas players provided the only talking points at Elland Road. Dowling followed his hat-trick of tries in the semi-final with an even more unlikely drop goal in the final. Ella, who had scored in every previous round, missed out for once. So did Shaun Edwards, who only came on for the last six minutes as a substitute for Gill. With Ella at stand-off and Mike Ford at scrum-half, Hampson's return as full-back meant Edwards was unable to claim a regular position. He could fill in on the wing while Ella was performing so well at stand-off, but for the JPS Trophy final Wigan had selected Gill and Mordt, the latter playing only his second-ever game of rugby league. A direct and forceful runner with a surprising turn of speed, Mordt's unusual habit of running straight into defenders rather than trying to evade them was probably more effective in union than league, where tackles tended to stick, but the winger could obviously play and would certainly get better. Like Du Toit, he put a lot of heart into his game, and his bristly, combative attitude instantly won the Wigan fans over.

Hull KR were beaten again in the league, just for good measure, before Wigan's unbeaten run came to an end at Widnes, where Dowling was temporarily blinded by lime used in the pitch markings. Widnes and Hull KR were seen as Wigan's principal rivals for the title. Halifax had topped the table in early January, but only, it was thought, because of Anderson's odd policy of fulfilling as many league fixtures as possible, even hiring alternative grounds to get matches played when games at Thrum Hall were lost to the weather. Halifax were a small club who had been in the second division more recently than Wigan. They were only in front because they had played more games, the others would eventually catch up.

Widnes's chances of taking the title, however, took a dive on 20 January, hours before the Challenge Cup deadline, when their star attraction, Joe Lydon, was sold for a record £100,000. To Wigan, obviously. No one else had that sort of cash, and no one else bought players who were not even on the transfer list. That Wigan had long coveted Lydon, a player they felt they should never have missed in the first place, was common knowledge. It was the manner of his capture which took everyone by surprise, not least Eric Hughes, who resigned as coach in protest when he discovered the player had effectively been sold behind his back. Had Hughes been consulted over the transfer, Widnes officials explained, he would most likely have refused to sanction it, so he might have had to quit anyway. Widnes, in dire financial straits again, needed £100,000 more than any player or coach, and the ever alert Lindsay had realised the time was right to swoop. £100,000 was a high price to pay, so soon after Hanley, Goodway and the other arrivals, but Lydon was a certain winner who at 22 had a lot behind him and even more in front. Wigan had just picked up £25,000 from Halifax for Whitfield (a record amount for the Yorkshire club to pay for anyone) and seen as a straight swap of one utility back for another, Lydon's acquisition made perfect sense. Whitfield had served Wigan well, but Wigan had moved on. Lydon was younger, faster and classier. More expensive, but Wigan could now afford to shop at the quality end of the market. 'We didn't do anything wrong or underhand when signing Joe,' Lindsay explained. 'I know the deal didn't go down too well in Widnes, but that was not really our concern. Every player is for sale, whether on the list or not. Knowing Widnes were strapped for cash, we simply made them an offer. If they had turned us down that would have been the end of it, but they didn't. They wanted to do business, or rather they needed to do business. We were being more predatory than we had been in the past, and perhaps a little more ruthless, but to get ahead you need to be. As with all our signings we were up front and above board about it.'

Lydon himself suspects Widnes had been discreetly advertising his availability, knowing they would have to part with either him or Tony Myler to raise funds for ground safety work. At least he suspects that now. He had no inkling of it in 1986. 'I was naïve then,' he said. 'The first I knew of the deal was a phone call from Jack Robinson, who asked me what it would take, wages-wise, to bring me to Wigan. I told him that to be honest I couldn't see Widnes selling me, at which point Jack told me they just had. I was a little bit shocked, but I soon got used to the idea. I knew Widnes were desperate for money. I had been there four years and enjoyed it, I wasn't exactly looking to leave, but it was no hardship coming to Wigan. Of course, in 1986 I didn't know what was around the corner at Wigan. Nobody did. If someone had told me then how many times I'd go to Wembley and how many medals I would end up with, I would have said they were barmy. Because I'd been to Wembley with Widnes, I knew how hard it was.'

Goodway, the first of the new batch of arrivals, had watched in amazement as the team he joined had been strengthened on an almost weekly basis. Six months after meeting Lindsay in Australia, an already strong Wigan had been comprehensively and expensively overhauled. 'The team was transformed by the signings that season,' Goodway said. 'Coming from Oldham, where money was always tight, I just wasn't used to it. I was already excited at joining a big club

like Wigan, and felt the team they started the season with was good enough to challenge for honours, but when they brought Ellery in and then Joe it took us to a different dimension. It was like all the best players in the country were playing for the same team. I began to realise Wigan were doing something different, that they had something bigger in mind than other clubs. It was about this time I stopped pretending to have a job and began to concentrate on my rugby. If I had been looking for a new challenge when I joined Wigan that was exactly what I got. We all did. The challenge was to stay in the team, because every week some terrific player, someone who cost a lot of money or would be a star turn at another club, would have to miss out.'

When the Challenge Cup trail began at second division Workington, this abundance of talent was very much in evidence, though Lydon was unavailable, his début delayed until March after undergoing a cartilage operation while still at Widnes. Wigan merely flexed their muscles to win by a colossal 56–12, with no fewer than eight players sharing a total of 12 tries and Du Toit kicking a rare goal late in the game. As a cup tie, such a cruel mismatch lacked any element of suspense, but the day out on the West Cumbrian coast was greatly enjoyed by travelling supporters. Cherry and white shirts spilled from every pub and café in Workington. Fans keen to repeat the previous season's Wembley experience also appeared keen to follow the team every step of the way, so as to be able to boast 'I was there' in the future. A couple of miles up the coast from Workington is a village called Flimby, an obscure place nevertheless familiar to every Wigan follower because it is mentioned in every programme and record book. In 1925 a Wigan side containing Jim Sullivan (22 goals) and Johnny Ring (seven tries) beat the hapless amateurs of Flimby and Fothergill 116–0 in a cup match, still the club's highest-ever score. Sixty-one years later it was clear Wigan had another extraordinary side whose exploits might go down in the game's history.

Back in the league, Wigan played to 18,450 spectators for the visit of the entertaining Halifax, though less encouraging was the way the visitors held the home side tryless in a 6–6 draw. An even bigger crowd saw St Helens despatched 24–14 in the second round of the Challenge Cup, which to Wigan's annoyance was broadcast live on television. No longer content with an attendance of a mere 18,553 the club felt the switch to Saturday and the presence of the cameras cost them up to 10,000 extra spectators. Wigan were not at their most convincing in the derby, twice having to come from behind and needing an interception try from Stephenson to swing the game in their favour, but they survived into the next round and were rewarded with a home tie against Castleford. Another 18,503 turned up in a jolly mood on 16 March, only for the atmosphere to turn funereal in the space of 80 minutes as Wigan turned in their worst performance of the season. A second-half try from David Roockley sealed a famous Castleford victory, after John Joyner had opened the scoring for the visitors. All the holders could manage in a miserable 10–2 defeat was a solitary Lydon penalty. The favourites were out of the Cup. Wigan's illustrious and expensive team had failed to score a try at home for the second time in four matches. That Castleford went on to win at Wembley was of no consolation to the losers. Wigan had not expected to go out of the Cup, but it was the manner of their exit which left supporters most perplexed. Wigan had failed to put up a fight. With normally reliable performers like Hampson and Hanley looking decidedly ordinary, they had simply surrendered to a better team. It was an unwelcome reminder of the way things used to be, all the more unpleasant for being unexpected. Those Wigan supporters who had already booked their Wembley hotel, or entertained visions of Ella emulating Kenny and claiming a second successive Lance Todd Trophy for Australia, were brought up short. The embarrassment was considerable, the excuses were few. The outcome might have been different had not Ella missed the game with an injury from the league match at Hull, but Wigan, of all clubs, ought to have been able to cope with the loss of a single player. It was clear, and St Helens supporters were not slow to point this out, that Wigan were not as good as they thought they were.

The season never really recovered from that shock discovery. It was fortunate that relatively easy league games at Dewsbury and Swinton followed the Cup exit, but Wigan completely failed to negotiate the hurdle of Easter, losing at St Helens on Good Friday and, even more disastrously, at home to Oldham on Easter Monday. A further point was dropped in the next home game, a 10–10 draw with Warrington, which significantly saw Wigan's home gate drop back below 10,000. All the grand plans were unravelling. Wigan won their five remaining league matches but it was too late. Halifax were champions by a single point, Wigan finished runners-up. Hull KR, in the time-honoured rugby league tradition, had to abandon hope of catching Anderson's team when forced to play nine games in 17 days after qualifying for Wembley. The fact that the title had been won by a deeply unfashionable and cut-price outfit now boasting former Central Park luminaries like Whitfield, Juliff, Scott and Stephens only made the situation harder to bear. There wasn't even a slightly happy ending, after Warrington denied Wigan the hollow satisfaction of reaching the Premiership final. After the Cup exit, it seemed any sort of satisfaction would be hollow. Scapegoats were needed, and the joint coaches were handily placed. Towards the end of the season it had been unkindly observed that Wigan were a million-dollar team with a ten-bob coaching partnership. No one could say quite what was wrong with what Clarke and McInnes were doing, but it was easy to draw the conclusion that in lavishly rebuilding the team, Wigan had overlooked the coaching department. Rumours began to circulate linking Wigan with Brian Smith, coach of perennial Winfield Cup wooden-spoonists Illawarra. The last four league attendances of the 1985–86 season, averaging only 8,500, represented failure for Wigan. There are only three things a failing club can alter – the directors, the players and the coach – and it is always easiest and quickest to change the coach. So on a Monday night in June 1986, despite the fact that the Lancashire Cup and the JPS Trophy sat on the Central Park sideboard, Wigan sacked Clarke and McInnes.

It was not a complete surprise to the two men, who had heard the rumours like everyone else, and had not been reassured by the somewhat lukewarm support from the direction of the boardroom. 'Lindsay and Robinson denied everything, but I knew they were talking to Brian Smith,' Clarke said. 'Getting an overseas coach now seemed to be the latest big idea, and I knew nothing could ever be the same again, even if the club had wanted Alan and I to stay on. Nothing lasts forever, especially in sport. I got a phone call from Maurice at the same time as Alan was getting one from Jack. That's how they did it. I could see they were trying to be fair, and I don't suppose there was an easy way of doing a job like that, but Alan and I were both bitterly disappointed. We had just had a bit of a wobble at the time Steve Ella was out of the team. It didn't seem a lot to be sacked for, after the tremendous season we'd had.'

Clarke and McInnes were so disappointed over their sacking, and what they considered inadequate compensation, that they took the matter to an industrial tribunal claiming they had been unfairly dismissed. The hearing agreed with their contention that while they might have been unsuccessful by Wigan's new standards, they had performed adequately by everyone else's, and Wigan were obliged to up their cash settlement. It was a tricky time for Clarke, in particular, whose son, Philip, was starting to earn rave reviews in playing for St Pat's junior teams, and was already interesting Wigan. 'I never actually fell out with Lindsay or Robinson,' he said, 'though obviously relations were strained for a while. It took a year or two for everything to get back to normal, but it's all water under the bridge now. The four of us bump into each

other quite often and there's no animosity. We all want the best for Wigan, we always did. But I wouldn't let even Wigan walk all over me. I went to court to get what was right. Anyone who knows me knows I will always stand up for myself if I feel I have a good argument.' Supporters were divided on the issue. Some felt the joint coaches deserved more loyalty after two seasons in which only the league title had eluded them, and that only by a point. Others felt a change was necessary and were curious to see what innovations an overseas coach could bring. The players, always conservative and fearful of change in these situations, were uneasy. Stephenson talked rather theatrically of quitting in protest, a threat he never carried out, but most were aware of how much Clarke and McInnes had put into the club and felt they had in some way let them down. 'Colin and Alan were great guys to work for,' Goodway explained. 'They actually complemented each other very well, and at the time I would have said Wigan's coaching was better than anyone else's. Alan was a thinker, reserved and quiet, who would come up with ideas and explain them coolly and patiently. Colin was closer to the players, very passionate and a bit emotional. He wore his heart on his sleeve, but players responded to him. He could wind us up a bit. I was sad when they got the push, I must admit, because I couldn't understand what they had done wrong. I was only 24, and I had just come to a club and won some trophies for the first time. I had been captain when we won the Lancashire Cup, and I had thoroughly enjoyed the John Player final. I was amazed when the club said they weren't satisfied. It had seemed like a marvellous season to me.'

Lindsay insists that at the time Clarke and McInnes left Central Park a replacement had not been found, though by that stage he knew Smith, of Illawarra, was not coming. 'We did make Smith an offer, 45,000 dollars a season if memory serves, but he turned us down because his wife wasn't sure about moving to England,' Lindsay said. 'We weren't all that bothered actually. Smith was an overseas coach, but apart from that he didn't seem to have a lot to recommend him. Illawarra had been wooden-spoonists three years on the trot, and his name had only cropped up because John White, the agent we dealt with when signing Brett Kenny from Parramatta, had suggested him. We didn't want just any Australian coach, we wanted a high-flyer, otherwise there would have been no point. Parting with Colin and Alan had been a terrible thing to have to do, and we felt we had to get someone demonstrably better or than just doing the best for Wigan. Someone had to do something for the good of the British game. As one of the few people in this country who realised how frighteningly we were slipping behind Australia, I was concerned for our game as a whole. The whole country needed to move on to a new level. I felt desperately sorry for Colin and Alan because they were performing to the best of their ability. It wasn't their fault they couldn't get up to the Australian level, no one in this country could. I knew that anyone we

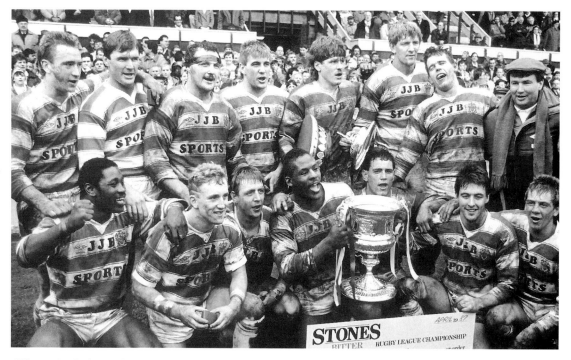

Wigan win the league by a street. Not surprising, really, looking at the talent in that team. Ray Mordt, second from left at rear, did not even need to get his shirt dirty, and Graeme West, fourth from right at rear, is also finding his first team place under threat.

risk losing face. Jack Robinson was very supportive of the plan to get a coach with Australian experience, but it was basically my decision. I was the one who had spent a lot of time in Australia. I had been on tour in 1979 when Eric Ashton was the coach and in 1984 when it was Frank Myler and I knew we were going backwards. The Australians were light-years ahead. I knew that the first club to import their methods and standards would clean up in Britain, but there was more to this got with Australian experience, on the other hand, would make a visible improvement on the pitch, which is why we talked to Smith. It wasn't going to be difficult for anyone coming from Sydney to have an immediate impact in England, because we were starting from such a weak base. We didn't know who to get though. The coach we fancied was John Monie, who had succeeded Jack Gibson at Parramatta and enjoyed considerable success, but we couldn't see him leaving. We were a little bit stuck, until we got a phone call from Colin Hutton [the Hull KR chairman] telling us Graham Lowe was coming over on holiday and had asked about a job in England. That phone call was like an act of God.'

Lowe was the coach of New Zealand, a confident Kiwi whose talent for self-promotion was nevertheless backed by results. His New Zealand had beaten Australia twice, a feat Great Britain could only dream of. He had experience of coaching in Australia too, but in Brisbane, not Sydney, which would have recommended him more highly to Wigan. And he was available. Lindsay agreed to meet him for a preliminary chat in Tom Rathbone's restaurant. 'It was a waste of time,' Lindsay said. 'Before we even sat down to eat I knew we had the right man. I don't think I'm the most impressionable person in the world, but Lowey just bowled me over. It took under ten minutes to find our next coach.'

First impressions can deceive, but not this time. Twelve months later Wigan were champions for the first time in 27 years and Lowe was at a reception in Manchester to pick up the coach-of-the-season award. 'Hey, Maurice, do you know what day it is?' he called, stepping down from the stage. 'It's exactly a year since we met to discuss the Wigan job.'

It had been quite a year for Wigan. Lindsay's contention that overseas coaching techniques could revolutionise club rugby in England had been, if anything, an understatement. Wigan won the league title by a clear 15 points, a ridiculous margin in a competition comprising only 30 matches. Wigan won no fewer than 28 of them, eight more than their nearest rivals St Helens, and set a series of new first division records along the way. No one else had ever scored as many tries (174) or points (941) or won as many league points (56). In addition, Wigan conceded only 29 tries and 193 points all season, both new lows, and after the only league defeats of the season, both at the hands of Warrington, was a run of 17 successive league victories. The Lancashire Cup stayed at Central Park, as did the John Player Special Trophy, and they were joined by the Premiership Trophy as Wigan finally gained revenge over Warrington at Old Trafford. Wigan had never had a more successful season. And Hanley, brilliantly switched to loose forward midway through the season, finished with a new first division record of 44 tries, including five in one game against his former club Bradford. Lowe's initial plan had been to play Hanley at stand-off, feeling he was not involved enough at centre. This meant either Ford or Edwards had to miss out, however, and Hanley's distribution was not up to the standard of either. When Wigan signed Andy Gregory for a record £130,000 in 1987, bringing the last homeboy back, the situation became critical. There was no room at half-back for Hanley, but by persuading him to join the pack, Lowe proved to everyone's surprise, including the player's, that what had happened so far was merely the prelude to the most successful phase of his career. 'I always think of the three positions of scrum-half, stand-off and loose-forward as a central triangle,' Lowe explained. 'If you have got good players in those positions, the team as a whole won't be far wrong. There were good players in those positions when I came to Wigan, but I think the triangle of Hanley, Gregory and Edwards is probably the best in the world.'

Lowe nevertheless managed to fall out with all three of those players during his time at Wigan, just as he almost fell out with a journalist at his introductory press conference. Legend has it that Lowe was accosted on his first day at Central Park by a fan who told him in no uncertain terms that nothing Wigan won would count for anything until they beat St Helens at Wembley. Pleasing though this version is, it is sadly not quite the whole truth. The point was put to Lowe in the Central Park boardroom by a member of the press, and the coach reacted huffily, insisting he would decide what constituted success and was not about to let anyone else set the agenda. He changed his tune eventually, of course. Coming all the way from New Zealand, and still finding his way about the place, he was not to know what a monu-mental significance Wigan's two Wembley defeats in the '60s occupied in the minds of the club and its supporters. But he soon did.

At the same press conference Lowe announced that two new players would be joining him. Dean Bell, the Kiwi centre who had already had spells at Carlisle and Leeds, and Ian Roberts, a then unknown prop or second row from South Sydney. Bell, who had been playing for Easts in Sydney, had previously agreed to return to Leeds for the 1986–87 season, but changed his mind given the chance to rejoin Lowe. 'Leeds had actually offered me £5,000 a season more, but I had to go to Wigan because Lowey was there,' Bell said. 'I looked at the players Wigan had and thought they could win more games than Leeds, but the fact that Lowey wanted me was the main thing. I've always been able to look back and say that was the best move I ever made for the sake of £5,000.' Roberts's principal attraction was an English passport. Having been born in London, he was exempt from quota restrictions, but he was far more than just a gimmick. Although he only played 19 games he must rank among Wigan's best value imports, and the club got him young. On his return to Australia, Roberts joined the more glamorous Manly side, and went on to become a Kangaroo tourist and regular inter-national.

Wigan's league season began with a 42–12 romp over an outclassed Salford at Central Park, although newly promoted Barrow, in the next match, appeared to present more difficulty. Wigan won 18–6, but the perform-ance was far from convincing. No flashy tries, little entertaining or open play, and a lot of time spent on the defensive against a side seemingly intent on keeping the score down. Wigan supporters were restless. Some left before the end. Was this what the new regime was all about? Dull, percentage rugby? Happily it was not, and the next game, when Bell made a scoring début in a 35–0 win at Leigh, banished any lingering doubts about negative rugby. Leigh, whatever their own circumstances, had always managed to rise to

Dean Bell scores his first try for Wigan, in the Lancashire Cup against Rochdale.

the derby occasion in the past. Wigan's record at Hilton Park was quite dreadful, but this time the bogey side were blown away. The fact that Wigan did not have a point scored against them was just as impressive as the 35 they posted on the scoreboard. Bell, meeting his new team-mates for the first time, was certainly impressed. 'I couldn't believe the class of the players around me,' he said. 'I knew straightaway I'd made the right decision. I saw Ellery Hanley score a try that day and I just thought, "Wow!" I'd never seen a player get rid of tacklers the way he did. It was a real eye-opener.' Suddenly it was clear what Lowe was all about. Wigan, quite literally, were playing a different game than Leigh. Whatever he had done, to basically the same team as the previous season, had been brilliantly effective. So what had he done?

'Organisation really,' explained Goodway. 'That was all. Graham was very good tactically, in a way we had never considered before. He basically introduced a defensive system that was all about work off the ball. No one was ever to stand still. We had formations for when we had the ball and formations for when we hadn't, and the speed of our line used to take everyone by surprise. We used to get in position before opponents realised what was happening, and then whatever they tried to do, we would be ready for them. It sounds complicated to describe, but it was quite simple to operate, and when it worked, of course, which it did from the very beginning, we used to do it all the more enthusiastically. Simply by splitting the game up between defence and attack, and making us think about what we did when he had the ball and what we did when we lost it, Graham took us on to a different level. There wasn't much else to it, but it took all the other teams ages to catch up.'

All the Wigan players were unanimous in praise of Lowe who, despite his reputation as a technical coach, seemed to have the happy knack of simplifying the game rather than overcomplicating it. Brian Case, player of the year in Lowe's first season, said: 'He makes ordinary players look good and good players look brilliant.' Part of the reason for Lowe's swift popularity was his engaging personality. A combination of show-off, comedian and natural communicator, Lowe the person was considerably more complex than his coaching philosophy. 'If you don't want to win things you might as well pack in, and if you don't enjoy it when you win, what's the point?' he once asked.

Enjoyment was important to Lowe, but not at the expense of a basic efficiency. 'Rugby league is a simple game, there really isn't all that much to it,' he explained. 'All the best games are fundamentally simple, but it is wrong to assume that because of that you can go out on the park and take it as it comes. You can do that if you wish, you might even enjoy it, but you will always find yourself second best to a team which has given a little more thought to organisation. All I tried to do at Wigan, just as at other clubs I have coached, was to make players more aware of what jobs they are supposed to be doing, and how they can help each other. No big secrets, no magic formulas, just that. You don't have to sacrifice your enjoyment of a game to play more effectively. In my experience, the more players put into a game, the more they get out.'

Lowe always wanted players to put more into their physical development, encouraging the shift to full-time training and regular use of the weights room. 'Too many English players are not as strong as they could be,' he explained. 'They should do a lot more to build themselves up. All players are born the same, but in Australia your starting weight is

Graham Lowe kisses the Lancashire Cup, his first trophy as Wigan coach, watched by his Australian captain, Ian Roberts.

just that, a starting weight. You don't have to tell Australians the advantages of building up extra strength and speed, in their league the players who don't do that just get left behind. Fitness levels are the reason for the gap between Great Britain and Australia. The Aussies have the advantage in strength and physique. Great Britain could beat Australia in the near future if they got their act together.'

One player aware this was not just coaching bluster was West, who had captained several of Lowe's New Zealand sides, notably to victory over Australia in Brisbane in 1983. What happened in the Kiwi dressing-room that night gives a clearer insight into Lowe's powers of motivation and inspiration than any amount of technical theory. 'Unbeknown to us, Lowey had turned the clock in the dressing-room back a few minutes,' West said. 'He only wanted us to go out at the last minute, and when the Australians took the field he told us they were trying to con us into going out early.' Lowe takes up the story. 'Australia were out there letting off fireworks and singing their national anthem, and I knew we would be booed onto the pitch,' he said. 'The crowds at Lang Park are always hostile to visitors, you always get an enormous boo, so instead of sending the team out together we sent them out one by one. As soon as they caught sight of Graeme they started to boo, but Westy just padded out to the middle of the field on his own. Then we sent out the next man, and the next, and the crowd couldn't keep up the noise. A small victory, if you like, but the big one came later. It's important not to let Australians have everything their own way. Give them an inch and they'll take a yard.'

Wigan could hardly fail to be emboldened by such talk, and when the 1986 Kangaroos opened their tour at Central Park in October a Test-strength side featuring Miles, Kenny, Lewis, Sterling, Roach and Cleal had to work for a 26–18 victory, with Bell, Lydon and Edwards scoring tries for the home team in an inspired second-half fightback. This was only the second defeat of the season (the first, away to Warrington, had been the previous Sunday) and Wigan had been running up some enormous scores against smaller clubs. But what stood out about the Australian game was the attendance. Wigan had promoted the fixture imaginatively, producing colour posters to commemorate the occasion and staging a gala lunch in the clubhouse prior to kick-off, and were rewarded by a crowd of 30,622. Only a couple of hundred more people turned up for the second Test at Elland Road. Less than a fortnight previously, 28,252 had packed Central Park to see a narrow Wigan victory over St Helens in the Lancashire Cup semi-final. Watching Wigan had never been so fashionable, and rarely so exciting. The rest of the game wondered where they were finding all their new fans. Money was pouring into Central Park, as the directors' initial gamble paid dividends beyond anyone's expectations. Wigan had never had it so good.

Oldham were beaten 27–6 in the Lancashire Cup final, and Wigan did not lose again all year, until Warrington came to Central Park and won a physical encounter 6–4. A week later the same two sides, easily the strongest around that season, met to contest the JPS Trophy final at Bolton. Warrington were installed as favourites, principally on account of their league double over Wigan and the fearsomeness of a pack of forwards which included Boyd, Tamati, Jackson and Rathbone. In the event it was Wigan's forwards who won the day, with West outstanding, Potter putting a recent knee operation behind him and Roberts playing on in spite of ten stitches in a cut lip at half-time. Goodway won the Man of the Match award, more for a 65-yard interception try than anything else, but Lindsay was most impressed with the overall look of the team. 'I watched Wigan and I saw Australia,' he said. 'Warrington were a good team under Tony Barrow, but we beat them with the kicking game. They were looking for the ball all the time but we wouldn't let them have it. I had seen Australia do that umpteen times to British teams, now we were doing the same thing. We had moved the game on a level. It was a proud moment.'

There were to be many more of those before the end of the season. Mordt, in perhaps his finest game for Wigan, took over where John Ferguson left off in tormenting Hull KR at Craven Park. No fewer than nine games through the season saw Wigan keep a clean sheet, including a 30–0 defeat of Leeds at Headingley which many fans rated close to perfection. Mordt and Richard Russell, Wigan's wingers, both scored hat-tricks, though there was no doubt the star of the show was Gregory, the scrum-half Wigan had finally brought back home after a prolonged dispute with Warrington had kept him sidelined for most of the season. Arguments were still raging in Wigan about why his home-town club missed him in the first place. 'As far as I know Wigan weren't interested in me in 1979, I never received an offer from them,' Gregory said. 'But that's academic anyhow, because I wasn't interested in joining Wigan in 1979. I've heard the tale that I was broken-hearted not to hear from them but it just isn't true. I wanted to join a successful club, and the best around seemed to be Widnes. I wasn't wrong either. Widnes, when I joined them, were so professional it was frightening. We knew exactly how to prepare, exactly what to do. Wigan were pretty cocky when we played them at Wembley in 1984, but deep down I knew they hadn't a cat in hell's chance. They came out to enjoy themselves and we just stuffed them. It all went according to plan. I didn't feel sorry for Wigan, not even for my mates among their supporters. We had put in the work and we reaped the benefit.

'Things change though, and Wigan became the ultra-professionals. Call me mercenary if you like, but I rate myself the best scrum-half in the game and I will always want to play for the best club. I don't see anything wrong in wanting to win, I'd hate to pull on a shirt every week and go out expecting to lose. I set myself high standards, and I only want to be involved in teams with the same attitude. Loyalty works both ways, after all. If Widnes were still the club I joined, if they had kept up their standards, I would probably still be playing for them. I won't accept anything less than the best, and Wigan are the ones who have got it right. They have even stopped me giving away half a dozen penalties a game. They have such a professional set-up, they will be winning things for years to come.'

With Gregory, Hanley and Wigan's entire back division running rampant in the 17-match winning sequence which saw the league title secured a fortnight before the end

Wigan had been chasing Andy Gregory long enough; no wonder Graham Lowe looks pleased to see him.

of the season with a 62–7 hammering of Featherstone, Wigan ended their campaign on a winning note with a tense 8–0 victory over Warrington in the first Premiership final to be staged at Old Trafford. It had been quite a season, with only one flaw. Wigan did not beat St Helens at Wembley, nor anyone else, since on 4 February 1987, in a rearranged first-round tie at Watersheddings, Wigan were dumped out of the Challenge Cup at the entirely unexpected hands of Oldham.

This, of course, was worse than the previous season's Cup disappointment. At least Castleford were a strong side who had the decency to go on and win the Cup. Oldham were relegated at the end of the season and lost in the next round of the Cup to St Helens. Wigan supporters then had to endure the dismal spectacle of St Helens failing to beat Halifax in the final, followed by that of Whitfield, Scott, Juliff, Stephens, Pendlebury et al parading around Wembley with the Cup. It was another big feather in the cap of Australian coaching as performed by Chris Anderson, and something of a facer for

Graham Lowe. It was only in the immediate aftermath of the 10–8 defeat at Oldham, in fact, that Lowe fully grasped what getting to Wembley was all about. 'It's hard for Antipodeans to understand our Cup tradition,' Lindsay explained. 'They don't have the same sort of thing over there, everything revolves around the league. Graham knew we wanted to get to Wembley, obviously, the fans, the players and the directors had made that perfectly clear, but I don't think he understood how much we all wanted to go. Then when we were coming home from Oldham, and the atmosphere on the bus was like someone had just died, he began to realise that even winning the league might not make up for this disappointment. It was quite a shock to him. That night was quite a shock to all of us.'

That night began well enough, with Bell scoring a try and Lydon kicking a couple of goals for an 8–4 lead, but Wigan were unable to find the points they needed for a comfortable margin, and were caught cold a minute from the end when Lydon knocked-on close to his line and Paddy Kirwan forced his way over. That levelled the scores, Mick Burke's successful goalkick gave the tie to Oldham with no time left for Wigan to argue. There were any number of points for disgruntled supporters to pick over on the way home – had Hampson not been substituted ten minutes from the end Wigan might have kept their noses in front, a still hot-headed Gregory hardly helped matters, and so on – but the overriding reaction was one of dis-

belief. In that respect, and with due respect to a real tragedy, it was like the sinking of the *Titanic* all over again, with Oldham as the iceberg. It was certainly a night to remember.

'The way it happened was terrible,' Hampson said. 'I never saw the try, I was on the bench with my head in my hands. I couldn't watch, but I knew they had scored, because of the din. It was a sickening feeling, much worse than losing to Castleford the year before. I can still remember the Oldham fans celebrating – they were that pleased about beating Wigan I don't think they minded getting relegated.'

Hampson was still wondering whether he would ever get to play at Wembley. So was Goodway, an ex-Oldham player for whom the experience was especially painful. 'Losses do happen, but I don't recall ever being in a match where the expectation was so high,' he said. 'I don't just mean that we thought we were going to beat Oldham, we were all convinced we would be going to Wembley that year. That was probably our mistake, looking past the first round, I don't know. All I know is that there are losing dressing-rooms and losing dressing-rooms but I've never known one like that night. When the result finally sank in all the players were bitterly disappointed. For themselves, of course, and for the fans, but mostly for the coach and the directors. We knew how much they had put into the club, we knew how much faith they had in us, and we felt they deserved better. It was just such an incredible let-down.'

CHAPTER SEVEN

Top of the World

'When we get it right like that, somebody suffers.'

Half-way through the 1986–87 season, at the end of the Kangaroo tour, Wigan signed Wally Lewis. Although he had had his nose pushed out by Kenny on the 1982 tour, the Australian captain had recovered the stand-off position, had performed and led superbly, and was generally reckoned to be the last word in rugby league players. So Wigan hijacked the *Grandstand* cameras again to show the nation the new heights of their ambition. Where Lewis was going to fit into Lowe's celebrated triangle was anyone's guess. How much he would earn, for what was only going to be a short stay, was another imponderable. Both questions turned out to be academic, however, for Lewis never came.

'Wally double-crossed us,' Lindsay explained. 'Or at least he went back on his word once he got back to Australia. We had the deal in writing, so we could have held him to it had we really wanted to, but once we were on two different continents that would have been a lot of hassle.' Lindsay had almost signed Lewis in 1985, when in Australia, only to return with Dowling and Ella instead. The Australian captain had in fact driven Lindsay to Dowling's home to set up the former's deal, and the possibility of joining him at Wigan had been discussed. But it was the presence of Lowe which brought Lewis and Wigan together. 'Graham was desperate to sign him, having been with him in his early Brisbane days,' Lindsay said. 'I don't think Wally was quite as keen on the plan, but he didn't want to say no to Graham. So he said yes and signed, but even as he did so I wondered if his heart was in it. I was filled with trepidation for the next month

when he went home, and knowing Wally's reputation, not entirely surprised when he didn't return. It said in the newspapers that he had a shoulder injury, which may have been convenient. It is also possible he got hold of the idea that Ellery Hanley was not happy about having him at Wigan.'

Strictly speaking, Wigan's transfer policy was none of Hanley's business, but there was an unwritten understanding that the former Bradford player was the highest-paid member of the Central Park squad. Lindsay protested that Lewis's proposed deal was comparable to Hanley's, not superior, and pointed out that it was only a short-term signing, but the Wigan man nevertheless deemed the time right to ask for a rise. A short dispute followed, during which Lowe refused to back down and Hanley stayed away from the club and missed a JPS Trophy game against Swinton, before both sides were placated. It was a warning of what was to come. Lewis stayed in Australia, but several years later Wigan received a letter from Australia, from the agency promoting the great player's testimonial. Would Wigan like to hold a dinner in his honour, it asked, a black tie event which Lewis would attend and meet all his friends and admirers in the area, who the agency were sure would be happy to fork out £100 a ticket to help raise money for such a fondly remembered former player? Lindsay wrote back, informing the fund-raisers that Lewis had never actually played for Wigan, adding that while such a dinner might be very pleasant, he could not guarantee any great demand for tickets as he was not sure Lewis was remembered with any fondness at all. 'He would have been though, had he ever come to play for Wigan,' he said. 'He would have been guaranteed success.'

No matter, Wigan had another cunning plan to make the world sit up and take notice and force Australia, in particular, to pay attention. Lindsay wanted to repeat the success of the previous season's tour game against the Kangaroos, without waiting four years until the 1990 party arrived. Looking at the fixture list, which might not throw up

Wigan's South African trio of the mid-'80s: left to right, Nick Du Toit, Rob Louw and Ray Mordt.

another Wigan–Saints semi-final in the Lancashire Cup this year, he was concerned at the lack of an early season glamour game, something to get the turnstiles clocking beyond the 12,000 and 13,000 crowds they were currently averaging. He had been to Australia again in the close season, failing once more to sign Gene Miles, but moving in altogether more elevated circles now as a result of Wigan's success and his own growing reputation. Even so, Ken Arthurson, the Australian Rugby League secretary, did not take him seriously at first when he suggested a play-off match, a World Club Challenge, between the English and Australian champions. To Lindsay's annoyance, David Oxley

and the English Rugby League were scarcely any more enthusiastic either. You had to hand it to Wigan, one championship in 27 years and here they were trying to use it as a foot in the door to something bigger, but few in England or Australia shared Lindsay's visionary desire. To their lasting shame, the administrators preferred neat, orderly fixture lists, and unadventurous separatism. In their defence, the logistical problems facing the proposed game were immense. The English season ended in April, when the Sydney Premiership is barely two months into its course. The Australian season ended in October, when the following English league campaign has already started. Apart from the fact that there was no convenient time when the champions of both countries were standing idle, with nothing better to do than to play each other, whichever compromise slot in the calendar was agreed upon, one team would always be coming off the back of a hard slog to the title, whereas the other would always be comparatively rested and fresh. These were serious drawbacks to what was undeniably an exciting idea, which the World Club Challenge was never completely able to overcome. Nor was a 13,000-mile flight and the attendant jet lag and dislocation easy to ignore. On the other hand, when Wigan finally played Manly on an unforgettable night at Central Park in October 1987, the plus points were obvious.

From a commercial point of view, the crowd of 36,895 exceeded everyone's expectations. Almost 30 years ago Central Park had once held 47,000 for a league match against St Helens, but in the modern era of seating and safety considerations, the night of 7 October 1987 saw the old ground as packed as it could possibly get. Many supporters had never experienced such a crush, and although just about everyone present still has a vivid recollection of an extraordinarily tense game and an atmosphere which positively crackled with excitement, a high proportion of spectators could only have glimpsed fragments of the action over someone else's shoulder. The sightlines at Central Park are not great for standing spectators, especially towards the end of the touch-lines and low around the corners, and so tightly was the crowd packed in that there was no possibility of moving to a better location. For anyone under 6 ft and without a seat it was a struggle to see all of the action, but no one was complaining. This, it seemed, was a taste of the old days. This was sport in the raw, the type of event our grandparents had told us about, which we could now claim as our own for the purposes of boring disbelieving youngsters in the future.

launched fireworks exploded into the night sky. All the game had to do now was live up to its billing and packaging. The World Club Challenge concept would have died on its feet that night if such an expectant crowd and such an extravagant fanfare had been rewarded with a mere sideshow, a glorified testimonial game with players going through the motions or operating at half pace, but in the event the two sides gave the best demonstration yet of why the idea had a great future.

Lancashire Cup celebrations, 1987.

future. It was obvious from before the kick-off that to be able to say 'I was at the Manly game' was going to be important in one's dotage.

Wigan, with Lindsay now fully into his stride as entrepreneur, impresario and circus-master all rolled into one, showcased the game stylishly. Once more a glossy, full-colour poster was produced to commemorate the occasion; once more a gala dinner was held in the clubhouse. Live music on the pitch preceded the entry of the teams, and when Hanley and Paul Vautin led out Wigan and Manly to tumultuous applause, mortar-

Wigan won a raw, physical and at times ill-tempered encounter 8–2. There were no tries, Stephenson scored four penalty goals to Michael O'Connor's one, but the excitement never flagged for a moment. It was obvious throughout that pride was at stake, and that rather than staging an exhibition or holding something back, both sides were doing their utmost to protect the honour of their country and competition. Rivalry of this intensity cannot be hyped or manufactured, and is central to the greatest sporting contests. When so much is at stake, and so many people have turned up to watch, you can be confident your main event will not be upstaged by the preliminary fireworks or cheerleaders. After about five minutes of the game, Lindsay must have known he was onto a winner. Manly came closest to scoring a try, when Dale Shearer was held on his back over the line, but they also helped turn the match

He thought the referee (English) had favoured the home side and penalised his players too severely. But Fulton always thinks that, no matter what the result or occasion. He was on more solid ground in arguing that, although the match had been for the right to the title of world champions, it was hardly a level contest.

Quite an atmosphere. Wigan take the field amid fireworks and fanfare for the World Cup Challenge game against Manly.

Wigan's way by repeatedly losing their discipline, notably when hard man Ron Gibbs was dismissed in the fifth minute for attacking Lydon with his elbow. One of Stephenson's penalty goals followed a fight between Edwards and Shearer, another came after Des Hasler had stamped on Wane. Manly also lost Cliff Lyons to the sin bin, and were undoubtedly unsettled by the hugely partisan crowd, but Wigan, too, were caught up in the mounting hysteria, losing Case for ten minutes in the second half and only just managing to hold out in his absence.

Bobby Fulton, the Manly coach, charac-teristically complained at the end of the game.

Manly had just completed a demanding season in Sydney, playing more matches than everyone else by virtue of going to a Grand Final with Canberra, and had been expected to produce their best form after flying 13,000 miles into a strange country to meet a partisan crowd and an unhelpful referee. He was not wrong, but Wigan were not slow to advertise themselves as world champions. The debate about the logistics of the event could go on elsewhere. Meanwhile, Lowe, whose coaching contribution to the victory over Manly cannot be overestimated, had something else to point out. The victory over Australia's champion side had been achieved by a team of exclusively British players. Of the 17 men named for the game, only West, a non-playing substitute, was not qualified to play for Great Britain. In the context of the tour Down Under the following year, and the continued failure of Great Britain to achieve any success at all against Australian teams at Test level, this was a considerable psychological boost. Lowe was not aiming to harm Australian chances – despite his Kiwi background he displayed no antipathy to the old enemy – merely to enhance the confidence and self-esteem of his own Wigan players. 'I've never known anyone better at making you believe in yourself,' said Goodway. 'And that's from someone who has always believed in himself. Graham would push you to do things you didn't think you could, then when you had worked your balls off to justify his faith in you, he would be sitting in the dressing-room afterwards relaxing, as if nothing had happened. He'd just smile and say he told us we could do it.' Whether turning clocks back at Lang Park, or sending out a team of Englishmen to beat Manly at Wigan, Lowe would try any trick to instil a psychological advantage. In point of fact, with Bell injured, the Iro brothers still to arrive, Mordt and Louw back in South Africa and new signing Adrian Shelford still contesting his registration with St Helens, Lowe was virtually forced to play a home-based team. It was just typical of him to try

and make it into an advantage. For the record, Wigan's team against Manly was: Hampson; Russell, Stephenson, Lydon, Gill; Edwards, Gregory; Case (Lucas 76), Kiss, Wane, Goodway, Potter, Hanley. Manly lined up: Shearer; Ronson, Williams (Ticehurst 54), O'Connor, Davis; Lyons, Hasler; Daley, Cochrane, Gately (Brokenshire 55), Gibbs, Cunningham (Shaw 21), Vautin.

The reason Mordt and Louw were back in South Africa was that Wigan had paid up their contracts at the start of the season. Partly this was because the restrictions on overseas players were now starting to bite (Du Toit had been offloaded to Barrow midway through the previous season), and partly it was because Lowe did not seem to rate the Springbok pair. Louw had only started 15 games in the 1986–87 season, and although evidently an intelligent and skilful player, had looked too old and inflexible to make an impact on rugby league, especially at the level at which Wigan were now operating. Mordt was a different matter. He had made only one start more, but had scored 15 tries, an impressive ratio by anyone's standards. Mordt, moreover, was still young enough and certainly fit enough to get even better. He had made mistakes, though demonstrated himself to be a quick and willing learner, but never seemed to enjoy the coach's full confidence. He was, in fact, treated rather shabbily by

The new electronic scoreboard at Central Park spells out the success of the Manly game.

Wigan, and only refrained from saying so because going quietly was a condition of his financial settlement. In August 1987, Mordt was ready to cut his losses. Wigan had to get Louw off their register and had made the forward a generous offer to leave. Louw accepted, and Mordt was quick to ask whether he could leave on the same terms. In

Nicky Kiss takes on Manly's Michael O'Connor.

different circumstances Mordt's English career might have lasted longer, although it was his determination to stay with Louw which created difficulties. Clarke, the former coach, was sorry to see Mordt go. 'Louw was not the awesome player I had been led to believe by some rugby union people,' Clarke said. 'But I think Mordt could have been one of the all-time great rugby league wingers. I can't believe he could not have been persuaded to stay, because I know how determined a player he is. He was doing all right, too, though by the time he left he couldn't see a future for himself at Wigan.'

Lowe always denied that the South Africans were shifted out to make way for more New Zealanders, but that is in effect what happened. Kevin Iro was the big Kiwi signing in 1987, a formidably built teenage centre who had already destroyed Australia

at Test level. New Zealand at that time were in the habit of hanging on to their youthful prodigies until they had played a certain number of internationals – realising their essentially amateur game would be quickly stripped if wealthy British and Australian clubs were allowed to sign the best young talent – but with Lowe at the helm Wigan had a useful connection when it came to capturing Kiwis. Iro, despite looking half asleep half the time, was a great success in British rugby, as was his brother Tony, who looked just as dozy but could suddenly wake up and inflict surprising damage from second row or three-quarter line. Taking their age, size and rugby league backgrounds into account, the Iros were more than adequate replacements for the South Africans. Seen as a direct trade, which it was not, Wigan were ahead on the deal. More complicated, in every respect, was the arrival of Shelford, a burly and ponderous prop forward whom St Helens thought they had signed. St Helens did in fact have a piece of paper to prove this, but so did Wigan. So, as a matter of fact, did Newcastle, in New South Wales, proving that traditional stereo-types in rugby are occasionally accurate. To paraphrase Wilde, while it might be considered an accident to sign for two clubs simultaneously, only a prop could be careless enough to promise himself to three. New-castle quickly dropped out of the race, but St Helens, who believed they had signed Shelford first, gained a court order to prevent him playing for Wigan, and eventually took the dispute all the way to the High Court, where at Christmas 1987, a judge ruled against them. Wigan had won, though the celebrations never got out of hand. Perhaps we had all been led to expect too much, but Shelford was no Dowling or Roberts, not even a Wane or a Case. Not a bad prop forward, but not noticeably better than many of the local alternatives around him, Shelford must have been extremely flattered to have three leading clubs fighting over his services. More significant than any contribution Shelford made on the pitch was the damage the protracted court battle did to relations

An all-British dressing-room – except for the coach – celebrates a ground-breaking win over Australia's finest.

between Wigan and St Helens. Previously always cordial, throughout the keenest of rivalries, directors from both clubs began to swap insults in the press, and an element of bad feeling crept in among supporters. St Helens may have been somewhat stubborn over a player who had clearly indicated that he wished to play for their rivals, and were probably ill-advised to pursue an expensive court claim when they were not certain of winning, but it is hard to escape the conclusion that for Wigan the whole business had more to do with spiting Saints than signing a talented player.

Lowe's second season at Wigan also saw some significant domestic arrivals. Freedom of contract had formally arrived in summer, with a transfer tribunal set up to arbitrate between clubs who could not agree a price for a player moving between them, and Salford's utility back Ged Byrne became the first player to make use of the system. Wigan offered £20,000 for the former St Patrick's player, Salford said they wanted £75,000, the tribunal fixed the deal at £40,000. Wigan got excellent value from the likable Byrne, even though he was signed as cover and rarely had a regular first-team shirt to call his own. Another signing, direct from St Pat's this time, was Phil Clarke, son of Colin, and highly promising as a stand-off or back-row forward. Clarke immediately began to attract attention in the Colts team alongside Denis Betts, another forward for the future signed the previous season from the Leigh Rangers amateur side. Betts once had trials for Manchester United and could undoubtedly have made his mark at some level of professional football, but opted for rugby league instead. Mark Preston, a slight but lightning-quick winger from the Fylde rugby union club, arrived to complete an impressive trio of local signings, as Wigan honoured their pledge to reduce their dependency on overseas over time and attract the best of the home-produced talent. They had no intention of sticking rigidly to the

Diligent as ever at identifying and developing amateur talent, Laughton had virtually laid siege to the Goulding household, but in the end could not match Wigan's financial clout. Goulding picked up £20,000 as a down payment for his first three years at Wigan, a considerable sum considering he would only be 19 at the end of that period and had no

Wembley 1988, and Ellery Hanley evades a despairing lunge from former Wigan player Gary Stephens on his way to the Halifax try line. Tony Iro and Andy Goodway keep their colleague company.

Wigan boundaries, however. In February 1988, Jack Robinson snapped up 16-year-old Bobby Goulding from the Widnes St Maries club. A precocious and obviously exceptional scrum-half, Goulding had more than once been described as the new Andy Gregory, and now his career was starting like Gregory's in reverse, being spirited out of his home town to join Wigan. Widnes, with Doug Laughton back in charge, were the most disappointed of the clubs who had been talking to Goulding.

realistic chance of dislodging Edwards or Gregory in the meantime.

Wigan's victory over Manly had been their tenth in a row stretching back to the start of the season, and in the Lancashire Cup final, four days later, they came up against another unbeaten side in Warrington. The exertions of the previous Wednesday night might have been expected to tell on the Wigan players, but thanks to Edwards's eye for a gap and Hanley's immaculate support play they collected their third consecutive county cup with a 28–16 win. This particular competition was becoming so familiar Wigan began to wonder how winning it had ever seemed difficult. Winning against Halifax was still as difficult as ever, however, and in their next match Wigan suffered a rare home defeat at the hands of the Yorkshire side, now featuring veteran Aussie Test full-back Graham Eadie.

The John Player Special Trophy, another competition Wigan were now starting to regard as their personal property, saw Sheffield, Castleford and Salford despatched to set up a semi-final confrontation with Leeds at Burnden Park. This was the meeting many had secretly hoped would grace the final. Leeds were resurgent under Maurice Bamford (his second spell at the club, having been in charge of Great Britain in between) and had twice broken the transfer record to sign Hull pair Garry Schofield and Lee Crooks. Leeds were foremost amongst several clubs trying to 'do a Wigan'. The Central Park club's remarkable success, and the income it was capable of generating, had not gone unnoticed by the rest of the league. The formula seemed to be simple enough – investment in the team leading to business at the turnstile leading to success on the field leading to even more business at the turnstiles – but other clubs experienced the greatest difficulty getting the elements in the right order and maintaining the smooth upward curve Wigan had demonstrated. Together with the new contract system, itself an inflationary influence full of pitfalls for the unwary or over-optimistic, the desire to match Wigan simply by taking the same financial risks led several clubs to the verge of insolvency. Very few of Wigan's major investments had actually been risks. They had simply managed to collect a nucleus of the best players in the country in a short space of time when the rest of the game was feeling complacent and conservative. Now their success was self-perpetuating, in that the best young players wanted to associate themselves with such a strong side, they were finding it easier to maintain a level of achievement and attract consistently high crowds. Many of their would-be emulators realised too late that there was only so much talent around, and Wigan had cornered most of it.

Still, Leeds had their moments under Bamford, and the Burnden Park semi-final was certainly one of them. Wigan were beaten 19–6 and knocked out of the competition they had dominated for the past two years. They had gone into the game strong favourites, though by the time of the semi-final, played on a crisp December afternoon, Leeds were probably the more settled side. Wigan had lost Bell and Kiss to injury, and Lowe had opted for youthful forwards Lucas and Gildart ahead of the vastly more experienced Potter and West. Leeds began the game badly, losing Crooks with a dislocated shoulder in the opening minutes and letting Hampson in for a try, but substitute forward Kevin Rayne proved a most effective replacement and another forward, Paul Medley, had levelled the scores by half-time. Leeds edged ahead with a drop goal early in the second half, but it was clear the game was still waiting for its decisive moment, and after Wigan had gone close with a couple of handling moves, Schofield picked his time perfectly to score a try fit to win any semi-final. The costliest player among two costly sides surged into a gap in front of Wigan's posts before leaving Hampson floundering with a thundering change of direction. Wigan were beaten, Colin Maskill's late try and goal only emphasising the fact. It was a sweet moment for Bamford. 'Graham Lowe calls himself supercoach, but I think I got his measure that day,' Bamford said. 'He made a fairly basic oversight in selecting his side, as soon as I saw those young, inexperienced forwards I told our lads to play on them. There's no substitute for experience in cup ties. Our forwards had it, and Wigan's didn't. They made it easy for us. Lowe is a clever fellow, and he has coached some superb sides, but he dropped a clanger that day.'

Wigan barely had time to get back to winning ways at Hunslet before facing St

Helens at Central Park on Boxing Day. With a certain amount of needle from the Shelford court battle enlivening the occasion, plus the fact that anti-hero Alex Murphy was now coach at St Helens, the game was watched by 23,809, a new first division record. It was also one of the most memorable of derbies, particularly for the St Helens contingent. Wigan led 22–6 at half-time, and the only person at the ground who did not consider their cause lost was in their dressing-room. 'If Wigan can score 22 points in 40 minutes, so can we,' Murphy told his players. By cutting out their mistakes and switching tactical kicking responsibilities to Loughlin, Saints actually scored 26, to no reply, winning 32–22 after one of the great fightbacks.

Potter and Stephenson both asked for a move at Christmas, the latter joining Leeds at the start of 1988, as the normally steady Wigan ship sailed into some turbulent waters. The Saints defeat was followed by a draw at Warrington, where the theatrical feud between Goodway and Paul Cullen led to both players being among four dismissed in the opening 20 minutes, a victory at Halifax and a defeat at Bradford, so there was some concern about Bradford's visit to Central Park in the first round of the Challenge Cup, particularly as Hanley had chosen this inopportune moment to fall out with Lowe. Hanley was mysteriously absent from the side which beat Bradford 2–0 in a mud-soaked exercise in defensive sterility. A long-range penalty from Lydon was the only score in a tryless, joyless encounter described by one critic as the best advert for rugby union in years. Bradford disputed the penalty and made half-hearted appeals for a rematch, but no one paid any heed. This was the least memorable of cup ties, yet it was the start of something big for Wigan. How big, no one yet realised.

Leeds were next, with Hanley now dropped for his disruptive attitude in training. Over 25,000 spectators at Central Park saw the Yorkshiremen race to a ten-point lead, prompting visions of Burnden Park all over again, but Wigan steadied, and first-half tries from Case, Goodway and Tony

Iro gave them a 16–10 interval lead, which Russell, Hampson and Iro again eventually improved into a convincing 30–14 victory.

Controversy arrived in the next round. Wigan were again drawn at home, although as their opponents were Widnes no one could say they were taking the easy way to Wembley. Widnes, imaginatively remodelled in a short space of time by Laughton, were shaping up as one of the teams of the season, with ex-Rosslyn Park rugby union wing Martin Offiah averaging better than a try a match, and Manly and Australia star Dale Shearer adding class to a back division already boasting Tony Myler and the Hulme brothers. By now Hanley was on Wigan's transfer list at a record £225,000, a price Wigan were surprised, but relieved, to find no one ready to offer, though Warrington did have a player exchange turned down and several Yorkshire clubs cheekily asked whether they could rent the loose forward on a match-by-match basis. Wigan won the Cup tie 10–1, but in all honesty Widnes were the superior side, and the outcome might have been wholly different had two apparently legitimate touchdowns by Mike O'Neill and Richard Eyres not been disallowed by Halifax referee Jim Smith. Wigan's tries, from Hampson and Tony Iro, both arrived in the final quarter, after the visitors' efforts had been refused, and after the home side had been outplayed for an hour. Widnes were furious, and asked that Smith be barred from officiating at their games in future, though there was nothing they could do to prevent Wigan taking their place in the semi-final.

At Burnden Park once again, Wigan met Salford, surprise conquerors of St Helens in the third round. The first surprise at Bolton, however, was the state of the pitch. Bolton Wanderers had played a match on it the night before, and it had not stopped raining since. The second surprise was the return of Hanley, who had made his peace with Lowe, and the third was the reappearance of Bell, named as substitute after a long injury lay-off. There were no surprises in the game itself. Salford conceded two early tries, pulled one back at

Lance Todd Trophy winner Andy Gregory celebrates with Graham Lowe at Wembley in 1988.

the start of the second half then saw the game turn Wigan's way when Hanley had the ball knocked from his grasp near the posts and Kiss kicked ahead to score while defenders appealed in vain for a knock-on. Three more tries arrived after that, the last made for Hanley by Bell, as Wigan ran out easy 34–4 winners. 'I thought we conceded an unlucky try at a bad time,' said Salford coach Kevin Ashcroft. 'But apart from that, Wigan stuffed us.'

Hanley was not particularly impressive at Bolton, as might be expected after a lengthy lay-off, but as Lindsay was later to say, he more than made up for it at Wembley. Few explanations for his conduct were forthcoming, but according to Lindsay, popular conjecture that he swallowed his pride in order to play at Wembley is wide of the mark. 'Nothing could be further from the truth,' Lindsay said. 'I don't think there is anything in the world that can make Ellery swallow his pride, and he certainly wasn't about to do it to play at Wembley. This was a player who had never appeared at Wembley at this stage,

remember, and I knew just how badly he wanted to be there, but would he budge? No chance.' The dispute arose out of a training ground argument over the captaincy Hanley had lost through injury, and escalated because Lowe, too, was possessed of roughly equal amounts of stubbornness and pride. 'Neither man would back down, it just got more serious and at the same time more ridiculous,' Lindsay said. 'I must admit I thought that the further we progressed in the Cup the more likely Ellery would be to come around to Graham's view, but I quickly realised I was mistaking him for an ordinary player. He was shocked when we put him on the list, but he still wouldn't budge. We didn't want to sell him of course, we just wanted to open up a dialogue again, but no one came in for him, even though £225,000 was far from a fencing price. That shocked me, a little bit. Had I been the chairman of a rival club I would have put in a bid right away, no matter what it took to raise the money.'

On the list with no takers, Hanley was effectively out of the game. Wigan were

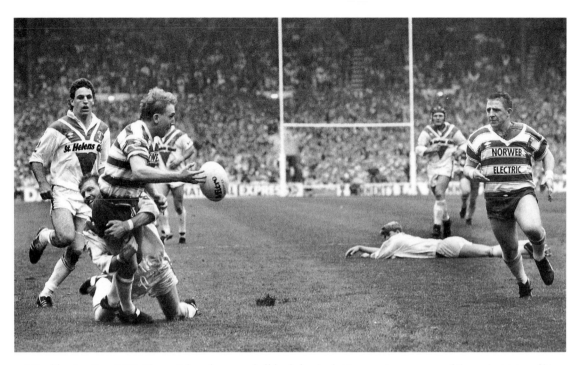

Wembley try time 1989. Shaun Edwards pops a ball back for Andy Gregory to score one of the easiest tries of his career, with the St Helens line just out of the picture and the grounded full-back Connolly out of the argument.

managing well enough without him, but Lindsay resolved to resolve the situation on receipt of a letter from a supporter. No ordinary supporter either but Cliff Barker, the town's chief police prosecutor, a learned and serious man and in some ways an unlikely ally of Hanley's. Barker argued that Hanley would have to be brought back into the fold because he was special to the club, its supporters, and the town as a whole. 'Wigan are still winning games, but the magic is missing,' he said, adding that it would be folly for the club to drive him elsewhere or force him to spend any longer on the sidelines. 'That made up my mind,' Lindsay said. 'I drove over to see Ellery at his home in Leeds, to plead with him, basically. He was very nice, asked me in, made me a cup of tea, but he absolutely did not want to know about climbing down. I was defeated. I drove home thinking the man would never be broken.' Nor was he, but Lindsay was not quite out of ideas. 'What I did was work on Graham Lowe, and in the end I persuaded him, for the club's sake and my sake, to eat a bit of humble

pie,' Lindsay said. 'Graham didn't want to do it, but to his credit he accepted he had a wider responsibility and telephoned Ellery. He only needed to give a little bit of ground, and Ellery was on the phone to me in a flash, telling me how much he respected Graham and how he would be happy to work with him again. It was only a personality clash, the sort you see ten times a season at any rugby club, but the two people involved were both fiercely proud. It was terrible while it was going on, but it was over in minutes. And when it was over it was over. Ellery flew out to New Zealand a few years later to take part in Graham's *This Is Your Life* programme. They are the best of friends now.'

Once back where they most wanted to be, Wigan suffered a bad attack of 'Wembleyitis', the rugby league term for putting all one's eggs in the Cup final basket, and lost their next three league matches on the trot, effectively leaving Widnes and St Helens to fight each other for the title. Wigan actually beat those clubs over the Easter period, and won all their four remaining league games, but the damage had been done. Worse, in the penultimate league game, at home to Salford, the terribly unlucky Hampson broke his arm. Not only did this put him out of the Wembley final for an unbelievable third time, it cost him his chance of touring Australia with Great Britain in summer. Hampson's storming displays at full-back had been a feature of the season, and he was the players' choice as first division Player of the Year. He was a certainty for the tour, where his performances against Balmain's Garry Jack would have been eagerly anticipated. For several years Jack had been regarded as the world's best full-back, but Hampson had improved, in defence and attack, to be within touching distance, and was poised to overtake him Down Under in 1988. Praise does not come any higher than that, and the whole of rugby league felt desperately sorry for a great player denied an opportunity he was so obviously ready to seize. The only, inadequate compensation was that Wigan were well covered for Wembley, with Lydon dropping back to full-back to accommodate the returning Bell in the centre. If that was an easy decision for Lowe, his forward selection was more complicated. Due to the non-availability of Hanley, West had appeared in all the earlier rounds. Now, with Hanley back in the pack after returning as a centre in the semi-final, West missed out on a forward spot, with Case and Shelford in the front row, Goodway and Potter behind, and Wane as forward substitute. The man who had lifted the Cup for Wigan three years previously would have to go to Wembley in a suit. This was undoubtedly hard on West, the most loyal of players who would not dream of staying away from the club to prove a point, and whose age was against him for future Wembley chances. The big man was not best pleased at Hanley's antics or his late return to the Cup final side, but diplomatically kept his thoughts to himself.

Back in the league, Widnes were champions by four points, St Helens pipped Wigan to runners-up spot on scoring difference. Not that Wigan were particularly interested in the runners-up spot. A first-round exit at home to

Warrington suggested they were not particularly interested in the Premiership either. Wigan had eyes only for the meeting with Halifax at Wembley on 30 April.

It was not the greatest of Cup finals. No 1985, certainly. There were some spectacular long-range tries in Wigan's 32–12 demolition of Halifax, but the final was too one-sided to be recalled with any great affection by the 94,273 present. Halifax, under Anderson, were supremely well organised, but susceptible to real pace, and a pitch as large as Wembley was always likely to expose that weakness. Wigan had pace in every department, and although the final got off to a slow start, their eventual try spree against a tiring Halifax highlighted the deficiencies of the St Helens side which had lost the Cup final to the Yorkshiremen by a single point the previous year.

Scoreless for almost half an hour, during which time Halifax lost their main playmaker and tactical kicker when Les Holliday twisted knee ligaments, the final was all but over by the interval. Three tries in six minutes, with a touchdown from Gill sandwiched between a pair from Kevin Iro, were followed by Lydon crossing by the posts on the stroke of half-time. The one consolation for Halifax was that Wigan kept missing the goals, even the last one, which Gregory, instigator of almost every try, slapped against an upright. The Halifax dressing-room must have been a forlorn place at half-time. It was already evident there was no way back for Halifax, and Wembley is a very public place to endure another 40 minutes of torment.

Gregory piled on the agony six minutes into the second half, floating a tantalising pass out to the right wing which Whitfield thought he could intercept but realised too late he couldn't, Tony Iro collecting the ball without breaking his stride to score. Gregory, a clear winner of the Lance Todd Trophy, had a hand in most of Wigan's most dangerous moves, but never was his positional awareness better demonstrated. Halifax wearily restarted the game, only to find themselves back under their posts in a matter of seconds.

*Popular try for Steve Hampson in his long-delayed Wembley début, against St Helens in 1989.
Phil Veivers can only watch.*

Gregory fielded the kick-off and fed Lydon, who cut an elegant swathe through the right side of the Halifax defence before unloading to Hanley, who kept out of reach of the cover in a sideways run to the posts. Gregory kicked the first Wigan goal from their sixth try, and with half an hour remaining, the final was beginning to appear like a case for the anti-cruelty league.

It did not quite turn out that way. Wigan's spate dried up as suddenly as it had started, and only one further try was added, a popular score from Bell, between the touchdowns from Tony Anderson and Neil James which allowed Halifax a vestige of respectability with a final scoreline of 32–12. There was so little drama towards the end that Edwards was able to withdraw himself to let his mate Byrne sample the atmosphere for the last five minutes. 'No one in the world would have beaten you out there today,' Lowe told his players after the lap of honour. Halifax were in no position to argue. 'Wigan were much too strong and fast for us,' Chris Anderson admitted.

As five of their players – Case, Edwards, Gill, Gregory and Hanley as captain – prepared to fly out to Australasia with Great Britain (Goodway was in the original party but pulled out for personal reasons, a decision he later came to regret; Lydon had to forego his place after a supporter pressed assault charges following an incident on the pitch at St Helens, the player was later cleared) Wigan could reflect on another satisfactory season. Not as successful as the previous campaign, which had brought in every prize available except the Challenge Cup, but Wigan could cope with missing out on the league title from time to time. It was Wembley they wanted to savour every year. Players like Hanley, Bell and Goodway were enjoying the experience for the first time, players like Case and Potter for perhaps the last, and the likes of Gregory and Lydon were reassuring themselves it was possible for Wigan to go as often as Widnes had. Goodway actually admitted he saw Wembley as an annual event in a programme interview soon after joining the club. In response to being

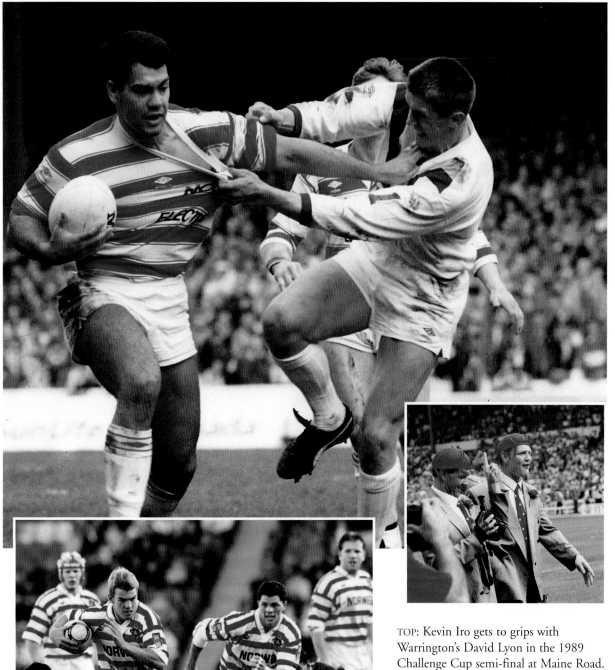

TOP: Kevin Iro gets to grips with Warrington's David Lyon in the 1989 Challenge Cup semi-final at Maine Road.

ABOVE: Billy McGinty and Neil Cowie stay in high spirits despite missing out on selection for Wembley 1993.

LEFT: Gary Connolly makes a break against Paris St Germain in the Super League in 1996, with Henry Paul in support.

The last Lancashire Cup win of all. John Monie and the Wigan team savour success against St Helens at Knowsley Road in 1992.

One for the Dorahy scrapbook. Coach John poses at Wembley with sons Dane and Jason and the 1994 Silk Cut Challenge Cup.

Henry Paul, resplendent in white boots, receives a pass from Mick Cassidy against Paris.

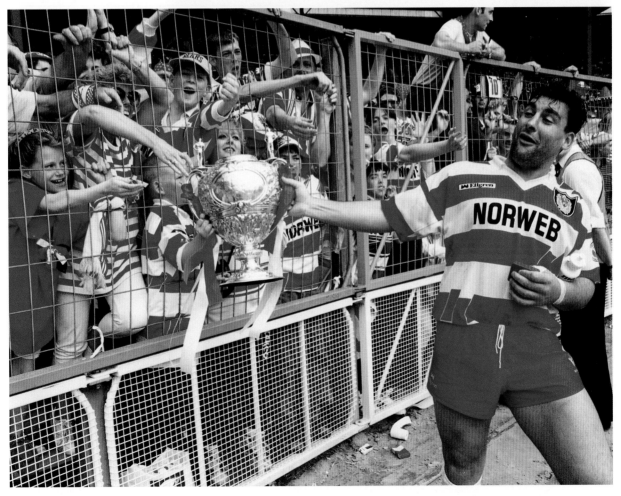

Give it back, it's mine! Kelvin Skerrett shows the Cup to eager Wigan fans after the 1993 final.

Can't catch me! Martin Offiah's length-of-the-field try at Wembley in 1995 against Leeds.

No old pals' act. Kelvin Skerrett fends off Ellery Hanley at Wembley in 1995.

Not bad for a beginner. Graeme West shows off the Central Park silverware after a grand slam in his first full season. Clockwise, from bottom left: the League Championship Trophy, the World Club Challenge Trophy, the Stones Bitter Premiership Trophy, the Silk Cut Challenge Cup, the BBC TV Team of the Year Award and the Regal Trophy.

Ouch! Henry Paul is collared by the Leeds defence in the 1995 Premiership final at Old Trafford.

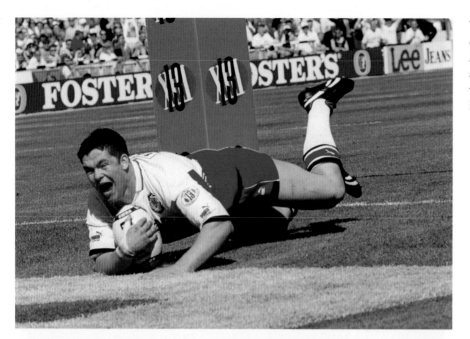

The loneliness of the long distance try-scorer. Not that Andy Farrell is complaining, as he crosses the Leeds line without a defender in sight in 1995.

Wigan win the shortened Centenary Championship in 1996, and get to keep the old League Championship trophy for good.

It's a lockout. Leeds defenders gang
up to keep out Neil Cowie in the
1995 Premiership final.

Jason Robinson directs Joe Lydon to
the try line in the 1993 Challenge
Cup quarter-final at snowy Halifax.

Denis Betts treats would-be tacklers with contempt in the 1995 Challenge Cup final against Leeds.

Maurice Lindsay. Yesterday Wigan, tomorrow the world. (Photo: Gerald Webster)

asked about his ambitions, he replied he would like to go to Wembley every single year. That was before he had even been once. 'I didn't know what it was like then,' he explained. 'It was just something I said off the top of my head. I mean, nobody goes to Wembley every year, do they? The very last thing I expected was for it to come true.'

Wigan knew that season 1988–89 would have to improve on the last, simply to avoid suffering by comparison. One of the penalties of aiming so high is that supporters expect a level of success every year, but Wigan thought they could provide it. There was plenty of improvement yet. The league and Cup double had never been achieved, for instance, and the league was the most obvious target to aim for after the Cup. Things did not go quite to plan. Widnes, after reinforcing their side with rugby union signings like Alan Tait, Emosi Koloto and, eventually, Jonathan Davies, were again the team to watch in the league, and the title race came down to a memorable showdown on the final day when Wigan were defeated at Naughton Park. Widnes were champions again, Wigan did not manage the double, and to cap it all Graham Lowe left for Australia at the end of the season. But his third season was as successful as every Wigan supporter wanted it to be. The Lancashire Cup arrived, as usual. The John Player Special Trophy returned after an absence of a year. Most important, the Challenge Cup stayed. And more important still, Wigan won it by beating St Helens at Wembley.

The season began ominously with defeat by Widnes in the Charity Shield match on the Isle of Man, the first occasion Wigan had failed to win one of these jaunts since their inception in 1985. Four of the Wembley side were missing, including Hanley, on his way to a losing Grand Final appearance in Sydney with Balmain, but Widnes had not managed to topple Wigan in four meetings the previous season, so it was odd they should start now. Offiah, the freakishly quick winger who had bagged 19 tries on tour with Great Britain, including one in the historic Test victory over Australia in Sydney, grabbed another one in Douglas. Several Wigan players had starred in the first British success over Australia for a decade, particularly Gill, scorer of two tries, Gregory, all-round inspiration, and Hanley, ditto and captain. The sight of Gill going round Garry Jack on the outside was a sight for sore British eyes, it was just a pity the victory came after Australia had secured the Ashes. Nevertheless, in 1988 it was apparent British rugby was on the right track. The Ashes series could have gone either way, and Wigan were chiefly responsible for the British revival. Indeed, had Goodway and Lydon been on the tour, the narrow defeat in the first Test might have been avoided and the outcome of the series altered.

Andy Platt, the St Helens back-row forward whose tour ended early with a wrist injury, was Wigan's big summer signing, moving between Knowsley Road and Central Park for £140,000. Saints fans were not happy. Although Platt had played at St Patrick's in his youth, he was St Helens born, and supporters felt his loss keenly, arguing, with some justification, that they would never match Wigan's standards by selling their best young players to the very club they were trying to catch. Platt was soon back at Knowsley Road, tasting the success only Wigan could promise. Wigan's fourth consecutive Lancashire Cup came after a 22–17 victory over Salford in the final at St Helens, the most significant obstacle having been cleared in the previous round when Widnes were beaten 14–10 at Central Park. Martin Dermott, beginning to threaten Kiss as first-choice hooker, scored Wigan's only try against Widnes, who were beaten by five goals from teenage full-back Sean Tyrer, whose father, Colin, once played for Wigan but was now on the Naughton Park coaching staff.

The JPS Trophy trial began in farce. Runcorn, Wigan's first-round opponents, surrendered ground advantage to play in front of a huge (for them) crowd of 7,233 at Central Park, but turned up with 12 regular first-teamers missing due to a players' strike. By scouring the amateur leagues and retirement homes for semi-senile professionals, Runcorn somehow fielded a side at Wigan, only to lose 92–2 in an embarrassingly one-sided game. No one demanded their money back, however, since the afternoon had its dramatic high point when former Wigan player and coach Bill Ashurst was dismissed for a blatant attack on Goodway, becoming the only born-again Christian ever to be caught on the nation's back pages in the act of head-butting an opponent. The 40-year-old Runcorn coach was banned for four matches by the league and fined £100 by his club. The ban didn't matter – 'I have no intention of playing again anyway,' Ashurst explained – but the fine rankled. 'It's a bit rum isn't it? I was only playing because the players walked out. They were only fined £50 for letting the club down; I showed loyalty and had to pay a ton.' Goodway, he said, had provoked him. He probably had. Goodway habitually called veteran players 'old fossils' and generally attempted to wind up opponents, but Ashurst seemed to seek out Goodway as if to remind him that he had once been the hard man on this patch, and perhaps prove to himself he still had it in him. Goodway just laughed. 'As a born-again Christian I should not have done what I did,' Ashurst admitted. 'I'm deeply ashamed and I'll regret it forever.'

Wigan needed a replay to see off Hull KR in the third round of the JPS Trophy, but otherwise progressed smoothly to a final meeting with Widnes, beating Halifax and Bradford on the way. Widnes, with Tait now looking a wonderfully complete full-back and Offiah an exceptional winger, behind a pack featuring Sorenson, Grima, Koloto and McKenzie, were already a formidable blend of uncompromising league players and exciting imports from union. But in the week preceding the final Laughton pulled off his biggest stroke yet by signing Welsh RU captain Jonathan Davies. The publicity alone appeared to edge Widnes ahead of Wigan as favourites to win the trophy. The Llanelli stand-off did not play in the final, despite mischievous speculation from Laughton that he might be named as substitute, but his presence in the stand at Bolton meant most of the outside broadcast equipment in the north of England turned up to record the meeting of Wigan and Davies's 'new team'. The slightly built Welshman's actual involvement in the day's events was limited to blinking under the television lights at an impromptu press conference, chatting to a BBC interviewer on the pitch and waving nervously to his new fans from his stand seat, but this arrival put the spotlight on the other union converts in the Widnes side.

To a man they failed to respond. Tait succumbed to nerves and lost his personal battle with Hampson, fit again and challenging for the Great Britain shirt. Offiah was starved of the ball and well policed on the few occasions he threatened. And Koloto, the big Tongan in the pack who had made giant strides in his first season in rugby league, had to be substituted early in the second half after conceding two expensive penalties, both kicked expertly by Lydon. The massive interest in Davies had concealed other Widnes weaknesses too. Sorenson was clearly not fit, and Myler, at stand-off, was all too easily dominated by the quicker, more alert Edwards. For a team which had promised so much, Widnes were a disappointment. Wigan, the side everyone had been prepared to write off, confounded their doubters in the most convincing way with a deserved 12–6 victory. Byrne, who began the match at stand-off with Edwards at scrum-half and Gregory on the bench, created the first try for Kevin Iro, then after Darren Wright had seized on a wayward pass from the otherwise impressive Shelford to level the scores with an interception try, Gregory took the field for the last half hour and conjured the winning try for Hanley with a pass round Grima. It had not been easy, in fact Davies's first question after the match was to ask if rugby league was always so hard, but Wigan had shown their nearest rivals they still had some way to go.

Smug smiles abounded in the winners' dressing-room afterwards. 'We all wish Jonathan the very best, but now he will know that Widnes are not the only team with great players,' Lindsay said. 'People seemed to overlook the fact that Hanley, Bell, Hampson, Goodway, Gregory, Lydon and the Iro brothers are all great players too. All we've heard this week is what a great team Jonathan Davies has joined. I think Widnes might have been victims of their own publicity.' Laughton was ready to concede the point. 'With

complaining of barracking from the home crowd and then objecting to being deposed as captain in favour of Hanley, but although he had asked for a move the club managed to keep him content. Gregory's beef was being left out of the starting line-up and only getting a game as a second-half substitute. He didn't mind at first, but after it had happened

Final hooter, Wembley 1989. Graham Lowe and the Wigan bench go up, Alex Murphy and St Helens stay down. Murphy's coaching career would never recover; Lowe's was about to take off in Australia.

hindsight, I think it might have been better to keep quiet about Davies until after the final,' the Widnes coach said. 'The whole thing came at the wrong time really. I was in Wales when I should have been helping our lads prepare, and the media fuss didn't help our concentration. The timing was unavoidable though, because we wanted Davies before the Challenge Cup deadline, and he couldn't have pulled out of the Welsh training squad without giving the game away.'

Gregory asked to come off the transfer list after the John Player final, having become the third point of Lowe's central triangle to find himself at odds with the coach. Edwards had had a couple of tiffs in late 1988, once

five times on the run, predictably earning Gregory the nickname Judge (because he sat on the bench), he went to see Lindsay. 'I can cope with being left out from time to time, but I don't want to make a career of it,' he told his chairman, Lindsay having by now taken over Jack Hilton's titular role as head of the club. 'If you don't want me, I'll go somewhere else.' Wigan definitely did want Gregory, but had no option but to accede to a transfer request from a player who was not in the team. So they made him available, and were immediately confronted with strong interest from Alex Murphy at St Helens. 'We would have been in trouble with the town again if we had let Greg go,' Lindsay said. 'It was another of those personality clash problems. Graham Lowe was trying to introduce a squad system, trying to use all his 15 players as imaginatively as possible, but was meeting resistance

Steve Hampson, a Wembley winner at last.

from players who were not as used to the idea as their counterparts in Australia. Virtually everyone had a sulk at one time or another about being left out of the team, I remember Andy Goodway once sitting on a ball like a spoilt child and refusing to take part in training, but it was because the team was so strong. Nobody wanted to miss a single game. It felt like a threat to be left out. We managed to explain this to Graham and patch things up with Andy. We would have needed a very good explanation for selling Andy to St Helens, and we didn't have one. Andy didn't want to go, and we didn't want to sell him. It was like Ellery all over again, but not as bad. Once we had resolved Ellery's situation, we felt better able to cope with smaller scale emergencies like Shaun and Andy.'

A feature of the Gregory dispute, however, was a certain amount of personal abuse

directed at Lowe, whose intransigence was perceived to be prolonging the argument. Nothing too serious, not that it is ever pleasant to receive hate mail and have your car daubed outside your home, but it affected Lowe, who was merely trying to assert his authority and take a principled stand. Here was an ironic twist to Wigan's rise to prominence. Ten years previously Wigan hardly had any supporters, and the men who almost led the club into extinction did so without any orchestrated public protest. Now the club was the most successful in Britain, arguably the world, and people were not satisfied with the way it was being run.

Gregory's dissatisfaction surfaced again when he was named substitute for the first-round Challenge Cup match at Doncaster, and even though Wigan improved noticeably when he came on, pulling away for a 38–6 victory, he missed the next round at Bradford amid talk of retiring from the game altogether. After an early season wobble in Yorkshire, when defeats at Wakefield, Castleford and Leeds cost them vital league points, Wigan put themselves back in the title frame by losing only one match between December and April, when they were surprisingly, but thoroughly, turned over at Central Park by Brian Smith's organised and efficient Hull. Perhaps Smith felt he had a point to prove. Illawarra might have been perennial wooden-spoonists in Sydney, but the English championship was a different matter. By virtue of a third-round victory at a snow-covered Oldham, where tries by Edwards and Kevin Iro helped ensure there was no repeat of the shock of two years previously, Wigan progressed to a Challenge Cup semi-final with Warrington at Maine Road. The larger venue had been chosen because a large crowd was anticipated, and 26,529 turned up to watch a Warrington side which fancied its chances of stopping Wigan's domination. In addition to Australian Test forwards Les Boyd and Steve Roach, Wire also boasted former Leigh favourites John Woods and Des Drummond, neither of whom had played at Wembley.

When the semi-final draw was made, it looked as though Wigan and Warrington would be fighting for the right to play Widnes at Wembley. Laughton's side were also chasing success on two fronts, and after blowing away quality opponents like Castleford and Leeds in earlier rounds, appeared to have a simple task against the fitful St Helens. At Central Park, however, fate conspired against Laughton's fast, entertaining side, destined never to grace Wembley until after it had started to split up. Richard Eyres was dismissed for a trip, an in vogue offence at the time, and Widnes were at a numerical disadvantage after 17 minutes, but that was not the only reason they failed to get into their stride. Perhaps they were still being unsettled by Davies, as yet unable to claim a place in the side. Perhaps the occasion got to them, as the John Player final against Wigan had. Murphy, the St Helens coach, was certainly not slow to talk up both these factors in his various media outlets, and Widnes failed to do themselves justice at Central Park. Even without O'Connor and Vautin, the two Australians whom Manly had refused to fly back for the game, St Helens won 16–14 through a late try by Les Quirk. Widnes claimed the match turned on Eyres's dismissal, St Helens could point, with at least as much justification, to a textbook tackle on Offiah by 17-year-old full-back Gary Connolly which saved a certain try.

The second semi-final had a lot to live up to, but probably managed it. The game was much tighter, hard fought and desperately close, so close, in fact, that it was decided by a drop goal, despite the eventual scoreline of 13–6 to Wigan. But this was no ordinary drop goal. Warrington, playing with a resolve which belied their lowly league status, were holding Wigan at 6–6 with less than ten minutes to go. Neither side looked particularly like breaking the deadlock, Warrington had stifled most of Wigan's attacking ploys and in Woods, had a player who could exploit the merest chink of an opening. Before the game Lowe had confessed to fearing Warrington, the one side who had beaten Wigan during his reign more times than Wigan had beaten

them. The tension was tangible, something special was needed to take either side to Wembley, but it was difficult to see what. Warrington had promised they would prevent Wigan scoring any of the flashy, long-range tries from their own half which had become their trademark, and they were as good as their word. Understandably though, they had overlooked the possibility of flashy, long-range drop goals from their own half. What took Wigan to Wembley in 1989 was an astonishing 61-yard pot-shot from Lydon which sailed between the uprights.

Lydon's monstrous kick dominated discussion of the match as completely as Eyres's dismissal had done in the earlier semi-final. 'I just hit it and hoped,' Lydon said with unconvincing modesty. 'I was going to kick for touch, but Hampo shouted to go for goal, and I thought, what the hell.' Lydon's effort was worth only a single point, but Warrington heads dropped, along with several thousand lower jaws, when the ball bisected the posts, and Edwards's late try, from Hanley's kick, was mere decoration. There were bruises in both dressing-rooms afterwards, and both sides acknowledged the efforts made by the other in one of the most draining of contests, but it was left to Lindsay to stress the significance of Wigan's achievement. Returning to Wembley was only part of it. 'Everyone knows that St Helens and Wigan have only met at Wembley twice, and that Wigan were humiliated on both occasions,' he said. 'Some of the most fervent of Wigan supporters believe nothing this club achieves will count for anything until we have set that record straight. The odds against both clubs making it to the final in the same year are very long, so I am delighted that we now have the opportunity.'

Both towns went mad with excitement and anticipation. It must be difficult for the rest of the world to comprehend, but for a small corner of what used to be south-west Lancashire, events do not come on a more global scale than Saints v. Wigan at Wembley. Before the oldest of rivalries could be resumed, however, there was some unfinished business with Widnes to resolve. Wigan won all their league matches after Maine Road, Widnes stuttered against Bradford and Hull then hit a winning streak which lasted all the way to the Premiership final. On one of the most exciting title climaxes for years, the destiny of the cham-

Nicky Kiss and Ian Lucas, Wembley 1989.

pionship came down to a last day meeting at Naughton Park, which Widnes won 32–18. Wigan were hampered by losing Kevin Iro to New Zealand Test duty and Edwards and Gregory to injury, and were not helped by what looked very much like a knock-on in the build-up to one of Offiah's tries going undetected, but could not really argue with the overall result. Offiah's third try alone was worthy of winning a championship. The winger sliced between Tony Iro and Bell and held off Hampson and Preston in a blistering 50-yard run to the line. Offiah's defence was criticised then as now, but any winger capable of scoring over 100 tries in his first two seasons, including such breathtakingly audacious finishes, had to be worth any coach's interest. Hanley tried his best to lead a fightback after Offiah's try, but Widnes held out. The Wigan captain had to be content

with a record third Man of Steel award. For Wigan, too, the season had to be judged a success. The average gate was now a healthy 15,000, a record for any club in the modern era, and Saints at Wembley were still to come.

That the first Challenge Cup semi-final had been something of a travesty was seen when Widnes played a league match at Knowsley Road a month in advance of the final and won 44–16, Saints' heaviest home defeat since the war. 'It looks like Wigan have got a bye at Wembley,' shouted one disgruntled spectator from the stand. He didn't know how right he was. Nor, probably, did Lindsay when he spoke of humiliation at Maine Road. By Murphy's own admission, Saints played like statues at Wembley and were totally humiliated in a shameful 27–0 defeat. Wigan, to be fair, would have given most other teams a similar mauling, but with a proud record, and the town's self-esteem at stake, St Helens completely failed their faithful supporters with a performance as abject as their opponents' was masterful. Long and loud were the recriminations in the local press, and the common themes were a sense of betrayal, and the pain which Saints, not Wigan, had inflicted on their followers at Wembley.

Eight miles away it was carnival time. Wigan, relieved to find that 1961 and 1966 were just defeats and not manifestations of some cosmic principle, celebrated in style. T-shirts bearing the simple slogan '27–0' appeared on the streets; the score, as Gregory pointed out after the game, expressing everything. 'I looked up at the scoreboard as I was leaving the pitch because I wanted to treasure the memory,' the scrum-half said. 'It seemed too good to be true, even then. I feel a bit sorry for St Helens, but I don't think anyone realises yet how well we played. It will take a while for our performance to get the credit it deserves.'

Gregory, Lance Todd Trophy winner a year earlier, was pipped on this occasion by Hanley, whose colossal impact on the final began in the second minute when Connolly, the 17-year-old full-back cruelly exposed on his biggest day, knocked-on to occasion a drop-out. Hampson, making a Wembley final appearance at long last, casually fielded the ball on half-way and fed his captain, who powered deep into the St Helens left flank, easily avoided an ineffective challenge from Roy Haggerty, drew the cover and released Kevin Iro to score through three players. The final was barely three minutes old, and St Helens fans would have no further cause for cheering.

Making 27 handling errors, missing tackles all over the pitch and looking clueless in attack, Saints became the first team for 38 years to fail to score at Wembley, only the fourth in history, and put up one of the most dismally inept performances in the history of the Challenge Cup. Wigan, by contrast, were almost perfect. Hanley played the game of his life, Kevin Iro was unlucky to miss out on the Man of the Match award after scoring two tries for a second time, and Edwards, Gregory, Hampson and Platt were all eye-catching in Wigan's disciplined yet dashing display. The forwards mowed down everything above grass height, while the backs darted purposefully through the numerous holes made in the St Helens defence. Hanley, of course, did both.

Hanley scored Wigan's second try in the 25th minute, the one which confirmed Wigan's superiority, sealed his Man of the Match award and probably still haunts St Helens to this day. Receiving the ball a couple of yards inside his own half, Hanley exploded again into the Saints defence, this time going all the way. Vautin, specially flown over from Australia with O'Connor, was effortlessly wrong-footed and left floundering, then as a quartet of defenders converged on the loose-forward 20 yards from the line, Hanley found extra speed and strength to burst out of custody and half stride, half stumble his way to a touchdown by the posts. Gregory dropped a goal next, as if anticipating a close contest, but the second half brought only further Wigan tries through Iro and Gregory himself, before Hampson completed the scoring with a popular touchdown.

Murphy's response to the embarrassing failure was predictable and rather lame. 'We

need six new players,' he said. 'Wigan were in a class of their own out there. We had pea-shooters to their cannon.' All true, but the coach needed to accept at least a portion of the blame for his initial selections, his failure to make changes when things started to go wrong, and the complete absence of any moves or tactical awareness in the St Helens display. Murphy's coaching career was effectively over. Few enough took him seriously after his Wigan dismissal, now his credibility, as well as his reputation as a Wembley magician, was in tatters.

Murphy, as is his wont, had started out by trying to ridicule Lowe and his clipboard methods. 'Wigan think you have to be miserable to win things, they are taking all the enjoyment out of the game.' Lowe's team had done his talking for him, but he was still magnanimous in victory. 'Saints made a lot of mistakes, but we forced them into errors,' Lowe said. 'We took hold of the game in the first minute and never let it go. It was as professional a performance as I've seen, we just didn't give St Helens a chance to play. That was the culmination of many months of hard work, and when we get it right like that, somebody suffers.'

Lindsay had to have the last word, as usual. A feature of the 1989 final was that Goodway only made the pitch as a substitute, such was the depth of talent in the squad, and Wigan's second substitute was the immensely promising Betts, still only 19 but certain of a big future. 'Wigan now have the best collection of talented players ever assembled at a rugby league club,' he said. Older generations of Wigan supporters might have taken issue with that contentious remark, but for once no one in St Helens had the stomach for an argument.

What Lindsay did not know at the time was that his collection of talented individuals had just lost its coach and inspiration. Lindsay knew that Lowe's three-year contract was up, and he knew his coach's stock had risen in Australia as a result of his Wigan success. He was slightly concerned that Lowe had not already brought up the subject of the future, but as the pair had never had a written agreement anyway, having proceeded from day one on the basis of a handshake, he was hopeful they could continue on the same footing.

He knew he was wrong, however, the day after Wembley when the fans lined the streets to welcome the Wigan team home. Just as the players were transferring from their motorway coach to the traditional open-topped bus at the usual point on the outskirts of town, Lowe caught sight of the crowds of cheering supporters and burst into tears. 'Graham was always the emotional type,' Lindsay said. 'But I sensed right away he was crying because he was leaving. Without being told, I just knew that he had signed up with an Australian club. I tackled him about it later in the evening and he admitted it. He had had a big offer from Manly, and had accepted it. I made a token effort at talking him round, but I knew it would be useless. Apart from the fact that he wasn't one for changing his mind, I knew he had always wanted to coach a big Winfield Cup side, and they don't come much bigger than Manly. I also knew his daughters from his first marriage were in Australia, and he hated being so far away from them, so it didn't seem right to stand in his way. Nor could we. He had done his three years, and done us proud.'

Still in tears, Lowe made an emotional speech to Wigan fans at the Cup homecoming – 'This is the best club in the world, thank you for having me as your coach' – which many supporters were almost as quick as Lindsay to interpret as his farewell. Few begrudged Lowe his chance to shine in Australia, and everyone in Wigan was sorry when ill-health curtailed his Winfield Cup career soon after it started. Lowe was a genuinely popular figure who, despite his various arguments, left no enemies in England. Once the immediate emotion of the parting was over, however, Lindsay went on the warpath. 'It turns out the English Rugby League had hosted an international board meeting in London,' he said, 'and during that period Ken Arthurson, the Australian representative, had tapped Lowey for Manly. I contacted him to register a complaint, about his using his official capacity to poach a coach from one club for another, but he said he was only carrying a message on Manly's behalf. A likely story. Everyone knows Manly is Arko's club. So I complained to David Oxley at rugby league headquarters, and he said he would look into it, but I doubt if he did anything. I certainly didn't hear any more of the matter, and it makes me laugh now, the way Arthurson gets built up as some kind of gentlemanly ambassador. That man pinched my coach.'

Lindsay's and Arthurson's paths would cross again in the '90s, at a time when Oxley's conciliatory, amenable approach was just a fond memory in rugby league, but we leave Wigan at the end of the '80s as world champions and conquerors of St Helens at Wembley. They had come quite a long way since beginning the decade as a complete and utter joke.

CHAPTER EIGHT

The Incredible Monie Man

*'I think a lot of English coaches do not pay enough attention to pure coaching,
to improving their own players.'*

Lindsay was despondent after losing Lowe, but far from defeated. He knew the next Wigan coach would be from Australia, where there appeared to be no shortage of bright, personable individuals with winning ways and thoroughly modern methods of communication with players. He was not sure if he could afford a top Winfield Cup coach, or even if he could persuade one to leave the sunshine of Australia for the winter of Wigan, but he felt such an appointment could build on the foundations Lowe had laid. 'The Graham Lowe era was a remarkable one for us, though at the end I never felt the only way to go was downhill,' Lindsay explained. 'I was still in the habit of going to Australia a lot. I used to go into dressing-rooms and see these coaches in action, and I was convinced there was still plenty that Sydney could teach England.'

Lindsay had one particular coach in mind, but doubted he would be able to get him until he read in *Rugby League Week* that John Monie was planning to retire. Monie had followed Jack Gibson, the most famous coach of all, at Parramatta and, initially at least, taken that club to new heights of success. Parramatta was the club which had supplied players like Kenny and Ella to Wigan, and Lindsay was on friendly terms with the club's agent, John White. Immediately he rang to check the situation. White was able to confirm that Monie was thinking of retiring after nine years with The Eels, and that he was still a great coach, just one in need of a rest. In White's opinion, Monie had simply been at the same club too long, and was getting out to make way for someone else. The great players

who had served Parramatta so well, the Kennys and the Sterlings and the Prices, were all approaching retirement and Monie felt he ought to be doing the same thing. 'Would he be good for Wigan?' Lindsay asked White. 'Maurice,' White replied, 'he would be absolutely brilliant for anybody.'

The only trouble was, Monie had his heart set on retirement. 'I'm just a beach bum,' he replied to Lindsay's first inquiry. 'I've been working hard for nine years and now I want to spend some time surfing. I think I've earned it.' Undeterred, Lindsay kept pestering his man, despite the wavering support of his fellow directors. 'Jack Robinson asked me why I was so insistent on getting Monie,' he recalled. 'He reminded me that Parramatta had not actually won anything for a few seasons. I knew that, but I knew there was something special about Monie. I had seen him operate, and wondered at the calmness of the man. Dressing-rooms of any sort are noisy, unruly places, rugby dressing-rooms especially. Yet I had seen Monie walking around one talking to players without even raising his voice. He had a presence which instantly commanded respect. And unlike some British coaches, when he talked it all made perfect sense. He made the game seem very simple, and he made sure each player knew his responsibilities.'

Lindsay knew Monie was cracking when he said he didn't know what England was like, but had never really fancied travelling that far. 'He told me he had only been out of Australia once, on holiday to Bali,' Lindsay said. 'He asked me if Wigan was anything like Bali. I must admit I was stumped for a minute. I'm quite a salesman, but I don't think I could have pulled that one off. But I didn't give up, I kept on at him, and eventually he said yes.' Monie duly discovered that Wigan was nothing like Bondi, let alone Bali, but he grew to like it anyway. He came for two years

Andy Platt, back-row ball-player at St Helens, turned into a first-rate prop forward at Wigan.

and ended up staying for four. He and his wife ensconced themselves comfortably at Wrightington, a small village at the rural end of the borough, where they quickly became involved in the local community. When the couple had a child, Lindsay was a godparent. And in the four years Monie was at Central Park, Wigan won the double of league and cup. Not once, but four times. Apologies for the sudden lack of suspense in this narrative, but Wigan were about to make suspense virtually redundant. In any contest involving Wigan when Monie was coach, it was never hard to pick the winner.

That there was something different about Monie was obvious from the day he walked in. 'The first thing you noticed was his immaculate grooming,' said Jack Winstanley, rugby league correspondent of *The Mail on Sunday*. 'His hair, his clothes, his whole demeanour seemed to belong to some other

occupation. He didn't look like any rugby league coach I have known, and he didn't sound like one either. He looked very smart, and that's the way he sounded. It could have been an act, but I didn't think so. He just projected class. He looked a winner.'

On the other side of the dressing-room wall, Goodway thought so too. 'We didn't know what to expect after Graham Lowe, obviously. It's always a bit of a worry for players when a new coach comes along. You don't know whether he'll rate you, he might have someone else in mind for your position, and so on. Usually you have an idea of what the bloke is going to be like from what he has done previously, but John Monie was a complete stranger to us.' In the summer of 1989, however, several Wigan players had been guesting with Australian clubs. Edwards went to Balmain, Gregory and Hampson played for Illawarra, Lydon was at Easts and Hanley, for a rumoured £4,000 a game, turned out for unfashionable Wests, and came back with a groin injury so serious Wigan eventually had to advertise in a national newspaper for a specialist competent to cure it. Before leaving for England, Monie made a point of meeting them all, so that as the Wigan players returned home, so did the first titbits of information about the new coach. 'The players who had been at home all summer were curious to know what Monie was like,' Goodway recalled. 'He had already been sending faxes to Westy detailing what he wanted doing in training, and we thought he might be a bit of an ogre. But the players who had met him said no, he's not like that at all.'

Goodway eventually met Monie, of course, and struck up a lasting friendship almost straightaway. Goodway had been closer than most to Lowe and was surprised to find another coach could command the same respect and admiration, although he recognised at once that Monie was a completely different animal from his predecessor. 'Graham's whole attitude was full of pride and passion, his feeling ran through the players,' Goodway explained. 'Monie made a point of not socialising with the players at all. He had a cut-off point. He'd say I'm going home, and leave us to it. It was like he only wanted to deal with us in working hours, and after that his life was his own. His approach worked, and I have tried to incorporate some

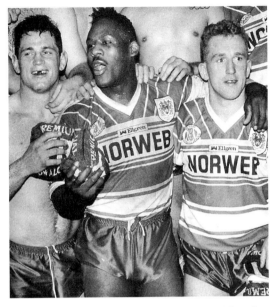

Andy Goodway, Ellery Hanley and Shaun Edwards.

of it in my own coaching career. I bet Dean Bell at Leeds is doing the same thing at Leeds.' Bell certainly is. 'Monie commanded respect but kept a distance,' Bell said. 'At first I thought it was just a quirk, but now I think it's important. It works. The other thing with Monie is that he never relaxed. Once we had a really good win and still got a 15-minute tape of our mistakes. But we never complained. You can't argue with results.' Every player who was under Monie will have been influenced by his style, Goodway reckons. 'I know I was. He is a man of few words, not a bit like Lowe, but he chooses his words carefully, and when you got a blast off him you knew you had stepped well out of line.'

Lindsay, having something of a way with words himself, describes Lowe as an evangelist and Monie as an educationalist. 'Graham was superb at putting belief into players, he could make the hair on the back of your neck stand on end, but he eventually got fed up

with the tantrums and petty squabbles in the Wigan dressing-room. He felt Australians were more professional, which is only true to a point. Their players can be just as difficult, but they don't have this British habit of sulking and refusing to play, taking their ball home, as we call it. In fact, I remember when Graham first arrived and asked why somebody or other wasn't at training, and his assistant, Geoff Hurst, told him it was because he had taken his ball home. Graham actually thought that meant he was training on his own at his home. He never got used to that sort of behaviour, he was very sensitive and used to get worked up if players wouldn't co-operate. John just let the players' problems wash over him. He deliberately kept a distance, and though he would come up to the boardroom and privately argue that we should keep such a player or sell another, he never showed his feelings to the players. His discipline was brilliant, mainly because the players were always in awe of his technical knowledge.'

Whether Monie's discipline would have been as brilliant if Wigan had been unsuccessful is an interesting question, but an academic one since it was never put to the test. Wigan just kept winning under Monie, despite losing their opening game against Warrington, and although his first few weeks were characterised, as Lowe's had been, by complaints of a rigidly defensive style which was alien to Wigan's attacking traditions, there were few dissenters left when the time came to count up the trophies at the end of the season. Wigan had missed out on the Lancashire Cup for the first time in four years, thanks to a surprise semi-final defeat by a single point at Oldham, but had retained the JPS Trophy, now retitled the Regal Trophy, by beating John Dorahy's Halifax in a bad-tempered final at Headingley. They had also retained the Challenge Cup for a third year, with a 36–14 rout of Warrington at Wembley after a terrific semi-final against rejuvenated St Helens at Old Trafford, and won the league title by four points, Preston scoring two tries to seal a 16–12 victory over nearest challengers Leeds in front of 24,462 at Central Park as the championship campaign reached its climax. The league and Cup double had previously been considered, if not impossible, an extremely tall order. Monie had managed it in his first season, seemingly by not changing anything.

'He didn't change anything for quite a while,' Goodway said. 'He told us he just wanted to watch us for a few weeks, to see how we worked, which seemed reasonable enough. He also told us we had been fooling

Joy from Bobby Goulding and the Wigan bench as Wigan beat St Helens in the Challenge Cup semi-final at Old Trafford in 1990.

ourselves if we thought we had been working with the weights, and wanted us to get stronger. Lowe had said more or less the same, but Monie gave us plans, detailed work-sheets to record our training, our targets and our progress. He also brought his own fitness expert over for a while, to show us what he wanted. He didn't leave much to chance. When he finally got round to discussing the way we played, he was just as meticulous. Out came the video, and we had to sit through the last game again. He would already have watched it a couple of times at home and prepared a script. Why did we do

that? Why didn't we try this? The way he broke games down was brilliant. There was nothing complicated about it, I just hadn't seen it done like that before. He didn't leave any room for argument, everything was all worked out. And though he said he didn't want to change much, and started us off sticking to a fairly rigid pattern, I think that before long we were playing to his exact instructions without even realising it.'

It wasn't quite all good news. Attendances at Central Park showed a fractional downturn for the first time in ten years, suggesting an average of 15,000 was what Wigan might have to settle for. Widnes, as champions, defeated Canberra in the second World Club Challenge, which produced a stirring contest at Old Trafford but no extra bums on Wigan seats. Lindsay though, was still hard at work at the ideas factory. His latest wheeze was to put Wigan in tight, shiny red shorts, figuring that sex appeal might pull in a few more female spectators. It is debatable whether this worked, although Lindsay says it did, but one or two traditionalists were seen shaking their heads in disbelief. Traditionalists were also beginning to worry about the Challenge Cup final. It wasn't that Wigan's unprecedented three wins on the trot represented unhealthy domination, several teams including Huddersfield, Wakefield, Widnes and Wigan themselves had come close to the feat over the years. It was more a concern that the last three finals had been one-horse races. Preston scored the most thrilling try against Warrington at Wembley, Kevin Iro scored twice yet again but saw the Lance Todd Trophy go to Gregory for a second time, and Edwards bravely played on despite the pain of a fractured eye socket. But the salient point from a neutral spectator's perspective was that the contest was over by half-time. The element of surprise and therefore excitement was missing. Wigan's three winning performances had been among the best in Challenge Cup history, but it was beginning to look as if no one else could live with them.

By 1990 Wigan were dominating every Challenge Cup draw, not just the competition's conclusion at Wembley. At each round of the tournament one club would receive the pairing it dreaded, the one that meant its Cup adventures were over for another year, while the rest of the game went through the motions of wondering whether this or that team could stop the Central Park juggernaut. The answer was always no. In 1990, Hull KR ran Wigan very close in a first-round tie on a muddy pitch at New Craven Park, but after that the holders had only to negotiate Dewsbury and Wakefield to book a

stage in the game, Hanley beat four defenders and presented Goodway with a try under the posts to clinch a dramatic 20–14 victory. After that, it was no surprise to find Warrington overawed and nervous at Wembley.

St Helens were the next to try, in 1991, but not even the old magic of Wigan and Saints at Wembley could quite lift the spell. There was little that was remarkable or memorable about the 13–8 victory over the old enemy at Wembley, except that Wigan, tired and injury-affected after a more than usually

The try that took John Monie to Wembley for the first time. Andy Goodway crosses by the posts, while Ellery Hanley, the architect of the score, looks satisfied with a job well done.

place in the semi-final. At Old Trafford, St Helens certainly gave them a game, but another factor in Wigan's domination began to reveal itself. The more high-profile, high-pressure games Wigan played, the more they thrived on them. Although Saints led for much of the semi-final, and were still hopeful of a replay when the game entered its final minute, they discovered their opponents had simply been keeping their powder dry. With an astonishing burst of energy for such a late

strenuous league campaign, gave their least convincing Wembley performance of the past four years. The holders looked vulnerable, and were possibly there for the taking, but St Helens could not raise their game sufficiently. It was a familiar story. No one could. There should have been no way for Wigan to retain their league championship in a climax to the season which saw them face eight matches in 19 days, even Monie called it 'Mission Impossible', but incredibly the Central Park supermen went through their punishing programme undefeated. To do so they had to call on all their resources, with Goulding deputising for the injured Gregory, Platt playing with pain-killing injections and even West emerging from semi-retirement, but

earlier, but there was no argument over a 26–6 victory in which the visitors were outscored by four tries to one. Little was seen of the explosive pace of Offiah, the brilliance of Davies or the strength of the Widnes pack, the factors which had taken Laughton's side

Andy Gregory scores against his old club Widnes in 1990. Bobby Goulding, who had to switch to hooker to play in the same side as Gregory, signals his approval, while new rugby league recruit Jonathan Davies lies down for a breather.

when it came to the games that mattered Wigan were still ahead of the rest. Closest challengers in the league were Widnes, and when the two sides met at Central Park in April for a match which Wigan needed to win to prevent the title returning to Naughton Park, the game attracted a lock-out attendance of 29,763, needless to say a new first division record. Wigan were slightly fortunate to meet a Widnes side still reeling from having their Wembley ambitions thwarted yet again by St Helens a few days

to within sight of another title. Instead, a Wigan side which had started the season sluggishly, with new signings Kelvin Skerrett and Frano Botica taking their time to bed down, burned at its brightest, with young forwards Betts and Clarke showing the shape of things to come.

Wigan now needed two points from their last two games to clinch the title, and since the final fixture was Leeds away, had to take something from the visit of Bradford two days after the Widnes match. When Bradford raced to an 18–2 lead against a visibly tired Wigan it appeared the 20,000 present would leave disappointed. Wigan would surely throw in the towel now. They were at Wembley, and had given the league title a good shot. No one would think any the worse of them for losing in any circumstances. In Hanley, however, Wigan had an individual unwilling to think of losing in any circumstances. Singlehandedly the Wigan captain inspired his side to a fightback in the last half hour, which saw Bradford denied and the score pulled back to 18–18. Wigan could even have won the game if a couple of late drop-goal attempts from Botica had succeeded. Bradford were amazed they could fail to win a game from such a position. Wigan supporters were equally surprised that one man could prove capable of winning it. Probably only Hanley could. He did not score, but he led by example in taking Bradford on and hurting them. All weary Wigan had to do was follow him. The game remains one of Lindsay's fondest memories. 'We have won cups, leagues, prizes, all sorts of things,' he said. 'But I have never seen anything like that before or since. I would say it was Ellery's finest hour. You could see the amount of pride and passion he has burning inside him. He just wouldn't lie down. He was incredible.'

Hanley had already shown his determination the previous season in coming back from a troublesome groin injury to lead Britain to victory over Australia at Wembley. He was now approaching the end of his playing career, but it speaks volumes for his durability and the sheer potency of his presence that Leeds were prepared to pay £250,000 for him later in the year. There will be few occasions in any sport in which the transfer record is broken for a 30-year-old player. But there are few athletes, in any sport, like Ellery Cuthwyn Hanley MBE. To journalists and reporters, indeed to the author who asked in vain for his assistance with this book, Hanley remains aloof, unapproachable, unwilling to communicate. I did interview him once, on the telephone, at the start of his

Wigan career when, oddly but consistently, he told me he enjoyed proving people wrong. 'Especially journalists. I like it when people put me down and I am able to make them eat their words.' To Malcolm Reilly, coach of Great Britain in 1991, he was a once-in-a-lifetime player. 'He's no trouble at all to me,' Reilly said. 'My only concern is to put out a

Ellery Hanley receives the Silk Cut Challenge Cup from David Oxley.

successful side, and he is my best player and a brilliant captain.' Lindsay argued he had earned the right to be accepted on his own terms. 'It is important to him to be totally independent, he likes to feel he doesn't have to do anything for anyone if he doesn't need it. He's a rebel, but a hard-working one, someone who does his work so well that he just gets left alone to go his own way. No one bothers him.' Like that other 'rebel' at the club, Goodway, Hanley was a non-drinking, non-smoking fitness fanatic who exerted a massive influence as a role model for younger players. Betts, one of a new generation of rugby players brought up to only know good habits, cheerfully admits to a reverence for both players bordering on hero worship. Goodway has possibly had a more practical influence on Betts's career, but Hanley remains his inspiration. 'You can't be in awe of anyone in this game, but I'll always be proud to have played alongside Ellery Hanley,' Betts said. 'He was a great professional who helped me a lot along the way. It doesn't bother me if he never says another word to anybody. He spoke for all of us players out on the pitch.'

Out on the pitch at Leeds, in the final game of the 1990–91 league campaign, Hanley had to leave early with a leg injury. Goulding, playing instead of the already injured Gregory, was the chief inspiration in a 20–8 triumph which ensured the championship stayed at Central Park. 'We feel we're the best team in the comp, and we didn't want the title stolen from us,' said Monie afterwards. 'But the rugby league isn't supposed to be an endurance type of thing, only a champion side like this could have done it.'

By the time the second league and cup double had been completed at Wembley a fortnight later, with 21-year-old Betts collecting the Lance Todd Trophy to cap a magnificent season, people were worrying aloud about the effect of Wigan's domination, though at least the league campaign, if not the cup run, had been a splendid series of exciting contests. *En route* to their fourth consecutive Challenge Cup, Wigan's first-round tie at Castleford was the only hurdle viewed with any concern, yet Darryl van de Velde's strong and capable side were blown away 28–4. 'Wigan were simply awesome,' the Australian coach admitted. In 1991, no one knew how long Wigan's superiority would last, and how damaging it would ultimately be for the morale and finances of their rivals.

In an editorial preface to the 1992–93 edition of the *Rothmans Rugby League Yearbook*, joint editors Ray Fletcher and David Howes mention that Wigan 'inevitably' dominate their review of the preceding season. 'We would endorse the view that Wigan's setting of high standards should set a challenge for others to emulate and surpass.' If this sounds a touch desperate, it needed to be. The championship and Challenge Cup had been secured again, but this time the margins were frightening. The gap at the top of the first division was eight points,

between Wigan and their nearest rivals St Helens, and Wigan had sealed the title by hammering Bradford 50–8 at Central Park with two games still to play. Now including a still muscular though not quite so pacy Henderson Gill on the wing, this was the same Bradford which had played with such

Happy homecoming. Once the players were content to wave the Challenge Cup around. By 1991 they had graduated to throwing directors in the bath. Jack Robinson looks cheerful enough despite the soaking. Maurice Lindsay is worried that this photograph might not be a good idea.

spirit the year earlier, but also the same Bradford which, in a travesty of a Challenge Cup semi-final at Burnden Park, had gone down to a record 71–10 defeat. Brilliantly though Wigan played that day, the evidence was staring the game in the face. Far from emulating, let alone surpassing, Wigan's standards, the rest of the game was actually falling further behind.

Perhaps this was not surprising, since Wigan were not standing still, waiting to be caught, but actively taking steps to stay ahead. The same edition of *Rothmans* shows exactly why the rest of the game was struggling to catch up. Between July 1991 and January 1992, Wigan signed 15 players. They included Martin Offiah, Gene Miles, Jason Robinson, Barrie-Jon Mather, Neil Cowie, Billy McGinty, Sam Panapa, Andre Stoop and, last but by no means least, a promising 16-year-old called Andrew Farrell. Anyone seeking to explain why Wigan stayed so long at the top need look no further. It is often remarked that Monie presided over a period when many of Wigan's big-name players left Central Park, and it is perfectly true that Hanley, Goodway, Gregory, Kevin Iro, Gill, Preston, Goulding and Wane departed on the Australian coach's watch. But this was a signing spree to match any in the club's history, and it was different in character to any which had preceded it. In the past, Wigan had prospered by simply going out and buying the best. This they did again with Offiah. No sooner had Hanley walked out of one door than the game's most lethal finisher walked in through another. Wigan had to pay Widnes £440,000 for the privilege, and for the first time in over a decade had to call in a few favours from sponsors and friends to raise the cash. Wigan had also had success in importing quality players from Australia, and did so again in finally capturing Miles for a single season, more than ten years after they first began talking to him. Doubtless the presence of Monie was a significant factor in the Brisbane centre's decision, and to a certain extent he was a vanity purchase – it was ironic that Miles finally came when Wigan were so strong they hardly needed him – though his partnership with Offiah was more than decorative. Lindsay himself could have scored tries from some of the gilt-edged invitations the giant centre sent out, and Offiah simply ran riot, scoring 30 tries in only 15 games, including five in the semi-final against Bradford and a ridiculous ten in a Premiership semi-final against Leeds, now coached by his old mentor, Doug Laughton.

Yet these were merely the famous names. No one had heard of Robinson, for instance, when Wigan pinched him from under Leeds's noses in 1991, but that soon changed when a rookie half-back was converted into a turbo-charged winger destined to electrify Wembley on more than one occasion. Mather was a tall, elegant centre or second row who came from a rugby union background but took to league straightaway. McGinty, Panapa and Cowie were steady performers for Warrington,

Wembley 1990. Andy Gregory is a Challenge Cup winner for the fifth time, and the first ever player to win the Lance Todd Trophy twice at Wembley.

Sheffield and Rochdale respectively whose careers were transformed at Central Park. Obviously they enjoyed more success than they had been used to, but it was more than that. Suddenly they appeared fitter, stronger, better players all round. It wasn't just the company they were keeping either. McGinty said that when he arrived at Wigan, saw what the players did and what he was expected to do, he realised that previously he had only been playing at being a full-time athlete. It was, he said revealingly, a bit like leaving an amateur club and joining the professionals. Wigan were now in the business of producing their own players. Betts and Clarke were the best examples, two players who would have made the grade wherever they happened to play, but who realised every ounce of their potential by beginning their careers at Central Park. Wigan had mastered the Australian concept of putting something extra into a player. Betts and Clarke represented a new breed of British rugby league player. Their development had been planned and monitored from day one, and it showed. Muscular but still fast, skilful, clever and enviably fit, they were state-of-the-art athletes for the game of the '90s. There was no doubt whatsoever that the precociously talented Farrell would follow in their footsteps, and sure enough the big back-row forward was a Wembley winner at the age of 17 and a Great Britain international a year later.

Wigan were so far ahead of the game in 1992 they could even afford to take time off to participate in the Sydney Sevens in between early rounds of the Challenge Cup, a competition they surprised themselves, and astonished everyone in Australia, by winning. Lindsay flew out with ten players basically to fulfil a flattering invitation – the Sydney Sevens might have been an event of some prestige Down Under but it meant little or nothing in Britain – and found, not for the first time, that the overwhelming expectation that Wigan would fail acted as a spur to the team. With Offiah in the side, of course, they happened to have a player guaranteed to run riot in a sevens tournament.

Andy Gregory takes up the story. 'Martin finished up as top scorer in the competition with ten tries, which pleased me because I'd had a bet on him to do just that. I'd seen what he could do for Widnes, so it seemed like a safe investment as long as we stayed in the competition. The funny thing was that David Myers fancied himself as top scorer too. He'd backed himself, and a few of the lads had backed him, but Dave didn't manage to score a single try in the whole competition. He took some fearful stick from Gene Miles about that. In fact, one morning he woke me up in the small hours. I heard a noise outside my bedroom door and went to see what it was, and it was Dave practising sprint training in the hotel corridor.'

Gregory was one of Wigan's best players, though he had had to be persuaded to go. 'I wasn't exactly the right size or shape for sevens, and I was reaching a stage in my career where I was slowing down a bit,' he explained. 'I only went because John Monie insisted, but I'm glad I did. It was a memorable experience. I'm very fair skinned, though, and everyone told me I'd suffer in the

Phil Clarke, one of the best players Wigan ever produced.

strong sunlight, because it was the height of the Australian summer. So I went on an intensive course under a sun-bed for a month to give myself a bit of colour. I was tingling with prickly heat all the way to Australia, then when we got there it poured with rain all week long. And I still got called a milk bottle because I looked so pale. The milk bottle managed to score a try though, which was more than Dave Myers did.'

Wigan were defeated by Cronulla in an early match and thought they would have to settle for the plate competition, but due to the complicated rules found themselves progressing to the knockout stage, where they won the trophy by beating Manly then Brisbane

Broncos. 'It was a great feeling,' Gregory said. 'Australians never give you any credit, so it's always a pleasure to wipe the smiles off their faces. But after getting beaten early on we didn't expect to win either. We were all lounging about at the back of the stand on the second day, drowning our sorrows with a few tins of beer, when Maurice came walking up, under an umbrella. We thought he was going to tell us which plane home we would be catching, but he came to tell us we had qualified. I doubt if a bunch of English rugby league lads has ever kicked their tins of beer away so quickly.'

Botica, the former New Zealand All Black who had become Wigan's first significant capture from rugby union for years a couple of seasons earlier, made a shrewd decision early in his rugby league career. 'I couldn't see where I was going to get in the team at first,' he said. 'I was still picking up the game, and I was surrounded by all these players who had been doing it all their lives, and they were so good at it. I used to watch the reserves and they were brilliant too. So I thought I would practise my goalkicking. I was asked to kick goals quite early on, and it surprised me that such a strong team did not seem to have a regular goalkicker, but I suppose Wigan figured they could always score enough tries to win matches. I still had the rugby union idea that a goalkicker is indispensable, so I thought if I worked hard enough and became good at it, they wouldn't be able to leave me out.' That is exactly how Botica's career turned out, though before long he was in the side for his general play, not just his goalkicking. But his unerring accuracy with the boot soon became one more factor in Wigan's impregnability. Botica could score from anywhere on the pitch, and usually did. Few could recall Jim Sullivan in his heyday for purposes of comparison, most were prepared to accept Botica as the best goalkicker they had seen. Certainly opponents were aware of the threat he posed. A try conceded against Wigan was always likely to cost you six points rather than four. Penalties would invariably be accepted. Wigan's score moving on in

multiples of six was the reason why so many huge totals were being run up. Botica scored ten goals in the 48–16 thrashing of Saints in the Premiership final, and nine in each of the 70-point romps against Bradford and Leeds. His accuracy also brought him six goals, and helped earn him the Man of the Match award, in a 21–4 success against Australian champions

Two men in suits. John Monie meets Prime Minister John Major after the 1992 Challenge Cup final.

Penrith in the third World Club Challenge, played at Anfield. Wigan were on top of the world again.

Playing on the right wing at Wembley, Botica kicked five goals and received a couple of nominations for the Lance Todd Trophy, but it was Offiah's match. The winger scored two tries which no one else could have managed in Wigan's comfortable 28–12 win over Castleford, and showed such lightning reactions in chasing and reaching Edwards's kick for his second that Prime Minister John Major, perhaps attending the game with a view to picking up a few tips on longevity, described him as 'faster than a camera shutter'. There could be no arguing with Offiah as Man of the Match, despite being only the second winger to receive the Lance Todd Trophy, the first being Saints' goalkicker Len Killeen against Wigan in 1966. In addition to being denied the first-ever Wembley hat-trick only by a debatable refereeing decision after another 50-yard run to the line, Offiah also used his speed to foil Castleford's Ellis in the 55th minute and prevent a certain try. John Major's surprise at Offiah's quickness was matched only by his shock at encountering a naked McGinty when the Prime Minister popped unannounced into the winning dressing-room. McGinty was returning from the shower wearing only a circular knee pad, which made a neat fit around what romantic novelists would refer to as his manhood. Mr Major appeared to take it for a piece of fruit. 'I'll never eat pineapple rings again,' he exclaimed.

There was another departure from Central Park in 1992. Maurice Lindsay stood down as a Wigan director and after spending part of the summer as tour manager with Great Britain in Australia (series lost 2–1; Offiah, Edwards, Lydon, Skerrett, Dermott, Platt, Betts, McGinty and Clarke all played in the intoxicating single success against Australia in Melbourne – the first time a Test side had ever fielded an entire pack from the same club) moved on to replace David Oxley as chief executive of the Rugby Football League. Monie was even less chuffed about this loss than the exodus of star players which he constantly grumbled about. He did not get on as well with Robinson, who now took over as chairman at Central Park, and was never likely to agree another extension to his contract once Lindsay had moved on to higher things. In fact Monie had higher things of his own to move on to, having been entrusted with the responsibility of taking Auckland Warriors into the Winfield Cup, and it became increasingly clear in his final season at Central Park that he would not be shedding any tears at leaving. For while the Warriors were a no-expense-spared opera-tion, with more than a year available to Monie to plan ahead and get his team together before New Zealand made its momentous entry into the newly expanded Australian competition in 1995, Wigan had suddenly started to count the pennies.

Partly this was the effect of spending nearly half a million on Offiah. Partly it was the draining effect on the club's finances of the new stand constructed at the pavilion end, a necessary and welcome bit of redevelopment which, due to unforeseen circumstances (though foreseeable, given that Wigan is a mining town literally built on unstable ground riddled with old pit shafts), took longer and cost considerably more than the £2 million which was first budgeted. And partly it was because the whole game was now struggling financially. In the past couple of years the league had been reorganised into three divisions, would shortly revert to two again, and was about to expel three of its most conspicuous under-achievers – Chorley, Blackpool and Nottingham – on the grounds that they contributed nothing and received grants which would be better spent else-where. Lindsay's reign as chief executive, it was already clear, would be markedly different in character from that of his predecessor, the friendly, tolerant but essentially ineffectual Oxley. Economies at rugby league headquarters began almost the day Lindsay walked in. Out went refereeing controller Fred Lindop, marketing executive Mike Turner and seven other members of the staff of 27. Like the clubs, Lindsay said, the league had to learn to live within its means. The game as a whole had been spending money it did not possess. Lindsay asked to see clubs' accounts, and was horrified at what he saw, where the accounts had been presented professionally enough to make them legible and coherent reading. In many cases they had not. With a mixture of shock, frustration and annoyance, Lindsay realised at once why the game was caving in around itself and why Wigan was compounding the imbalance by being so much better than everyone else. The calibre of administration at most of the lesser clubs and even some of the large ones was, in Lindsay's own words, 'quite abysmal'. He had always taken it for granted that clubs would see what Wigan were doing and start to do the same thing. He now understood how important his own input had been in Wigan's success. No one else happened to possess a workaholic chairman with an accountancy background, a flair for PR and marketing and a dazzling record in the transfer market. The gulf between Wigan and the rest on the pitch was only half the story. Off the field, with a few notable exceptions such as Leeds and Castleford, no one appeared to have even been watching the Wigan revolution, let alone learning from it. The attitude of several clubs, in fact, seemed to be one of hoping Wigan would simply go away. Having brought Wigan out of the dark ages in the early '80s, Lindsay now saw he would have to repeat the process for the rest of the game. He began to work on a policy document eventually called *Framing the Future*, which basically instructed clubs to get their financial and administrative acts together, to improve their grounds and try to attract spectators, rather than simply expecting the loyal few to continue turning up. 'Presented with a choice between a chief executive and a scrum-half, most of our clubs would go for the scrum-half every time,' Lindsay said. 'They would ignore the fact that the scrum-half has possibly only two seasons left in him and was a flop at his last club. They simply assume that by associating themselves with a certain name, and buying a hope of future glory, however remote, they will impress their supporters and be deemed ambitious. It never seems to worry them that they might be paying out dead money, whereas investing in quality management or improved facilities would bring money into the club. We have wasted the last 20 years and now the situation is critical. Unless we get organised quickly there may be no future for rugby league.'

This was common sense and simple business sense, but Robinson, struggling to cope with some extremely inflated players'

contracts at Central Park, could be excused a wry smile. 'Maurice is a good talker,' he said. 'In fact he rates himself as a top negotiator. He used to say there was no player or coach he couldn't persuade to come to Wigan. That made me laugh a bit. It's easy to negotiate deals if you have an unlimited budget. When Maurice encountered any opposition, he

Faster than a camera shutter . . . Martin Offiah bursts between former Wigan player Mike Ford (7) and the grounded Jon Wray to reach Shaun Edwards's kick and score in the 1992 Challenge Cup final, despite starting his run half the field behind the Castleford defenders.

would simply up the money. Every professional has his price, but it's much harder to get the people you want if funds are limited. Funds are limited at Wigan at the moment because we are paying out more than we can bring in. Our spending has got to be brought under control, and I've been left with the responsibility.'

Had Wigan made an early exit from the Cup or begun to perform poorly in the league at this delicate stage, the blow to their finances would have been severe. For several seasons now the club's accounts had been geared to large crowds, prolonged cup runs and a big Wembley pay-day. Speculation had been mounting as to what might happen if all this predicted success was suddenly interrupted, and now Lindsay had jumped ship before having to find out. Robinson, more cautious by nature, was simply exercising prudence in taking in some sail, but the crisis never arrived while Monie was in charge. Even though he bitterly opposed the release

a bookie's stand at Cheltenham races. Saints had to be content with getting the better of Wigan on three of the six occasions on which the clubs met in 1992–93, and holding their rivals to an honourable draw in the Good Friday derby at Central Park. Unfortunately, Wigan won when it really mattered. After losing the last ever Charity Shield game to Saints at Gateshead, Wigan won the last ever

Mr Popular. Wigan's £440,000 winger is mobbed by fans after the 1992 Challenge Cup final.

of Gregory, Goodway, Iro and Miles, the coach brought in another league and Cup double to order before leaving for 'a very long holiday'.

Wigan only won the league title on points scoring difference from St Helens in 1993, the first time a championship had been decided in such a way. St Helens made a half frivolous suggestion that a play-off should be arranged, because the principle of differentiating by scoring records was fundamentally flawed in a season which had seen relegation abandoned at the half-way stage. The argument was lost, but it was a good point. Anything now seemed possible in rugby league, even its chief executive was momentarily embarrassed when Alan Sherratt, chairman of the Blackpool club the league was trying to forget about, photographed Lindsay taking bets on

Lancashire Cup final. Only the rugby league would abolish a 90-year-old competition after it had just attracted a lock-out crowd of over 20,000 to a breathtaking final, but life under Lindsay was making post-revolutionary France seem ordered and rational by comparison. In fairness, there were several good reasons why the county cups had to go, but no one at Knowsley Road could remember what they were as Wigan beat Saints 5–4 in a tense, tryless final thanks to two goals and a drop goal from Botica. It was ironic the final should be so low scoring, since Wigan had amassed a total of 162 points in the three earlier rounds, Edwards becoming the second player in a year to score ten tries in a 78–0 rout of Swinton.

The next meeting was at Knowsley Road on Boxing Day, and the outcome was very different. Wigan were thrashed 41–6, the sort of tanking to which they and their coach were unaccustomed. When St Helens were drawn at Central Park in the second round of the Challenge Cup, Wigan supporters were understandably worried. Was this going to be the end? St Helens were not going to have to raise their game, Wigan would need to raise theirs. Few Challenge Cup ties in recent years had been as keenly anticipated on one side of

Martin Offiah, Jason Robinson and John Monie with the Challenge Cup in 1993, the coach's fourth and last. Wembley visit.

Billinge and as nervously awaited on the other. A crowd of 21,191 turned up to watch. Saints and their fans could not possibly have been any more fired up, yet within minutes of the kick-off they knew they were not going to Wembley. Wigan simply flew at them, and from the opening exchanges, with Clarke and the forwards leading the charge and Saints being forced backwards against their will, it was clear the holders intended to stay in the competition. Saints were well beaten, 23–3. No surprises this year either, although Wigan just as quickly lost their steely Cup resolve and were slightly fortunate to win by a single point in the next round at a snowy Halifax. But Wigan could obviously respond when they perceived their supremacy to be threatened. How did Monie motivate them for the Cup tie

against St Helens? By rerunning the video of the Boxing Day defeat, of course.

Monie could have done with doing the same thing before the Good Friday encounter, an entertaining 8–8 draw, and a game which drew a crowd of 29,839 to Central Park, creating a first division record likely to stand for some time. Wigan should have won the game, since a Lydon drop goal in the closing stages was discounted on the spurious grounds that Gus O'Donnell had got a hand to it in flight, a claim later disproved by television. In the long run it mattered little, since Saints needed to beat Wigan to retain a realistic chance of the title. Having failed, they could only watch as their rivals won their remaining two league matches against Warrington and Castleford to overhaul them at the top of the table on the final day.

Widnes, at Wembley, contributed to one of the most memorable finals in years. True, Eyres became only the second player ever to be dismissed in a Cup final, for elbowing Offiah in the head as his former team-mate hurtled past him, and that fact almost certainly saved the hot-headed Goulding, now playing for his home-town club after a brief and stormy sojourn with Laughton at Leeds, from becoming the third. Goulding escaped with a warning for a foul on Robinson which was just as cynical and which, as the scrum-half's temper had been ticking away like something unpleasant in an Alfred Hitchcock film, quite possibly contained an element of malice aforethought. When Goulding finally let his frustration get the better of him, Andrew Farrar, the big Australian centre who was effectively a cut-price replacement for Miles, had to be restrained by his teammates from picking up the little menace, possibly with a view to impaling him on the perimeter fence. Passions certainly ran high, but so they should in a Cup final, and after the lifeless processions of previous years this was much more like the real thing. To an extent Widnes's frustration was understandable. Having been cited for years as the only side capable of giving Wigan a game at Wembley, they eventually got there to find Offiah on the

The secret of Jason Robinson's elusiveness. Keep both feet off the ground.

opposing side, Koloto and Myler retired, Sorenson and the Hulmes at the veteran stage and Tait with Laughton at Leeds. But they still managed to score the first try, something no one else had managed since Wigan's dominance began in 1988, and took the lead again in the first half before Panapa claimed the game's most crucial touchdown early in the second half, taking a pass from Man of the Match Bell to score under the posts and celebrate with the biggest smile since Gill's in 1985.

With Monie having reacquainted himself with the Regal Trophy earlier in the season, as well as winning the Lancashire Cup for the first and last time, Wigan were now in a position to secure an unprecedented grand slam of every available domestic honour if they could carry off the Premiership Trophy at Old Trafford. The World Club Challenge

trophy had gone back to Australia, Brisbane Broncos having achieved the first-ever win on British soil at Central Park in November, but a domestic clean sweep would have been a perfect farewell for Monie. It nearly happened, Wigan were strong enough to beat Castleford six days after Wembley, but ran out of steam against a highly motivated St Helens in the final. Monie was not about to get upset over a sideshow like the Premiership. 'It's your game, and perhaps not my place to comment, but I really think the season should be organised so that it finishes with a bang at Wembley,' he said. 'When the players have built themselves up for that high, they don't really want to know anything else until it starts again after the summer break.'

Unknown to Monie, Lindsay and the league would eventually come round to his way of thinking, even though they did not follow his instructions to the letter. It was impossible to predict, as Monie departed in 1993, that within two years the game would have shelved the summer break, moved Wembley to the start of the season and repackaged the end-of-season play-offs as the climax to the whole event, but the Australian did prophetically warn that the English game would have to do something. 'There are too many easy games in England at the moment,' he said. 'That is probably the biggest single reason why overall standards are behind those in Australia. But even at a domestic level, easy games are frustrating for quality players and ultimately a turn-off for spectators. Sydney is tough because teams are strong all the way down the comp. Over here when top plays bottom you know who will win. In Sydney you don't. There are some very good English clubs, the standards at the top are comparable, but the big difference is the number of bad ones. Competition is healthier in Australia, coaching is more of a challenge.'

That said, coaching at Wigan had occasionally been a challenge for Monie, who had lost a lot of his favourite players against his will, and had had Botica foisted upon him by Robinson, who had simply been keen to take a risk on a rugby union player for a change. At that very time, Monie had already lined up the purchase of Phil Blake, a tried and tested rugby league utility back from Australia who had already proved a success in a short loan spell at Wigan. Monie was not in the habit of seeking recruits from rugby union, and thought a player of 26 was too old to teach new tricks. 'I just don't rate rugby union very highly,' he explained. 'I'm sure they have plenty of talented athletes in their ranks, but you could say the same thing about football, and we don't sign any of their players. Rugby union is not played at the same intensity as rugby league, you just know, watching that game, that the rules do not allow the players to be fully extended, and that even an average bunch of rugby league professionals would blow them off the park. I haven't got a bee in my bonnet about this, it's just a question of attitude. In my opinion the people with the best attitude to play rugby

league are rugby league players. They know how uncompromising the game is but they have willingly embraced it. Rugby union players always get a shock when they realise how different the games are. You are never sure whether they will be able to cope. It would be foolish to say none can make the transition, some of the very best league players have come from union, but as a coach, given a choice between a proven rugby league player

Frano Botica. The rugby union convert John Monie didn't fancy at first, but changed his mind about later.

and a promising rugby union one, I don't see the point of taking a risk.'

That attitude fairly represents the Australian outlook, where league is the dominant code and feels it has nothing to learn or gain from union. The British attitude is more pragmatic. Without an abundance of talent to go around, league has often looked beyond its northern confines to bring in talent from the 15-a-side game, especially from Wales, where good players are looking to make a living from their skill. Relatively few union converts make it to the top in league, however, and only Doug

The one that got away. Shaun Edwards looks exhausted after the 1993 Premiership final.

Laughton's string of successes at Widnes could be said to have been worth the time and trouble in recent times. Too many club chairmen appeared prepared to waste money on union captures for reasons associated with personal vanity, or the nebulous benefits of a few days of publicity. Prior to signing Botica, Wigan had wisely stayed out of the debate, and did not seem to have suffered by signing only league players. But Robinson had been excited by a glimpse of Botica he caught on video sent up by Wigan's Welsh scout. He was supposed to be assessing a Welsh forward, playing against the All Blacks, but he was most impressed by the tourists' lively half-back, and he reckoned it was about time Wigan took a gamble.

'Monie wanted risk-free signings all the time, he did exactly the same thing when he got to Auckland Warriors,' Robinson said. 'It's one way of ensuring you will never get tanked in a game, and as a rugby league man myself I've got a bit of a bias towards home-grown players too. If a lad's been playing league since the age of seven or eight he knows it backwards, you don't need to teach him the game, just show him the disciplines of playing in a professional team. But at the same time there's a big wide world beyond rugby league and some very talented individuals. Speaking as a fan, more than a director, I thought it was time to cast our net a bit wider.'

Monie could have quit in a huff when he found out he would have to telephone Blake and tell him he was surplus to requirements after all, but that was not his way. He felt just as angry about Gregory and Goodway leaving Central Park, but he always maintained the first duty of a coach was to work with the players he has, not the ones he would like. 'It's always my philosophy that you never sack a champion,' he said. 'I came back from Australia for my final season at Wigan, having spent two weeks persuading Gene Miles to re-sign for us, and immediately had the embarrassment of phoning him up to tell him the deal was off. Apparently he and Andy Gregory were both luxuries we could no longer afford. I was unhappy, to say the least. I had to go and say my piece to the board. I disagreed with them, and let them know, but once I had done that it was over. I'm a coach. I'm not paid to make business decisions, and neither would I want to.

'A club's books have got to balance, and as Wigan got a good price for Ellery Hanley, for example, it probably made sense to let him go. Personally, I would never agree to a player like that leaving, but a coach must work with what he has. I think a lot of rugby league coaches in England style themselves on football managers. They are often good at spotting talent and building sides, but possibly don't pay enough attention to pure coaching, to improving their own players. Wigan were pretty successful when I joined the club, but I reckon we made our biggest gains in my first 12 months, just by working on the weights and making sure the players stuck to the training disciplines. Wigan claimed they already had a weights room, but it was more like a brothel. They were only playing at it.'

Bell, the Wigan captain in Monie's final year, admits the truth of this. 'It never really struck me before, but John is right,' he said. 'He was ever so clever, saying he didn't plan to change anything at first but overhauling the fitness routines from day one. He was at the club so long it was easy to forget we hadn't always done things the way he showed us, but a lot of the disciplines we came to take for granted were his innovations. And he introduced them all in his first season.'

As Goodway said, no player who worked with Monie would regard him with anything less than admiration, with the possible exception of Preston, a winger whose defence was seen as a weakness but whose Central Park career might have been longer under a less demanding coaching regime. Even Botica quickly grew to like Monie, and more surprising still, the feeling was mutual. When Monie finally decamped to Auckland Warriors he took several Wigan players with him. Bell was an obvious choice as captain of the Warriors. Platt and Betts, the voracious workhorse who had responded most enthusiastically to the demanding training routines to pump himself up into one of the best prop forwards in the world, and the still-improving second-rower who already seemed to have a lifetime of achievement behind him at Wigan, were English players with big reputations Down Under. But Monie also took Botica, a big name in New Zealand for sure, but not initially a big favourite with the coach.

But typically, Monie had been instrumental in getting the best from his new player. Without rancour or further recrimination, he had introduced Botica on the wing, then gradually brought him inside to stand-off, allowing the player to develop at his own pace as his confidence increased. 'I could have sulked and thrown him in straightaway to see if he was as good as he was supposed to be, but that would have reflected poorly on both of us,' Monie said. 'You can crucify players that way.' Botica, an extremely good learner as well as a highly competent player, survived and prospered. He even turned up in a dream team of Parramatta and Wigan players Monie was asked to contribute to an Australian newspaper. 'Like Jack Robinson said all along, Frano is a very good player,' Monie said. 'I'm not right all of the time.'

For four years he had everyone in Wigan fooled.

CHAPTER NINE

Trouble and Strife

'How do you find the right person to deal with a dressing-room full of world-class psychopaths?'

Joe Lydon took quite a bit of ribbing from his team-mates when the identity of John Monie's successor was revealed. In the 1990 Regal Trophy final he had had a running battle with John Dorahy, and at one point was penalised for stamping on the Halifax player-coach. Dorahy had also been the player responsible for altering Shaun Edwards's youthful good looks when the Wigan teenager lost a front tooth at an early stage in his career. The Wigan players wondered if their new coach would hold these grudges against them. He didn't, although Dorahy might feel the Wigan players held plenty against him.

The Australian had failed to get Halifax out of the second division in his one season coaching in England – not that there was much chance of promotion when players were on strike over unpaid wages at Thrum Hall – and had returned Down Under to take up a position as assistant at Newcastle. He was a low-key appointment to follow Monie and something of a surprise choice. Dean Bell had bumped into him the day he was interviewed at Central Park without putting two and two together, because the names being mentioned in connection with the Wigan vacancy included those of Warren Ryan and Tim Sheens, the leading club coaches in Australia. Everyone assumed Wigan would continue to shop at the very top end of the market, forgetting that they only got Monie because he had decided to quit Parramatta, and even then he took a lot of persuading. The difficulty facing Jack Robinson was not merely money either. The whole relationship between Britain and Australia

Welcome to Wigan. Directors Robinson, Rathbone, Hilton and Martin greet Va'aiga Tuigamala.

had changed. In the '80s several coaches – Lowe, Anderson, Smith, even Monie to an extent – had used clubs in this country to enhance their reputations and advance their careers in Australia. British league was then a land of opportunity, Australian league was a tight little élite centred around Sydney which was difficult to break into. By 1993 all that had changed. The game in Britain was shrinking, in Australia it was growing fast. The Auckland Warriors were not the only new club due to come on stream in 1995, there were also extra teams planned for Queensland and Perth as Australian rugby league went transcontinental and trans-Tasman at the same time, fuelled by large amounts of television money.

Australia was the place to be, and Robinson would have had little chance of persuading Ryan or Sheens to try winter in Wigan even had he been willing to enter an open-ended auction. Which he was not. Budgetary constraints were a consideration, although Wigan still found the cash to purchase Gary Connolly from St Helens and Nigel Wright from Wakefield that summer for £250,000 and £140,000 respectively, but basically Robinson did not want to throw money at a coach to bribe him to make a move he did not fancy. He wanted someone who wanted to come to Wigan, and Dorahy fitted the bill perfectly. He was Australian, with English experience, his terms were acceptable and he gave a very good interview. Bell did not realise it that day at Central Park, but Dorahy had already made a sufficiently favourable impression on Robinson and the board to be offered the job a couple of days later.

'He was just the type of fellow we were looking for,' Robinson said. 'Young, with something still to prove, very pleasant and articulate, but with an obvious inner strength. We knew it was going to be a tough call following Monie. The people going around at the time saying coaching Wigan was the easiest job in the world simply didn't have a clue what they were talking about. For seven years we had a team full of top-class players who had known nothing but success under top-class coaches. The senior pros in the side would almost certainly have won more and done more than any coach we could bring in. Those players would spot any defect immediately, in fact they would probably be looking for signs of weakness. That may sound intimidating, but that's the way it is with sportsmen at the top of their profession. It's not a bed of roses. Dorahy knew the score, it was precisely because we thought he would be able to handle that situation that we gave him the job.'

Dorahy may not have known the whole score. He could not have known, for instance, that Wigan would lose four players to the Warriors and that Robinson and Monie would become involved in an international slanging match. The Wigan chairman did most of the slanging, accusing his former employee of reneging on a gentlemen's agreement not to poach contracted players and signing deals in secret, while Monie contented himself with clipped comments of the 'Jack Robinson should grow up and stop whingeing' variety. But despite the fact that Bell, Platt, Betts and Botica were available to Dorahy throughout the season, the Warriors

Steve Hampson towards the end of his Wigan career.

were always a distraction, particularly in the case of Bell, who was unavailable most of the time through injury. Bell is rightly indignant at the suggestion he was saving himself for the Warriors that season, his last at Wigan, but whether intentionally or otherwise his off-the-field presence acted as a focus for dressing-room discontent and a reminder of the way things used to be, thereby helping undermine Dorahy's authority. Bell had been Monie's captain, for instance, and when Dorahy offered the job to Platt in his absence, the forward declined out of loyalty to his friend. The coach ended up choosing Edwards, the very player with whom he had been at loggerheads for much of the season.

Perhaps most important, Dorahy could not have realised the significance of being the first coach employed by Wigan after Lindsay had left. Robinson had not appointed a coach on his own since Bamford, and even then he had had Lindsay at his side to help out when the going got rough. No one expected anything like that to happen to Wigan in 1993, the general perception was of a well-oiled machine which would continue to run smoothly, but as soon as Dorahy saw the club from the inside he began to appreciate it was not as substantial as it appeared to outsiders. That season, Wigan announced a £300,000 loss on a turnover of £3 million. Worryingly, wages alone were costing the club almost £2 million. The club's financial situation was delicate, to say the least. And when Dorahy went to meet Robinson at his place of work, an unprepossessing warehouse almost Dickensian in its dusty disorderliness, he was slightly taken aback. 'I was surprised that a club like Wigan could be run out of a place like that,' he said. 'My first thought was I had come half-way around the world to work for Steptoe and Son.'

Robinson's down-to-earth nature always used to be balanced by Lindsay's eloquent charm, but what Dorahy found in 1993 was a club chairman who was not only on his own but feeling lonely. When Lindsay left in 1992 he allowed a majority shareholding to pass to Robinson, and his seat on the board and the remaining shares were taken up by Melvyn Leatherbarrow of Oldham, better known as John Martin of the Riverside. The latter was the cavernous nightclub and architectural carbuncle built into the front of Central Park, unwisely sold into private hands by the club in a period of penury in the '70s. Martin was the entertainer cum entrepreneur who had made it work, packing the place out every weekend with a combination of cabaret kitsch and harmless ribaldry which Wiganers on the razzle found went just right with a dozen pints of lager and a few dodgy cocktails. For a few years in the early '80s the Riverside was undoubtedly more famous than the rugby club, which had frequently been berated for

letting such a reliable source of revenue slip away. Having Martin on the board brought the two interests closer together, which was desirable, although the immediate advantage to Robinson was in thwarting the ambitions of millionaire businessman Dave Whelan.

After several years of hovering in the background, Whelan now wanted to buy into Wigan in a big way, and had anticipated

Hampson's replacement, the elegant and enviably talented Gary Connolly from St Helens, sets off on a run with Martin Offiah in support.

taking Lindsay's seat on the board. The club could certainly have done with his money, but Robinson believed Whelan would demand a high price for any cash injection. 'Dave wanted to take over, I don't think anyone can be in too much doubt about that,' Robinson said. 'He's a clever chap, saying he only wants to help us out, but I know the way he operates and he would insist on sole control. But he didn't build this club up from nothing, did he? Where was he when Wigan were in the second division?' In selling his shares to Robinson, Lindsay appeared to endorse this opinion, and when Whelan discovered he had been out-manoeuvred he was furious. He could still have bought up a minority shareholding, but said he had changed his mind about joining the board and revised his opinion of the present directors, following their scandalous treatment of Steve Hampson.

This was transparently a convenient excuse, though it did highlight a public relations bungle which did not augur well for Robinson's period in sole charge. At the end of the 1992–93 season Hampson had been unceremoniously dumped by the club, first placed on the list at £15,000 and then given a free transfer, as Wigan prepared to bring in Connolly from St Helens. Hampson was 30 and not quite the player he used to be, still reliable but lacking the dash and impudence of old, whereas Connolly at 21 was an enviably complete player with a lot of experience behind him and clearly a great future ahead. As a swap, it made sound sense, but that was not the point. Hampson was due a testimonial. And he was a very popular player. Every Wigan supporter had a soft spot for the player who had suffered such cruel luck with injuries and missed the first three Wembley visits. The lad who originally did not appear to realise how good he was yet had climbed to the very top of his profession, only to be struck down by injury again. Hampson had never fallen out with any of his coaches either, and because he arrived with no reputation and stayed loyal to the same club, he was never able to profit from a fat transfer fee or demand a substantial pay rise. He was, in short, the most deserving case for a testimonial imaginable, and his benefit would certainly have been well supported, yet Wigan turned him down.

Whelan was not exaggerating the situation, the town was shocked. Hampson himself was angry and confused. 'They have taken away my pension,' he said. 'I don't think I ever did anything to deserve such treatment, you wouldn't do that to your worst enemy. You normally need 300 games for a benefit, I did 306, and obviously I would have managed more but for missing a whole season through

injury. Or you can have a benefit after ten years. I did nine years eight months and then they just said: "Sorry, you're not involved with us any more." I was on tour with Great Britain a year ago and won the Man of the

A study in concentration from Shaun Edwards.

Match award this year in the Challenge Cup semi-final against Bradford, so I can't be all that washed up. I loved playing for Wigan, I never wanted to play for anyone else, but I would never have expected a kick in the teeth like this.'

The conclusion Hampson drew, along with the vast majority of supporters, was that such an injustice would never have happened had Lindsay still been at the club. Perhaps that is not strictly true. As we shall see, Robinson was always the ruthless partner, sticking to his principles and often prevailing over Lindsay's tendency to complicate matters with a more conciliatory approach. With Lindsay departed, the ruthlessness was still there but without the sugar coating. Hampson might still have been disappointed had Lindsay still been around, but he would not have been so stunned. Lindsay would have found some way of stage-managing the affair so it all ended happily. Martin, his replacement, was merely a figure in the background at this stage. He had neither the knowledge nor experience to offer Robinson useful

Another Wembley homecoming, another spot of controversy. John Dorahy answers his critics.

support on rugby matters, though he would soon boast a prop forward as a son-in-law when Neil Cowie married his daughter.

Dorahy probably paid little attention to this local drama on arrival at Wigan, when in fact it could have told him much about what would later unfold. After three wins in the league, the first sign of trouble arrived with a 35–22 defeat at Featherstone. Wigan supporters thought they had put this sort of thing behind them but accepted it without too much grumbling, until Dorahy criticised Wright's performance in the press, singling out the player's defensive lapses as a factor in the defeat. Letters arrived in bundles at local newspapers. Criticising one's own players, Dorahy was swiftly informed, was not the Wigan way.

League form swiftly picked up, and the only defeat in the next five matches was at home to the New Zealand tourists. When the Kiwis met Great Britain at Wembley, Robinson scored two typically alert tries on his Test début, and with the series won, 18-year-old Farrell was called up for the third Test. It was the international in between, played at Central Park on 30 October, which caused all the fuss. Wigan had four players involved – Edwards, Offiah, Clarke and Connolly – and a few extra injury problems as well, but Dorahy decided against postponing the fixture at Castleford a day later. From the comments made by Edwards and Offiah after the international at Wigan, it was clear the decision to play the following day had not been a popular one. The same two players subsequently pulled out of the Castleford trip, citing injuries from the international, for which they were disciplined and dropped by Dorahy. The coach was within his rights in asserting his authority here, and both players accepted their punishment without demur, but it was too late. Wigan were thrashed 46–0 at Wheldon Road, and not even the absence of Edwards and Offiah, the tiredness of Clarke and Connolly or the presence of raw reserves like Murdock, Radlinski and Haughton could explain a result like that. Something was wrong.

As if chastened, Wigan won their next nine games in a row, including a big Boxing Day win in front of 29,100 at Central Park, and although some of the performances had been less than vintage, the problem seemed to have gone away until Castleford cropped up again, this time in the Regal Trophy final at Headingley on 22 January. Wigan had never lost a Regal final before, but they were never in this one. Castleford played superbly, Wigan were deservedly beaten 33–2. Any team might have struggled against Castleford that day, but Wigan were not just any team, and it was unusual to see them so comprehensively outplayed. So not only had Dorahy's team just lost its first Regal final in seven, it now trailed to Castleford by an aggregate score of 79–2 after two meetings.

Unless Wigan were simply allergic to Lee Crooks, something was very wrong.

Watching the Headingley débâcle from the stand was Va'aiga Tuigamala, the All Black barrel of a winger who had just become Wigan's second high-profile rugby union signing. Robinson had been so impressed with Botica he had decided to go back for another of New Zealand's finest. Inga the Winger was probably the most famous rugby player in the world at the time, but Robinson reported disappointingly little in the way of clandestine meetings or patient stalking of the prey. 'We just dealt with his agent,' he explained, matter of factly. 'There was none of the cloak and dagger stuff we had with Frano, when we had to smuggle him out of the All Black camp and up to Wigan for a day. Inga wanted to join us, so it was all pretty straightforward.' When Botica had arrived he expressed the fear that he might have come too late to share in Wigan's success. 'I knew I was joining a good team, but kept thinking it would be just like me to join them the year they didn't get to Wembley,' he said. Botica needn't have worried, all his seasons at Wigan were phenomenally successful. But Tuigamala must have been thinking similar thoughts as he watched his new team fail to make an impression on Castleford. Was this really the unbeatable Wigan he had heard so much about?

The Challenge Cup got under way the following week, and although Wigan beat Wakefield 24–16 at home, the performance was far from convincing and only an interception try from Wright made the game safe. The Wigan crowd were thrilled by the lively and elusive Henry Paul, a young Auckland Warrior on loan to Trinity, but audibly critical of their own team. Wigan's confidence seemed badly affected. Tuigamala made a surprise début at Widnes, scoring a try in an easy win watched by 5,772 spectators, but was left out of the next match, a Challenge Cup tie at Hull, when Wigan scraped through by a single point after trailing 21–2 in the first half. Tuigamala made his home début in the following game, at

home to Wakefield in the league, but again the only New Zealander worth watching was Paul, who was even more prominent than before in helping his side to a shock 20–13 win. Dorahy criticised referee Robin Whitfield after this game, for which he was fined £250 by the League, and when Wigan and Featherstone players were fined for brawling in the Cup quarter-final (Skerrett literally flying into the action in one of the season's few moments of comedy) it was noticeable that the coach could not quite distance himself from the controversy, blaming opposition players and exonerating his own. Disparaging opposing teams was now a more or less weekly routine. It was clear that Dorahy, for better or worse, was doing things differently to the almost painfully discreet Monie.

So unconvincingly were Wigan playing that for the first time in half a dozen seasons supporters went into a Challenge Cup semi-final with something approaching trepidation. Even a bad Wigan side could still get to Wembley most years, but this year the opponents were Castleford, at the same Headingley venue which had witnessed the Regal Trophy reversal. No one was rushing to back against Wigan, any gambler had to respect the record of a side which had succeeded in its last six semi-finals, but if this one went to form, Wigan would be out of the Cup, and that was not something anyone had been heard saying for the past seven years.

Wigan did not go out of the Cup. They raised their game considerably, and put in one of their best performances of the season to sweep past Castleford 20–6. 'We will always raise our game in the Cup,' Denis Betts explained. 'Especially if there is an expectation or a fear we might lose. Because we are all scared stiff of losing. The longer this record goes on, the more powerfully it grips the players. No one wants to be in the team that finally loses it. New players are coming in all the time, and they don't want to be held responsible for letting the side down either. It's a sort of pressure really, when we come to the end of another Cup win we feel relief more than enjoyment. But that's what keeps us going. Fear. It's a self-perpetuating thing.' While the wider game sighed with disappointment after Headingley, Wigan followers travelled home wondering what all the fuss was about. Was there anything wrong with the team after all? Or was it just the coach? Before the Headingley car park had emptied, stories were circulating about Dorahy asking the players to pick the team themselves.

Stranger still, Wigan slumped quickly back into lethargy, losing four out of five away matches after the cup semi-final and all but throwing away their chance of the league. Had they lost at Knowsley Road on Good Friday they would almost certainly have left themselves too much ground to make up, but they were able to win the hardest fixture, despite it cropping up in the middle of the sequence of five, and took six points from their last three league games to secure a fifth successive championship on points scoring difference in a three-way split with Warrington and Bradford. The catalyst for the late spurt seemed to have been the appointment of Bell as coaching co-ordinator. The appointment was short-lived – 'I only took it because I thought they were going to get rid of John,' Bell said. 'I didn't realise he would be standing behind me when I went back to all our old moves.' – but the message got through to the players that Dorahy's days were numbered, and the effect was startling. Dorahy must have picked up exactly the same signal, yet his message in the final league game of the season at Oldham – 'To all doubters – suck!' – could only have hastened his demise.

The coach cut a less controversial but equally forlorn figure at Wembley, after the victory against Leeds which brought Offiah two splendid long-range tries and his second Lance Todd Trophy. Unsought by congratulatory handshakers, uninvited into any of the celebratory antics, Dorahy only just managed to get involved in the team photograph, and everybody used to get on that. He did get hold of the Cup for a short time, to show it off to his family in the crowd and pose briefly for photographs, but he was all too clearly alone in his moment of triumph. Those newspaper photographs were to come in handy when Dorahy was sacked two days later.

By the end of the season there was little doubt that Dorahy would not be around the following year, but few expected his tenure to end quite so suddenly and messily. The Australian felt insulted at the post-Wembley club dinner when, with his family present, he was pointedly snubbed by Robinson, who thanked everyone at the club but failed to even mention the coach. The following day, on the coach back to Wigan, a scuffle broke out between the two men. Like the Lindsay-Murphy-telephone tale, the idea of Dorahy and Robinson rolling around in the dusty aisle of a coach was too good not to be true, and contemporary accounts ranged from a heated argument to a full-scale punch-up. Bell, in his book *Ultimate Warrior*, describes it as a bit of pushing and shoving. Both Robinson and Dorahy deny there was any physical contact at all. Robinson complains of 'a torrent of abuse', Dorahy says he was 'verbally attacked'. Each insists the other was the instigator. But the upshot was Dorahy's departure, sacked for 'gross misconduct' at first, later toned down by Robinson to the less challengeable 'unhappy differences'.

All that remained was to sort out the severance. Dorahy expected compensation to reflect his three-year agreement, and was stunned to hear Robinson talking of a 12-month trial period, with an option of a further two years. 'That was definitely not the agreement we started out with,' Dorahy said. 'There is no way I would have dragged my family across from Australia just for 12 months. We agreed to a compromise and the settlement was progressing fairly amicably until Wigan moved the goalposts again while I was out of the country. I ended up with more than I was originally offered, but less than I was entitled to. Old man Steptoe did me in the end.'

Dorahy is keen to correct several false impressions of his turbulent season at Central Park, beginning with the idea that it was all a painful mistake. I apologised in advance in case the title of this book caused him to wince,

Henry Paul in defence.

but he said no, he regarded his time at Wigan as one of the best years of his life too. 'It had a mixed finish, to say the least, but it was one of the most challenging and satisfying years I've known,' he explained. 'I felt I had been thrown into a position on a par with the supercoaches of the world, knowing how demanding the job of coaching a top team can be, and I think that despite limited coaching experience I handled it quite capably. I'm not saying I didn't make mistakes or that I didn't have to learn quickly. But I thought I was coping. I didn't want out. I could only have got better the following season.'

The popular notion that Dorahy never saw eye to eye with Edwards is also wide of the mark, Dorahy claims. Edwards will actually confirm this, maintaining that while he found some of Dorahy's actions hard to understand, he respected him then and still gets along with him now. 'I did have some set-tos with Shaun, he is an outspoken member of the team and we did not always agree,' Dorahy said. 'I had battles with Dean Bell and a few others as well. That's par for the course. But while on occasions I was disappointed with the attitude of some of the so-called professionals at the club, Shaun was never one of the players who spat the dummy. I knew he'd fallen out with Graham Lowe and John Monie in his time, but he never refused to play for me, even when I pulled him off for the first time in his career at Wakefield. He told me that had never happened to him before – I didn't expect him to be thrilled – but after that he was fine.'

Dorahy's only real regret, the only thing he would have done differently had it been possible, was leaving before the end of the season and allowing Graham West to reap the benefit of the glorious World Club Challenge. 'It was a mistake not to finish the season, I would have liked the opportunity to take the team on, but it was out of my hands,' he said. 'I think Graeme West got a lucky break there, but fair play to him, he saw his chance and took it. Jack Robinson once told me that Graeme West would never be coach at that club as long as he was chairman. That was about a month before he appointed Graeme West as coach. But I'm not bitter. I understand that it is easier to have a yes-man as coach than someone who is prepared to put his foot down and make a stand. It might not be the best thing for the club, but it is easiest in the short term. My mistake was to assume that Wigan wanted a coach to stand up to the players. I'm a fairly easy-going sort of person most of the time, but I can make hard decisions. The main trouble was that some of the players couldn't take them. They didn't like the straightforwardness I applied. Some of those players with quite big egos didn't like to be constructively criticised. They didn't like the way I operated. So I had to go, but the daft thing is I'm sure the situation at Wigan is worse now than when I was there. I'm sure the players are trampling all over the coach and from the sound of it the chairman is digging an even bigger hole for himself.'

At Wigan, according to Dorahy, the politics come from the dressing-room as well as the boardroom and the coach is usually caught in the crossfire. He accepts, with hindsight, that playing the game at Castleford the day after the Kiwi Test was a costly mistake which would perhaps have been best avoided. 'But we needed to get games played, and I think we could have given Castleford a pretty fair run for their money had we not had a mutiny on our hands,' he said. 'I was very upset at the scoreline. I didn't like the Regal Trophy final result too much either, though at least Castleford had played well. Sometimes games go like that. Asking the players to pick their best side before the Challenge Cup semi-final against Castleford was all to do with politics. As a psychological exercise it was quite useful, I am always interested to know how players respond to each other and rate each other, but the main reason why I did it was to show the board that the players wanted Platt and Skerrett to be in the front row. I had been put under pressure to include Cowie, ostensibly because he would be with us for the future and not going to Auckland, but in reality because he was related to one of the directors.'

Dorahy dropped Cowie for the Headingley game and left him out of the starting line-up at Wembley too. 'I could hear the jungle drums beating for me after that, but I still wasn't expecting the freeze-out at the hotel. Whatever I was supposed to have done, that was out of order. I don't think Jack could have made me feel any worse if he'd told me not to turn up next season or sacked me on the spot. It wasn't even as if we had lost. When I came to Wigan I knew that anything less than league and Cup was likely to be regarded as failure, and naturally I was worried that I wouldn't be as successful as John Monie. But Jack gave me so much support it wasn't funny. He was a model of patience and understanding when things began to go wrong. He was almost too kind. I remember sitting in his car for about an hour one night after training, discussing plans for next season. He told me not to get too upset about the way things were going, because he knew how hard it was to step into Monie's

shoes, and I couldn't be expected to pick it up straightaway. And when we won at Wembley I thought: "Well, it's been a pretty up-and-down season, but here we are with the double again, I've not done too badly after all." But Jack had completely changed his attitude by the time of the Cup final. He had set his face against me. I knew him sufficiently by that time to recognise that was how he operated – he was a wheeler-dealer in business and he would make the same sort of instant decisions in life, but I was still hurt by his rudeness at the banquet. That was simply un-English.'

Even Bell, by no means Dorahy's biggest fan, said Robinson's behaviour spoiled the celebration. 'There was a real tension in the air, it was very awkward,' he said. 'That's a very chivalrous thing for Mean Dean to say,' Dorahy acknowledged. The coach still blames his captain for coming to see him late in the season with the news that 80 per cent of the players were against him. 'I asked him to name names, and Dean started to squirm a bit,' Dorahy said. 'He said he didn't know how he had got himself into this predicament.' What Dorahy didn't know was that Robinson had pushed Bell into this meeting, doing his dirty work for him as the player would later describe it. Dorahy and his family eventually left the banquet, but they were not the only ones discomfited. 'John Martin was so embarrassed he went to bed early,' Dorahy said. 'Tom Rathbone and his wife came over and apologised. They said they were totally embarrassed and bewildered.'

Despite all this Dorahy, who took up a post at Warrington just over a year after leaving Central Park, says he bears no animosity to anyone at Wigan. 'I can hold my head up high whenever I go back there, because I did my best and said whatever had to be said to people's faces,' he said. 'I don't think everyone at the club when I was there could necessarily say the same. I think one or two of the people who helped shaft me might want to look away. But I just feel sorry for people who have to be devious to get what they want. It's a matter for God and their conscience.'

Edwards, a Christian with a conscience

who might nevertheless be included in the scope of this remark, is unrepentant about Dorahy's fate and the players' part in his downfall. 'Basically John tried to fix something that wasn't broken,' he said. 'When he first arrived he came to see me and my dad and asked us to mark his card about the team and the club. Which we did, but did John take the advice? No. He changed almost everything. Much too quickly. Including things that didn't need changing at all. He would have us calling our old moves new names, for example. He changed most of our moves, even the ones we knew and could rely on to work. He made training a real pain, sessions were much longer and much more boring. We just couldn't see the point. It wasn't as if we were doing badly when he arrived. I don't dislike the bloke, and I wish him well at Warrington, because he can make an improvement there. Without wanting to sound big-headed, I don't think he knew how to improve us, so instead of leaving us alone he tried to control us.'

The situation never got to the stage where Edwards felt like refusing to play for Dorahy, though the latter confronted a more mature individual than had either Monie or Lowe. It is doubtful whether a younger Edwards would have taken his substitution at Wakefield so calmly, particularly as his version of events differs significantly from Dorahy's. 'We were winning and he pulled me off,' Edwards said. 'So I sat on the bench and asked him why he had done that. He said he was just resting me, nothing to worry about. The game was won and he was bringing me off as a reward, to save my legs for the next match. That sounded fair enough, so I thought no more of it until I picked up a paper the next day. The reporter had asked John why he had pulled me, and he'd told him it was because I had been trying to do too much on my own and it wasn't working. So I had spent a day thinking the coach thought a lot of me and then I find he's having a go at me in the press. I tackled him about it and he said it had just been a mistake. But it was in another paper later in the week. I gave up in the end. What can you do with someone who bangs on about honesty and plain speaking all the time yet says different things to different people?'

Robinson, for his part, says he regrets nothing except his perceived rudeness at the post-Wembley function. 'I didn't purposely set out to make John feel uncomfortable,' he said. 'I did actually thank the coaching staff as a unit, without singling out any names. But I didn't single out many players either, only the ones who were leaving. It was a difficult situation that year, we all knew what had taken place and it would have been silly trying to pretend everything was wonderful.'

Dorahy is correct, Robinson confirms, in saying he had support from his chairman for 95 per cent of the season then the 'bum's rush' at the end. 'That's pretty much the way it was, I can't deny that,' Robinson said. 'Because I had recruited John, and because I knew exactly how hard his job was, I gave him all the support I could. Once it became clear at the end of the season that the team would go down the tubes if we didn't sort out the situation, I acted quickly. I had a decision to make, so I made it. That's what chairmen are for. It might sound brutal, but it is much easier to replace a coach than a dozen-and-a-half world-class rugby players. What had happened had to be John's fault. I daresay the players weren't blameless, but I couldn't very well sack them, could I? Maybe we were partly at fault for recruiting the wrong man, I don't know. How do you go about finding the right person to deal with a dressing-room full of world-class psychopaths? Is there a manual? Every single coach to come down here has had grief from our players, and some have been nearly broken by it. The only person who wasn't affected was John Monie, who was totally ruthless and wouldn't stand any nonsense. He actually terrified the players, I'm not sure how, but he did have the benefit of a big squad which was probably one of our strongest. I often wonder how he would have coped had he come to Wigan before Graham Lowe. Like I said, it's a very difficult job. All those coaches in charge of

Martin Hall makes a run against the Sheffield Eagles.

players who don't mind if they don't win anything don't know how lucky they are.'

So while Robinson was sympathetic to John Dorahy's predicament, he still had to go. 'I would say his man-management skills let him down,' Robinson said. 'He tried to change too much in too short a time. Whatever he did, he put the players' backs up, and that wasn't a situation we could tolerate. As much as I disliked the idea of player power, I knew what I had to do. I had done it before. I was the one who insisted Colin Clarke and Alan McInnes had to go when we were bringing in Graham Lowe. Maurice wanted to keep them on as assistants, because he didn't think they deserved to be sacked. I wasn't sure they deserved to be sacked either, but I was positive that if we were bringing a coach from New Zealand to take us on to a new level, he deserved to be given a free hand. Once we had made the first decision the other

followed on from it. It would have been easy to mess that whole thing up by trying to be too kind. It cost us a bit of money, sacking Colin and Alan, and our friendship took a bit of a knock, but I think in the long run it was the right thing to do. If I wanted to be popular I wouldn't do this job.'

Robinson has lost count, he says, of the number of people who no longer speak to him. 'I was the one who got shot of Goodway and Gregory, and Case and Potter before them, and none of them liked it. I'm pretty ruthless in that respect, but I think it's necessary. The minute you start running an old pals' act or a rugby players' social club, you're in trouble. The hardest part of running a rugby club is arranging a smooth turnover of players, but if you can crack that you're economically viable as well as strong on the field. If we had kept Case and Potter on longer, for instance, Gildart and Betts would not have come through in the same way. You don't want to move out your best players too soon, but you don't want good lads mouldering in the "A" team either. Too many clubs do that, and I think it's almost immoral. When we sign a junior player at Wigan we don't just give him a cheque, we give him a commitment that if he makes satisfactory progress, he'll get a chance in the first team when he's ready. Personally I don't think clubs should sign youngsters on any other basis. The ideal is to have a successful first team where the average age remains about the same every year, and the faces change but not the quality or the style of play. I reckon Liverpool Football Club came nearest to that in the '70s and '80s, but I think we have been pretty close in the last few years.'

Dorahy's sudden exit after Wembley saw Graeme West take over as caretaker coach until the end of the season. There were a maximum of four matches left – three possible rounds of the Premiership, and a decidedly attractive fixture in Brisbane, where the World Club Challenge was being played for the first time on Australian soil at the ANZ Stadium, home of the Broncos. West was lucky enough to take over a team on a roll, and smart enough to realise it. Once the players worked out that Dorahy was a lame duck, the improvement was marked. Suddenly Wigan showed their best form of the season, and West was the unanimous dressing-room choice as coach. Possibly the players thought they would get their own way under the devil they knew, possibly they were keen to show the indifferent displays of earlier in the season were down to Dorahy rather than themselves. Either way West did the right thing in immediately declaring his desire to do the job on a full-time basis. Not even Robinson could sack two successful coaches in the same year, and West had a shrewd idea that the way Wigan were playing, at least one more trophy might arrive by the end of the season, if not two.

If Dorahy was a low-key successor to Monie, West was even more so. He had no front line experience, just an easy rapport with the Wigan fans, a job in the club's pools office, and responsibility for coaching the 'A' team. He had done well in the last respect, though he was a far cry from the super-coaches Wigan were being linked with less than 12 months previously. West had, nonetheless, been sounded out as a possible replacement by Monie himself. 'John said he would recommend me to the board as a successor, if I wanted him to,' West said. 'I was flattered, but I had a testimonial that year, and I couldn't see how I could do both things at once. So I passed up his invitation, and they got Dorahy. Then when my testimonial was over, with Dorahy being taken on for three years, I started to listen to coaching offers from other clubs. I couldn't see me getting any further at Wigan, and people were saying I needed some first division experience before I could be a serious candidate for any of the top clubs. I agreed with that, although it struck me that Dorahy hadn't got any, so I was talking to Hull and Wakefield and wondering if I dared apply for the St Helens job, when things started to wear so thin at Wigan I thought I might get a look in after all. I wasn't sure I was quite ready for clubs like St Helens or Wigan, but what happened towards the end of that 1993–94 season made my mind up for me. I just thought: "Gee, if I can't do better than this bloke I might as well pack in."'

West was perfectly well aware that he was seen as a soft alternative by the players, who were responding so well only because the pressure on them had been lifted, but he managed to turn this to his advantage. 'The players were enjoying being able to express themselves again,' he said. 'Dorahy had been a bit like a strict schoolmaster, and now it was the end of term. I didn't see any reason why they shouldn't be treated a bit more like adults. I just tried to let them keep their freedom, with a bit of control. They do know what they are about, after all. Shaun Edwards, for instance, knows an awful lot about the game. I don't mind taking his views on board. When you have such experienced players it makes sense to listen to what they have to say.'

The Premiership is not normally a competition Wigan care much about, but for some of the players the season was only just starting. St Helens and Sheffield were beaten in barnstorming fashion to secure yet another appointment with Castleford in the Old Trafford final. Wigan won more comfortably than the 24–20 scoreline suggests, with Edwards controlling the game with his kicking and Panapa picking up the Harry Sunderland Award for Man of the Match, and departed for Brisbane on a high. The only downer was leaving Skerrett at home with a broken jaw, the result of a collision with Dean Sampson's elbow which the Wigan player did not seem to regard as accidental. As Platt had already made himself unavailable for the Brisbane game, that meant Wigan would have to face the Broncos' front-row giants, Lazarus and Gee, with Cowie as the only recognised prop in the side. Ironic, considering the difficulty Dorahy had experienced in leaving Cowie out.

But Cowie was outstanding on the night, ably supported by McGinty and Cassidy as West used his squad substitutions intelligently. More than 54,000 people in the ANZ Stadium believed the Broncos couldn't be beaten, and just as many back home thought the same thing when they heard McGinty, who hadn't played for six weeks, was in the side at prop forward. But if Wigan were makeshift up front they were solid in the back row, where Betts, Clarke and Farrell all excelled, and in Robinson they had a match winner.

'The gods were with us that night,' said Lindsay, present in his official capacity of RFL chief executive but really there to see the final fruition of a seed he had planted seven years previously. 'The Broncos were unlucky to lose Renouf and Kevin Walters, two of their most important players, early in the game, and Sailor was a bag of nerves all night. But nothing had prepared them for Billy Whizz. They think they have got all the best players, you see. It never occurs to Australians that someone might come along and surprise them. That's why it was such a pleasure to be there. I'd never seen 54,000 people gobsmacked all at once. The spirit in the Wigan side was phenomenal.'

Robinson only scored one try in the 20–14 victory, but it was the early one Wigan wanted, and once Mather had taken advantage of Sailor's hesitation to add a second, the visitors had a lead they were able to defend. By the end of the game they were defending quite desperately, yet the overriding image everyone took home was of Robinson's incredible energy and elusiveness. The winger began the game as one of the smallest men on the pitch, in reputation as well as physique, but finished a colossus in both respects. It was a trick he would manage surprisingly often throughout his career. No one ever seemed to be ready for the damage the deceptively diminutive Robinson could cause.

The winger's inclusion was a personal triumph for West. Dorahy had preferred Tuigamala at Wembley, upsetting Robinson by leaving him out. 'Basically I was lied to,' Robinson said. 'The coach told me to prove my fitness in the "A" team. I did, and he still left me out.' West was unlikely to make the same mistake with a player he had brought through the 'A' team and long regarded as a favourite. In Brisbane it was Tuigamala who was out in the cold, the coach reasoning that after a none-too-impressive first six months in which fitness appeared to be more of a problem than the usual positional uncertainty, the New Zealander was not ready for such a demanding game. Tuigamala sought out West afterwards and asked him what he had to do to make a position his own. He was serious, and gave West a solemn commitment he would do whatever was necessary. 'I never even thought of not believing him,' West said. 'I knew from the way he said it he would be as good as his word, and if anything he was better. If only everything in life was so straightforward. Inga worked his socks off in summer and won a place in the team for the following season on merit. He has never looked back since, he has consistently been one of our best players.'

On his return from Brisbane, West, now confirmed as permanent coach, would do exactly the same for Scott Quinnell, a Welsh rugby union forward who initially found rugby league difficult but blossomed under the coach's patient guidance into the type of player to strike fear into opponents' hearts. West was also quick to play Henry Paul in the first team as well, once Robinson had pinched him from Wakefield and by extension the Warriors. It might sound ridiculous to keep a player of Paul's extravagant ability out of the team, but Peter Fox managed it for long enough with his brother Robbie at Bradford. Paul is up there with the best signings Wigan have ever made, when Robinson is playing in the same team the jack-in-the-box factor is unbeatable, yet incredibly he agreed to stay in England because he did not think Monie rated him highly enough to give him first-team football so early in his career. If that is true, Monie might not be the judge of a player we all thought he was, and Wigan might be profiting from one of his mistakes after four years of perfection. West can also congratulate himself, since he knows the importance his chairman places on bringing young players through the ranks, on the exemplary development of Kris Radlinski and Simon Haughton in the first couple of seasons, with Rob Smyth and Andy Johnson not far behind.

Radlinski and Haughton, Paul and Tuigamala were all prominent as Wigan swept to another league and cup double in 1994–95, with Robinson winning the Lance Todd Trophy for destroying Leeds singlehandedly at Wembley. With two more Regal Trophy successes in addition, one low-key game against Warrington at Huddersfield and one snorting contest against St Helens at the same venue, no one can say West has let the side down over silverware, even if he does strike Dorahy as a yes-man. 'If it works, don't fix it,' West said. 'I don't feel I have to defend my methods. I'll let the record speak for itself.' Interestingly, both Dorahy and Robinson had to revise their opinions of West when he took his players out to Australia for the World Club Challenge. The game in Brisbane was on

a Wednesday, and Wigan had a week to kill beforehand. West had the players training on the Thursday and Friday, then gave them Friday night and all day Saturday off, with the proviso that they returned to work on Sunday. It was a toss-up between the British and Australian press as to who was most astonished to see Wigan players preparing for the Brisbane game in the bars and nightclubs of Queensland's Gold Coast, but West had told them to let their hair down and do as they pleased. 'Jack Robinson was tearing his hair out, and Dorahy actually told me he would never have let the players go to the Gold Coast on their own,' West said. 'But as soon as I saw the efforts they put in at training on the Sunday I knew we were on a winner. Graham Lowe did the same with the Kiwis in Brisbane in 1983 when I captained the side to victory against Australia. He reckoned we would just get bored training all the time and building the game up in our minds. A little relaxation never did anybody any harm, and it can actually improve team spirit if players are treated as adults once in a while.'

Last word on the subject of World Club Challenges goes to Lindsay, however, without whose drive and determination the series would never have got off the ground, much less reach such a rewarding conclusion in Australia. 'I was very proud that night in Brisbane,' Lindsay said. 'Not just of the Wigan lads either. I had always been aware that the World Club Challenge would never be taken seriously by the Australians until a British team went out and beat them in their own backyard. I never imagined for a moment it would happen the first time the match was staged in Australia, and neither did the Australians, I can tell you. I was at a function prior to the game, and the Australian Rugby League administrators were being their usual selves. Polite, hospitable, but faintly patronising. No, on second thoughts just patronising. Ken Arthurson slapped me down a bit at one point, just enough to make me squirm in public, and I thought: "You arrogant sod. I'd love it if our lot stuffed your lot tonight." And our lot did.'

Lindsay had had to put up with much the same thing back in 1987, when the Australians failed to see the point of a proposed challenge which they were sure to win. David Oxley and David Howes, at British rugby league head-quarters, were not enthusiastic either, and though Lindsay fired off several letters to the ARL in Sydney, he received only one non-committal reply, and telephone calls only convinced him the idea was not being pursued. 'I could see if I was going to get any-where it was going to have to be a face-to-face job,' he recalled. 'So I jumped on a plane, and found Bob Abbott, Ken Arthurson and John Quayle together, as usual, in a NSW box at the Sydney Cricket Ground, watching a boring game between Norths and Souths. Because not much was happening on the pitch there was a lot of talking being done, and a lot of wine being passed around. They gave me a big hello, and called up a few more bottles, and it was all very convivial until around midnight, when I told them what I had come for. As soon as I mentioned the World Club Challenge their faces fell and there was a lot of harrumphing and head-shaking, but I had been expecting that. I had a trick up my sleeve ready. I told them I had a sponsor lined up, and that Foster's were willing to put up £50,000 prize money. "What do you think," I asked them, "of playing on a basis of winner takes all?" Well, Arthurson's eyes lit up then. Manly were almost in the Grand Final, and if they won

they would be sure to beat Wigan, and all that money would end up at his club. He told me he was sure we could do business on that basis, at which point I put my drink down and fled. I told them I had a taxi waiting outside. Next morning I announced the game to the Australian press, before anyone had a chance to sober up and change their mind.

'Back in Britain, I had the same battle all over again with the BBC to get the game covered, only I had to admit defeat with them in the end. They really were arrogant and patronising in those days. Worse than any Australians. I think they gave it about 15 seconds on *Sportsnight*. I had to get pictures from Channel 10, from Australia, to fulfil my contractual obligations. I can still remember the Aussie commentator when the teams walked out. "Here comes the Manly team," he said. "What a treat this Wigan crowd is in for." Nobody thought we had a prayer. And no one imagined for a moment we would get 37,000 spectators. The Rugby League sud-denly took an interest after that, and took over the running of the event. They staged the next one at Old Trafford. The World Club Challenge was a winner after all. So yes, I had a big smile on my face at Wigan against Manly, and another one at Brisbane against Wigan. You don't often get the chance to say "Told you so" to people who have been scoffing at your ideas, but when it happens, it's a bloody marvellous feeling.'

CHAPTER TEN

Look Back in Anger

'You didn't want me, did you, Jack?'

One morning in early 1995, Maurice Lindsay had an unusual appointment in his Chapeltown Road office. His secretary showed in Phil Clarke, who came to say he had had enough of winning medals in British rugby league and wanted to try his hand in Australia. Clarke was 24. He was in his fifth season as a Wigan first-team player and was on his way to his fifth Wembley winner's medal and his fifth league championship. Clarke had plenty more trophies besides, as did most of the Wigan players, but he explained the excitement was beginning to wear off.

'He said he was playing in too many games where the result was not in doubt, and as a consequence was not enjoying his rugby as much as he once did,' Lindsay said. 'He said the challenge was no longer there, it had all become too mechanical. He had come to see me because I was the person who had signed him for Wigan, and he wanted me to be the first to know he was leaving. I thought that was very nice of him, but told him it was Jack Robinson's problem really. I didn't want to see him leave, obviously, and I tried to persuade him to stay, but I could see he had been doing his homework very thoroughly. That was typical of the bloke, I should have known he wouldn't do anything at half-cock, or on the spur of the moment. He told me he had had an offer from Easts, and was looking forward to proving himself in the Sydney Premiership, and that he had been discussing a move into sports broadcasting in Australia with James Packer. I could see this was a career move he had thought all the way through, and I could see his heart was set on it, so I simply wished him well.'

Clarke was hugely disappointed with the way British rugby league had turned out, and by this time he was not the only one. 'Compared to what it was ten years ago, it's crap now,' he told me in 1995. It was impossible to argue. In some ways Clarke's perspective was personal to him, in some ways he shared the frustrations of spectators. A competitive individual, he hated the idea of cruising through a game or a season. In a way he wanted to play against himself. He was distressed to find his standards and those of his team so far ahead of everyone else's that his efforts in training were rendered almost meaningless. Matches were too easy, even Wembley was becoming almost meaningless. Clarke was constantly complaining, for instance, about the number of non-players and assorted hangers-on who would crowd into the celebratory team picture on the Wembley turf at the end of every season. A small thing, perhaps, but Clarke hated anyone taking Wembley for granted. He wanted to keep it pristine, as it had been in his youth. For winners. And having the same winners every year just wasn't right. 'I wish it could be like 1985 again,' he said, 'when there were plenty of good teams about and you had to play your socks off to win anything.'

Ten years after the 1985 spectacle, David Stephenson, one of its participants, was of the same opinion. 'Wigan have killed the game,' he said. 'They haven't done anything wrong, in fact they have been absolutely brilliant to watch, but no sport can cope with the same team winning everything. I don't see anyone catching them up either. In fact I would say a lot of teams have gone backwards.'

Surveying British rugby league in 1995, there was plenty of evidence to support this view. Only two teams were full time – Wigan and Leeds – and it was no accident that the same teams contested the 1994 and 1995 Challenge Cup finals. The fact that Wigan won on both occasions could be traced to the start they gave themselves by going full time first – back in 1985. It was at least five years before Leeds got the message, let alone began to implement it, and by that time players like Clarke and Betts were rolling off the Central Park production line. Stephenson moved from Wigan to Leeds in 1988 precisely because they tolerated a more flexible training regime. 'I had quite a good job, which I wanted to keep,' Stephenson explained. 'When Wigan started arranging training sessions in the afternoon I was having to make excuses. I could only take so much time off work without jeopardising my career. Wigan were not sympathetic to my situation, but I don't blame them. I think full time was the way to go. I might have been tempted to pack in the day job myself had I been a bit younger at the time. But Wigan weren't on such big wages then either. It would have been foolish to put 30 years of future employment at risk for the few seasons I had left in the game. But you only have to look at the athletes Wigan have produced to understand the point of the exercise from the club's point of view. Phil Clarke was always going to be a good footballer, but Wigan turned him into one of the best players in the world. There is simply no way he would have developed to the same extent under the old system.'

In 1995 the majority of rugby league clubs were only just waking up to the reality that for the past ten years they had been chasing the unattainable. Wigan were not playing by the same rules. They were hardly playing the same game. It was professionals v. amateurs.

Whether the game should have taken so long to recognise this fairly obvious imbalance is a moot point. Whether Wigan should have been allowed to go it alone in the first place is another delicate question. With hindsight, it might have served the overall

game better had David Oxley forbade any unilateral switch to full time and insisted that Wigan wait until the game was ready to go forward together. In 1985 this would have struck Wigan as unwarranted interference from above and an unexpected departure from Oxley's *laissez-faire* policy, though compared to what would happen to clubs ten years later it would have looked like the most

Eight and out. Martin Offiah and Shaun Edwards don't know it in 1995, but they won't be doing this in 1996.

gentle and well-meaning of restraints. There is no doubt the two questions are related. Wigan's unhealthy dominance was not the reason for the Super League coming into being, although many in the game welcomed the levelling effect of the reorganisation and saw it as a chance to compete with Central Park on an even footing. But Wigan's continued stranglehold on success, with its legacy of disillusioned supporters and demoralised competitors elsehere, was a significant factor in the spiritual and economic despondency which left rugby league in 1995 ready to embrace any source of salvation.

Hindsight, though, is never available when it is needed. In 1985 the question of going full time was not so cut and dried. Even Wigan only did it in piecemeal fashion, taking a few years and ending up full time almost without realising it. It was not immediately clear what the benefits would be, nor would it be for another few years. In 1985, rugby league had been in existence on a part-time basis for precisely 90 years. Not every club wanted to go full time, and not every club could afford to. When the game's centenary arrived in 1995, however, the impact of Wigan's decade of doing things differently was all too clear. No one talked about catching them any more, with the single exception of Leeds, who only talked about it quietly. Castleford and St Helens could give the big-shots a game, on their day, but the rest of the game appeared to have given up the ghost.

Framing the Future, the policy document Lindsay presented in 1994, was partly in recognition of this. The game had always dreamed of expansion, now it was admitting that contraction and consolidation would be necessary. Mergers were mentioned for the first time in September 1994, when Lindsay and Rodney Walker, the RFL chairman, floated the opinion that Hull and Hull KR might be better joining forces in an attempt to rekindle interest in rugby league on Humberside, rather than fighting separate losing battles against declining crowds and disappointing results. Both Humberside clubs, doughty opponents of Wigan in 1985, had fallen on hard times ten years later. Rovers' new stadium was a sad, charmless place, and a recent Hull coach had resorted to running marathons to raise money to buy players. Neither had been to Wembley since 1986 and 1985 respectively, and neither looked likely to. It was the same elsewhere. Featherstone, Wakefield and Castleford had all had financial problems, as had Widnes

and Warrington. Swinton had lost their ground, while Salford had one they couldn't fill. Most of these neighbours were only half a dozen miles apart. On their own they were never going to manage the standards laid down in *Framing the Future*, even though they were only being asked to bring their grounds up to a minimum capacity of 10,000 and appoint some full-time marketing and administrative staff. So would it not make sense to unite and survive?

Inga the Winger. Or centre, as he quickly became under Graeme West's tutelage.

That survival was at stake was spelt out quite clearly in *Framing the Future*, a report based on a year of independent research into clubs' finances and future viability. Too many clubs, it concluded, were fighting for too few spectators in too small a catchment area. This was not startling news, but before allowing clubs to dismiss the report as another expensive exercise in stating the obvious, Lindsay wanted to use it to force the game to confront issues it would normally prefer to ignore. Such as the fact that 60 per cent of all those who attended league games came from just four postal districts along the M62 corridor. And that 17 of the 32 member clubs happened to be technically insolvent. Stadiums and facilities were woefully inadequate – 'philistine' was Lindsay's exact word – and clubs were selling their grounds at an alarming rate. Finally, while there had been a 3 per cent growth in gross income over the previous three years, players' wages had increased by 10 per cent.

'It doesn't take a genius to understand why change is necessary and urgent,' Walker commented in 1994. 'The game is currently losing £3 million a year. The situation is unsustainable, it's only a matter of time before you go bust.' Not before time, the game was facing up to the fact that the quality of the product on the pitch could not mask significant inadequacies elsewhere, and that the slick image successful clubs like Wigan and Leeds presented to the TV cameras was misleading in terms of the sport as a whole. A salary cap was debated, some form of central control to prevent clubs spending too high a proportion of their income on players, and inevitably Lindsay was accused of preaching now what he had failed to practise at Wigan. Had not Wigan created this crisis, he was asked, and might it not be easier and simpler just to cap that club's spending to give everyone else a chance? 'No,' Lindsay said. 'You cannot penalise success. But I do understand that the imbalance of power is harming the sport. It is bleeding us to death, everyone's enthusiasm is waning. A whole generation of supporters, kids who were seven or eight when Wigan won at Wembley in 1988, are probably smoking cigarettes and drinking in pubs now, without ever having seen anyone else win the Cup. It must be debilitating for all the other clubs and I admit I don't know the answer. I seem to have created a monster.'

The tentative remedy hinted at in *Framing the Future*, some sort of super league involving ersatz amalgamations of clubs, did not convince anyone. 'Shuffling the deckchairs on the *Titanic*,' opined one rugby union correspondent, hoarily but not unfairly. Even rugby league diehards doubted whether the game possessed 16 clubs willing, let alone able, to join the modern world as well as the entertainment industry. 'You had better hurry up and get your book out,' John Stopford, the former Swinton and Great Britain winger, informed me that week in Smith's bookshop in Wigan. 'There will be no such thing as rugby league in ten years time.'

Inga the Dad. Va'aiga Tuigamala and family at Wembley in 1995.

Officially, such pessimism was frowned upon, but there was no doubt Lindsay and Walker were desperate. They knew the severity of the situation, they also knew that the game would talk it over for a few days then forget about it, which is exactly what happened. But even had everyone in rugby league acted together, immediately, and in the game's best interests; even had the polite suggestions in *Framing the Future* been adopted with alacrity; Lindsay and Walker were both aware that intervention might come too late to save the patient. Both admitted at the time of *Framing the Future* that the game should have been doing this 20 years ago. Lindsay, ever the optimist, felt the game might not be tapping all the potential support in its traditional areas, whereas Walker was more concerned that it might be. 'The game's traditional areas are mining communities, and for the most part they are depressed,' Walker explained. 'I thought it was sad, but very revealing, that a couple of weeks after that marvellous win against Wigan in the Regal Trophy final last season, Castleford's home crowd was back under 4,000. Our game needs to work hard just to hold its audience share, never mind increase it.'

It is against this background of realism bordering on gloom that the advent of the Super League must be judged. *Framing the Future* was conveniently forgotten about as the 1994–95 season got under way, with Wigan once more winning the league and cup double in Graeme West's first full season as coach, but as the year turned, attention strayed to the game's centenary, 1995 being the 100th anniversary of the birth of rugby league in Huddersfield, and to events in Australia and New Zealand, where Auckland Warriors and the other new clubs joining the Winfield Cup, were at last ready to commence playing. The Warriors' inaugural game was a tremendous success. Despite losing the match 25–22 to Brisbane Broncos no one in the 31,500 crowd at the Ericsson Stadium doubted this was the start of something big, yet the future was not as secure as it seemed. For Auckland, for Brisbane, for anyone. Even as Australian administrators were congratulating themselves on a brilliant opening weekend, trouble was brewing away from the pitch. Television magnate Rupert Murdoch had already had one bid for Australian Rugby League (ARL) turned down, by an administration happy to stay with his rival, Kerry Packer. It had been Packer's television company which had helped rugby league in Australia reinvent itself as a successful television sport in the early '80s, and a decade later the arrangement was mutually profitable. But Murdoch had long been convinced that

sport was the best tool to drive satellite and subscription TV, and knew rugby league was the sport that counted in Australia. Having once been rebuffed, he was quickly back again, and this time he was not talking to the ARL. He was talking directly to the clubs and the players.

For a few weeks British observers watched in fascination as the Australian game tore itself into two. To over-simplify matters slightly, the new, out-of-Sydney clubs like the Warriors and the Broncos aligned themselves most firmly with Murdoch, accepting lucrative contracts to play in his proposed Super League, while the older, Sydney-based sides like Manly and Easts stayed loyal to the ARL. Some clubs did not know which way to jump. Some clubs went one way and found their leading players had signed individual deals to go the other. The situation quickly descended into anarchy, as friends and clubmates found themselves on opposing sides of a money war. Clarke and Betts, still in Wigan but contracted to clubs on opposite sides of the divide, followed events from afar with a mixture of bafflement and concern. 'Neither of us know how it's all going to end up, I don't think anyone does,' Clarke said in early 1995. 'People keep saying one side or the other is going to win, but it changes every day, and it looks as though rugby league is going to be the only loser. I reckon we'll both be back in a couple of years, playing for Bath or somebody. Rugby union clubs will soon be the only ones with any money to spend.' Fuller details of the rights and wrongs and twists and turns of the ARL–Super League battle can be found elsewhere. For the purposes of this book it is necessary only to know that the row became very messy indeed, and that Murdoch seemed absolutely determined to win, whatever the cost. And that the war arrived in Wigan on 8 April 1995.

It had been obvious for some time that Britain was not going to escape the ructions in Australia, particularly when both sides of the argument began throwing silly money at players and attempting to sign anyone and everyone capable of counting in a propaganda war. For league in this country to do nothing was to risk being systematically asset-stripped by either or both parties. Agents were already understood to be over here, and anyone remotely famous could expect to be contacted and offered the sort of money it was hard to turn down. At a Rugby League Council meeting at Headingley on 5 April, where the feasibility of a switch to summer rugby was one of the items due to be discussed, Lindsay was called to the telephone and found himself speaking to Murdoch in person, calling from Washington. Lindsay was able to tell council delegates a Super League deal was available if they wanted it, but at that time did not know precisely how much money was on offer or what any conditions would be. At a league game at Central Park that evening between Wigan and Doncaster, members of the press were similarly in the dark. Clearly what had just happened in Headingley was of more immediate concern to the game than the outcome of Wigan's match with Doncaster (44–4 home win, since you ask) but no one knew exactly what had happened. 'It was bedlam in the press box that night,' recalled Martin Richards, of *The Daily Mirror*. 'Everyone was trying to file stories, but no one had any concrete information. Sports editors were screaming for copy, and all sorts of rumours and wild guesses were flying around. It didn't help that some people appeared better informed than others. When we all heard Dave Woods do his Radio 5 report, for instance, everybody started scribbling out what they had written and beginning again. He seemed to have a more up-to-date version of events, but no one knew whether or not it was accurate. We had worked out that a lot of money might be on its way from Murdoch, but beyond that, confusion reigned. When the game kicked off, hardly anyone noticed.'

Loose ends were tied up the following Saturday, when a meeting of club chairmen was convened at Central Park. Considering what was decided that day, the meeting was surprisingly short. It began at 10 a.m. and was over at noon, at which point Lindsay and Walker were able to adjourn to an adjoining room to inform the press that the news was good and bad. The good news was that Murdoch's News Corp was willing to invest £75 million in British rugby league over the next five years. The figure later rose to £77 million and then £87 million, and the deal would involve a switch to summer rugby, so that a play-off could take place at the end of each season between the leading Super League clubs in Britain and Australia, whose seasons would now be aligned. The bad news was that mergers were back on the agenda. The European Super League, as it was to be called, would comprise 14 clubs, including two from France and one from London. The other 11 places would include five new clubs to be created by the merging of 15 existing ones.

Some of the proposed mergers were bizarre in the extreme. Castleford, Featherstone and Wakefield were to join forces as Calder, for example, an amalgamation which might make geographic sense, but only to a geographer unaware of the intense rivalries between those towns. 'Fev is Fev, Cas is Cas,' as the protest banners would later shriek. 'Stick your mergers up your arse.' The suggested combination of Carlisle, Barrow, Whitehaven and Workington to form Cumbria was just as improbable, though for different reasons. In no sense are those towns close (try driving from Barrow to Carlisle), and neither was there an obvious location convenient for all four. Hull and Hull KR might have been weary enough to jump into bed together, but Warrington and Widnes hated each other. And the idea of Salford and Oldham combining forces as Manchester was a transparent attempt to hijack a big city name, when the reality was that both clubs were outside Manchester and proud of it.

Even as Lindsay related these details to the assembled media it was obvious there were serious flaws in the scheme. The entire plan had been hatched and approved in under 96 hours, he was later to claim. It showed. The miracle was that the club chairmen had approved it, but as we have seen, they were

Kris Radlinski, one of the exciting young talents Graeme West helped bring through to the first team.

desperate, and between them Lindsay and Murdoch held a gun to the game's head by announcing a decision was needed within 24 hours, otherwise the money might no longer be on the table. It transpired that a secret, preliminary meeting for first division chairmen only had already been held in Huddersfield the night before, and second division chairmen, like Featherstone's Steve Wagner, deeply resented being given only a couple of hours notice on the Saturday over such a momentous decision. 'I couldn't believe I was being asked to vote on something that would radically alter the future of my club, and the game as a whole, with hardly any notice,' he said. But like every other chairman, he voted in favour of the Super League proposal. The money on offer seemed staggering, the future secure if not straightforward. None of the chairmen needed any reminding of the financial hard-ships of the present, and in the unusually fraught and highly irregular circumstances, perhaps none can be blamed for their decision. There seemed no alternative.

Thus did rugby league turn itself upside down within hours in the very year it was supposed to be celebrating a century of solid tradition. The game is nothing if not acrobatic, however, and shortly it began to turn itself inside out as well. The fans – that small, dwindling band of people who actually went to games – did not like the idea of mergers at all. And they absolutely hated mergers which were foisted upon them, with seemingly no forethought or prior consultation. It was remarked more than once during the stormy month of April that if half the number of people currently engaged in protests as diverse as pitch invasions, radio phone-ins, television forums and questions in the House of Commons actually attended matches on a regular basis, rugby league would have no need to merge any clubs. But this misses the point. Which is that mergers were not necessarily a bad thing, the economics and the thinking behind them were sound. 'We don't need any of Wakefield or Featherstone's players,' said Lee Crooks, the Castleford captain. 'But we are all in the same metropolitan area and we have to stop

fondly recalled his team's giant-killing act over then mighty Hull 12 years earlier at Wembley, failing to appreciate that Hull themselves would never reach those heights again unless they found a way to compete with full-time clubs like Wigan. Never mind a pit village of 11,000 like Featherstone. The irony was that if any area produced enough rugby league players to challenge Wigan's

Scott Quinnell. One of the last Welsh internationalists to 'go north', and one of the first to return to rugby union in time to resume his representative career.

fighting each other for the same sponsors and spectators. If we are going to go full time, and we must, because Wigan will never be caught by part-timers, one club for the city of Wakefield makes sense. I feel desperately sorry for all the players and spectators, but everyone has to stop and ask themselves what they want to carry on. Their sporting rivalry or their sport.'

Not everyone grasped the seriousness of the situation so quickly. Ian Clayton, a Featherstone fan who enjoyed brief celebrity as an outspoken opponent of the mergers,

supremacy it was the Castleford–Feather-stone–Wakefield triangle. One full-time club in that area would have had enormous potential. But the proposed mergers were incredibly badly handled, to the point where thousands of Yorkshire fans imagined it was Murdoch, rather than Lindsay, who was attempting to trample on tradition and cheat them of their birthright. And perhaps because they were cobbled together so quickly, many of the proposed fusions were unworkable as well as unwanted. Jim Quinn of Oldham and John Wilkinson of Salford spent four hours discussing merger proposals and failed to agree on a single thing. Not even the colour of shirt the proposed new club might adopt. Backtracking on mergers began almost immediately after the Central Park meeting broke up. 'I didn't vote to merge with Widnes,' said Warrington director Peter Higham. 'I voted for the £75 million. In the overall interests of the game, I felt I had no choice.' Just about the only good thing anyone had to say about the Super League plans as initially drawn up – apart from welcoming the cash injection – was that at least some of the new super clubs should be able to give Wigan a game.

But in the face of continued squabbling among clubs – 'News Corporation must think they are dealing with a crowd of idiots,' remarked Workington's Kevan Gorge at one point – and adverse publicity which was beginning to worry Murdoch's Sky TV representatives, a compromise was eventually adopted. Mergers were off for the time being, unless any clubs wanted to pursue the option voluntarily. The Super League would go ahead with 12 clubs for the time being, comprising London, Paris, and the ten leading English sides. Clubs missing out, like Widnes, Salford and Keighley, were pacified with the reinstatement of promotion from the first division, allowing them a path to join the élite. An opportunity had been lost, but the money was still there. All that was actually new about the Super League was a single French team of doubtful pedigree, giving the venture a tenuous European dimension, and the end-of-season Anglo-Australian play-offs, which at least would be jolly for the likes of Wigan and St Helens. Hardly a brave new world, but a reasonable compromise which might just stop British rugby league going out of business.

The only worry was that no compromise had yet been reached in Australia, where the ARL and Super League were still going at it hammer and tongs. At the time of signing the British Super League deal, Lindsay appeared supremely confident he had backed the right horse, and that the ARL would eventually have to concede defeat. 'News Corp are bound to win in time, because even if the worst comes to the worst they can simply wait until players come out of contract and sign them up,' he explained. Naturally this was not an approach which endeared Lindsay to Ken Arthurson, his counterpart in Australia and orchestrator of the ARL resistance. Arthurson felt Lindsay had betrayed their personal friendship and rugby league in Australia by selling out the British game. Lindsay disagreed. 'What right has he got to ask us to turn down £87 million?' Lindsay demanded. 'What did the Australian Rugby League ever do to take the game around the world? When they got a £40 million television deal we never saw a penny of it in Britain and France. The ARL is a very insular organisation, and that's why it is being routed by someone with a global outlook.'

By 1996 it was much less clear the ARL was being routed at all. Arthurson was still hanging in, and was fighting Murdoch through the courts and Lindsay through the world's media. 'David Oxley was an outstanding ambassador who did much to elevate the status of international rugby league,' Arthurson said at one point. 'Virtually overnight Maurice Lindsay has erased that good work with his lack of judgement and mismanagement.' There was still a chance that Super League might not succeed in Australia, and as even Lindsay accepted that Murdoch's generosity towards British rugby league had only been to gain a lever in that wider struggle, the future for the £87 million investment was far from certain. Committed to commencing their new, summer Super League in March, the RFL had decided to fill in the gap between the old season, which ended in April 1995 with Wigan winning the title for a sixth consecutive time, with a shortened 'Centenary Championship', which to no one's great surprise, Wigan won as well. It filled an awkward longueur, though there was another gap of just under two months before the summer season started, during which the Challenge Cup provided the only fixtures. They were waiting in Australia as well, waiting for the ARL to give up the fight, waiting for the New Super League to start, and waiting for Justice James Burchett to give his ruling on the legality of the whole enterprise.

In February he did. Super League in Australia, it appeared, was wholly illegal. Murdoch had no business, Justice Burchett effectively ruled, in trying to appropriate someone else's business without their approval. News Corp lawyers immediately lodged an appeal, but initial indications were that Super League is dead Down Under until the year 2000. There would be no Anglo-Australian play-offs at the end of Britain's first Super League season, or perhaps any other. British rugby league was left with an 11-match summer league programme followed by a domestic play-off which it already had, and £87 million over five years.

Back in Wigan, Jack Robinson was also experiencing a February from hell. Probably the only thought that cheered Lindsay up during the month was that at least he was not in quite the same pickle as his former co-director. Having won the Centenary Championship, with a squad which West had politely warned on several occasions was getting dangerously small – Clarke, Betts, Bell, Platt, Mather and Botica had all left without being replaced – Wigan went to Salford in the second round (fifth round proper) of the Challenge Cup. The Pope was still a Catholic, ducks could still swim and it still went dark on the night of Sunday, 11 February, but by the time the first stars began to twinkle, Wigan were out of the competition they had dominated for the past eight years.

Salford, coached by Andy Gregory and boasting former Wigan favourites Sam Panapa, in the forwards, and Steve Hampson, at full-back, deservedly won 26–16. It was not even an especially tight game. After so long, everyone imagined it would take a super-human effort to dislodge the holders, but it turned out not to be so. Salford simply played well, with another Central Park reject Steve Blakeley outstanding at stand-off, and were never in much danger. Without the injured Cassidy's tenacious tackling the home side

were able to establish an early superiority, and tries by Young and Naylor (a fifth Wigan old boy) to one by Tuigamala allowed Salford to turn round 14–4 in front. If Wigan were not panicking at that stage, they were when Naylor scored a second after the interval to put Salford 20–4 in front. Offiah claimed a try which Wigan supporters hoped would signal the fightback, but Martin merely responded with another for Salford. With Blakeley kicking six goals, Tuigamala's second try, just before the end, came far too late to keep Wigan in the Cup.

The run had to come to an end sometime, and it seemed appropriate that a team coached by a graduate of the Central Park university should have finally brought the curtain down on one of the longest-running shows in sport. 'The lads were up for this one,' Gregory explained. 'We wanted to show Wigan how good we were. Right from the time the draw was made, we never felt "Oh, no, that's us out of the Cup". It was more a case of "Let's get them down here and show them what we can do".' It was a continuity of sorts, and with Goodway at Oldham, Bell at Leeds, Lucas at Leigh and Dorahy at Warrington, the game was not short of clubs doing things the Wigan way. As even some of Wigan's supporters had begun to wish for a change of script at Wembley, Salford were regarded as having done the game a favour. Naturally there was a sense of disappointment, but most fair-minded fans felt happy for Hampson and Gregory.

At full-time at the Willows, however, Hampson looked far from happy. As the Salford players celebrated a famous victory, and supporters hugged each other with surprise and joy on the terraces, Hampson walked slowly and purposefully towards the main stand and the Wigan directors' box. 'You didn't want me, did you, Jack?' he roared from the touch-line. 'You thought I was finished, didn't you?' The Salford main stand is not on an impressive scale and there was no chance of Robinson not hearing the volley of angry words aimed in his direction. Using language considerably stronger than it

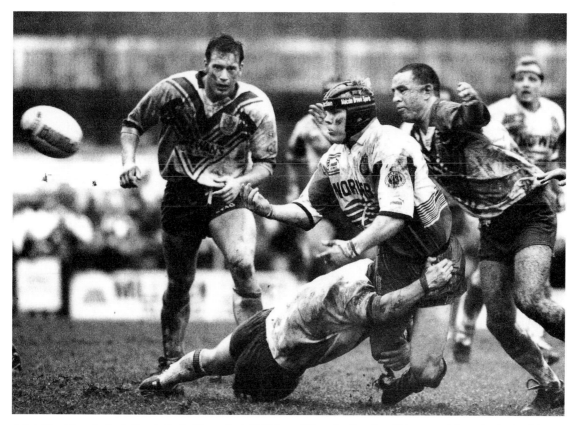

Mick Cassidy gets the ball out of a tackle against St Helens. Wigan badly missed his cover defence in the fateful cup tie at The Willows.

would be wise to reproduce here, a clearly emotional Hampson said he was glad to have turned the tables and deprived Robinson of some money he thought he had coming to him. One of the spectators within earshot was Lindsay, who had attended the game in his official capacity, and whose sympathy was now torn between an old friend and a player with a legitimate grievance. 'It was an eerie moment,' he said. 'Hampo wasn't just jeering at Jack, his face was contorted with anger, there were tears in his eyes and he was almost bawling. It looked like he'd had this stuff bottled up inside him for three years, and now it was all boiling to the surface. He'd been calm during the game, in fact he played brilliantly. It was like watching him play for Wigan again. But inwardly he must have been angry all the time. I doubt if he planned that outburst at the end of the game. He probably just couldn't help himself.'

Hampson was calm soon afterwards. 'I had been carrying a grudge,' he explained. 'Not against the Wigan players or the supporters, but against the chairman. I've got rid of that grudge now, I feel a lot better for getting it off my chest.' Perhaps Hampson should have kept hold of his grudge for a little while longer. Salford were beaten by St Helens in the next round of the competition. But Lindsay was worried about Robinson. Hampson's harsh treatment of three years earlier was only the first in a series of odd decisions and erratic stances from the Wigan chairman. In 1994 Wigan signed Daryll Lacey, a 12-year-old St Helens schoolboy. Apart from the legal, ethical and local difficulties this caused, the decision appeared to have been made by Robinson alone, who had now added the duties of chief scout to his portfolio. Robinson appeared to be making a lot of decisions alone. There had been the about-turn over

Dorahy, signs of paranoia in the complaints over Monie at Auckland Warriors, and any number of abrupt changes of direction over the question of a new ground. Wigan fans no longer knew whether they were leaving Central Park or staying.

Robinson did not appear to know either. Having originally been in favour of moving to a purpose-built stadium and selling Central Park to a developer, he went cool on the idea when the prospect of sharing with Wigan Athletic was raised by the town council. Dave Whelan, now owner of the football club, was strongly in favour of a joint use scheme which would attract significantly more grant assistance, but Robinson doggedly insisted on going it alone, even if it meant Wigan and Latics both moving to brand new stadiums. 'I think it would demean a club of our stature to share our ground with anyone,' he said. 'We are the most famous club in the world at what we do, and our supporters do not want to see us move in with a third division football club.' When consulted via a questionnaire, the near unanimous verdict of supporters was that the club should stay at Central Park, despite its unsuitability for modernisation. Robinson decided to carry on looking for a new site regardless.

Lindsay was beginning to be concerned about how Robinson was coping alone with so much responsibility. 'I don't think he's getting enough advice,' Lindsay said. 'Instead of bringing in some new blood to the board he's absorbing everything himself. We used to help each other and get a lot of support from Jack Hilton and Tom Rathbone. Now I've gone, Jack's getting old, and Tom has business worries. I wish he would share the responsibility more, get some solid business people around. Wigan is too big for one man to run by himself.'

The Wigan players accepted defeat at Salford with dignity, though several people thought they had failed to do themselves justice on the pitch. It was not the sort of performance which the eight-year-old record had been built on. 'I had a feeling that this game might be the one all along,' said Lindsay. After the event, of course. Not too many people fancied Salford for an upset prior to kick-off. 'No, even before the game I wondered if Wigan's preparation was right,' Lindsay explained. 'They had finished the Centenary Championship a fortnight earlier, and a lot of their players had been abroad on holiday in the meantime. They hadn't all been away together, either. They had been away alone, with their wives and girlfriends, or in small groups of friends. Everybody doing their own thing. What they would normally do at the end of the season, in other words. Only this season wasn't quite over. I knew I was right once the game started. I've seen Wigan pull through enough scrapes to know that nothing is over until it's over, but I've also seen Wigan go out and kill opponents in the first quarter of many a cup tie. They didn't do that on this occasion. Everyone seemed to be looking to someone else to take the initiative, but before they realised what was happening Salford took it instead.'

Robinson agreed. 'We lacked our usual intensity even in the warm-up,' the Wigan chairman said. 'We had the capability to win, but not the desire. I think we are at our best when we are under pressure, playing two or three games a week. Having a fortnight break did not do us any good at all.' Crucially, however, that was not all Robinson had to say on the subject of the two-week lay-off. Noting that Cassidy, whose workrate had been sorely missed, had put himself out of the cup tie by breaking a toe while swimming off a Mediterranean beach, Robinson questioned Graeme West's wisdom in allowing his players to go off around the world before an important cup game.

This was not the most gracious response the Wigan chairman could have made at the conclusion of a cup run that will never be equalled, and Robinson's comments did not look any better when they were used prominently in that week's edition of *The Wigan Observer*. Supporters recognised there was some truth in Robinson's remarks, but believed he should share some of the blame.

A lively debate ensued, over who bore responsibility for the team's actions, which Robinson blamed the newspaper for stirring up. The players themselves largely escaped censure, it being recognised that if they were now expected to play throughout summer there would be limited opportunities available to take holidays, until the *Observer* was contacted by a reader who had been in Tenerife at the same time as a party of Wigan players including Edwards. Their behaviour, it was alleged, had been boorish at best, and the amount of alcohol consumed not conducive to winning a cup tie on their return. One player, it was claimed, had collapsed at the poolside due to excessive drinking.

The *Observer* checked this story with the hotel manager in Tenerife, and received sufficient confirmation to run it front page, thereby curtailing an already cool relationship with Robinson. No one at Central Park was exactly delighted with the messenger or the message, though Edwards did admit there was an element of truth to the tale. 'For the first three or four days of the holiday, I do not deny that we did drink and party,' the Wigan captain said. 'And yes, one player did fall asleep while he was at the side of the pool. Who doesn't fall asleep in the sun when they have been on the ale?' Events were moving on, however, because the *Observer* had made a potentially damaging mistake. In naming the five players involved in the Tenerife trip, they had incorrectly included Cowie, who had been on holiday elsewhere and was only too happy to prove it. If Cowie sued, the damages could be considerable, and he had a very strong case. The newspaper's natural

exhilaration at a scoop quickly turned to unease. A couple of days went by anxiously until the word came. Cowie was going to sue.

What happened next surprised everyone. Almost literally, since this obscure and slightly petty argument suddenly spread to involve the Leeds board of directors, the Wigan police, and was flashed across the nation's television screens on the main news bulletins. When the *Observer* received the communication they had been expecting, after a nervous wait of a fortnight, it was not from Cowie after all but from the club. The *Observer*'s inaccurate exposé, it was claimed, had cost Wigan a great deal of money, since a proposed transfer of Cowie to Leeds had now fallen through. Wigan, as opposed to Cowie as an individual, intended to seek redress from *The Wigan Observer* for this financial loss, greater than any the player would have been able to claim for the damage done to his reputation.

Though worried at first, the *Observer* thought it odd that their sports desk had no inkling of any transfer of Cowie to Leeds. A simple check call to Headingley established that Leeds knew nothing of such a deal either. And yes, they would tell the police the same thing should they ask. Eventually the police did ask. On the morning of 3 April, Robinson, Martin and Cowie were arrested at their homes and taken to Wigan police station for questioning. Cowie was subsequently released, but Robinson and Martin were remanded until 8 May, the day of Wigan's historic game against Bath rugby union club, when they were formally charged with conspiracy to defraud *The Wigan Observer*.

CHAPTER ELEVEN

Look Back with Pride

'I only gave Ged Byrne five minutes at the end and he creamed about three of their players. He was really fired up.'

Eight years, 43 ties, eight Wembley wins in a row, no one in rugby league is ever going to top Wigan's Challenge Cup exploits between 1988 and 1995, and few other sports will ever witness such extraordinary consistency and regular brilliance. The Wigan team altered considerably over the years, going through four coaches and countless changes of personnel, but one player appeared in every game, even including the two unexpected defeats at Oldham and Salford which framed the record-shattering run. Shaun Edwards became the most decorated rugby player of all time in the process, and it is unlikely anyone else will come even close to touching his unique achievement. Here, he looks back on the greatest cup run in history.

1987
Round 1: Oldham 10, Wigan 8
'Not a great performance, but the reason we lost at the end was because Joe Lydon, who had just fielded a deep kick, had the ball pulled out of his hands after being tackled. The referee didn't see it, and he didn't get any help from his touch judge. We complained, of course, but had to get on with it. That's how Oldham came to get the ball on our line, and as everyone knows, Paddy Kirwan managed to get through. It's too late for excuses now, though. We lost and we had to suffer. It was awful in the clubhouse that night; we just wanted to slip away, but Oldham were having the biggest party of their lives. They got relegated at the end of the season too. I think we all discovered that night how much everyone else hates Wigan.'

1988
Round 1: Wigan 2, Bradford Northern
A very muddy pitch and the usual hard game against Bradford. It was a disputed penalty, and I think we conned an extra ten yards out of the referee which made Joe's kick easier. It was only the pitch that kept the scores so close, though. Pressure-wise, we were all over them.'

Round 2: Wigan 30, Leeds 14
'A massive game in front of a packed house. Leeds had a good team at the time and they went 10–0 in front. We showed tremendous character in coming back, but our season was on the line. Our fitness showed in the end, and we began to run away with it late on. A fantastic game, though.'

Round 3: Wigan 10, Widnes 1
'They had two tries disallowed and they didn't like it. I can't say I blamed them either, because I think they were probably valid tries. But the referee didn't give them, so we got on with the game. Whether those decisions affected the outcome, who knows? But I remember Hampo having a brilliant game and clinching a place in the semi-final with a try at the end.'

Semi-final (Burnden Park): Wigan 34, Salford 4
'Very heavy going again, but this time the mud didn't stop us. We dominated throughout, I think it was a bit one-sided really, for a semi. I scored an easy try from a miskick by Andy Gregory. I had my photograph taken celebrating a try with Henderson Gill, and because of the way we looked with all the mud, the picture won an award.'

Final (Wembley): Wigan 32, Halifax 12
'It was nil apiece for ages, and then we just blasted them before half-time. It was an all-round top display really, everything we tried came off once we got started. I was lucky to be playing, actually, because the day before the game I had been larking around with Ged Byrne and Shaun Wane and had kicked a kerb. I almost broke my toe, and needed an injection to play. I would have looked pretty silly if I had missed the game, as I was captain at the time. I enjoyed lifting the Cup. I came off five minutes from the end to give Ged a go, and I told Graham Lowe to send Shaun Wane on as well, because I know how bad it is getting to a cup final and just sitting and watching. Ged

Shaun Edwards lifts the Silk Cut Challenge Cup as Wigan captain in 1988.

was only on for five minutes but he creamed about three of their players with really big hits. Nothing illegal, but considering the Cup was won, it was quite funny. He was really fired up.'

1989
Round 1: Doncaster 6, Wigan 38
'Joe Lydon scored four tries. There was a bit of turmoil at the club at the time and Andy Gregory only came on at half-time. Not one of our best performances, but it didn't need to be. Doncaster tired badly in the second half.'

Round 2: Bradford Northern 4, Wigan 17
'Very tough game. Probably our best perform-ance of the whole campaign. Bradford had an awesome pack, with Skerrett and Hill and some really big lads, and everyone thought we would try to keep the game in the backs and try to run them around. We didn't though, because we reckoned that might be playing into their hands. We decided to take them on up the middle to try and tire them out through tackling. It took a lot of guts to play that way, and some of our forwards took an awful pasting, but our tactics worked. It was my dad's idea actually, not to run them around, and I mentioned it to Graham Lowe, who agreed it was worth a try.'

Round 3: Oldham 4, Wigan 12
'Played in snow. I scored the first try and slid about ten yards to cross the line. In fact, there's a funny moment on the tape of the game when Nicky Kiss pats me on the head after scoring and about half a ton of snow appears to fall out of my ear. We ran from dummy half a lot in that game, because in those days there was only one marker. We were all aware of what had happened in the last cup tie at Oldham, but we were able to use that as motivation.'

Semi-final (Maine Road): Wigan 13, War-rington 6
'Incredibly tough game. I know all cup ties are tough, and semi-finals especially, but this really was exceptional. The two sides were evenly matched, the rugby was of a very high

standard, it was more like a Test match than anything else. John Woods had an excellent game for Warrington, we were nervous of him all the time. The scores were locked at 6–6 and then Joe launched that drop goal. I was as surprised as anyone else. I'd never seen anything like that before. Warrington had to play catch-up then, and we saw them off. I scored late in the game from a cross kick by Ellery Hanley, another thing you don't see too often.'

Final (Wembley): Wigan 27, St Helens 0

'We dominated from the start. Saints were very poor. They made loads of mistakes which made our job easier. The game might have been a bit one-sided for neutrals, but it was fantastic for the Wigan fans. Some people thought we would never beat Saints at Wembley, and we had played them the week before in the Premiership and lost. The Wigan record against Saints at Wembley was at the back of our minds, to be honest. You think it's only superstition, but you never quite know. What we realised after only a few minutes

was that we had prepared for the final and Saints hadn't. Perhaps Alex believed Saints were invincible at Wembley, because he had changed his winning team. The Australians they brought in were a big disappointment. O'Connor was particularly poor, I thought, and after Vautin took a big hit off Platty early in the game he didn't want to know. But we scored some fabulous tries, especially Ellery's. To do Saints at Wembley like that was just a dream.'

1990

Round 1: Hull KR 4, Wigan 6

'The great escape. A very muddy, slippery pitch and a narrow one too. The wind was blowing a gale right down the length of the pitch, it was very difficult to play in such inhospitable conditions. I put up a kick and Dave Marshall reached it for the try which saw us through, but I don't think we would have scored it at any other ground. The in-goal areas at New Craven Park are unusually long, and the ball stayed in play whereas at other grounds it would have gone dead.

Old Trafford 1990. Ged Byrne congratulates Andy Goodway on his last-minute try. Gary Connolly and George Mann of St Helens are studies in dejection.

Painful memory. The 1990 final was going like a breeze for Shaun Edwards up to this point in the first half, when he became the meat in a Bob Jackson-Gary Sanderson sandwich. Edwards suffered a fractured cheekbone and eye socket, but stayed on for the rest of the game.

Anywhere else, in those conditions, and we might have been out of the Cup, except I don't think you would get those conditions anywhere else. We kept taking drop-outs from under our posts, and neither Ged Byrne nor me could get the ball further than ten yards up the pitch, so Rovers were straight back at us every time. Joe Lydon had come off injured, but John Monie sent him back again just to get a bit of distance on our kicks into the wind.'

Round 2 : Wigan 30, Dewsbury 6

'Dean Bell got sent off and picked up a ten-match ban. Felt sorry for him about that because the bloke he hit was asking for it. Not a great game. Dewsbury came to spoil, and used niggling tactics to keep the score down.'

Round 3: Wakefield Trinity 14, Wigan 30

'Hard game, Wakefield fancied themselves a bit. They had Ray Price that year, though he didn't last long. We didn't get everything our way, and we had to play in our half of the field quite a bit, but our pace was decisive. Kevin Iro scored one long-range try, and I got a couple.'

Semi-final (Old Trafford): Wigan 20, St Helens 14

'It turned out all right in the end, but this wasn't one of our best games. We played quite poorly, especially in the first half, when I think we were a bit too fired up. We went behind, but gradually clawed our way back when we stopped running all over the place and settled into our usual pattern. It was still looking like a replay though, until Ellery made this unbelievable run right at the end and made a try for Andy Gregory. Saints were gutted at the end and I felt for them a bit. They had played really well, a million times better than at Wembley the previous year, and we had got out of jail.'

Final (Wembley): Wigan 36, Warrington 14

'Still a painful memory. I was already playing with a broken hand, which needed a pain-killing injection before the kick-off, when I got my face smashed in after about eight minutes. It was incredibly painful, and I couldn't see properly out of one eye for the rest of the game. I thought at first I'd broken my jaw, but it turned out to be a cheekbone and eye socket fracture. It's funny but I never thought of coming off. I'd trained so hard to get myself fit, and worked particularly hard in the week leading to the final. I thought I would be in just as much pain sitting on the bench, and really fed up at not being on the field, so I stayed on. I could still run and everything, and I think I only made one mistake, kicking too early in the tackle count. I stood wide and didn't do my share of tackling though. Dean Bell helped me out a lot in that respect.'

1991
Round 1: Castleford 4, Wigan 28
'An absolutely awesome performance, probably the best of the whole eight years. I'm really proud of it even now. Castleford were pretty confident, and we were quite worried about them. They had a strong side and were going well under Daryll van de Velde. But our defence, in the first half especially, was the best I've ever seen from a Wigan team. The big hits were unbelievable. I think we would have beaten anyone in the world that night, playing like that. Australian club teams, Test teams, anybody. We absolutely battered Castleford.'

Round 2: Rochdale Hornets 4, Wigan 72
'Not a complete walkover, despite the scoreline. Rochdale had been saying they thought they could beat us, and they didn't play too badly at first, but our forwards were always on top and we blasted them in the second half. I got sent off for retaliation.'

Round 3: Wigan 32, Bradford Northern 2
'Again, sounds easy looking at the scoreline, but it wasn't. There was no such thing as an easy game against Bradford in those days, you were always counting the bumps and bruises afterwards. Bradford are not quite so physical nowadays, although I don't think anyone is. The game has changed because of the five-metre rule. It's more about fitness now than strength. We had the fitness back in 1991, and it told in the second half. We used to do a

few teams like that back then. We would find opponents could compete for 50 minutes or an hour, but couldn't go the whole distance.'

Semi-final (Burnden Park): Wigan 30, Oldham 16
'This was pretty low-key as semi-finals go. It was a fairly comfortable victory, and we played within ourselves a bit because we knew what was coming up in the league. We had what John Monie called Mission Impossible in front of us. Even in the dressing-room afterwards the atmosphere was a bit subdued. We were all knackered that season, we were just getting on with it.'

Final (Wembley): Wigan 13, St Helens 8
'The most miraculous of all our wins at Wembley. How we managed to stay on our feet, never mind beat St Helens, I'll never know. About eight of us were on pain-killing injections, some of us could have done with crutches afterwards. Half the team couldn't even run properly, but we were lucky enough to get a couple of tries on the board early on and somehow we managed to hang on to our lead until the end. Definitely the longest final I've ever played in. Saints were quite pleased with themselves afterwards, because it had been a close game and they had managed to keep the score down, but the truth is that they were beaten by a team of cripples.'

1992
Round 1: Salford 6, Wigan 22
'A few days before we flew out to play in the World Sevens in Sydney. I remember scoring a try, but not much else. The Sevens dominated that week, but although we won in Sydney, and it was a terrific adventure against the odds, we knew the Challenge Cup was more important.'

Round 2: Wigan 14, Warrington 0
'In the circumstances this was a great win. We had only just arrived back from Sydney, and the trip, more than anything, had taken it out of us. I remember looking up at the clock thinking there were only about five minutes

Martin Offiah shows Shaun Edwards the way to the Castleford try line in the 1992 final.

left, and getting a shock when I realised we were only ten minutes into the second half. With 25 minutes left my legs had gone, and there were a few others who felt the same way. Exhausting.'

Round 3: St Helens 6, Wigan 13
'A brutal game, with a lot of fighting. We never felt we had the game safe, this was one of the occasions we came closest to going out.

I scored a disputed try. Saints claimed a double movement, but I thought it was all right, and I got away with it.'

Semi-final (Burnden Park): Wigan 71, Bradford Northern 10
'Pretty close to perfection, I reckon. One of the best two Wigan sides I have played in, 1994 being the other. The standard of our football was excellent. Bradford just couldn't get near

Dean Bell with John Major at Wembley in 1992. There is a banana in the picture, but no sign of Billy McGinty and his pineapple ring.

us. We all knew we were amassing a pretty big score, obviously, but playing so well was exhilarating. I didn't feel sorry for Bradford at all. Maybe after the game I did a bit, when I saw how fed up Karl Fairbank looked, but on the field it was different. We just went for it.'

Final (Wembley): Wigan 28, Castleford 12

'One of my favourite finals, I really enjoyed it, possibly because it was the first for a while when I hadn't been carrying an injury. We played really well in the first half, I put in a kick and Martin Offiah scored a try that no one else in the world would have scored, but we couldn't get hold of the ball after half-time. We did quite well to keep our heads in front, because Castleford were hitting us with everything, and I thought St John Ellis was certain to score and make things even more difficult before Martin came to the rescue,

chasing back to clear. He deserved the Lance Todd just for that. I've never seen anyone run as fast on a rugby field in my life.'

1993
Preliminary round: Wigan 40, Hull 2

'We didn't think we should be in a preliminary round, and we probably took it out on Hull, who actually didn't deserve to be in this situation either. They were quite a good team then, this was a good display by Wigan. We had just been annihilated by St Helens in the league, but we were starting to put a bit of form back together.'

Round 1: Dewsbury 4, Wigan 20

'I had almost forgotten about this game, and I don't particularly want to dwell on it now. An awful game, an awful place. The pitch was just disgraceful.'

Round 2: Wigan 23, St Helens 3

'One of the very best performances of the whole eight years, up there with Castleford in 1991. Saints were red-hot favourites to beat us after the result on Boxing Day, but I think they handled that pressure less well than we coped with being underdogs. We went out with an unbelievably positive attitude and just swarmed all over them. We didn't do anything too fancy, we didn't let them play their expansive game, we just pasted them in the middle.'

Round 3: Halifax 18, Wigan 19

'What happened to consistency? We were always struggling here, on a wintry day, and at one point we were quite a way behind. One of our closest shaves, but probably not the closest. We clawed our way back level before the end, when Andy Platt put in a big run to set up the position for Joe to drop a goal. It was about 30 yards out, and not an easy opportunity, but Joe snaffles those no bother.'

Semi-final (Elland Road): Wigan 15, Bradford Northern 6

'A very bruising game, probably not all that thrilling for spectators. We lost Dean Bell, injured early on, which didn't help. But we were always in control, and I scored my first ever drop goal. I must have tried dozens down the years, but this was my very first success.'

Final (Wembley): Wigan 20, Widnes 14

'A very hot day, and we went down twice in the first half, which wasn't something that normally happened at Wembley. We were

Close call at Halifax. Neil Cowie looks to unload the ball in the 1993 quarter-final.

back on terms before half-time though, then Sam Panapa scored a try just after half-time which sealed the victory. I was made up for him, it couldn't have happened to a nicer chap. Dean Bell backed himself to win the Lance Todd and managed to collect. Richie Eyres got himself dismissed. I think he deserved it, it was a bad foul. Widnes got a bit wound up before the end, but I think the heat might have been partly to blame. It was very sapping, and couldn't have been much fun if you were losing.'

1994
Round 4: Wigan 24, Wakefield Trinity 16*
'We were in a rough patch here, it was a terrible time at the club with morale at a very low ebb. Henry Paul had a brilliant game for Wakefield, and we only won through a Nigel Wright interception try. One of the few times we had been worried at home. I was worried because for the first time ever I was no longer enjoying my rugby. It was a worrying season all round.'

* Challenge Cup format amended in 1994 with seeded clubs entering at fourth-round stage.

Round 5: Hull 21, Wigan 22
'The greatest escape of all. Our second-half performance was one of our best ever. I was on the bench in the first half as I had been dropped, and when we went 21–2 down I remember thinking this year I would be going to Wembley on a coach with my mates for a change. But B-J got a try just before the interval, I played in the second half and we stormed right back. Andy Farrell got the winning try. We showed a lot of character that day.'

Round 6: Wigan 32, Featherstone Rovers 14
'We were playing a little better now, though we were not too happy about letting Rovers score 14 points against us. This was the game with the brawl though, the one that everyone remembers Kelvin Skerrett coming flying into. Very amusing that, we all thought afterwards.'

Semi-final (Headingley): Wigan 20, Castleford 8
'We had been written off for this one, which I suppose was understandable, given our two earlier performances against Cas. I think we must perform at our best when under fire, because our first half was as good as anything I have seen. I think we dropped the ball once, and went in 18–0 up. The game was as good as over. This was the time John Dorahy asked us to pick our strongest team beforehand, an exercise which some of us, I'm sorry to say, did not take very seriously. I don't think there was any harm in it.'

Final (Wembley): Wigan 26, Leeds 16
'The hottest conditions for a game I've ever known in England. It was more like playing in Queensland or New Guinea. I don't think we played particularly well, but Martin scored one of the best tries I've ever seen. It must have been an entertaining final, because Leeds came back at us at one point and got quite close. Martin Dermott put in a massive hit on Ellery Hanley though, he spilled the ball, Mick Cassidy made a run and we scored as a result. But it was close, we could have lost.'

1995
Round 4: Wigan 16, St Helens 16
'Out of jail again. Very muddy pitch, we failed to adapt, trying to play our expansive game when the conditions didn't allow it, and nearly came a cropper. Bobbie Goulding's attempted drop goal hit a post and bounced back, otherwise it might have been the end.'

Replay: St Helens 24, Wigan 40
'An awesome display – our speed was breathtaking. I reckon there are four stand-out Wigan performances in the whole of our eight-year run, and two came against Castleford and two came against St Helens. This was the fourth. There was a massive crowd in, people were still queuing outside, and the Saints supporters were very confident. But we raced to 20–0 up in almost no time, and that quietened them. A great win, though we

Botica the boot. Frano pops over another Wembley winner.

shipped a few too many points after our initial burst. Saints had a very strong side though.'

Round 5: Batley 4, Wigan 70

'The weather let Batley down for this one. Jeff Grayshon had been shouting his mouth off after a good performance against St Helens in the Regal, saying Wigan would get stuck in the mud. But it didn't rain for days beforehand, and the pitch was baked rock hard. No grass to be seen, but we didn't mind that. We just ran Batley ragged.'

Round 6: Widnes 12, Wigan 26

'Wet conditions, tough opposition, and again we didn't adapt very well. We went down 12–0 and only got on top late in the game. Widnes gave us a lot of problems.'

Semi-final (Huddersfield): Wigan 48, Oldham 20

'One-sided game, must have been disappointing for spectators, not that very many turned up. Almost embarrassingly low-key for a semi-final. We played all right, not very happy with letting them score 20. We seemed to be making a habit of letting teams come back at us instead of finishing them off.'

Final (Wembley): Wigan 30, Leeds 10

'Probably my favourite final. There was a lot of bad feeling at the time about Super League. Several players had received loyalty payments, and I hadn't. I wasn't very happy about that, but it was a pleasure to be able to turn on our best form and dominate a final against a Leeds team I rated as stronger than the year before. Jason Robinson was our match-winner, but his place was in doubt beforehand because of a foot injury. I helped persuade Graeme West to let him play. We were all glad about that afterwards.'

1996
Round 4: Wigan 74, Bramley 12

'I nearly missed this game, because I had been banned for a tackle on Robbie Paul that I only just managed to overturn on appeal. The video evidence showed quite clearly I was not guilty, and fortunately the appeal board could see that for themselves. Then I won the Man of the Match award and everyone started saying I shouldn't have been playing. I was concerned about a suspension costing me my unbroken cup run, but more concerned about being punished for something I hadn't done. The game was straightforward enough, no indication of what was to come.'

Round 5: Salford 26, Wigan 16

'The end. We played poorly, there's no doubt about that. And we missed Mick Cassidy. There were also two tries we had disallowed, I think a little harshly. But I don't want to be accused of sour grapes. Salford deserved their win, I just wish we had gone out playing well instead of playing badly.'

CHAPTER TWELVE

Full Circle

'We're handing everything to rugby union on a plate.'

Something else of significance had occurred in 1995. In one of those cosmic coincidences which will delight future historians, almost one hundred years to the day after the northern pay rebels first split from their arrogant and élitist southern masters, rugby union announced to the world, from a flashy hotel in Paris, that it too was finally ready to grasp the nettle of professionalism. 'We had a situation which tended to make honest men dishonest,' admitted International Board secretary Vernon Pugh, not before time. 'We want an end to the hypocrisy.'

The possible impact of such a step on rugby league had long been a subject for discussion among adherents of both codes. Rugby union writers, often as keen to toe the Twickenham party line as any buffer in a blazer, were fond of advancing the argument that once the senior code began paying its players, there would no longer be any need for rugby league. This red flag was always eagerly charged at by the more bullish among league's supporters, who pointed out that thousands of BARLA's true amateurs played the 13-a-side game every week for nothing, and that rugby union could not sustain professionalism without doing something to make the game more attractive and well-supported at the turnstile. Rugby union would have to start paying spectators, not just players, it was sneeringly remarked, if it seriously imagined people were going to give up watching Wigan and Leeds in favour of Orrell and Otley.

All too plainly, however, these were merely stock responses from both sides of a century-old cultural divide. Rugby union

enjoyed rubbishing rugby league, and vice versa, and always had done. One could imagine how a level, professional playing field might subtly alter that age-old antagonism, but no one knew exactly what would happen because no one could foresee how professional rugby union would work. Even now, more than a year after the Paris declaration, that is still more or less the case in Britain. Professionalism in the Southern Hemisphere has gone much more smoothly, perhaps because Australia, New Zealand and South Africa were already some way down the track in 1995, with a realistic schedule of what they wanted to achieve, but in the Five Nations countries, confusion reigned. Wales were all for derestriction and unfettered financial freedom, and within weeks of Paris had begun the process of getting former favourites like Jonathan Davies and Scott Gibbs back to the valleys. Scotland and Ireland were less enthusiastic and proposed to carry on pretty much as before. France, as usual, made their own arrangements. All the surprises happened in England, where it is not too much of an exaggeration to say that the world as we thought we knew it was stood on its head.

It all began predictably enough. No sooner had professionalism got the green light than Sir John Hall, the millionaire behind Newcastle United, began paying football-type wages and transfer fees to assemble a formidable rugby union side in the north-east. Dazed and confused, Twickenham hastily imposed a 12-month moratorium on the professional era. This was the reactionary RFU stance everyone had come to expect,

The history men . . . Andy Farrell of Wigan and Phil De Glanville of Bath lead their teams out for their match at Twickenham. Bath were the victors on this occasion, after losing the opening encounter at Maine Road.

from an administration memorably characterised by Will Carling as '57 old farts'. Yet within the year, the Twickenham which had once sanctimoniously espoused the pure milk of amateurism had embraced the ethos of professionalism so thoroughly that it had signed its own exclusive deal with Sky TV, much to the chagrin of the other home unions, and declared its intention to go it alone even if it meant the scrapping of the Five Nations Championship. Yet even this level of professionalism was not enough for the leading players and the wealthy businessmen who had invested heavily in clubs in the top two divisions. Sensing that Twickenham was more concerned with paying its own bills and looking after the essentially amateur game nationwide, these clubs were now threatening to break away on their own.

From a rugby league perspective, of course, this was highly amusing. As Lady Bracknell nearly said, to have one breakaway over professionalism might be considered unfortunate, to have a second sounded like carelessness. It was also deeply refreshing to hear the shortcomings of the Five Nations Championship being discussed for a change, after years and years of the most fawning, deferential coverage this side of a royal wedding. For anyone from rugby league to suggest that the Five Nations was a parochial event of little global relevance which annually failed to rise above the obvious limitations imposed by its repetitive format and was quite possibly holding the Northern Hemisphere game back, had always been tantamount to treason. Now here were people in rugby union saying exactly the same thing. When you have put up with the amount of nonsense rugby league has had to put up with over the years, small victories for truth and reality are seized upon with relish.

Except that rugby league did not feel much like celebrating. It seemed ominous, to say the least, that rugby union should start living in the real world just as rugby league was moving into the realms of fantasy. The nearer the first summer of Super League came, the less sense it all made. Despite the bold front put on by Lindsay and his friends from Sky, Super League's sums did not appear to add up. The switch of seasons alone was a massive risk, a desperate gamble which would have been tricky enough to pull off had everything else been equal. But everything else was far from equal. In just about every direction one cared to look, the odds seemed to be stacked against the new enterprise. Even as Sky plumbed new depths in tastelessness by depicting players in rugby strips leaping over the trenches on a mock First World War battlefield, one wondered how much of rugby league would emerge unscathed after going so remorselessly over the top.

There was, for a start, the question of club finances in what was now an alarmingly short season. The play-offs with Australian clubs, the glamorous, end-of-season money-spinners which had been the real *raison d'être* for the switch to summer, had now gone by the board. With just 12 teams in the Super League, that meant a mere 11 guaranteed home fixtures, 12 if you finished first or second and earned a play-off semi-final. People used to talk of streamlining the fixture list back in the days when the season was cluttered with county cups, Regal and Challenge Cups and the rest, but this was drastic pruning. In the 1991–92 season, to take an example at random, Wigan had played a total of 43 games, of which 20 were at home and four were at neutral venues. This was a season which featured a World Club Championship game, but not a Lancashire Cup final or a match against a Kangaroo or Kiwi touring side. In 1996, Lancashire Cup finals, Kangaroo touring teams and World Club Championships had all been consigned to history. It occurred to more than one club

chairman that Murdoch money or not, a season of only 11 home games was going to be a financial struggle.

It certainly occurred to Jack Robinson. Wigan's crowds had nose-dived during the Centenary season. Everybody's had. Perhaps this was inevitable. Even Lindsay had half-apologetically admitted the truncated Centenary championship, which Wigan won to keep the old trophy in perpetuity, was a mere stopgap. When many coaches began talking of the Centenary season as an experimental period, a dry run for Super League, it was only natural that fans too should start to pick their matches. 'The Centenary season was an absolute disaster for us,' admitted Robinson, then going on to outline some of his ideas for making things better in Super League, suggesting the Central Park faithful might go for country and western themed afternoons or Elvis look-alike competitions. When everyone stopped laughing, a few went on to consider that Wigan, from the sound of things, were in big trouble already.

The trouble was that having offered the public the distinctly lacklustre Centenary season, the Super League had a credibility problem. Apart from Paris St Germain, themselves a fairly major credibility problem, Super League had very little new to offer. If spectators did not fancy Wigan against Oldham in the Centenary competition, why should they go for Wigan against Oldham in the Super League? Inevitably, it would be another one-sided contest. And unwisely, though perhaps just as inevitably, Wigan had put up their ticket prices for Super League. Most clubs were now asking more money for what was basically the same show. Except in many cases it wasn't even that. Several rule changes, most notably the one that kept a defending team ten yards back at the rucks, had none too subtly speeded up the game and led to a proliferation of tries. As far as anyone was aware, there had been no dissatisfaction expressed over too few tries being scored in rugby league – as we have seen, two of the most memorable games in Wigan's recent

Jump! Just one of the things people imagined they would never see. Wigan challenge (not very expertly) for lineout possession in the game against Bath at Twickenham.

history, the Manly match and the last Lancashire Cup final, had both been tryless though by no means joyless encounters – but supporters were suddenly presented with a situation in which ten or twelve tries per game was quite normal. The purist/progressive argument over whether this is a good or bad thing is largely irrelevant. Defences now have an almost unmanageable job – it is not physically possible to repulse a decently organised team for a whole 80 minutes – and this is certainly a shame. But two evenly matched teams can still produce a high-speed, high-skill contest, and no one really objects to high-scoring games if they are as absorbing as the 1996 Challenge Cup final between Bradford and St Helens, or the same year's Premiership semi-final between Wigan and Bradford.

One had to feel for Robbie Paul of Bradford, who in 1996 became the first player ever to score a hat-trick in a Wembley final, yet still climbed the steps on the losing side, and for Scott Quinnell, Wigan's Welsh recruit who claimed that he was just coming to terms with the pace of his new code when rugby league became twice as fast overnight, but by and large the new rules did not harm the top tier of competent clubs. The problems came when top met bottom. There was already a vast gulf in capability within the Super League, all the way, so to speak, from Wigan to Workington, and this was one of its identifiable weaknesses. The new rules and the increased scoring rates only magnified this inequality. It was bad enough when the weaker teams in the league got on the end of 40-point hidings; why anyone should imagine there was a market for 70- or 80-point winning margins was a mystery. This was less of a problem for teams like St Helens and Bradford, who were enjoying long-awaited success and did not mind winning by cricket scores, but at Central Park the novelty of winning too easily had long since worn off. Throughout the country, older spectators and traditionalists were uneasy at the way the game seemed to be mutating into a form of basketball. The quote from Wigan schoolteacher Derek Birchall at the start of this book happens to encapsulate a simple truth about rugby league. You do have to be brave to play it, and while you don't have to be brave to watch it, you respect the players as much for their bravery as for their skill or their speed. The last thing a rugby league match should be is easy. My father paid his senior citizen's rate to watch St Helens against Sheffield in the Super League, but walked off in disgust at half-time. 'Saints were already leading by 30 points,' he said. 'It was a travesty of a contest.'

To recap, then, the first summer season of Super League had the following obstacles to surmount. One: the change of season itself. Any business reliant on building an audience knows better than to muck the customers about, and rugby league consumers were now being asked to ignore the traditional

Jason Robinson, seen here in typical 'Billy Whizz' form against St Helens. The winger made a great impression in the rugby union games, but had long been one of Wigan's most explosive performers.

routines and familiar rituals of winter and turn out instead in the holiday season. Quite apart from taking holidays in summer (most people still do, and this factor alone would hit season-ticket sales), rugby league fans were just as likely as anyone else in this cold country to want to make the most of fine, warm weather. It was one thing to enjoy spending a cold winter's afternoon at an antiquated rugby league ground of old England, with pungent steam rising simultaneously from the scrum on the field and the urinal at the back of the stand, but summer was a different proposition. English grounds had all been built with a view to keeping the weather out.

Two: the season was a short one, and it was likely that if your team lost a couple of games early on, it would be out of the running for the rest of the campaign. Lack of overall competitiveness, the chief failing of the British game for over a decade, was just as evident in the Super League as it had ever been. Bradford proved surprisingly strong, Leeds disappointingly weak, but it was essentially the recipe as before. London and Bradford provided nuisance value, but the title race, almost from the word go, was between Wigan and St Helens. Outside the top four clubs, from Warrington downwards, no one had anything remotely super to offer. Worse, an inferior side would now find itself up against an insurmountable points deficit as early as 15 or 20 minutes into the game. The greater ease of try-scoring did allow some notable fight-backs – a team 20 points down in the first half was no longer necessarily out for the count – but these were the exceptions rather than the rule. All too often, all hope of a contest would evaporate inside the first quarter. And many clubs had raised admission prices. There were some notable exceptions, but a lot of the time clubs were asking spectators to pay more to see less. All this during the summer of 1996, which did happen to feature the odd counter-attraction, such as the European Football Championships, staged for the first time in England, and the Olympic Games from Atlanta. The former event completely dom-inated the early part of the summer to such an extent that even a traditional favourite like Wimbledon struggled to get a look in. If Super League was hoping to win new friends as well as hang on to old ones, it could scarcely have picked a worse summer to start. Its media profile was constantly disap-pointing, even on satellite TV.

Which brings us to perhaps the biggest drawback of all. As adverse circumstances go, the above list is quite substantial, yet Super League might still have been a success had it not been handicapped by the very agency which brought it into being. It was easy to forget, in the rush to grab Murdoch's £87 million, the confusion of the ARL–Super League struggle and the novelty of changing seasons, that what Lindsay and the club chairmen had put their names to was a television deal. There was no chance of forgetting when the Super League eventually began. Not only were there more matches covered live on television than ever before, it suited Sky to shift kick-off times to 6.30 p.m., and sometimes switch games from Sunday to Friday evening at short notice.

What this meant for the game as a whole was another poor deal for season-ticket holders, who could no longer rely on games kicking off at three in the afternoon, or even taking place on a Sunday. What it meant for Wigan, a leading club who had always attracted more than a strictly fair share of television coverage, was that nearly all their quality fixtures were screened live on Sky.

One scarcely needed a diploma in marketing to spot the perils in this arrangement. The same spectators who were being asked to put up with season changes, rule changes, price hikes and new timetables, were simul-taneously being told they could stay at home if they liked, and watch the game in the comfort of their living-room. Or meet in the pub – well, it is Friday night, after all – and watch the game with friends and a few beers.

It was not long before Robinson, showing a fine disregard for the rules of the television sportscasting game, began questioning the role of the major partner in the Super League enterprise. 'Too many people are watching games on television,' he said. 'Real sup-porters come down to the ground and watch the match live. Our success in the last decade has been achieved through spectators sup-porting the club at the turnstile, not couch potatoes tuning in at home. I believe television is having an adverse effect on our attendances, and although we do receive money from Sky it is not enough to keep a team of this quality together indefinitely.'

This was at the start of the Super League season, when it was already clear that the considerable outgoings of a club like Wigan were not going to be wholly offset by television revenue. The Murdoch millions might have been a godsend to the type of club which was rarely on the television anyway, but Wigan, for one, still needed a game to pay at the gate. The club was budgeting for an average gate of around 14,000 during Super League, something of an ambitious break-even point considering the switch to summer, the disappointing crowds of the Centenary season, and the fact that the club's average league attendance had risen through the '80s but peaked at 14,500 by the mid-'90s. The great hope was that fewer games, though of better quality, would prove attractive to spectators. There was nothing wrong with this theory, except that as Super League neared and finally arrived, it was still only a theory. The only certainty was that the new rugby league season would involve sub-stantially fewer games.

It was during the jittery period between the Centenary season and Super League, when club accountants were beginning to express concern about revenue forecasts, that Wigan received an offer of help from an unexpected source. Rugby union was also in a period of limbo, looking at an uncertain future, and facing unprecedented wage bills. Bath, as dominant a force in rugby union as Wigan were in league, were looking for a money-spinning fixture. Alan McColm, Martin Offiah's agent, was able to put the two parties in touch with each other. Having eagerly embraced the new era of professionalism, and gone to some expense in preparing for it, the West Country club was interested in using some of the new-found freedoms to recoup some of their outlay. How would it be if Bath played Wigan at rugby league, then staged a return match under union rules?

By March 1996, this was far from an outlandish suggestion. At any other point in history it would have been laughed at, or turned down out of hand by Twickenham, but the best indication of how much had changed between the codes, and how quickly, was that when the Bath–Wigan challenge was first mooted, the RFL was more resistant to the idea than the RFU, because it was reluctant to disrupt an early Super League weekend. Once that difficulty had been ironed out, the Bath–Wigan challenge took its place in history, or at least in a rapidly evolving sequence of ground-breaking events which was changing the whole rugby landscape.

Maurice Lindsay and Vernon Pugh had set the ball rolling with an informal meeting in January 1995. Arising from this entente was a lifting of the IRFB life ban, in March 1995, on anyone who had ever played league, though a three-year stand-down period, widely thought to be unenforceable in law, would have to be observed. In June 1995, on the eve of the Rugby Union World Cup final in Johannesburg, Murdoch's News Corporation announced a £360 million deal for the television rights to rugby union in South Africa, Australia and New Zealand. Apart from dwarfing the amount of money paid out to rugby league and subsequently rugby union clubs in England, this also put most global rugby of either code – with the exception of that under the dogged control of the ARL – in the hands of Murdoch. In October 1995 the three-year stand-down period was scrapped, the IRFB having been informed that a test case it would certainly lose might be imminent, and by the following month Jonathan Davies, Cardiff rugby union club's first-ever £90,000 capture from rugby league, was playing against Aberavon in front of a crowd of 7,000. Davies was followed home by Jonathan Griffiths, and eventually Scott Gibbs of St Helens, while John Devereux of Widnes signed for Sale and Leeds lost Jim Fallon to Richmond and Craig Innes to Australian Rugby League. In a gesture of friendship, Twickenham invited the Rugby League to send a team along to the annual Middlesex Sevens, and Lindsay handed the invitation along to Wigan.

In April 1996, Wigan supporters received a shock when Scott Quinnell announced his Central Park contract had been bought out and he too would be moving to Richmond. The Welsh forward, after a slow start, was by this time regularly winning rave reviews as Wigan's strongest and most effective pack member, and the club could have done without losing his immense contribution so soon after saying goodbye to Denis Betts, Phil Clarke and Andy Platt. Quinnell was one of the replacements who were enabling Wigan to carry on as normal. Without him the pack began to look dangerously lightweight. But what worried Wigan supporters most was that the club did not appear to put up much of a fight to keep Quinnell. Rather, they seemed to accept with unseemly haste that some rugby union clubs now had greater financial clout, and appeared to be congratulating themselves on saving the expense of Quinnell's contract. For the Welshman, one of the last of the breed to come north and one of the most hard-headed and realistic about his reasons why, had not succumbed to homesickness or nostalgia. He came to Wigan for the money and the career advancement, and went to Richmond for the same reasons. It was true that the possibility of renewing his Welsh international career was a factor in Quinnell's decision, but no one was pretending the financial deal was not attractive. Wigan had simply been outbid. 'We couldn't match the money Richmond were offering,' Robinson said. Had a rugby league club come along with the same sort of offer, Wigan supporters would have expected to see it rejected out of hand, yet for several seasons now this theory had never been put to the test. Wigan had the best players in rugby league, they won all the prizes and paid the highest wages. Their players did occasionally join other clubs, but only when Wigan wanted them to, having had the best of them or decided they were surplus to requirements. Players like Offiah, Edwards and Connolly were assumed to be at Central Park for life, for the simple reason that no one else could afford them.

The new money swilling around rugby union changed all that, and from the alacrity with which Wigan accepted Richmond's offer for Quinnell, Wigan were more relieved than aggrieved. Supporters were asked to accept that the club was having to tighten its belt, not just because of the loss of revenue at the turnstile, but because the RFL were now talking of introducing a salary cap for the following season. Quinnell, who actually played his last game for Wigan at Twickenham, was on one of the biggest contracts at Central Park, so it was prudent to let him go.

Salary caps, however, are there to be dodged and defied, or 'rorted' as they described it in Australia, after a tentative stab at central control of finance in rugby league was comprehensively routed by the ingenuity of club accountants. What no one has ever done, when confronted by a salary cap, is blush like a guilty schoolboy and agree to slash the wage bill. Wigan kept saying they were worried about the salary cap, but they were not widely believed. It was assumed instead they could not afford to keep their contract payments.

This was in fact the truth, since Wigan found themselves in a uniquely uncomfortable situation once their crowds began to fall. What clubs normally do when confronted by loss of expected income is sell a player or two, thereby realising some cash and at the same time reducing the overall wage bill. But Wigan's players were all tightly bound by contracts, all freshly negotiated and newly topped-up as a result of the ARL–Super League dispute. And while contracts can be bought out, there wasn't a single club in the Super League capable of matching the money Wigan's stars were being paid, even had one been able to persuade a Connolly or an Offiah to leave Central Park. So Wigan had no option but to grin and bear a tight financial situation. Even the first couple of tranches of Murdoch money had been swallowed up by loyalty payments to players. News International funded the generous payments to all the first-team players who signed up with the Super League, but Wigan were effectively penalised because the quality of reserves like Haughton and Murdock meant they too were targeted by the ARL, and to ensure their long-term future lay in this country the club had to outbid the Australians out of their own pocket. Small wonder that Wigan almost snatched rugby union's hand off when it arrived waving wads of notes. Robinson was desperate to do business. Shem Tatupu was next to leave, giving up Wigan's Alliance team for the delights of Northampton, and it was widely predicted that Va'aiga Tuigamala would soon follow. But an exodus of star names to rugby union was the last thing Super League needed or expected.

These very points were put to Lindsay on the occasion of the historic Bath game, when Wigan and their rugby union opponents met under rugby league rules at Maine Road, Manchester, on 8 May 1996. 'If we are no longer able to sign players from rugby union, that's no great loss,' Lindsay said. 'We've been raiding rugby union for the last 50 years, but only cherry-picking players – we haven't got them wholesale. That situation is reversing now, but if only the ex-rugby union players leave our game, I don't think it will be an irretrievable loss. I would only worry if rugby union clubs started to offer handsome contracts to our original players. Even then, they would have to go up a bit, because people like Gary Connolly and Andy Farrell are on big, fat contracts anyway, bigger than Richmond, but that's commonplace in rugby league.'

These were brave words, though Lindsay must have realised at the time that Wigan were finding it difficult to meet their contractual obligations, and of course a salary cap, were one ever to be introduced, would virtually force leading rugby league players to take up more lucrative offers from union. But in May 1996, despite the thaw between the codes and the astonishing rate at which events were unfolding, rugby union clubs waving attractive contracts under the noses of born and bred league players such as Connolly and Farrell still seemed an unlikely prospect. The old snobbery still existed towards rugby league and northerners in general, but beyond that there was still precious little evidence that anyone in rugby union even rated rugby league and its players. Mike Burton, the corporate entertainment specialist, ticket broker and occasional player's agent, was one of the few men who moved freely between both codes. 'The overall rugby union market is bigger, and so is the game's potential for growth,' he said. 'But most rugby union types haven't got a clue how far their game is lagging behind rugby league in almost every other respect. You would be amazed how little most union people know about league: the level of ignorance is staggering. There is actually an immense depth of talent in league not recognised by union, mainly because it has always turned its back on anything north of Coventry.'

This was the situation more or less as it always had been. Rugby union only wanted its old boys back; it had no further interest in rugby league. But this situation changed dramatically when rugby union took a look at Wigan. One could say opinions were revised

overnight, except that strictly speaking the conversion happened on two separate nights. The first was the Wigan–Bath game under league rules on 8 May. The second was three days later, when Wigan made history by taking up their invitation to the Middlesex Sevens and actually playing rugby union at Twickenham. In terms of the collision of the two cultures, Wigan entering the union citadel for the latter event and emerging triumphant after beating all-comers in an alien code was probably the most memorable, treasurable occasion. Maurice Lindsay said Nigel Starmer-Smith's half-astonished, half-affronted commentary for the BBC's *Rugby Special* was something he would treasure for the rest of his life. But first things first. No rugby league club had ever met a rugby union club before, let alone champions against champions, until Wigan and Bath took the field at Manchester City.

Wigan won 82–6. It was not, in all honesty, a very exciting game. Bath took most of the first half to come to terms with the rules, and Wigan eased off a little in the second half, not wishing to run up over a century of points against opponents who impressed everyone with their guts and determination. Wigan had not expected to lose; Bath had not expected to win. The margin of victory was not all that surprising to Wigan, who regularly racked up almost as many points against bona fide rugby league teams, and while Bath were almost certainly not expecting to lose so heavily, they emerged with credit for learning the game on the hoof and for not letting Wigan have everything their own way, whatever the scoreline might suggest. It was a brave performance. In similar circumstances, one or two other famous rugby union sides, perhaps not so strong on pride and team spirit, might have let their heads drop and really been embarrassed.

The one-sided nature of the game rather deflated the occasion and devalued the exercise, however, and the critics who felt disposed to dismiss the experiment as a meaningless charade began to do so. Jeremy Guscott, Bath's international centre, had

Gary Connolly: the best centre in Britain, according to Will Carling. Few in Wigan would disagree, and neither would his former club St Helens, against whom he scored this blistering try in the 1996 Premiership final.

declined to take part in the game for reasons of cowardice or prudence, depending on whether you read the rugby league or rugby union press. But even as their words went to print, it became apparent from the Manchester City dressing-rooms that Wigan's points avalanche had been far from pointless. The Bath players were extraordinarily generous in praising their opponents. 'Wigan were awesome,' said Jon Callard, their lone try-scorer. 'I had a huge amount of respect for them before the game but now they are bordering on being godlike. I would like Bath to do one rugby league training session a week. If we did that, we would be a far better side than we are at the moment.'

At risk of becoming repetitive, this was one of the things no one in rugby league ever expected to hear from anyone in rugby union. And what was even more astonishing, given the appalling anti-league bias many leading rugby union writers had been happy to display over the years, was to see the Bath players' fair-minded enthusiasm echoed by some of the very same people whose self-appointed function it had been to pour scorn on rugby league at every opportunity. 'Bath played well, they really did,' said Paul Ackford in *The Sunday Telegraph*. 'Even the official statistics said so. Yet Bath were buried, completely overwhelmed by Wigan's sheer footballing ability, and this is where rugby union begins to eat buckets of humble pie. Wigan were not better because they were fitter, or more used to rugby league rules. Those were factors on the night, not reasons. Wigan were better because they are better rugby players. Full stop.'

If there were a few retired colonels choking on those words over breakfast in the southern shires, there must have been just as many northerners spluttering into their cornflakes. Ackford was not finished. 'Wigan were light years ahead of Bath, who are light years ahead of their rugby union peers. We knew all about Tuigamala, but Jason Robinson was something else. If he ever decides to latch on to rugby union's ridiculously over-inflated gravy train, the Wigan winger could name his own price. On the evidence of Wednesday's *tour de force* he's worth about three Ben Clarkes.'

Never mind who Ben Clarke is, for by the time these words appeared, Wigan had made another indelible impression on rugby union sensibilities. One of the immediate effects of the rout of Bath on the Wednesday was a sharp intake of breath at Twickenham on the Saturday. Wigan were quickly installed as favourites for the Middlesex Sevens. On the face of it this was ludicrous, since Wigan would this time be playing union, not league. What the bookmakers knew, however, was that union clubs were in the habit of sending along weakened sides and not taking sevens too seriously. Wigan were unikely to do the same. As soon as the bookies discovered Robinson, Tuigamala, Edwards and Connolly would be in the party for Twickenham, the odds came tumbling down.

Touchingly, the Twickenham faithful did not share this hard-nosed realism. They were all in favour of Wigan being beaten, and could hardly contain their excitement when Harlequins took a 12–0 lead against the northerners in the second round, or when Wasps went 15–0 ahead in the final. But these deficits were occasioned only by Wigan's inability to get hold of the ball. Once in possession, they knew how to make it count, and after surviving against Quins, they actually managed to score on every single occasion they received the ball in the final against Wasps, running out 38–15 winners. Twickenham did not know whether to laugh or cry.

Middlesex Sevens spectators are not normally the most disciplined of audiences, the whole event being something of an end-of-season party, and it was widely reported that only when Wigan were in action were the bars empty and the stands full. This was true, but according to Lindsay, present in his official capacity as RFL chief executive, it would be a mistake to imagine everyone was draining their glasses and rushing back to their seats to admire Wigan's expansive style

of rugby. 'No, it wasn't quite like that,' Lindsay explained. 'The fact was that no one in the ground wanted to be absent when Wigan took a beating.'

Anyone who has been paying attention to the earlier chapters of this book will recognise a familiar scenario here. Once again it was Lindsay, and Wigan, against an army of non-believers. The calibre of opposition in the Middlesex Sevens might not have approached the daunting standards set in the past by the likes of Manly and the Broncos, but the depth of anti-Wigan feeling in the crowd was stronger than ever. 'It was just like the old days,' Lindsay said. 'Jack Robinson had rather a lot on his plate at the time [the Wigan chairman had made his first appearance in court earlier in the week] so the club had just sent a small squad of players down and put Joe Lydon in charge. I was there anyway, sitting in the posh seats, but because Wigan were not involved all the time, I kept nipping down to the dressing-rooms, keeping the lads in touch with the other scores and generally geeing them up. It took me back a bit that; made me quite nostalgic.'

It was the experience of watching Wigan's games from the posh seats, however, that Lindsay enjoyed most. 'I was never worried,' he said. 'Even when we went a few points down in a couple of games I was unconcerned, because I knew the lads were not concerned. All they wanted was the ball, and they would be able to show what they could do. I did initially wonder whether it might be possible for the union sides to keep hold of the ball for the entire duration of a game, but it wasn't. We had to wait patiently for possession, but almost as soon as it came we were in business. From the very first try we scored, I knew everyone from Wigan was in for a very enjoyable afternoon.'

Lindsay's neighbours in the Twickenham stand made his afternoon all the more enjoyable by being less adept at reading the script. 'It was very funny,' Lindsay said. 'When I first took my seat, among the other club owners, officials and administrators, I was greeted cordially, but a little stiffly, which was understandable – I wasn't altogether sure of how chummy to be myself. Anyway, we were all conversing reasonably freely, until Wigan came out and beat Richmond 48–5 in the opening game. Everyone shut up then: it all went very quiet. It remained quiet until the point in the next round when Harlequins went 12–0 up. Then, suddenly, everyone was talking to me. They were saying things like: "Well, Maurice, this is interesting, isn't it?" But before I had time to answer, Wigan had begun their fight-back, and by the time I had thought of something to say, we were back in front and I realised silence had descended again.'

That silence lasted throughout the semi-final, where Wigan beat defending champions Leicester 35–2 to secure a final meeting with Wasps. Once the final got under way, Wasps' first try was greeted with only guarded enthusiasm, but by the time Gomarsall and Scrivener had added to White's initial touchdown to take the union side 15–0 in front, triumphalism returned to Twickers. The strains of 'Swing Low, Sweet Chariot' rolled down from the stand. In the posh seats, Lindsay was positively regaled by people venturing the opinion that Wigan were at last meeting a real rugby union team. On the BBC's commentary, Starmer-Smith was ill-advisedly saying the same thing. Ill-advisedly, because Wigan had literally not touched the ball yet. Once they did, Offiah, Tuigamala, Connolly, Robinson and Edwards joyfully ran in the tries to leave Wasps floundering. 'Well,' said Lindsay, turning to those sitting in shocked silence all around him. 'That was quite interesting, wasn't it?'

The next couple of days were interesting as well. Some of the loyalists in the rugby union media attempted to argue that the Middlesex Sevens was only a meaningless jolly for vets, kids and second-teamers, and virtually accused Wigan of cheating by sending their strongest side. This was the way rugby union always used to have it. When in doubt, retreat to amateurism and claim it is only a bit of fun. More sensible observers were aware that union was now in the professional era, and

Wigan were the only side at the Sevens who had represented themselves like professionals. 'I was very proud of the way the lads represented themselves, rugby league and sport in general,' said Lydon, after picking up the trophy and a cheque for £20,000. The latter had to be donated to a charity of the winners' choosing, and duly boosted the coffers of a surprised but delighted Wigan Schools Rugby League Association. Twickenham was probably just as surprised, but less delighted. The winners of the Middlesex Sevens are back by invitation the following year, however, so unless rugby union sides become a lot more professional in a short space of time, this unlikely arrangement may continue for some time.

To their credit, most rugby union correspondents gave Wigan the credit they deserved. Once again, some of the about-turns in the press had to be seen to be believed. Fulsome praise from Stephen Jones, of *The Sunday Times*, for rugby league was almost as disorientating as Wigan running round Twickenham with the cup. 'Wigan would have knocked over anyone,' Jones wrote. 'When they won the ball they often took the breath away. A combination in their outside backs of Offiah, Robinson and Tuigamala would simply threaten the most serious damage to any team ever assembled in any code of rugby.' Steve Bale, of *The Independent*, went further. 'Some of us will never look at rugby union skills in the same light after what we have seen over the past week from Wigan,' he said. 'They graced Twickenham and lent quality to an event that would otherwise have had little. Even if we accept that sevens more closely resembles their own code, the superb athleticism, strength and speed of every one of the rugby league champions' players in each of their games provided hundreds of object lessons. Their first appearance at HQ was an outright celebration. For union it is a time for humility. There were long periods against Wasps when Wigan were incapable of laying their hands on the ball, yet they made a virtue of this problem by ensuring that every time – this is

Celebration time again . . . this time after the trouncing of St Helens in the 1996 Premiership final at Old Trafford.

no exaggeration – possession was secured they exploited it by scoring. As a missionary expedition, or a foray into the shop-window if you prefer, this was faultless.'

Praise indeed, and there was much more in a similar vein from television, radio and a broad selection of ex-players, writers and commentators in the press. Wigan's performance had simply not left any room for argument. People in rugby union were now holding up their hands and admitting they had been wrong. This should have been rugby league's moment of triumph – many people had been waiting a lifetime to see union eating such copious quantities of humble pie – yet even as the superlatives flooded in for the skill and athleticism of performers like Robinson, Paul and Connolly, a jarring note could be discerned. How was it that rugby union, and the nation as a whole, had managed to remain so ignorant of rugby league and its practitioners? It was not as if

Wigan players were exotic visitors, making a brief visit from some planet of rugby perfection. They plied their trade week in, week out, in exactly the same small country. Why, only a year previously they had finally been installed as the BBC's team of the year, largely on the back of adding the World Cup championship in Brisbane to their clean sweep of domestic silverware. So had no one been watching when Robinson played the game of his life against the Broncos, or did people only pay attention when he began to run rings round rugby union players? Similarly, anyone who had witnessed the try Paul scored against St Helens in the Centenary season, running from his own line without a single Saint even getting so much as a hand on him, would have been aware that here was an exceptional athlete and rugby player. Or was no one watching rugby league? Anyone who had been following the 13-a-side code could have listed a dozen superlative displays by Connolly, yet at the southern end of the country, more used to regarding people like Guscott and Carling as the last word in centres, the Wigan player's prowess seemed to come as a revelation.

'It was annoying, after a while,' said Lindsay. 'Praise is always pleasant, and rugby league has never had anything like the praise it deserves, so it was great to hear people saying nice things about us for a change. But it did make you wonder what these so-called rugby people had been watching over the years. They certainly could not have been watching our game. Jason Robinson was brilliant in all the rugby union games, but that's nothing new. Jason was doing all that stuff against rugby league teams when he was still a little lad living at John Monie's house, because he didn't know anyone else in Wigan. The Wigan players might have humbled their rugby union counterparts, particularly in the Sevens at Twickenham, but the publicity we got was a double-edged sword. It was humbling for us to realise that, up till that point, we had been to all intents and purposes invisible beyond the north. We knew we had a winning game, but it appeared no one else did. We could only hope that Super League would be a more effective vehicle in helping us sell our product to the country as a whole.'

Were this a movie or a television drama instead of merely a written account of another eventful season in the life and times of Wigan and rugby league, the music would now be building up to a meaningful mini-crescendo. For we have reached what might be termed the nub of the issue. Super League was already carrying rather too much on its back; it needed no additional weight of expectation. For even as Lindsay spoke, the signs were that Super League was going to be a struggle. The new season was six matches old by the time of the Middlesex Sevens, and what Lindsay knew, though he was not about to admit it, was that in terms of a new departure, a bold and adventurous step which captured the public imagination and guaranteed a publicity splash, Wigan's Super League

exploits were already running second to their adventures in rugby union.

The crowd of 20,418 for the game at Maine Road, for example, had only half-filled the stadium and had generally been regarded as disappointing. Yet nothing in Super League matched it until nine more spectators turned up at Central Park in June for the top-of-the-table encounter with St Helens. And the 42,000 who saw the return Bath–Wigan game at Twickenham was more than double the best attendance Super League could offer. There is perhaps more to a successful season than crowd figures, and after beginning with two away games, one of them a pulsating Good Friday match at St Helens which saw the home side run out 41–26 winners, Wigan had no particular reason to be worried when 14,620 turned up for the first home match, the traditional Easter Monday meeting with Warrington. This attendance was bang on Robinson's schedule, Wigan won 42–12, and everything looked rosy.

But the next home match was a Friday evening kick-off, and despite quality opposition in Bradford, the attendance was only 9,872. This was distinctly worrying. Apart from the most meaningless of Centenary season fixtures, no one could remember the last time Wigan's gate had dipped under 10,000, and failure to reach five figures in only the second match of the season was unheard of. Robinson expressed his concern in the local press and asked for more support at the next game, and 10,675 duly turned up against Paris. Unfortunately, the easy 76–8 victory was not the most persuasive argument for the advantages of live rugby league, and neither were any of the remaining three games in May. After Wigan had beaten Bath at Maine Road they travelled to Halifax and won 50–4 at Thrum Hall; then to Workington, where just 3,176 spectators watched them beat the home side 64–16, and finished the month with a 50–6 home defeat of Sheffield. Significantly, the last attendance was again below 10,000.

On a brighter note, May also saw Wigan back at Twickenham for the second leg against Bath, where the rugby union side salvaged some pride with a thoroughly deserved 44–19 victory. Encouraged by the earlier performance at Twickenham, many Wigan supporters fancied their side to produce a result that would really make rugby union sit up and take notice, but the 15-a-side version of the game was as alien to Wigan as the running angles of rugby league had been to Bath. Reasoning that they would need height in the lineout to win the ball, and a trusty boot to play Bath at their own game, Wigan brought Graeme West out of retirement and gave Lydon a run at stand-off. These bizarre and faintly insulting selections (West was 43) were in the end as irrelevant as Gareth Chilcott would have been in the Maine Road match, had Bath decided they needed a little pantomime villainy to mix it with the early-bath brigade. Neither West nor anyone else in a Wigan shirt won any amount of ball to speak of, so Lydon's kicking function became superfluous. Wigan might have been better sticking to what they knew best and filling the side with runners able to make constructive use of what little ball arrived. Revelling in more possession than they would normally see in a whole season, Bath put the Wigan line under siege straight-away, and not even Connolly's tackling could keep them out. Towards the end of the game Wigan managed three tries through Murdock (two) and Tuigamala, which enabled their supporters to claim they had not only scored the best tries of the afternoon but adapted to the new code better than their opponents had adapted to rugby league. There was some substance in both these assertions, though it was really time to be as generous to Bath as Callard and his colleagues had been to Wigan. Neither of the two games had proved satisfying, both failing in their different ways to rise above the artificiality of the exercise, but both teams could hold their heads high as worthy representatives of their respective codes. The history was being made by getting both teams on to the same playing field; it seemed unreasonable to expect to be richly entertained as well.

Back in the Super League, rich entertainment was also at a premium. Wigan won convincingly at Leeds to keep in touch with St Helens at the top of the table, but on the evening of 9 June were held at 18–18 at Central Park by London Broncos. After racing to an early lead, Wigan found the Broncos' defence a solid barrier, and gradually the deficit was chipped away until Terry Matterson's last-minute goal gave the Londoners a share of the points. St Helens were still unbeaten, so this lost point was always likely to cost Wigan dear. What the Central Park spectators thought of it was evident the following Sunday when another Sunday evening kick-off, against Oldham, attracted just 7,228. If gates of 10,000 were considerably below Wigan's expectations, gates of 7,000 were closer to starvation level. Wigan were not even all that convincing in a 44–16 victory, although it is possible they were saving themselves for the visit of St Helens the following Friday.

Taken in isolation, the crowd of 20,429 for the Saints game, and the way in which the leaders were taken apart in a 35–19 defeat, with Robinson outstanding once again, represented business as usual. But it was becoming more difficult, as the dire financial situation at Central Park began to bite, to take anything in isolation. Robinson's pleas to the fans took on a more haranguing note, and supporters began to resent being asked to subsidise a club which was doing too little to replenish itself. With Quinnell gone and Skerrett missing since April, the pack was now visibly labouring; the famous Wigan strength in depth just a memory. It was clear that replacements for Quinnell and Skerrett would not be forthcoming, just as Platt, Clarke, Betts et al had never been replaced. Connolly, Robinson and Hall were still tied up on ARL contracts which would ultimately see them leave the club for Australia, and Jack Robinson made no secret of that fact that players like Tuigamala, Offiah and Paul were in discussion with rugby union clubs over possible winter contracts. The Wigan chairman went so far as to welcome union interest in his players, pointing out that it would be a considerable saving to the club if someone else took over the onerous contract payments during the fallow months of winter. Because of the ridiculously short season, and Wigan's apparent inability to fill Central Park even during the brief flurry of activity that was summer, another sacred cow was swiftly slaughtered. Robinson announced that a feasibility study into a ground-sharing scheme with Wigan Athletic, something he had always fiercely resisted, now had his blessing. The sale of Central Park was on the agenda again.

Wigan were not the only club in difficulty. For all the upbeat talk from Rugby League HQ, who insisted most Super League clubs were showing a rise in attendances (the Centenary season was bound to come in useful sooner or later), a majority of sides were growing ever more reliant on the monthly cheque from central funds. One such was Warrington, and around half-way through the season their director of football, Alex Murphy, began to ask some pertinent questions. Crowds, he said, were disappointing. It could be that summer rugby was not the answer after all, and a move back to winter might be worth discussing. The idea of a long, empty winter stretching from September until the following March clearly filled Murphy with dread and foreboding. In all fairness, a lot of rugby league followers, including this one, felt the same. Summer might have been an experiment worth trying, but it was surrendering the winter to football and rugby union which was the real worry, even before some of rugby league's biggest names began fixing themselves up with union clubs. This latest development clearly caused Murphy most concern. 'I've got to say I'm worried about the direction our game is taking,' he said. 'It seems to me that we are handing everything to rugby union on a plate.'

To some, this was mere common sense. To others, it was insurrection. Bradford chairman Chris Caisley was one of the quickest to respond to what he saw as backsliding by Murphy and Warrington. He pointed out that a quite revolutionary change was still in its infancy, and clubs should be trying their best to make Super League work, rather than giving up the struggle after a matter of weeks. Bradford, he said, were making a go of Super League and reaping the rewards with some significantly improved crowds. Clubs incapable of attracting a minimum of 10,000 spectators, Caisley remarked, should really be questioning whether they belonged in the Super League in the first place. If Warrington couldn't do it on their own, then perhaps the sensible option was to merge or move and find a larger catchment area, which, after all, was the original Super League idea.

By that reckoning, however, Wigan were only borderline Super League candidates. Their Friday night game against Castleford at the beginning of July produced a crowd of only 8,180 and a not terribly convincing 26–25 win. The only good news for Wigan was that mighty Bradford had beaten St Helens, throwing the title race wide open again. But July was not Wigan's month. The following Friday took Wigan to Bradford, where in front of a magnificent crowd of 17,360, Graeme West's players gained a close-up view of the shifting balance of power in rugby league. The Bulls had embraced Super League in a big way: marketing strategies, pre-match entertainment, the lot. Odsal, never a particularly appetising venue in winter, had definitely benefited from the switch to summer. With Brian Smith in charge of the team, the Bulls were not merely a publicity gimmick either. Wigan were turned over 20–12, their second defeat of the season, and the championship faded from view. Sky Television and its indefatigable commentary team did their best to inject life into the remaining six Super League weekends, but neither Saints nor Wigan lost again, and by the end of the season the false hype about the campaign going right to the final day had worn more than a little thin. Supporters were not fooled. A paltry 7,810 turned up for the penultimate home game against Leeds, unhelpfully shifted from Sunday to Friday at Sky's request and shown live on television, and just 6,466 diehards turned up for the final match against Oldham. Saints won the title by a single point, having also been beaten only by their close rivals and Bradford.

The point Wigan dropped at home against the Broncos effectively cost them the title. Even Bradford's joy was curtailed when Smith announced, long before the end of the season, that he planned to return to Australia. The man whom Wigan had sounded out before Graham Lowe – 'I turned them down; I had just started a family and I wasn't ready for it then' – was understood to have joined Bradford because he was fed up with the ARL–Super League situation in Australia, and the most credible explanation for his return so soon after revitalising the Bulls was that he was none too impressed with what was happening in England either.

He was not on his own. Following the Bradford defeat, Wigan's season lurched from bad to worse. The team kept winning, so as not to let St Helens in sooner than necessary, but the manner of their 24–20 victory in Paris and the 34–26 defeat of Halifax was unimpressive to say the least. With Wigan's blessing, Tuigamala fixed himself up with a winter contract at Wasps. Paul and Robinson opened negotiations, eventually to prove fruitful, with Bath. Offiah was talking to Bedford, despite his likely selection in Great Britain's party to tour New Zealand, New Guinea, Fiji and anywhere else where Super League was not a problem. This conflict of interests was pointed out to Clive Griffiths, the Great Britain assistant coach. 'If we've reached the point where Offiah doesn't want to tour with Great Britain because he's more interested in playing second division rugby union, we all might as well pack our bags and go home,' he said. This was a brave stance by a principled man, but a naive one. When the tour party was announced, Offiah's name was not on the list. 'We doubt if he would be sufficiently motivated,' was the new, emollient official line.

Shaun Edwards was not going on the tour either, having an old injury to clear up, and the long-serving scrum-half also appeared to have a few old grievances to sort out at Wigan. Clearly involved in a clash of personalities with West, he reacted angrily to being dropped to the substitutes' bench for a couple of games, and picked this far-from-convenient moment to demand a 12-month extension to his contract. Edwards, who had, after all, captained England at rugby union as a schoolboy, was possibly upset at missing the rugby union gold rush. A year earlier he had been similarly miffed when his lack of popularity in Australia meant he missed out on a Super League loyalty bonus. No offers of winter work came in 1996 from rugby union, and there were no firm bids from rugby league clubs either when Edwards talked of leaving Wigan. He never went on the list, though it was obvious to everyone in the game by now that Wigan would listen to offers for any player. Despite the fact that there appeared to be a rift between Edwards and club captain Farrell, not to mention coach West's obvious willingness to play Murdock at scrum-half if necessary, the 29-year-old eventually won his 12-month extension, signing a deal which effectively tied him to the club for the remainder of his career and possibly presaged an interest in the coaching job.

Edwards responded with some of his best rugby of the season in his final few games, though during his stand-off with the club, with other big-name players decamping to rugby union, performances on the pitch suffering and attendances continuing to decline, Wigan had a crisis on their hands the like of which had not been seen for over 15 years. Returning from a short holiday in July, I was brought up short by evening paper billboards claiming the fans were calling for the board to resign. A brief perusal of headlines and features that week would have included 'Wigan in Crisis', 'What's Gone Wrong at Central Park?' and 'Robinson Must Go'. There were even letters from supporters in local papers claiming that Wigan had become a laughing stock. It was like stepping into a time-warp, straight back into the second division.

But Wigan were not in the second division.

They were second in the table with what was still a very strong and enormously talented side. Yet in a way it was like being in the second division. Once the two league games with St Helens were out of the way, there was no one else to play. It was an odd limbo, made all the more unusual because of the change in season. One Central Park employee, who had better remain nameless, told me that staff continually had to remind themselves it was not the close season. It was so quiet at the club between games, they kept finding themselves imagining the real season was still a couple of weeks away. This was when the Super League season was, or should have been, at its height. And what was really round the corner, of course, was nothing at all: just five empty months stretching from September to February.

Belatedly, the RFL appeared to realise this. 'I am sick of reading about all our best players moving to rugby union,' said Lindsay, in a half-hearted attempt to block the signings of Tuigamala, Paul and Connolly by Wasps, Bath and Harlequins respectively. 'The Wigan v. Bath games look to have opened up the floodgates. Now we must close them again. We received £87 million from News Corporation to go full time, not part time.' David McKnight, agent to all three players, was quick to point out that Connolly was not even a Super League player, being contracted to join the RFL in 1998. Warning, as if Lindsay did not know, that any such block would be unlikely to survive a legal challenge, McKnight stressed none of the trio had any desire to leave Wigan or to quit rugby league. 'They are merely looking for the opportunity to play for five months when there is no rugby league whatsoever,' he said. Jack Robinson thought it was a little late in the day for the ARL to be wringing its hands over problems it ought to have envisaged much earlier. 'We cannot have a retrospective agreement after other players have been allowed to go to union,' Robinson said. 'I doubt if we could legally stop them anyway. I have to side with the players in this argument. It is the RFL's fault for this season being so short.'

If anyone was still in any doubt about why Robinson was so keen to wave his players goodbye, all was revealed when Offiah became the next departure, this time for good. Neither Bedford nor London Broncos could afford him outright, so after some protracted negotiations, during which it became clear that Wigan were practically giving the player away, both clubs signed him jointly. Offiah would play Super League for the Broncos during summer, and union for Bedford during winter. The overlap between the two seasons was what caused the two buying clubs most concern. London thought they had first call but Bedford appeared to be putting up most of the money. None of this worried Robinson, who could scarcely hide his relief when the Offiah contract – the player's existing deal would have kept him at Wigan until 1999 – had gone south. At a stroke, he told local newspapers, the club had just saved itself £700,000 in wages. Supporters were thus able to work out for themselves that Offiah's contract at Wigan was around £200,000 per season. That might represent the going rate – Lindsay himself had claimed 'big, fat contracts' were 'commonplace in rugby league' – but on the other hand Wigan's most recent home attendance had been 7,810. That is not the sort of figure to support too many big, fat contracts, and attendances were hardly likely to rise if Wigan continued to jettison their star names or loan them out to rugby union. Wigan had been caught in a vicious circle.

At least the season ended on a high note. Wigan survived a thrilling Bradford fightback to reach the Premiership final at Old Trafford and another match against St Helens, who were now claiming to have won the double, as both Challenge Cup and Super League Trophy resided on the Knowsley Road sideboard. Some of the more pedantic among Wigan supporters attempted to argue that this did not really count, as the 1996 Challenge Cup competition properly belonged to the 1995–96 Centenary season, when Wigan won the league, but this was no more than a reflex instinct to deny St Helens their deserved glory. One only had to pause to reflect that Saints could win the 1997 Challenge Cup in addition and still be unable to claim a true double, to realise that none of the old certainties applied any more. Confusion reigned: the game was in a mess. Wigan managed 80 minutes of brilliance at Old Trafford to see off an outclassed St Helens side 44–14, with Offiah's wing replacement Danny Ellison scoring a hat-trick of tries, but there was no point pretending it was like the old days. Some chose to interpret Farrell's Man of the Match award as a political decision, feeling that his Super League credentials had earned him the nod over the more deserving Connolly, who of course was an ARL player. Farrell was now the Great Britain captain, and a couple of weeks earlier had picked up the Man of Steel title, amid general surprise that the award had not gone to someone from St Helens. The most convincing explanation, it was felt, was that rugby league was afraid of losing Farrell full time to rugby union, and were consequently trying to shower him with every available honour.

There may have been no truth in either of these allegations, but the point is that they are not the type of allegations which used to enter into rugby league conversations. No sport can flourish in an atmosphere of suspicion, intrigue and mistrust. Just as Betts and Clarke had flown into a political minefield in Australia when all they were attempting to do was further their rugby careers, so the poison of an essentially Australian dispute had spilled over to sully rugby league in this country, which was even less well equipped to resist it. Clarke actually flew into something worse than disappointment. In one of his first games for Easts, playing against the North Queensland Cowboys under Graham Lowe, he broke his neck in an innocuous tackle. The early prognosis was that he might never walk again, let alone play again, and, as he lay immobile in bed, Clarke's first visitor was Betts, soon followed by Platt and Monie. He missed the whole of the 1996 season – not that it was one of Australia's vintage years – but has now recovered from a broken

vertebra to the extent of joining in with light training, and was hopeful of competing in 1997 if clearance by medical specialists had been forthcoming. Unfortunately this was not the case, and Clarke has had to announce his retirement.

While waiting for the decision, Clarke had been filling in with television and media work for Kerry Packer's Optus company, which involved keeping an eye on the situation back home in England. 'But I would be doing that anyway,' Clarke said. 'I used to joke about playing for Bath, but now Jason and Henry are doing it. I see they both scored a couple of tries in their first game too. But what really made me sit up and take notice was a quote I read after Gary Connolly joined Harlequins. Will Carling described him as the best centre in Britain. I'm not saying I disagree, but it's not something you ever used to hear, is it? I think we'll all be playing one game soon, and I don't think it will be rugby league. The way things are going, unless we get ourselves sorted out very quickly, it's going to be a total takeover.'

Clarke bowed out at Wigan after the 1995 Challenge Cup final. A commemorative poster produced for that occasion, featuring 16 of Wigan's top players, now acts as a useful benchmark for how much has changed. At the end of the first Super League season, some 16 months after Wigan's defeat of Leeds at Wembley, six of the players (Atcheson, Betts, Botica, Clarke, Mather and Offiah) have left the club, while Skerrett is understood to have played his last game. A further three – Connolly, Hall and Robinson – are contracted to the ARL, and Connolly, Paul, Robinson and Tuigamala are currently playing rugby union. Farrell may or may not be considering a full-time switch, which would come as a devastating blow to his original game, but the way things stand at present it would be a surprise if such a young and talented individual did not give the other code a try at some stage. The horizons appear to be boundless. Henry Paul had played just one game in Bath's colours when Jack Rowell, the England coach, began to hint at an international call-up. Paul is a New Zealander, but having only represented that country at league, and possessing an English grandparent, there would be no obstacle to his playing union for England. There are even fewer obstacles in the paths of Connolly and Robinson, and though it might be unduly pessimistic to pose the question, the RFL must be a little worried that some of its best players might not come back. There is a real danger, for the first time in over 100 years, that rugby union offers a higher standard of competition than rugby league, as well as some serious money and a wealth of fringe benefits. Certainly the RFL would be worried if they heard, as one does from time to time in Wigan, that such-and-such a young player, the most promising of his age group, does not intend to sign forms at Central Park but keep his options open for possible rugby union interest.

Full circle? 'I'm not quite sure,' said Jack Robinson. 'In our case it's more of a vicious one. In the beginning we didn't want to let anyone go – we fought tooth and nail to keep Denis Betts and Phil Clarke – but in the end I had to accept they had a point. To understand the intensity those two put into their preparation you would have to watch them training. They wanted to be the best, and then get even better. To keep improving you need new goals, and our game just wasn't giving them any. It's very hard to motivate yourself to train as hard as those two did when you know you have an easy game at the end of the week. They wanted life to be harder; they just weren't being challenged enough here. But then we changed to summer and Super League, and whenever you change anything completely there's always an element of risk. I think it's fair to say the Super League didn't work as well as we had hoped it would at Wigan. We had had a long period of feast, and we went straight into a period of famine. With the level of contractual payments we were paying, plus the loyalty bonuses we had to give our young players, we were on a very tight margin from the outset, and there was no way we could absorb losing four or five thousand spectators a game.'

Robinson does not believe all is necessarily lost for rugby league, but admits time is running out. 'Super League was supposed to be the answer to our problems, but it posed some problems of its own,' he said. 'I'm full of admiration for what Bradford have done, but I'm not sure we could do exactly the same here at Wigan. Bradford were building interest and attendances up from a fairly low base. We started with good crowds, and we started with seven or eight years of winning absolutely everything in sight, but the Super League did not offer the level of competition necessary to sustain that. We will be suggesting to the RFL that next season should be longer. We need to play more games, and we need them to be of a higher quality.'

This last, as usual, will be the tricky one to pull off. Now, more than ever, talent seems very thinly spread through rugby league, with the best concentrated at two or three clubs. Robinson appeared on television towards the end of the 1996 season, berating the Wigan public for failing to support their club and arguing that in America, where sporting operations are run on a franchise basis, the owners would have upped sticks by now and taken the club off to some more deserving location. 'You only get what you deserve,' he said. 'If the Wigan public don't want to come down here and watch the world-class players we've got, after all the success we've had, then it's very disappointing. We need a certain level of support to remain a top-class force in rugby league.'

This was, if you like, the antithesis of the argument advanced by Robinson and Lindsay in the early chapters of this book, that the Wigan public would always watch a successful team. That theory held good for 15 years, but was ultimately undermined by Wigan becoming the only successful team. When Wigan were successful beyond anyone's wildest dreams, to the extent of reducing the rest of the game to also-rans, the game was up. In the end it became impossible to gauge Wigan's success, except on the rare occasions they played Leeds, St Helens, or the Australian champions, because the greater factor in a match would always be the relative weakness of the opposition. With this kind of success, Wigan supporters were sated, and though it was ingenious of Robinson to suggest relocation to somewhere – Milton Keynes or Leeds, perhaps – where people would be more appreciative, it is doubtful whether the same recipe would have been received any better. The basic faults lay in the structure of the game.

Robinson now appears to accept this, and has stopped giving the Wigan public such a hard time. 'It's up to the game to come up with a more attractive formula,' he said. 'We have suggested splitting the Super League into two at the half-way stage, and having the top clubs playing each other twice in a sort of extended Premiership, and the bottom clubs playing off to avoid relegation. We need at least another five games, preferably of high quality.'

Robinson may get them in the second Super League season, following News Corps's surprise victory in the Australian court of appeal in October 1996. All manner of inter-hemisphere challenges and new competitions are now being considered again, but the relative weakness and uneven quality of the European end of the operation are issues which still need to be addressed.

It is typical of Robinson that he is still battling away on Wigan's behalf, still trying to find solutions to the game's intractable problems, when he has more than enough worries of his own. The last two difficult years at Central Park, with Robinson first fighting a takeover from Dave Whelan and then facing falling gates and fielding flak from every conceivable direction, almost certainly took a toll on the amount of time he could devote to business. He finally had to face the police charges alone, after Cowie was released without charge and eventually police announced that Martin had no case to answer either. The subsequent relationship between those two directors can only be guessed at, and Jack Hilton finally retired from the board in 1996, a further break from the original gang of four. Robinson pleaded not guilty to charges of attempting to pervert the course of justice and incitement to create a false instrument at Bolton Crown Court on 1 October 1996. The case will come to trial in the spring of 1997, coinciding with the second season of Super League, but Robinson appeared more concerned in 1996 with the court proceedings in Australia. And at Old Trafford on 8 September, he sat back and enjoyed the sight of Wigan winning against St Helens.

'I enjoyed the Premiership final more than any game for many years,' he said. 'After all the incredible hassle and aggro, it was pleasant to prove a few critics wrong and watch Wigan doing what they do best. We have still got a great, great team. I must admit there have been times when I have thought about quitting. When a small group of fans began chanting that I should resign, and the local paper appeared to be pursuing a vendetta against me, I did ask myself why I was carrying on. But then I asked myself why I had ever started, and reflected how far we had come since the second division. And then I thought, 'I'm damned if I'm going to resign because Wigan are second in the table, with players like Tuigamala, Paul and Farrell.' I remember wanting the original directors to resign in 1980, but if they had put a team like ours on the field I would have been singing their praises.

'I admit I don't know the answers to some of the problems facing rugby league at the moment. A lot of it is tied up in the court battle in Australia, and the chances are that we won't hear the last of that this year or even next. What I do know is that we can't afford to make any more mistakes. The next thing we do, we've got to get it right. To some extent I don't believe the judicial ruling on Super League even matters that much, because if the two sides are still arguing as a result, we will waste more precious time. What needs to happen is for everyone with an interest in rugby league to get together, put their differences to one side, and get on with life. We are in a very competitive situation at the moment with regard to rugby union, and we are in danger of losing the initiative I believe rugby league has always held. We need to sit down, learn from all our mistakes, and work out how to be a better sport.'

Amen to that. Except that the lesson of the last year or so might simply be that rugby league is incapable of becoming a better sport. Anyone brought up in Wigan would tell you it is practically perfect as it is. Any attempts to improve it only end up making it worse. The only drawback is that Wigan, sadly, is not typical of the rest of the world. Neither is St Helens, Castleford, Brisbane or Sydney. The rest of the world prefers football, which is erroneous but understandable, or rugby union, which is unfathomable. Or at least it was. That code's rules are swiftly changing in rugby league's direction, and when the new English season got under way in 1996, most of the star performers picked out in the newspaper supplements were rugby league players. Maybe, as Phil Clarke fears, we will all be playing rugby union soon.

Maybe it will resemble rugby league, and maybe it won't. Maybe the money will run out sooner than anticipated, as the rugby union entrepreneurs begin to comprehend the difficulty of filling stadiums on a regular basis. Maybe the new professional game will seize the public imagination; maybe rugby league will make a comeback. No one knows. These are exciting times, but not as exciting as

the last 15 years in one small former coal town in Lancashire. Whatever happens in rugby union or in rugby league in the future, it is unlikely to match winning at Wembley eight years on the trot, or hold a candle to the imperishable memories of Kenny and Ferguson in 1985. Will anyone, ever again, put together a three-quarter line to rival Robinson, Tuigamala, Connolly and Offiah? Will there ever be a rugby side so strong, so finely balanced, as Wigan's of 1990, with its peerless triangle of Gregory, Edwards and Hanley? Try to form a dream team from the last 15 years. How could anyone choose between Hampson and Lydon at full-back? Or between Clarke, Betts and Goodway for second row, or Hanley and Farrell at loose forward? Take any one of these players and put them in a rugby union side and they are considered remarkable. At Wigan, a team of quite incredible talents has long been taken for granted. But then rugby league has often been taken for granted. It is ironic that the game is only now getting the recognition it deserves when it seems to be facing a real danger of extinction, but there is no chance of memories or video recordings fading away. One way or another, an era seems to be ending in Wigan. Who knows what will survive this bleakest of winters? Time might be running out, but what a time we all had. The best years of our lives.

CHAPTER THIRTEEN

Heroes in Hoops

There follows a complete list of the players to have represented Wigan between the second division season in 1980-81 and the 1996 Super League. Qualification is eight games. Seasons spent at the club are indicated, except where players joined Wigan prior to 1981, in addition to source. Honours are also listed where relevant, using the following key: WC = World Cup Challenge; CC = Challenge Cup; Ch = Championship; P = Premiership, T = John Player/Regal trophy; LC = Lancashire Cup. Sevens tournaments and Charity Shield matches are not included. Players who have appeared in a minimum of ten games in a championship season are credited with having a championship honour, though this is somewhat arbitrary. The Rugby League used to allow medals for a minimum of six games, but there is no strict procedure and quali-fication rules have varied over the seasons.

I am indebted to Anne Dempsey, mainstay of the Wigan Supporters' Club and enthu-siastic keeper of Wigan rugby records and statistics, for her help in compiling the following list. For the information of anyone wishing to quarrel, the stats are Anne's, the descriptions the author's.

ASPEY, Mal 1981-82. Fulham.
One of the great modern centres. For Widnes and Fulham, that is.
ATCHESON, Paul 1992–93 to 1994–95. Widnes. WC1, CC1, Ch2, P1, T1.
Industrious and energetic full-back. Strong tackler whose own size made him hard to stop.
BAMBER, Lee 1982–83 to 1983–84. Blackpool Borough.
Short career, short fuse, short life.

BELL, Dean 1986–87 to 1993–94. Eastern Suburbs. CC7, Ch6, P2, T4, LC4.
Tough, uncompromising Kiwi centre with real pace. One of Wigan's best overseas buys.
BETTS, Denis 1986–87 to 1994–95. Leigh Rangers. WC2, CC7, Ch6, P3, T4, LC2.
State-of-the-art second row with the strength of a forward allied to the pace of a back; a thoroughbred in a team of champions.
BIRTS, Jimmy 1981-82. Halifax.
Legendary under-performer at a time when Wigan were famous for under-performing.
BLAKE, Phil 1989–90. South Sydney. Ch1.
Ultra-short-term Aussie signing who nevertheless did plenty to impress. Would have returned on a more permanent basis but for board signing Frano Botica.
BLAKELY, Steve 1990-91 to 1992-93. Leigh Rangers.
Slightly built stand-off with deceptive pace. Lack of size probably persuaded Wigan to let him go, but has since proved himself to be an excellent player.
BOTICA, Frano 1990-91 to 1994-95. North Shore RU, NZ. WC2, CC5, Ch5, P3, T2, LC1.
'A gamble' was how Jack Robinson described this signing, but there was surely never much risk involved with this supremely gifted half-back, a prodigious goal kicker as well as a natural runner and handler of the ball.
BRAITHWAITE, Ronnie 1983–84 to 1986–87. St Patrick's.
Reserve winger whose first-team chances were strictly rationed.
BYRNE, Ged 1987–88 to 1990–91. Salford. WC1, CC2, Ch1, T1, LC1.
Mad window-cleaner and occasional pianist. Seriously nice bloke, though, and a more-than-useful squad player.

CAMPBELL, Danny 1981–82 to 1985–86. New Zealand. CC1, T1.
Rough-and-ready Kiwi, deservedly popular with the supporters.

CANNON, Mark 1983–84 to 1984–85. St George.
Golden boy back in the days when Wigan used to lose at Wembley.

CASE, Brian 1982–83 to 1988–89. Warrington. WC1, CC2, Ch1, P1, T2, LC3.
Unspectacular but hugely effective prop forward.

CASSIDY, Mick 1991–92 to present. St Judes. WC1, CC2, Ch4, P2, T2.
On the small side for a forward but one of the best 'engines' at the club. Conspicuous for his cover tackling, Wigan always know when he is missing.

CLARE, Jeff 1982–83 to 1985–86. St Patrick's. T1.
Talented athlete who never quite made it as a rugby player.

CLARKE, Phil 1988–89 to 1994–95. St Patrick's. WC2, CC5, Ch6, P3, T2.
Son of Colin, and the very model of a modern league player. Desire to keep improving took him to Australia, with near tragic consequences.

CONNOLLY, Gary 1993–94 to present. St Helens. WC1, CC2, Ch3, P2, T2.
Lavishly gifted centre or full-back with deceptively lazy running action and extremely strong defence. A complete and virtually flawless rugby league player.

COURTNEY, Neil 1983–84 to 1985–86. Warrington. CC1.
Old-fashioned prop who enjoyed injury-curtailed Indian summer at Wigan.

COWIE, Neil 1991–92 to present. Rochdale Hornets. WC2, CC2, Ch5, P3, T3, LC1.
Rough, tough but inconsistent performer. Up with the best on his day.

CRAIG, Andy 1993–94 to present. Blackbrook. Ch1.
Home-grown winger or centre, steadily coming through the ranks.

CROMPTON, Martin 1992–93 to 1993–94. Warrington. Ch1, LC1.
Useful scrum-half Wigan bought but never really needed.

CUNLIFFE, Geoff 1981–82 to 1982–83. St Patrick's.
Big lad, short career.

DAVIDSON, Les 1989–90. South Sydney. Ch1.
Accomplished Aussie Test forward who came on same return ticket as Phil Blake.

DERMOTT, Martin 1984–85 to present. St Patrick's. WC2, CC5, Ch7, P1, T5, LC3.
Modern hooker with half-back's skills, butt of much Central Park dressing-room humour.

DONLAN, Steve 1984–85. Leigh. CC1.
Always seemed a more dashing and dangerous player for Leigh than Wigan, but gave his best for a short time in 1985.

DOWLING, Greg 1985–86. Wynnum Manly. T1, LC1.
Tough Aussie prop who missed out on the major prizes.

DUNN, Brian 1982–83 to 1984–85. Pilks Recs. CC1.
Unremarkable second row lucky to be in the right place at the right time for 1985 Challenge Cup final.

DU TOIT, Nick 1984–85 to 1986–87. CC1, T1, LC1.
Enormous running centre or second row with heart to match and crowd-pleasing style. Only age was not on his side.

EDWARDS, Shaun 1983–84 to present. St Patrick's. WC3, CC9, Ch8, P4, T7, LC5.
Pound for pound, medal for medal, flawless game after flawless game, has to be Wigan's best-ever signing.

ELLA, Steve 1985–86. Parramatta. T1, LC1.
Excellent Aussie half-back who deserved better than watching Wigan crashing out of the Challenge Cup when he missed a game through injury.

ELLISON, Danny 1993–94 to present. Golborne Parkside. Ch1.
Big lad for a winger, with a lot still to do to make a place his own at Central Park.

ELVIN, Wayne 1983–84. Cambelltown.
Feisty little barrel of a loose forward.

FAIRHURST, Jimmy 1982–83 to 1985–86. Blackpool Borough. T1.
Entertaining performer in an era before rugby league players started taking themselves so seriously.

FARRAR, Andrew 1992–93. Cronulla. CC1, Ch1, T1, LC1.

Craggy Aussie bought as a cut-price alternative to Gene Miles, but who didn't appear to mind a bit.

FARRELL, Andy 1991–92 to present. Orrell St James. WC1, CC3, Ch4, P2.

Precocious giant who looked the finished article while still in his teens, and has since managed to get even better. Has size, strength, quickness of thought and action; the sort of complete player we used to think only the Australians could produce.

FERGUSON, John 1984-85. Eastern Suburbs. CC1.

Simply stunning. Of all the players in this book, and that's quite a roll-call, the author suspects he is not alone in feeling most privileged to have watched this one.

FORD, Mike 1982-83 to 1986-87. Oldham St Annes. CC1, Ch1, T2, LC2.

No razzle dazzle, according to Graham Lowe, but plenty of clubs were willing to try this clever scrum-half organiser who found himself up against Shaun Edwards and Andy Gregory at Central Park.

FORD, Phil 1984–85 to 1985–86. Warrington.

Unpredictable Welsh winger who performed unevenly for long list of clubs, but who was actually quite good in his short time at Wigan.

FORSHAW, Mike 1989–90 to 1992–93. St Patrick's. WC1, Ch3.

Rare example of a useful player Wigan allowed to go elsewhere.

FOY, Martin 1981–82 to 1983–84. Saddleworth. T1.

Classy stand-off when he wanted to be, which, disappointingly, was not all that often.

GILDART, Ian 1986–87 to 1993–94. Wigan Colts. WC2, CC1, Ch5, T1.

Well-built prop or second row, never managed to stand out in period when Wigan squad was at its largest and strongest.

GILFILLAN, John 1989–90 to 1990–91. Orrell RU. Ch1.

Somewhat ambitious signing from local rugby union who found first-team opportunities predictably scarce.

GILL, Henderson 1981–82 to 1989–90. Rochdale Hornets. WC1, CC2, Ch1, P1, T3, LC2.

Inspired wing signing who in turn inspired a hundred happy memories.

GOODWAY, Andy 1985–86 to 1992–93. Oldham. WC1, CC5, Ch3, P1, T4, LC4.

Powerful back row with attitude and elegant running style.

GOULDING, Bobby 1988–89 to 1990–91. Widnes St Maries. CC2, Ch3.

Firecracker of a scrum-half, too hot for many clubs to handle, including Wigan.

GREGORY, Andy 1986-87 to 1991-92. Warrington. WC2, CC5, Ch4, P1, T2, LC2.

Inimitable and unmistakable scrum-half who called the shots on and off the field.

HALL, Martin 1992–93 to 1995–96. Rochdale Hornets. WC1, CC1, Ch4, P2, T2.

Stocky hooker, clever at the rucks and a model of consistency over the years.

HAMPSON Steve 1983–84 to 1991–92. Vulcan RU. WC2, CC5, Ch5, P2, T4, LC5.

One of the great uncoached naturals with a soaring style of his own.

HANLEY, Ellery 1985–86 to 1990–91. Bradford Northern. WC1, CC4, Ch3, P1, T4, LC4.

The one and only. The most remarkable player of the last 20 years, at Wigan or anywhere else.

HAUGHTON, Simon 1993–94 to present. Dudley Hill. Ch2, P1, T1.

Made The Guinness Book of Records *for his schoolboy try-scoring exploits in Yorkshire, and made a very quick impression as a back row forward at Wigan.*

HEMSLEY, Kerry 1983-84. Balmain.

First short-term Aussie capture after lifting of international transfer ban. Not actually one of Wigan's best, but looked the part, which at that time was the important thing.

HENLEY-SMITH, Gary 1985–86. New Zealand. LC1.

Only seven appearances, but included in this list because his double-barrelled name gave him a curiosity value beloved of quiz-masters, and because he did play on the wing in a winning Lancashire Cup side.

HODKINSON, Alan 1981–82 to 1982–83. Rochdale Hornets.

Old school prop who could still look after himself at veteran stage.

HOLDEN, Keith 1983–84 to 1986–87. St Patrick's.

Doubly unlucky scrum-half. Had persistent knee injury to cope with as well as Mike Ford, Shaun Edwards and Andy Gregory.

HORNBY, Jimmy 1981–82 to 1982–83. Wigan Colts.

Useful winger whose best years unfortunately coincided with Wigan's worst.

IRO, Kevin 1987–88 to 1990–91. Mount Albert, NZ. CC4, Ch2, T2, LC1.

Fitful centre who did not always produce as much as his enviable physique promised, but could be devastating on his day. No other player is likely to score twice at Wembley on three separate occasions and still miss out on the Lance Todd Trophy.

IRO, Tony 1987-88 to 1988–89. Mount Albert, NZ. CC2, T1, LC1.

Slightly narrower version of above, with quicker football brain but similar inability to concentrate.

JOHNSON, Andy 1994–95 to present. St Patrick's. Ch1.

Neat, clever second row who looks slightly small for the role.

JULIFF, Brian 1982–83 to 1984–85. Wakefield Trinity. T1.

Mad Welshman.

KENNY, Brett 1984–85. Paramatta. CC1.

The sort of stand-off you would be in your dreams.

KISS, Nicky 1981–82 to 1989–90. Saddleworth. WC1, CC3, Ch1, P1, T2, LC2.

Robust, uncomplicated hooker with boyish enthusiasm and permanent sense of surprise at his own success.

LOUW, Rob 1985–86 to 1986–87. Defence RU, Capetown. Ch1, T1, LC1.

Ball-playing forward probably wasted in union but too late a convert to league.

LUCAS, Ian 1985–86 to 1992–93. Wigan Colts. WC2, CC2, Ch4, T1, LC1.

Steady if unspectacular prop, career ended by highly dubious Australian tackle just as international career looked set to take off.

LYDON, Joe 1985–86 to present. Widnes. WC2, CC5, Ch6, P3, T4,LC4.

Class act virtually anywhere in back line; speed, strength, style and a top kicking game.

McDERMOTT, Barrie 1994–95. Oldham. Ch1, T1.

Wild-man prop forward with only one good eye but a sure nose for a punch-up.

McGINTY, Billy 1991–92 to 1993–94. Warrington. WC2, CC1, Ch2, P1, T1, LC1.

Popular and versatile pack grafter who surprised everyone, including himself, with rate of development and success after joining Wigan from Warrington.

McLOUGHLIN, Brendan 1981–82 to 1982–83. Blackbrook.

Limited player with limited appearances.

MARSHALL, Dave 1987–88 to 1990–91. St Patrick's. Ch1, T1.

Quick and alert winger who never realised his full potential, principally due to injury.

MATHER, Barrie-Jon 1991–92 to 1995–96. Arnold School. WC1, CC1, Ch3.

Tall, rangy centre or second row named after the Welsh rugby fly-half, but a considerable talent in his own right.

MAYO, John 1984–85 to 1986–87. St Patrick's.

Honest, hard-working forward who never quite made first-team mark.

MELLING, Billy 1981–82. Leigh.

Promising centre who ended up in the pack. Might have been much more famous had he been ten years younger.

MILES, Gene 1991–92. Brisbane Broncos. CC1, Ch1, P1.

Wigan waited long enough to sign this giant centre and were not disappointed, even though he was almost a veteran when he finally made it.

MORDT, Ray 1985–86 to 1986–87. Wanderers RU, SA. Ch1, T1.

Came to Wigan too late in the end, but still showed potential to be an outstanding winger.

MURDOCK, Craig 1993–94 to present. Hensingham. Ch2.

Quality Cumbrian scrum–half with try-scoring habit. Small matter of Shaun Edwards standing between him and a big first-team future.

MYERS, Dave 1990–91 to 1992–93. Warrington. WC1, CC1, Ch2, P1.

Well-built but still-speedy winger who was making a name for himself before the arrival of Martin Offiah.

NANYN, Mick 1981–82 to 1983–84. Saddleworth.

Fast but unaggressive running forward.

NICHOLSON, Steve 1981–82 to 1982–83. Bramley.

Another of Maurice Bamford's disappointments, quick enough for a centre but not classy enough for Wigan.

O'CONNOR, Terry 1994–95 to present. Salford. Ch2, T1.

Inspired and scandalously underrated front row signing. Most consistent prop on Wigan's books in Super League season; deserved 1996 tourist.

O'DONNELL, Augustine 1988–89 to 1991–92. St Patrick's. Ch1.

Gutsy but unlucky half-back who never quite made it at Wigan or Saints.

OFFIAH, Martin 1991–92 to 1996. Widnes. WC1, CC4, Ch5, P3, T3, LC1.

Wigan's record buy, and likely to remain so for some time. Freakishly quick winger with good hands and instinctive nose for the try line. Can be marked out of a game, and has his critics over defence, but few coaches ever leave him out of their dream teams.

O'NEILL, Paul 1984–85 to 1985–86. Salford.

Local hooker who was always surplus to requirements when Nicky Kiss was back in contention.

PANAPA, Sam 1991–92 to 1993–94. Sheffield Eagles. WC2, CC2, Ch3, P2, T1.

Versatile Kiwi who got lucky after being bought as a back-up player. Made more than one place his own, and graced some of the game's biggest occasions.

PAUL, Henry 1994–95 to present. Auckland Warriors. CC1, Ch2, P1, T2.

Superb athlete, sublime rugby talent. In spite of Jack Robinson's anger at losing Andy Platt, Dean Bell and Frano Botica to Auckland, when Wigan prised this gem from John Monie's grasp they got the better of the exchange.

PENDLEBURY, John 1981–82 to 1984–85. Leigh Miners. T1.

Intelligent, creative loose forward who must have grown tired of coaches telling him he was not big enough for the position. Now a coach himself.

PLATT, Andy 1988–89 to 1993–94. St Helens. WC1, CC6, Ch5, P1, T2, LC2.

Handy back row forward at St Helens who transformed himself into one of the world's biggest and best props.

POTTER, Ian 1983–84 to 1988–89. Leigh. WC1, CC3, Ch1, P1, T3, LC3.

Strong and silent type capable of turning average pack into an excellent one.

PRESTON, MARK 1987–88 to 1990–91. Fylde RU. CC1, Ch1, T1.

Flair winger with lightning turn of speed, whose alleged defensive deficiencies failed to impress John Monie. Lack of size and rugby union background might also have had something to do with early departure from Central Park.

QUINNELL, Scott 1994–95 to 1996. Llanelli RU. Ch2, T1.

Wigan waited an awful long time to sign a Welsh forward, and Quinnell took almost as long to adjust to league. But he made it in the end, and looked so impressive running with the ball that rugby union promptly claimed him back again.

RADLINSKI, Kris 1993–94 to present. Wigan Academy. Ch1, P1, T1.

Sparkling performer at full-back who seized his first-team chance with both hands.

RAMSDALE, Dennis 1981–82 to 1984–85. Whelley. T1.

Somewhat fragile winger who nevertheless developed strong defence.

ROBERTS, Ian 1986–87. South Sydney. Ch1, T1, LC1.

London-born player who enjoyed memorable season as Graham Lowe's protégé; one of the very few Australian Test forwards to come out of the closet as gay.

ROBINSON, Jason 1992–93 to present. Hunslet Boys. WC1, CC2, Ch4, P2, T3, LC1.

Jet-heeled winger who lived with John Monie for a while, so young and inexperienced was he when he first burst onto the scene at Wigan. Signed as a half-back, and intends to return inside, but explosive in any position. Arguably the most exciting player of the last 20 years.

RUSSELL, Richard 1985–86 to 1988–89. St Patrick's. WC1, Ch1, P1, LC1.

Incredibly versatile performer who cheerfully operated as winger, half-back or hooker.

SCOTT, Mick 1981–82 to 1984–85. Halifax. T1.

Third time lucky for Bamford, this tireless second-row grafter was worth every penny.

SHAW, Glyn 1981–82 to 1984–85. Widnes. T1.

Superb grizzly pack veteran with good handling skills to boot. Wigan career sadly curtailed by injury.

SHELFORD, Adrian 1987–88 to 1989–90. New Zealand. CC3, Ch1, T1, LC1.
Big but somewhat ponderous prop, who was always going to find it hard to live up to his advance publicity.

SKERRETT, Kelvin 1990–91 to 1996. Bradford Northern. WC1, CC4, Ch6, P2, T1, LC1.
Archetypal prop forward and caricature hit man with enough faith in his own ability to pioneer the personal contract system which let him deal with clubs as a free agent.

SMITH, Malcolm 1981–82. St Helens.
Handy occasional hooker.

SMYTH, Rob 1995–96 to present. Rose Bridge. Ch1, T1.
Local winger who seized his chance when Jason Robinson moved inside, and immediately began to outscore Martin Offiah. Small and nippy, with ability to duck under and out of a tackle, and real pace when in clear.

STAZIKER, Ged 1987–88 to 1990–91. St Patrick's. Ch2.
Capable forward used mainly as a squad player.

STEPHENS, Gary 1981–82 to 1983–84. Castleford.
Scrum-half with attitude.

STEPHENSON, David 1981–82 to 1987–88. Salford. WC1, CC1, Ch1, P1, T3, LC3.
Stylish and strong international centre with rugby union background.

STOCKLEY, Trevor 1981–82. St Patrick's.
Home-grown centre with pace and flair.

STOOP, Andre 1991–92 to 1992–93. Wanderers RU, Namibia.
Competent full-back prone to occasional costly aberration.

STOTT, Phil 1985–86 to 1986–87. Vale of Lune RU.
Handful of games on the wing.

TAMATI, Howie 1983–84. Waitara, NZ.
Neat hooker signed for no apparent reason.

TRUNDLE, John 1981–82. Kirkby Rangers.
Better forward than his name suggests.

TUIGAMALA, Va'aiga 1993–94 to present. New Zealand RU. WC1, CC2, Ch3, T2.
From the would-be tackler's point of view, just about the most fearsome sight in world rugby, and that includes Jonah Lomu. Fast, skilful and almost unreasonably strong, New Zealand's Big Black Bus was transformed by Wigan's training and fitness regime into something more along the lines of an express train.

TYRER, Sean 1988–89 to 1990–91. Leigh Miners.
Son of Colin, capable full-back offered limited first-team chances.

WALSH, David 1981–82. Wigan Colts.
Not terribly quick stand-off, but nonetheless popular for it.

WANE, Shaun 1981–82 to 1990–91. St Patrick's. WC1, CC1, Ch1, P1, T3, LC2.
Top local talent, would have been even better prop but for perennial problems with injury.

WEST, Graeme 1982–83 to present. WC1, CC1, Ch1, P1, T3, LC2.
The Big Fella. The definition of a far-sighted signing.

WHITFIELD, Colin 1981–82 to 1985–86. Salford. T1, LC1.
Quick and stylish centre or stand-off with most laborious goal-kicking technique since Colin Tyrer.

WILLIAMS, Barry 1981–82 to 1984–85. Bold Miners. T1.
Cheap and cheerful full-back.

WOOD, David 1981–82 to 1984–85. St Patrick's.
Utility back who struggled to meet Wigan's rising standards.

WRIGHT, Nigel 1993–94 to present. Wakefield Trinity. Ch1.
Still one for the future, but time beginning to run out for this classy but injury-prone stand-off.

Afterword

Peter Aspinall, *Wigan Evening Post*

It was around 1987, and I hadn't been covering Wigan rugby for very long. I suppose I was keen to make an impression. The opportunity seemed to present itself when the club installed some fancy new floodlights at the cost of several thousand pounds, and Maurice Lindsay mentioned in passing that it might be a good idea to invite some sort of celebrity to officially switch them on.

Just prior to my appointment as the paper's rugby league writer, I'd struck up a useful working relationship with one Fred Dibnah, the flat-capped Bolton steeplejack whose chimney-topping exploits were in the process of being made famous by the BBC. My idea was as brilliant as Wigan's new floodlights. I would persuade Fred to climb up one of the stanchions and turn on the new lights in a blaze of publicity just prior to a big game. Seizing the initiative, closely followed by the telephone, I got Fred on the line and excitedly put my plan to him.

'Sounds allreet to me,' he replied, in that earthy Bolton accent. How much, I inquired, would he want as a fee? 'Oh, let's see narr. I might want abaht fifty pund for't job. 'Ow does that sound?'

I told him it sounded fine, and immediately rang Maurice at the club to tell him of my grand design and the groundwork already done. He seemed both pleased and impressed, so I allowed myself a smug glow as I put down the receiver. About an hour later, the telephone rang. It was Fred Dibnah.

'Narr, Peter,' he said. 'I've been thinkin' about this 'ere job at Wiggin. I reckon I might be doin' meself out of a few bob. I mean, they're not strapped for cash, them rugby league buggers, are they? I bet they'll have a big crowd on too. I think I might want four or five hundred quid for t'job now. Tell 'em I'll do it for that.'

I was unable to persuade Fred to change his mind, though I went to some lengths in trying. Eventually, completely crestfallen, I rang Central Park to tell Maurice the bad news. He listened in silence – always a sinister sign – but as my feeble excuses trickled to a close, I thought I could hear someone sniggering in the background.

Maurice finally spoke. 'Mm . . . That does seem like bad news, Peter. But tell me, did Fred sound anything like this?' I listened, squirming with embarrassment, as yet another earthy Bolton accent came down the line. 'Narr, Peter. I reckon I might be doin' meself out of a few bob . . .' The background sniggering had now turned into gales of laughter, which I recognised as club secretary Mary Charnock enjoying a joke at my expense. The second Fred Dibnah had been Maurice all along, and I had been completely duped.

I was still speechless on the other phone when I heard a dull crash and even more hilarity. Maurice obviously performing to an audience. 'What was that?' I asked. 'Nothing to worry about,' he replied. 'Just Mary falling off her chair laughing.'

Even in the depths of my humiliation, I sensed that life with Wigan rugby league club was not going to be dull. Maurice may be regarded as a tyrant by some and a megalomaniac by others, but underneath the crusty exterior there lurks a sense of humour befitting of Dick Dastardly. And a terrific Bolton accent . . .